Confucianism · Nation · Uniqueness

Diverging Discourses on Chosŏn History between Korean and Global Scholarship

Sogang Korean Studies 01

Confucianism · Nation · Uniqueness
Diverging Discourses on Chosŏn History
between Korean and Global Scholarship

First Published 7 November 2025
Publisher Jong Hyuk Shim
Director Shang E. Ha

Editors Seung B. Kye, Hohyun Nam
Contributors Joon Hur, Seung B. Kye, Hyunchae Lim, Chaeyoung Choo, Karam Kim, Kunha Kim, Hohyun Nam, Dawoon Jeong

Published in Sogang University Press
35 Baekbeom-ro, Mapo-gu, Seoul 04107, Korea
Tel +82-2-705-8212 Fax +82-2-705-8612

ISBN 978-89-7273-538-0 94910
ISBN 978-89-7273-537-3 (set)
₩30,000

Sogang Korean Studies 01

Confucianism · Nation · Uniqueness

Diverging Discourses on Chosŏn History between Korean and Global Scholarship

Edited by
Seung B. Kye and Hohyun Nam

SOGANG UNIVERSITY PRESS

Introduction

Confucianism · Nation · Uniqueness
Diverging Discourses on Chosŏn History between Korean and Global Scholarship

Understanding the history of the Chosŏn dynasty (1392-1910) is essential to comprehending the historical consciousness and identity of contemporary Koreans. Situated at the crossroads of tradition and modernity in Korean history, the Chosŏn era not only laid the foundations for the lifestyles and mindsets of modern Koreans but also contributed to the factors behind Japanese colonial rule. The challenges faced by the Chosŏn dynasty provide valuable historical insights into longstanding issues such as the division of the Korean peninsula and Korea's position within the rapidly shifting geopolitical landscape of East Asia. Interest in these topics is expected to continue growing, driven by the rise of Korean studies and the global popularity of Korean culture, symbolized by the 'K' prefix.

Scholarly interest in the Chosŏn dynasty emerged with the early efforts of the so-called "first-generation" scholars in the United States. Pioneering works such as Martina Deuchler's *The Confucian Transformation of Korea: A Study of Society and Ideology*(1992) and James B. Palais's *Confucian Statecraft and Korean Institutions: Yu Hyŏngwŏn and the Late Chosŏn Dynasty*(1996) have been highly influential, not only advancing the study of Korean history but also contributing to a broader understanding of East Asian political structures and lifestyles. These seminal studies have profoundly shaped subsequent generations of scholars in Korean studies and continue to serve as important reference points for understanding Korea within the global academic community. Their influence has also been keenly felt within Korean academia, where scholars such as the late Professor Chung Doo-hee of Sogang University introduced trends in Chosŏn studies abroad and promoted active academic exchange and collaboration between Korean and international scholars.

However, despite these efforts, more than two decades later, it is difficult to assert that communication between Korean and global scholars on Chosŏn history has become truly robust. While the necessity of such dialogue is widely acknowledged, little critical examination has been undertaken regarding the differences in perspectives between the two groups and their historiographical implications. Ironically, the current environment—where research from both sides is readily accessible without intermediary works like those of Professor Chung—has contributed to this gap. Although researchers increasingly refer to international studies relevant to their fields, they often pay insufficient attention to the underlying discourses and historiographical views embedded in these works.

This book was conceived by scholars who share such concerns. Whereas previous works have primarily focused on introducing the trends in English-language scholarship on Chosŏn history, this volume aims to highlight the historiographical differences between Korean and global scholarship on key issues. Today, Chosŏn studies are no longer the exclusive domain of Korean scholars, nor are Korean scholars mere passive recipients of international perspectives. The current research landscape reflects a far more complex and dynamic interaction.

The volume is divided into two parts. The first part (Chapters 1-4) addresses topics where significant differences between Korean and global scholars have emerged. In Chapter 1, Joon Hur explores differing perspectives on the founding of the Chosŏn dynasty, emphasizing that while Korean scholars tend to emphasize "change" in Korean society, Western scholars highlight "continuity" in their interpretations, challenging the conventional binary framework of the "new scholar-official" interpretation (*sinjin sadaebu ron*). In Chapter 2, Seung B. Kye critically examines assessments of the sarim faction, dominant in early Chosŏn politics, and introduces the concept of a "Confucianization movement" to frame political transformations as generational shifts. Chapter 3, authored by Hyunchae Lim, analyzes scholarly discourse on the Imjin War since the 2000s, highlighting the war's role as a turning point in Chosŏn history and its lasting impact on Korea's diplomatic outlook toward China and Japan. Finally, in Chapter 4, Chaeyoung Choo investigates monarchical theories concerning Kings Yŏngjo (r. 1724–1776) and Chŏngjo (r. 1776–1800), critically assessing conventional portrayals of them as a "Confucian Sage" and a "Reformer," respectively, while exploring the historiographical trends underpinning these evaluations.

These four chapters vividly illustrate how Korean and global scholars differ in their interpretations of Chosŏn history and offer a historiographical analysis of these divergent viewpoints.

The second part (Chapters 5–8) of the book introduces emerging research trends that invite renewed scholarly attention from both Korean and global perspectives. In Chapter 5, Karam Kim revisits the topics of family and women in Chosŏn society, drawing on newly discovered case studies from the 21st century and advocating for more vigorous scholarly discussion. In Chapter 6, Kunha Kim examines the applicability of the "military revolution" thesis to Chosŏn history—a theory originating in Western historiography that posits military reforms as drivers of societal change. In Chapter 7, Hohyun Nam calls for greater attention to church history within Chosŏn studies, emphasizing its "East Asian" characteristics and the global dimensions of the Chosŏn Catholic Church, especially as Western scholarly interest in Chinese Catholic history rises. Finally, in

Chapter 8, Dawoon Jeong discusses the True-View(*Ching'gyŏng* 眞景) painting tradition, critiquing the somewhat uncritical reception of this concept in Korean and English-language scholarship and highlighting recent research trends to promote a more balanced understanding of Chosŏn art history.

The eight chapters in this volume, while not exhaustive, reflect each contributor's careful review of the historiographical currents related to their chosen topics. By presenting balanced perspectives from both Korean and global scholarship, the authors aim to offer English-speaking readers more accessible and nuanced entry points into the study of Chosŏn history.

Before its English-language publication, this manuscript underwent several rounds of review within Korean academic circles. The contributors regularly held seminars to refine their drafts, and some chapters were presented at an academic conference supported by the National Institute of Korean History in October 2024. Additionally, the publication of this book was made possible through the Academic Publishing Support Program of the Sogang University Press. On behalf of all the contributors, I extend our sincere gratitude to these two institutions for fostering scholarly dialogue between Korean and international academics.

While some contributors have prior experience writing for English-speaking readers, for others, this marks their first attempt at composing an English-language manuscript. Although the contributors have made every effort to refine the prose, any remaining infelicities or inaccuracies are solely our responsibility. We respectfully ask for the readers' warm interest and generous understanding.

We sincerely hope that this book will promote greater interest in the history of the Chosŏn dynasty—characterized by Confucianism, nation, and uniqueness—and lay the groundwork for further research endeavors.

On behalf of the contributors,
Hohyun Nam

Contents

1

The Foundation and Founders of the Choso̎n Dynasty

Joon Hur

Yonsei University

1 The Foundation and Founders of the Chosŏn Dynasty

Joon Hur (Yonsei University)

1. Introduction

It is widely acknowledged that during the time of Korea's victimization in the era of imperialism and during the Cold War, in the process of overcoming these difficulties, various historical discourses on Korea were constructed by different historians and scholars for their socio-political purposes. Especially, the colonial experience under Japan led Koreans to form negative memories of their past. The emergence and continued influence of Eurocentrism and Orientalism in the field of history has exacerbated this situation.

Since Japanese colonial historiography defined Korea as a society culturally behind and historically subservient to China and Japan, there have been many attempts among Korean scholars to prove Koreans' historical independence and cultural superiority. It was in this context that South Korean nationalist historians attempted to explain the establishment of the Chosŏn dynasty as Korea's social development that is in line with a law of universal history relying on linear development. The historians suggested the idea that it was the medium and small landlords in the late Koryŏ who defeated the large landlords and eventually established the

Chosŏn dynasty. According to this view, the establishment of the Chosŏn was the result of the conflicts and struggles between different socio-economic classes. The foundation of the Chosŏn dynasty was a "revolution" resulting from "class struggle," which was seen as working as the prime moving force in Western history and a significant proof that Korea was on the track of universal historical progress.

This view of history, known as the "new scholar-official" interpretation (*sinjin sadaebu ron*)," received positive evaluations and soon became the dominant view in Korean historiography on the establishment of the Chosŏn dynasty, probably because of its attempt to find a fit between Korean history and the concept of universal history relying on linear development.

Despite the positive impacts of the "new scholar-official" interpretation, it is still questionable whether such an emphasis on linear "progress" is the best way to effectively explain Korean history without serious distortion. As a matter of fact, attempts to mechanically apply Eurocentric conceptualizations of social development to Korean history have, in many cases if not always, ended up confirming certain limitations on the Korean version of progress despite their initial intention to reveal Korea's potential for development comparable to that of European states. It is natural therefore that in such studies trapped in the framework of linear development, the "failure narrative" of Japanese colonial historiography has often been repeated.

Moreover, the "new scholar-official" interpretation emphasizing "class conflict" as the main driving force behind the establishment of the Chosŏn dynasty has been strongly challenged by critics who questioned the possibility of a radical social revolution in fourteenth-century Korea. Since then, subsequent discussions of the founding of Chosŏn have been divided into two main approaches: those that focus on discovering the "changes" of social elements that characterize Korean society during the Koryŏ-Chosŏn transition period, and those that emphasize the "continuity" of social systems and structures. This division means that the "new scholar-official" interpretation is now subject to discussion and reexamination.

However, it is also true that this conventional view still holds influence on Korean historiography. This highlights the lasting impact of nationalist historiography, which sought to overcome colonial historiography, and underscores the ongoing need for in-depth discussion and examination of the founding and founders of the Chosŏn dynasty.

In light of this, this chapter examines the "new scholar-official" interpretation and its criticisms, and discusses appropriate approaches to the history of the establishment of the Chosŏn dynasty. Since much of the scholarly discussion up to the early 2000s is already well known, this chapter will focus more on relatively recent studies. This chapter attempts to explore the scholarly exchanges and discussions between various historians both in Korea and in the West. At the same time, it also touches upon the validity of nationalism-based historiography, particularly in the context of a true "post-colonial" discourse.

2. Different Interpretations about the Founders of the Chosŏn Dynasty: the "New Scholar-Official" Interpretation and Its Critiques

It is well known that the "new scholar-official" interpretation (*sinjin sadaebu ron*) began with Yi Usŏng's study which defines the *sadaebu* as the group of new bureaucrats in late Koryŏ under military rule who were "skilled at both letters and administration" (*nŭngmun nŭngni*) and had *hyangni* backgrounds.[1] Yi's study was followed by Min Hyŏn'gu, who introduced the concept of *kwŏnmun sejok* (powerful houses and strong families), typically defined as pro-Yuan large landowners. According to Min, they rose to positions within the central bureaucracy, often relying on a "protected appointment" system (*ŭmsŏ che*), and became a conservative power group that frequently found themselves in political conflict with the "new scholar-officials."[2]

Since then, the binary framework of the *sinjin sadaebu*, a newly emerged political power with local origins, and the *kwŏnmun sejok*, the conservative political groups struggling against the "new scholar-officials," has influenced later studies of the Koryŏ–Chosŏn transition. The late Koryŏ politics have been described as a struggle between conservative and reformative factions, or the pro-Yuan and pro-Ming groups.

This framework was further elaborated by Yi T'aejin, who identified the *sadaebu* as the small and medium landlords in the local society. According to Yi, small- and medium-sized landowners emerged through the development of agricultural productivity in late Koryŏ, ultimately dominating local society by promoting Neo-Confucian philosophy and culture. They evolved into "new scholar-officials," distinct from the earlier *nŭngmun nŭngni* literati during the late Koryŏ under military rule.[3] It has become a common trend in Korea to explain the founding of the Chosŏn dynasty as the result of the victory of the "new scholar-officials," who were primarily small and medium landowners, over the "aristocratic" large landowners: conflicts arose between socio-economically different groups in the late Koryŏ and early Chosŏn, and the outcome of these struggles ultimately led to the founding of the Chosŏn dynasty. This interpretation allows for viewing the founding of the Chosŏn dynasty as a societal revolutionary event driven by "class struggle," portraying Korea as a society that has progressed steadily through "universal stages of development."

Korean scholars have positively received the "new scholar-official" interpretation because it defines the establishment of the Chosŏn dynasty, described in colonial history as nothing more than a "court rebellion," as a revolutionary event that brought about significant social change.[4] During the 1980s and 1990s, Korean historians felt compelled to identify "developments" within late Koryŏ society. In this social context, it was challenging to criticize the "new scholar-official" interpretation, which highlights the growth and political empowerment of small and medium landowners and the rise of Neo-Confucianism as a new ideological framework.[5] Criticisms questioning the claim that the "new scholar-officials" originated from small landowners were not entirely absent.[6] However, due to the academic tendencies, not many studies directly challenged the crucial arguments of the "new scholar-official" interpretation.[7] Nevertheless, several studies have criticized the claim that the newly emerged *sadaebu* dismantled existing conservative political forces and ultimately established the Chosŏn dynasty; both Korean and Western historians of Korean history have questioned the binary framework in the "new scholar-official" theory, which emphasizes the conflicts between *sadaebu* and *kwŏnmun sejok*, or "emerging reformers" and "powerful conservatives." While these criticisms did not present a systematic alternative to replace the prevailing theory, they highlight its fundamental problems with dichotomy and are thus worth examining here.

In his book *Chosŏn ch'ogi chŏngch'i seryŏk yŏn'gu*, Chŏng Tuhŭi posits that many of the merit subjects of the Chosŏn dynasty were minor aristocrats in Koryŏ, and they rose through their own efforts and abilities. This seems like typical nationalist historiography, which asserts that the founders of the Chosŏn dynasty were not important members of the Koryŏ official establishment and thus, can be categorized as a newly emerging group. It is notable, however, that Chŏng points out that these merit subjects had different origins in the old dynasty after examining the backgrounds of the merit subjects of three reigns of Kings T'aejo, Chŏngjong, and T'aejong.[8] He suggests that some of the merit subjects, particularly civil officials, were Koryŏ aristocrats with prominent family backgrounds.[9] Although this study does not provide a definitive explanation for the origins of the Chosŏn founders,[10] it indicates that there is a probability of socio-political continuity between Koryŏ and Chosŏn ruling strata. According to Chŏng, the establishment of the Chosŏn should not be simplified as a radical change arising from the conflicts between the "old" and "new" groups.

Kim Tangt'aek presented that the established central-official descent groups used such terms as *sadaebu* and *sajok* to differentiate themselves from new elements of low social origins. He concludes that these *sajok* or *sadaebu* in the late Koryŏ were those who had been in power since early Koryŏ. According to his explanation, the official descent groups felt the need to redefine themselves as a socio-political group in opposition to men of more humble origins, such as slaves and eunuchs, who had elevated their social status in the Mongol period.[11] Kim showed that there was the advent of non-aristocratic elements in the late Koryŏ. At the same time, however, he also demonstrated that the established official decent groups never accepted these new elements among themselves. This calls into question the premise of the "new scholar-official" interpretation, which posits that the "new" men of humble origins became the *sadaebu* in the central bureaucracy who later experienced political conflicts with the old power group, known as *kwŏnmun sejok*.

Kim Kwangch'ŏl's study also challenges the conventional use and understanding of some terminologies. Demonstrating that the words *kwŏnmun* and *sejok* were never used together, Kim suggests that terms such as *kwŏnmun* and *kwŏnsega* were used in a pejorative sense to refer to particular individuals or families who were obsessed with monopolizing political power in the central government. In this sense, much of the criticism directed towards *kwŏnmun* or *kwŏnsega* in the late Koryŏ was not targeted at the central bureaucracy as a whole. Rather, the criticism was aimed at those who violated acceptable norms of power-sharing among Koryŏ elites. Kim's study also suggests that the term *sejok* refers to prominent families from the late Koryŏ period, while the term *sadaebu* encompasses all bureaucrats of the Koryŏ dynasty. This proves that *sejok* and *sadaebu* cannot serve as an effective pair of terms to describe competing political rivals. Ultimately, the study suggests that the political aggression against *kwŏnmun* and *sejok* in the late Koryŏ period should not be oversimplified as the attacks by the "new scholar-officials" on the established official decent groups that held power in the central bureaucracy of late Koryŏ.[12]

The critiques mentioned above highlight shortcomings of the binary framework that contrasts the "newly emerging groups from humble local families" with the "conservative elite from prominent families," which is central to the "new scholar-official" theory. Considering the composition of the founding forces of the Chosŏn dynasty and the actual instances of the usage of terms such as *sadaebu*, the criticisms directed at the "new scholar-official" theory appear convincing. Nevertheless, there has also been countercriticism that defends the "new scholar-official" interpretation, at least in part, if not entirely. However, it is still debatable whether this countercriticism directly addresses the "logical" issues raised by critiques of the conventional view. For instance, Yi Ikchu acknowledges that the terms such as *sadaebu* and *kwŏnmun sejok* have often been misused, and agrees with the criticism that the explanation that *sadaebu* originated from small and medium landlords or *hyangni* origins lacks evidence.[13] At the same time, however, Yi argues that "defining *sadaebu* as general bureaucrats disregards their historical significance and makes it difficult to explain the social transformations and resultant political changes of the late Koryŏ period."[14] Moreover, regarding the "new scholar-official" interpretation's emphasis on "the growth of small and medium landlords and their evolution into a political group," he contends that "the absence of evidence proving that *sadaebu* were small landlords does not mean that the theory should be discarded."[15] In doing so, Yi takes a stance supporting the main arguments of the "new scholar-official" theory without presenting substantial evidence.[16] This approach seems to stem from the view that, unlike "new scholar-official" interpretation, which is "capable of explaining the social development of late Koryŏ," its critiques fail to provide an account of "historical progress."[17]

Studies supporting the "new scholar-official" interpretation assume that historical "progress" is universally inevitable and then seek evidence from Korea's past to support this notion. In this context, the *sadaebu* had to exist as the driving force of historical and national development. There have been numerous attempts to define the *sadaebu* of late Koryŏ as either leaders of anti-Yuan movements or agents of social reform, despite the lack of concrete evidence.[18] This fact demonstrates that the raison d'être of the "new scholar-official" theory is to prove Korea's historical progress. Since the theory became widely accepted, the majority of historical narratives of the Koryŏ–Chosŏn transition period have largely adhered to the framework of "change and progress," in which the "newly emerging social forces" could be explained as the problem-solvers of "social contradictions." Consequently, the studies that criticized logical inconsistencies of the "new scholar-official" interpretation were often faced with demands to clarify how their criticisms could contribute to finding "progressive" elements in the past that "should" be found in Korean history, rather than being met with counterarguments based on substantial logic and evidence.

3. Responses from the West

When he "new scholar-official" theory was being criticized in Korea by scholars such as Chŏng Tuhŭi, John Duncan in the United States also questioned this conventional theory. In his article published in 1988, Duncan conducted a statistical analysis of the leading clans of the Koryŏ and Chosŏn dynasties. Based on this analysis, he argued that there was no significant change in the composition of the ruling stratum during the transition from Koryŏ to Chosŏn. First, this study reveals that a small number of clans held high-ranking official positions in the Chosŏn bureaucracy–especially the senior and junior first- and second-grade posts; this pattern was not significantly different during the Koryŏ period. The proportion of high-ranking positions held by certain leading clans increased steadily, suggesting that their political influence had grown by the late 14th century. Duncan also points out that access to political power had become more exclusive rather than open over time.[19] This study also indicates that 24 out of the 32 major clans, identified as important ruling elites in early Chosŏn, had already held significant official posts during the Koryŏ period. Only four clans–Changnyŏng Sŏng, Ŭiryŏng Nam, Ponghwa Chŏng, and Sŏngju Pae–fit the new scholar–official mold.[20] These four clans accounted for less than 10 percent of the officials from the entire thirty-two leading clans, and when limited to leading clan grade one and two officials, the percentage of the officials from these four clans was not significantly different.[21] By contrast, the five clans from the list of King Chungsŏn's "great ministerial families (*chaesang chi chong*,

宰相之宗)"[22] accounted for about 20 percent of both the officials from the thirty-two leading clans and the leading clan officials of grades one and two. The inclusion of other prominent members of the late Koryŏ aristocracy further increased the proportion of Koryŏ-origin elites in the early Chosŏn bureaucracy. This suggests that only a small amount of new blood emerged as notable political forces during the Koryŏ–Chosŏn transition; they were merely added to a largely self-perpetuating central aristocracy.[23] Based on this analysis, Duncan argued that while some individuals from new backgrounds appeared in central politics in late Koryŏ, they did not form "new political forces" capable of replacing the existing ruling elite. Moreover, the persistence of influential Koryŏ aristocratic families in early Chosŏn suggests that the new dynasty was more focused on joining these families rather than displacing them.

Duncan's work is notable not only for its reexamination of the commonly accepted definition of the "new scholar-officials," but also for its challenge to the conventional emphasis on "progress" and "change" in Korean historiography by nationalist historians. By demonstrating the that only four clans fit the new scholar-official mold and emphasizing that Yi Sŏnggye was building alliances with Koryŏ's ruling elite when he planned to establish the new dynasty,[24] Duncan argued that the emergence of a "new class," as suggested by nationalist historians, did not occur in the late Koryŏ period.[25] In this sense, his study contrasted sharply with the conventional progressionist view of Korean nationalist historians who saw the founding of Chosŏn as a "revolutionary" social change.

This study, which challenged the progressionist view of nationalist historians more directly than any other, was soon criticized by Korean historians, many of whom saw "progress" and "change" as essential elements of Korean history.[26] Probably because of this, in his book *The Origins of the Chosŏn Dynasty*, Duncan repeatedly emphasizes that the historical transition from Koryŏ to Chosŏn was a significant turning point in Korea's institutional transformation, emphasizing that Korea was not a "stagnant" society.[27] Nevertheless, in this book, his criticism of the main argument of the "new scholar-official" theory (which sought to confirm universal "progress" in history during the Koryŏ–Chosŏn transition) is strengthened rather than weakened.

Since Yi T'aejin elaborated the "new scholar-official" theory, the new scholar-officials have been defined as a "class" consisting of "small- and medium-sized landlords."[28] By explaining the founding of the Chosŏn dynasty as the emergence and triumph of this new "class," "class conflict" was presented as the main driving force of Korea's "progress." By explaining that "class conflict," which was proposed as a prime moving force of Western progress in the Western studies such as Marxist history, ultimately caused the establishment of the Chosŏn dynasty, the "new scholar-official" theory became an important historical discourse in Korea. This is because this discourse could show that Korea's premodern history was not fundamentally different from or inferior to that of the so-called "advanced" European societies, and that Korea followed a universal trajectory of historical development. However, according to Duncan, late Koryŏ and early Chosŏn society exhibited a very low level of social differentiation; in Chosŏn, where agriculture was the main industry, the yangban aristocrats monopolized important resources such as land and slaves, and thus there were no other significant social strata capable of challenging *yangban*, and *yangban* "stood alone at the apex of the Korean sociopolitical order."[29] In this context, it is futile to try to apply a "class conflict" mode of analysis to a society such as that of Koryŏ and early Chosŏn Korea.[30]

In fact, even among scholars in Korea, questions have been raised about the validity of the key premises of the "new scholar-official" theory such as "agricultural development" and "the rise of small- to medium-sized landlords." In addition, Duncan's study posed a fundamental question: Were there any "socially and economically heterogeneous" groups that could develop into significant social strata capable of challenging the established aristocracy of late Koryŏ society at the end of the 14th century? This study explains that at the end of the Koryŏ period, the ruling elite strengthened, rather than lost, their aristocratic privileges, as evidenced by the fact that only a very small number of families could newly become part of the power groups at the time. Therefore, it seems more appropriate to believe that the scholar-officials in the political "center" selectively absorbed new local elites as needed, rather than following the conventional notion that scholar-officials of *hayngi* origin overthrew the central aristocracy to seize power.

Nevertheless, studies that fail to find any alternatives to the "teleological" premises of the conventional interpretation–in other words, studies that fail to demonstrate "progress" and "change" in Korean society–may still be criticized as "stagnationist" studies that do not clarify the significance of the historical event of the Koryŏ–Chosŏn transition. In response to this criticism, Duncan sought to identify the significance of the historical event of the founding of Chosŏn in the transformation from a decentralized, locally particularistic sociopolitical order to a centralized system by the bureaucratic aristocratic elites. According to this interpretation, the transition from Koryŏ to Chosŏn at the end of the fourteenth century was not the result of a radical "revolution," but rather a gradual change. At the same time, this historical event demonstrates that there had been a fundamental and far-reaching social transformation over a long span of time, which eventually led to the establishment of a centralized bureaucratic system in Korea.[31]

4. Recent Discussions on the Establishment of the Chosŏn Dynasty

Recently, historians have reexamined the validity of the "new scholar-official" interpretation, which lacks sufficient evidence to support its main argument.[32] However, this does not mean that the theory has entirely lost its influence. For instance, Ch'oe Idon, in his recent work, defines the "new scholar-officials (*sinjin sadaebu*)" as intellectuals who grew up amid the "economic development of late Koryŏ" and held official positions in the central government "through the state examination system"; they grew to become a new political force, *sinjin sadaebu*, the social reformers who opposed the "exploitative aristocratic elite (*kwŏnmun sejok*)," and eventually established the Chosŏn dynasty "through revolution." Simply, Ch'oe maintained and repeated the conventional view of the "new scholar-official" interpretation.[33] Moreover, there are still a considerable number of newly produced local histories based on the conventional view of *sinjin sadaebu* as local elites (*chaeji sajok*).[34] The fact that even in the 2010s, many middle school textbooks explain the history of the Koryŏ–Chosŏn transition through the conflict between *sinjin sadaebu* and *kwŏnmun sejok*[35] also demonstrates that the conventional narrative still has some influence.[36] This situation seems to stem from the belief of numerous historians that revisionist studies, which critique the "new scholar-official" interpretation, have not successfully suggested meaningful "changes" during the Koryŏ–Chosŏn transition nor adequately explained their historical significance, contrary to the conventional view of nationalist historians. Nevertheless, due to the skepticism about the validity of the conventional definition of the "new scholar-officials" as "small- and medium-sized local landlords" and the doubts about the explanation that the "changes" in the political center were caused by the local agents, only a small number of historians have recently repeated the idea that the establishment of the Chosŏn dynasty was the result of a "social revolution by small and medium landlords." In this context, it would be more worthwhile to discuss here some of the recent studies on Chosŏn's founding forces that support or extend the critique of the "new scholar-official" theory.

Criticism of the conventional interpretation has mainly focused on revealing the inadequacy of the explanation that the Chosŏn dynasty was founded by the "new scholar-official class." This revisionist critique has prompted counterarguments that raise questions about who exactly founded Chosŏn, if not the *sinjin sadaebu*, and how the political and social nature of the founders should be understood. In addition, questions have arisen about how to "rescue" the "history" of the founding of the Chosŏn dynasty from the colonial historiographical framework of "stagnation theory," and which of "progress" and "continuity" should be more emphasized for a better understanding of Korean history. In this context, recent studies seem to go beyond merely negating the existing narrative of *sinjin sadaebu* and focus more on redefining the founding forces of the Chosŏn.

Kim Tangt'aek is one of the scholars who have insisted that the early Chosŏn ruling stratum has shown a substantial continuity between the Koryŏ and Chosŏn periods. In his recent study, Kim again claims that the majority of social reformers in late Koryŏ, who later became the founders of the Chosŏn, were not a discrete group from the members of the central bureaucracy. Additionally, Kim proposes a new interpretation of the founding of the Chosŏn dynasty that could be an alternative to the "new scholar-official" thesis, by addressing the question of who founded the Chosŏn dynasty.[37] According to him, the establishment of the Chosŏn was the result of repeated conflicts between the civil and military officials, rather than the struggle between the old aristocrats and the newly emerging scholar-officials. When political instability was exacerbated by the conflicts, Yi Sŏnggye received the support from civil officials who criticized the politics dominated by military officials and was able to establish a new state.

Kim also points out that the main cause of the political conflicts in the ruling stratum during late Koryŏ was not the political struggles between pro-Yuan officials and anti-Yuan officials, contrary to many existing studies' explanations. Rather, the ruling elites in late Koryŏ, including both military and civil officials, originally shared a common anti-Yuan attitude when the Yuan empire began to be dismantled. However, after they began to dominate the state politics through the Supreme Council (Todang, 都堂) and the Personnel Authority (Chŏngbang, 政房), which served as their institutional base, the military officials sought to normalize relations with the Yuan. This led to several conflicts between the Koryŏ and the newly emerging Ming dynasty during the late period of King Kongmin's reign. The civil officials, who had passed the civil service examination and mainly held pro-Ming attitude, challenged the political power of the military officials by criticizing their pro-Yuan politics. The officials demanded the abolition of Chŏngbang and undervalued the achievements of the military officials against foreign aggressors such as Japanese pirates. When numerous civil officials were purged by the military officials led by Ch'oe Yŏng, they sought help from Yi Sŏnggye, who was also a military leader but was marginalized from the political center at the time. After his return from Wihwa Island in 1388, Yi's faction gained a monopoly on political power in late Koryŏ and eventually established a new state.

It was a victory of the civil officials after prolonged struggles against the military officials. After the establishment of the Chosŏn dynasty, the civil officials dominated the state politics. The founders of the Chosŏn were not a separate political entity from the civil officials of the previous dynasty. Most of them were the civil officials in late Koryŏ who eventually took the power from the military officials. Many military officials in of Koryŏ were purged during the establishment of the new state. As a result, military personnel did not become a dominant political group in the Chosŏn, unlike the military officials of the late Koryŏ period.

Based on this explanation, Kim's study defines the founding of the Chosŏn as the political achievement of civil officials (*munsin*) who emerged victorious from protracted conflicts with military officials (*musin*). The group that established the Chosŏn dynasty shared a common identity as civil officials within the Koryŏ dynasty. By the late Koryŏ period, civil officials had already triumphed over military officials in the struggle for power, making them the political victors and the primary actors in the founding of the new dynasty. In contrast, most of the military officials who did not belong to the "Yi Sŏnggye faction" were purged during the political struggles and, as a result, could no longer be a significant part of the ruling stratum in the new dynasty. Therefore, the founding force of the Chosŏn should be understood as the "Yi Seonggye faction," centered on civil officials. Naturally, they should be regarded as a continuation of the civil official aristocracy of Koryŏ. As shown in this recent study, Kim emphasizes "continuity" as one of the important social characteristics of late fourteenth-century Korea.

Kim Kwangch'ŏl, who was also skeptical of the "new scholar-official" theory, has recently presented an expanded analysis of the political forces that dominated the late Koryŏ period. Although this study does not directly address the founding forces of the Chosŏn dynasty, it is still noteworthy as it discusses the social nature of the transitional period between Koryŏ and Chosŏn. According to this study, the late Koryŏ politics were dominated by numerous "close aides (*ch'ŭkkŭn*)" of the kings.[38] These royal aides used their own extrainstitutional agencies, such as *pich'ikch'i* (the scribe, *bičeči*, 必闍赤), to strengthen their political power and monopolize economic privileges. As a result, the late Koryŏ faced abnormal political situation in which political struggles were prevalent. Whenever a new king ascended to the throne, he would bring his own aides to replace the previous ones. Those who lost in the competitions often became supporters of the kings of the Shenyang (*Simwangp'a*, 瀋王派), and even attempted to make the Koryŏ a part of the Yuan empire.[39]

The abnormal political situation, dominated by a small number of royal aides and their extrainstitutional agencies, had a negative impact on the stability of the state and worsened the living conditions of the people. Many people suffered from a variety of economic problems, such as the unequal distribution of arable land and high taxes. In response to these social problems, the kings in late Koryŏ and ruling elites launched various reform projects. Although it is true that many of the ruling elites were landlords and their social reforms were inherently limited in solving the problems, it is still significant that the social reformers finally put an end to abnormal politics and their reform projects contributed to building a better society.

It should be noted that in this study, Kim asserts that the social reformers of the late Koryŏ period consisted of various groups.[40] The social reformers included not only men of humble origins, who had newly entered the central government, but also descendants of hereditary families (*sejok*), who had held political power and prestige. This suggests that the social reforms implemented in late Koryŏ were not solely the work of "new" members of the government.

This study also indicates that although the social reformers in late

Koryŏ had different origins, they shared some commonalities. Most of them were landlords, regardless of their level of land occupation, and passed the civil service exams. In this context, the political struggles in the late Koryŏ central government were not feuds between old aristocrats and new scholar-officials. Rather, the political conflicts in late Koryŏ were caused primarily by the social reformers' criticism of the close associates around the throne who attempted to monopolize political power and economic privileges. Kim offered a positive evaluation of the social reformers of the late Koryŏ period, arguing that these reformers expanded the pool of talent from which the central government could choose officials. If it can be said that the outcome of such social reforms and changes ultimately led to the establishment of the new dynasty, the founding of Chosŏn can be understood as the result of collaboration among those who shared common political goals and visions, not merely the achievement of the "new scholar-officials" alone. In this context, this study can serve as an important reference for understanding the founding of Chosŏn not as a revolutionary achievement by a new socio-political force, but as a continuation of the ongoing political actions of the ruling elite from the Koryŏ dynasty.

The two studies mentioned above, which contribute to a better understanding of the late Koryŏ politics, are significant for two main reasons. Firstly, they attempt to identify the causes of the political struggles in late Koryŏ, not only from an internal perspective, but also from an international one, focusing on the decline of the Yuan dynasty. Many historians have previously explained the struggle within the ruling stratum during the late Koryŏ period solely in terms of internal factors, such as the development of agricultural techniques and resulting economic growth. However, these studies demonstrate how the Koryŏ elite were both consolidated and fragmented by their desire to strengthen their power and secure strong patrons from international powers such as the Ming and Yuan. Secondly, these studies reveal that Korean elites continuously maintained their status as the political and intellectual leaders of society. While previous critiques of the "new scholar-official" theory, such as Duncan's study, focused on revealing the "socioeconomic homogeneity" among the ruling elites during the transition from Koryŏ to Chosŏn, these two studies delve deeper into the political actions taken by the ruling forces of late Koryŏ and early Chosŏn in order to identify the commonalities among the elite, ultimately aiming to clarify the nature of the political forces that contributed to the establishment of Chosŏn.

However, despite these academic contributions, there seems to be a need to debate whether these studies have achieved their original purpose –namely, to provide a new and clear definition of the founding forces of Chosŏn and to offer a new historical perspective that could replace the "new scholar-official" interpretation. For example, Kim Tangt'aek attempts to deconstruct the discourse of the "new scholar-officials" and redefine the founders of the Chosŏn dynasty. However, he does not seem to have succeeded in constructing a new historical discourse regarding the dynasty's establishment. It is true that Kim successfully avoids using the nomenclature of "new scholar-officials" when providing explanations about the founders of the Chosŏn. However, his study does not show any significant difference from previous criticisms of the "new scholar-official" interpretation. Kim merely states that the founders of the Chosŏn were a mixture of military officials under Yi Sŏnggye and the civil officials who joined Yi's group. Since Duncan had already pointed out that Chosŏn was founded by a coalition of the existing Koryŏ power group, the military forces including Yi Sŏnggye, and a small number of "newly" emerging scholar-official group, the conclusion that Yi Sŏnggye and the civil officials were the primary forces behind the founding of the Chosŏn does not seem particularly novel.

A more fundamental problem with the studies of Kim Tangt'aek and Kim Kwangch'ŏl is that by overemphasizing the "homogeneity" between the political forces in late Koryŏ and early Chosŏn, or the "continuity" of their political behaviors, they failed to properly characterize the social reformers of the Koryŏ and the founders of the Chosŏn. For example, the political conflicts identified in both studies are represented as "civil officials" versus "military officials" in Kim Tangt'aek's study, and "close aides of Koryŏ kings" versus "reformist forces" in Kim Kwangch'ŏl's study. These studies seem to attempt to show important "changes" in Korean history from Koryŏ to Chosŏn through the various political behaviors by different historical agents, and to present historical significance of the era. At the same time, they likely emphasize that the reformists in late Koryŏ and the founding forces of the Chosŏn were not distinct from the existing Koryŏ central aristocracy, thus highlighting the "continuity" in the composition of the ruling forces in late fourteenth-century Korea. The problem here, however, is that the overemphasis on this "long-term continuity" makes it difficult to clearly characterize the political groups presented in the two studies, such as "civil officials" and "reformist forces," with consistent definitions.

For example, although Kim Tangt'aek insisted that the Chosŏn was founded by the "civil officials," presumably to emphasize the conflict between the military and civil officials during the Koryŏ era, he also stated that the civil officials had different political careers during the late Koryŏ; the category of "civil officials" is overly broad, making it difficult to classify them as a single and coherent political group. Furthermore, according to Kim's study, those who eventually led the founding of Chosŏn were those who entered government through the civil service exams and later allied with Yi Sŏnggye, which does not clearly differentiate his work from previous studies. The main difference between this study and the "new scholar-official" interpretation is that Kim proposed that even some old aristocratic officials who had been hostile to Yi Sŏnggye later contributed to the establishment of the Chosŏn. However, this does not represent a significant departure from Duncan's explanation, which suggests that "the early Chosŏn bureaucracy may have been something of a mixed bag, including both new blood and old aristocrats."[41]

Kim Kwangch'ol's study is not significantly different. According to his research, the political powers at the end of the Koryŏ were heterogeneous as the leading officials, important political offices, and policies were constantly changing, influenced by the changes in the Koryŏ kingship. Given this, terms such as "close aides of Koryŏ kings (*ch'ŭkkŭn seryŏk*)" and "reformist forces (*kaehyŏk seryŏk*)" seem useful to explain that there were opposing political groups in the late Koryŏ, but they still do not clearly reveal who they were and what they did. In this context, even if the study suggests that the reformist forces probably contributed to "social stabilization" through their efforts such as improving the taxation system, it provides no more insight than the obvious conclusion that Koryŏ politicians tried to solve the social problems they faced. Even though this study successfully argues that there was a "continuous" and "repetitive" pattern in late Koryŏ politics, it seems to only reveal that there had been a "continuously repeated abnormal politics," raising questions about the historical significance of the late Koryŏ period.

Due to the failure to clearly define the political powers of the late Koryŏ and early Chosŏn, both studies, despite their academic contributions, have the problem of simplifying the politics of the Koryŏ–Chosŏn transition period as a "continuous power struggle" between "opposing groups." If the political history of late fourteenth-century Korea is simply explained as a struggle between "military officials and civil officials," or feuds between "different royal aides around the Koryŏ rulers" and "reformist forces that rose and fell according to political situations," it becomes difficult to understand this history as anything other than a power struggle between various political groups with different desires. Therefore, it must be carefully reconsidered whether the excessive emphasis on "continuity" only leads to the negative result of understanding Korean history as "a history stagnated in power struggles." The attempt to criticize the weakness of the "new scholar-official" theory should not, contrary to its original intention, regress into another form of "stagnation theory."

5. Conclusion

The continued influence of the "new scholar-official" theory, despite Duncan's direct refutation of its main arguments, is probably due to its "positive" historical narrative. In other words, the desire of historians to explain Korean history in terms of "development" and "change" remains influential even today, where the concept of "universal historical development," emphasized in Marxist historiography, has significantly weakened.[42] This is understandable given that the discourse of nationalist historians, which projected the concept of "universal historical development" based on the assumption of a "linear development of history" onto Korea's historical experience, had long dominated the narratives of Korean historiography.

Even the revisionist studies criticizing the "new scholar-official" theory also could not be completely free from the discussion of "change" and "development" in Korean history. Studies critical of the conventional theory that emphasizes the "change of the ruling classes" also seem to aim at finding some aspects of change and development of "Korean society" itself. Therefore, recent criticism of the conventional studies focuses on redefining the late Koryŏ reformers and the founders of Chosŏn as an important way to replace the "new scholar-official" theory; by presenting a new definition of the founders of Chosŏn, these studies also seem to aim at exploring the "progressive changes" in history that occurred in the late Koryŏ and early Chosŏn periods.[43] In other words, it seems that in many cases, the emphasis on "continuity" during the Koryŏ–Chosŏn transition in critical studies of the conventional theory is not only an attempt to reject the premise of "revolutionary change through class struggle" of the progressionist view, but also part of an effort to identify a more rational form of "change" in Korea's past. Since historians became interested in the establishment of the Chosŏn dynasty, "continuity" and "change" have consistently been central issues of discussion.[44]

Both the conventional view and its criticisms are clearly not free from the theme of "change and development" in Korean history. However, "continuity" and "change" do not exist in complete separation or opposition. A society characterized by strong "continuity" is not devoid of "change," and the society undergoing "change" also retains political, social, and cultural elements of "continuity." As Duncan aptly pointed out, the claim that the founding of Chosŏn was not a "revolutionary" change does not mean that there were no significant changes or developments in Korean society. On the contrary, it suggests that fundamental social change of fourteenth-century Korea occurred gradually over a long period.[45] However, there is still a tendency in Korean studies to focus on finding more distinct and short-term social changes; this tendency seems to need to be reconsidered and changed.

It seems that Korean history studies on the establishment of the Chosŏn dynasty needs to first overcome discussions based on the dichotomy of "continuity" and "change." The emphasis on the "development" and "change" advocated by the "new scholar-official" theory was part of the "post-colonial" effort to overcome the "stagnation theory" left by Japanese colonial historiography. However, if such efforts are distorted by the concept of "universal historical development" from the Western historical discourse that justified the rise of imperialism in the nineteenth century, the result will contradict the original intention of the nationalist historians' "decolonization" and their "new scholar-official" theory.

The revisionists and critics of the conventional view need to think carefully about the purpose and direction of their criticism. For example, if their focus remains on finding "historical change" during the Koryŏ–Chosŏn transition while rejecting the Marxist theories embedded in "new scholar-official" interpretation, their studies will likely fail to produce a better narrative or an insightful discourse that clearly distinguishes them from the "new scholar-official" approach. Similarly, emphasizing "continuity," the opposite of "change," without clearly defining the concept can also lead to problems. This approach risks reducing various events in Korean history to mere "cyclical fluctuations"[46] and may even be linked to the so-called "stagnation theory," potentially misinterpreting Koryŏ–Chosŏn transition as a "meaningless" event of power struggles.

The prevailing trend of discussing Korean history in terms of "progress" and "change" should now be overcome. Only then can we avoid the oversimplified understanding of historical agents and their behaviors in the fourteenth and fifteenth centuries by freeing ourselves from the binary framework of "change" and "continuity" or "development" and "stagnation." Historians should also approach the history of the Koryŏ–Chosŏn transition not by analyzing only the small number of elites in a particular period but by examining the much broader "social context."[47] Now, the field of history needs studies that go beyond the dichotomy of "continuity" and "change" and examine the various factors and variables that contributed to the social landscape of Korean society in the fourteenth and fifteenth centuries, which will help us gain a broader understanding of this period.

Note

1 Yi Usŏng, "Koryŏ ŭi 'i' e taehayŏ" (On the "clerks" of the Koryŏ dynasty), *Yŏksa hakpo* 63 (1964), pp. 21-26.

2 Min Hyŏn'gu, "Koryŏ hugi kwŏnmun sejok ŭi sŏngnip" (The rise of the late Koryŏ powerful families), *Honam munhw yŏn'gu* 6 (1974).

3 Yi T'aejin, "14·15 segi nongŏp kisul ŭi paltal kwa sinhŭng sajok" (Advances in agricultural technology and the new scholar-officials in the fourteenth and fifteenth centuries), *Tongyanghak* 9 (1978); Yi T'aejin, "Koryŏ mal·Chosŏn ch'o ŭi sahoe pyŏnhwa" (Social change between late Koryŏ and early Chosŏn), *Chindan hakpo* 55 (1983). Yi also explained that the *sarim* faction, which had been engaged in its political struggle with the *hun'gu* faction since the reign of King Sŏngjong, also originated from the small- and medium-sized landowners. Regarding this, see Yi T'aejin, *Han'guk sahoesa yŏn'gu: nongŏp kisul ŭi paltal kwa sahoe pyŏndong* (Studies in Korean social history: Advances in agricultural technology and social change), Seoul: Chisik Sanŏpsa, 1986.

4 It is well known that Japanese colonial historians attempted to explain the establishment of the Chosŏn as merely a result of a "court rebellion" that held no historical significance; this narrative was intended to emphasize the "stagnancy" of Korean society. Since Korea's liberation, Korean historians have sought to overcome this perspective. However, North Korean scholars still did not agree with the idea that founding of the Chosŏn represents historical progress. For example, in the *Chosŏn T'ongsa*, the establishmenf of the Chosŏn is described as simply a reinforcement of the feudal system, which did not lead to any significant historical evolution (*Chosŏn T'ongsa* (History of Korea), P'yŏngyang: Sahoe Kwahagwŏn, 1977). Regarding the Japanese colonial historiography and reactions from both South Korean and North Korean scholars, see John B. Duncan, *The Origins of the Chosŏn Dynast*, Seattle: University of Washington Press, 2000, pp. 3-5.

5 For instance, while pointing out the weaknesses in Yi Usŏng's hypothetical study, Yi Ikchu still acknowledges its validity, noting that "recent studies successfully revealed how new agricultural methods in late Koryŏ significantly

improved the economic independence of small landlords and, at the same time, how Neo-Confucianism, which reflects the interests of the landlords, was accepted as the dominant ideology." Yi Ikchu argues that these recent studies "strengthen" the "new scholar-official" interpretation, suggesting that he ultimately supports its main argument. (Yi Ikchu, "Koryŏ hugi sadaebu wa kwŏnmun sejok e taehan saeroun ihae: A book review of Kim Kwangch'ŏl, *Koryŏ hugi sejokch'ŭng yŏn'gu*" (A new understanding of the scholar-officials and the powerful families in late Koryŏ: A book rebiew of Kim Kwangch'ŏl, *Koryŏ hugi sejokch'ŭng yŏn'gu*), *Yŏksa wa hyŏnsil* 8 (1992), p. 321.

6 Yu Sŭngwŏn, *Chosŏn ch'ogi sinbun yŏn'gu* (Studies on status strata in the early Chosŏn dynasty), Seoul: Ŭlyu Munhwasa, 1987. For details, see particularly Chapter 5 "Sadabu kyech'ŭng kwa yangch'ŏn sinbunje."

7 The argument was essential to explain the "development" that is believed to have occurred–or that "should have occurred"–during the transition from late Koryŏ to early Chosŏn.

8 Chŏng TuHŭi, *Chosŏn ch'ogi chŏngch'i seryŏk yŏn'gu* (Studies on the political power of the early Chosŏn dynasty), Seoul: Ilchogak, 1983, pp. 54–55. Two main categories of the merit subjects were Yi Sŏnggye's military allies and civil officials in the central government in late Koryŏ.

9 Chŏng TuHŭi, *Chosŏn ch'ogi chŏngch'i seryŏk yŏn'gu*, pp. 54–55.

10 According to Duncan, there are two important problems with Chŏng's study. First, he assumed "talent" and "hard work" were exclusive to humble origins. More importantly, he failed to examine the entire officialdom of late Koryŏ and early Chosŏn (John B. Duncan, "The Social Background to the Founding of the Chosŏn Dynasty: Change or Continuity?" *Journal of Korean Studies* 6 (1988-89), p. 40.).

11 Kim Tangt'aek, "Ch'ungnyŏl wang ŭi pongnip kwajŏng ŭl t'onghae pon ch'ŏn'gye ch'ulsin kwallyo wa 'sajok' chu'ulsin kwallyo ŭi chŏngch'i chŏk kaltŭng: 'sadaebu' kaenyŏm e taehan kŏmt'o" (Political conflict between officials of mean origins and officials of *sajok* origins as seen in the reenthronement of King Ch'ungnyŏl: An examination of the *sadaebu* concept), *Tonga yŏn'gu* 17 (1989), pp. 195–232.

12 Kim Kwangch'ŏl, *Koryŏ hugi sejokch'ŭng yŏn'gu* (Studies on late Koryŏ

hereditary descent groups), Pusan: Tonga Taehakkyo, 1991.

13 Yi Ikchu "Koryŏ hugi sadaebu wa kwŏnmun sejok e taehan saeroun ihae," pp. 321-325; Yi Ikchu, "Kwŏnmun sejok kwa sadaebu" (The powerful families and the scholar-officials), in *Han'guk yŏksa immun 2. Chungse p'yŏn* (A guide to Korean history, part 2: the Middle Ages), ed. Han'guk Yŏksa Yŏn'guhoe (Korean History Research Society), Seoul: P'ulpit, 1995, pp. 86-93.

14 Yi Ikchu "Kwŏnmun sejok kwa sadaebu," p. 89.

15 Yi Ikchu "Koryŏ hugi sadaebu wa kwŏnmun sejok e taehan saeroun ihae," p. 321.

16 He insists that the increase in agricultural productivity and the introduction of Neo-Confucianism could be evidence. However, these merely restate explanations from the conventional theory which lacks sufficient evidence.

17 Yi Ikchu "Koryŏ hugi sadaebu wa kwŏnmun sejok e taehan saeroun ihae," p. 325.

18 Min Hyŏn'gu, "Sin Ton ŭi chipkwŏn kwa kŭ chŏngch'ijŏk sŏnggyŏk" (The rule of Sin Ton and its political nature) Parts 1 and 2, *Yŏksa hakpo* 38, 40 (1968); Yi Kinam, "Ch'ungsŏn wang ŭi kaehyŏk kwa Sarimwŏn ŭi sŏlch'i" (King Ch'ungsŏn's reforms and the establishment of the Sarimwŏn), *Yŏksa hakpo* 52, (1971); No Yongp'il, "Hong Chabŏn ŭi 'p'yŏnmin sip'alsa' e taehan yŏn'gu" (Research on Hong Chabŏn's "The Eighteen Ways of Caring People"), *Yŏksa hakpo* 102, (1984).

19 John B. Duncan, "The Social Background to the Founding of the Chosŏn Dynasty," p. 40.

20 Duncan classified eight clans as relatively new forces. However, he added that four of them–Chŏnju Yi, Hanyang Cho, Andong Chang, and Yŏngch'ŏn Hwangbo–should be categorized as military clans rather than scholarly official families.

21 John B. Duncan, "The Social Background to the Founding of the Chosŏn Dynasty," p. 59. Even including the four military clans in the note 20, the eight clans account for about 25 percent of the officials and about 30 percent of grade one and two officials, which hardly seems disproportionate for a group that makes up 25 percent of the thirty-two leading clans, especially when that group includes the royal family, the Chŏnju Yi clan.

22 The five clans are P'ap'yŏng Yun, Hwangyŏ Min, P'yŏngyang Cho, Ch'ŏngju

Yi, and Haeju Ch'oe (John B. Duncan, "The Social Background to the Founding of the Chosŏn Dynasty," p. 51.).

23 John B. Duncan, "The Social Background to the Founding of the Chosŏn Dynasty," pp. 59-60.

24 John B. Duncan, "The Social Background to the Founding of the Chosŏn Dynasty," p. 79.

25 According to Duncan, the rise of the small number of clans that fit the new scholar-official mold should be understood as "a continuation of the established pattern of recruitment" of the Koryŏ dynasty, which looks like "continuity" of social, political and institutional structures rather than "change" in them.

26 Korean history scholars in the United States, who emphasized "continuity" over "change," were got suspected of viewing Korea as a "stagnant" society. Regarding the suspicion, see Han Honggu, "Miguk han'gukhak ŭi sŏn'guja James Palais: chŏngnyŏn kinyŏm taedam" (James Palais, Pioneer of Korean studies in the United States: A dialogue in honor of his retirement), *Chŏngsin munhwa yŏn'gu* 24-2 (2001), p. 211. Duncan was no exception. In a special article in *Yŏksa pip'yŏng* in 2002, Michael Shin introduced Duncan's *The Origins of the Chosŏn Dynasty* and described his historical view as "a fundamentally more complex form of stagnation theory" that embodies the notion that "there was change in Korea, but no progress." (Michael D. Shin, "Migungnae han'gukhak kyebo" (The genealogy of Korean studies in the United States), *Yŏksa pip'yŏng* 59 (2002), pp. 84-85. In this writing, Michael Shin seems to support the view of Korean nationalist historians by showing a favorable stance toward the "internal development theory" (*naejaejŏk palchŏn non*). By showing the attitudes of "possessive exclusivism," Shin seems to frame much of Korean scholarship in the United States as influenced by Orientalism. However, one should be wary of approaching Western studies of Korean history from such an ideological perspective, given the substantial criticisms that have been directed at Said's concept of "possessive exclusivism," as well as the fact that Said himself later retracted it. For more details, see Edward W. Said, *Orientalism* (New York: Pantheon Books, 1978), p. 204; Edward W. Said, "Orientalism Reconsidered," in *Literature, Politics, and Theory*, eds. Francis Baker et al. (London: Methuen, 1986), p. 229.

27 John B. Duncan, *The Origins of the Chosŏn Dynasty* (Seattle: University of Washington Press, 2000), pp. 9, 275-278.

28 This definition is explicitly stated in Yi T'aejin's representative research, translated into English, where the "new scholar-officials" are described as "the small- to medium-sized landlord class." (Yi T'aejin, *The Dynamics of Confucianism and Modernization in Korean History* (Ithaca, New York: Cornell University, 2007), p. 3.) Here, one of the most significant changes during the Koryŏ–Chosŏn transition is presented as the rise of small- to medium-sized landlords who formed a new ruling class.

29 John B. Duncan, *The Origins of the Chosŏn Dynasty*, p. 276.

30 John B. Duncan, *The Origins of the Chosŏn Dynasty*, pp. 9, 278-283.

31 John B. Duncan, *The Origins of the Chosŏn Dynasty*, pp. 9, 278-283.

32 Song Ungsŏp, "Koryŏ mal–Chosŏn chŏn'gi chŏngch'i seryŏk ŭi ihae tasi pogi" (Reexamining the understanding of the political power in the late Koryŏ and early Chosŏn dynasties), *Yŏksa pip'yŏng* 120 (2017), p. 28.

33 Ch'oe Idon, *Chungse rŭl nŏmŏ Kŭndae rul pumŭn Chosŏn* (Chosŏn, the beginning of the modern era after the medieval period), Seoul: Yŏksain, 2021, pp. 62-82.

34 For example, Hong Cheyŏn, "Yŏmal sŏnch'o Kŭmsan chiyŏk ŭi chaeji seryŏk kwa sinjin sadaebu ŭi chŏngch'ak" (The movement of the local noble family and the settlement of the new scholar-officials in the Kŭmsan area from the late Koryŏ period to the early Chosŏn period), *Chŏnbuk sahak* 52 (2018).

35 For more details, see Kim Kwangch'ŏl, "Pokkop'ung sinjin sadaebu ŭi chaehyŏn–hyŏnhaeng chunghakkyo yŏksa kyokwasŏ ŭi 'sinjin sadaebu' sŏsul kŏmt'o" (The reappearance of the retro theory of the new scholar-officials– a survey on the description of the new scholar-officials in the current middle school history textbook), *Sŏktang nonch'ong* 62 (2015).

36 For instance, Kim Yunju, in her doctoral dissertation, explains the ruling forces during the Koryŏ–Chosŏn transition as follows: "As long as the class system did not collapse, the ruling class would have similar socio-economic backgrounds." That is, she critiques the conventional view, which emphasizes conflict within the ruling class, dividing it into two distinct socio-economic groups. At the same time, however, she argues that the theory of *sinjin*

sadaebu can still serve as a "valid methodology," revealing her somewhat contradictory stance. Kim Yunju, "Chosŏn T'aejo–T'aejong dae chŏngch'i wa chŏngch'i seryŏk" (The politics and political power in the reigns of King T'aejo and King T'aejong), PhD diss., Sŏul sirip tahakkyo, 2011, pp. 1-15.

37 Kim Tangt'aek, *Yi Sŏnggye wa Cho Chun· Chŏng Tojŏn ŭi Chosŏn kaech'ang* (The foundation of the Chosŏn dynasty by Yi Sŏnggye with Cho Chun and Chŏng Tojŏn), Kwangju: Chŏnnam tahakkyo ch'ulp'anbu, 2012.

38 Kim Kwangch'ŏl, *Yuan kansŏpki Koryŏ ŭi ch'ŭkkŭn chŏngch'i wa kaehyŏk chŏngch'i* (Politics of royal aides and politics of social reform in Koryŏ under the intervention of the Yuan empire), Kyŏnggi to: Kyŏngin munhwasa, 2018.

39 Kim Kwangch'ŏl, *Yuan kansŏpki Koryŏ ŭi ch'ŭkkŭn chŏngch'i wa kaehyŏk chŏngch'i*, p. 398.

40 Kim defines them as "liberal reformist political forces (kaebang chŏk chŏngch'i seryŏk)" that defeated "conservative political forces (p'yeswae chŏk chŏngch'i seryŏk)," for their common political goal. See, Kim Kwangch'ŏl, *Yuan kansŏpki Koryŏ ŭi ch'ŭkkŭn chŏngch'i wa kaehyŏk chŏngch'i*, p. 402.

41 John B. Duncan, "The Social Background to the Founding of the Chosŏn Dynasty," p. 51.

42 Hobsbawm, while criticizing the ahistorical elements and the risks of simplification of mechanistic models (E. J. Hobsbawm, *On History* (New York: New Press, 1997), pp. 34-36, 109-111, 122-123), also argued that the "change" with a certain "orientation" proposed by the Marxist model is the essential element of history (E. J. Hobsbawm, *On History*, pp. 150-156). For many historians who are opposed to seeing the historical past as a meaningless "cyclical fluctuation," the influence of the developmental models is still considerable, and it is also true that historians' narratives can be consciously or unconsciously influenced by such models.

43 For example, Kim Tangt'aek suggests that the political victory of the "civil officials" over the "military officials" represents a progressive change, while Kim Kwangch'ŏl describes the collapse of closed, kin-based political powers and the emergence of more liberal political forces as such a change.

44 This is evident in the subtitle of a recent book on the Chosŏn dynasty which poses the question of whether the Koryŏ-Chosŏn transition period was one

of "change" or "continuity." See Chŏng Yogŭn ed., *Koryŏ esŏ Chosŏn ŭro: yŏmal sŏnch'o tanjŏrin'ga kyesŭngin'ga* (From Koryŏ to Chosŏn: Does the transitional period between the Koryŏ dynasty and the Chosŏn dynasty mean discontinuity or continuity?), Seoul: Yŏksa pip'yŏngsa, 2019. This study emphasizes the need to move away from the progressionist view and examines the late Koryŏ and early Chosŏn periods from the viewpoint of "continuity."

45 John B. Duncan, *The Origins of the Chosŏn Dynasty*, p. 283.

46 E. J. Hobsbawm, *On History*, p. 153.

47 There have been numerous studies on Korea in the 14th and 15th centuries, examining various aspects including political forces, ideology, culture, institutions, and diplomacy (Chŏng Yogŭn ed., *Koryŏ esŏ Chosŏn ŭro: yŏmal sŏnch'o tanjŏrin'ga kyesŭngin'ga*, 2019). However, it should be noted that if such studies only serve to challenge the progressionist view, they will still have limitations in broadening the discussion on the late Koryŏ and early Chosŏn periods. For instance, in his study, Kang Munsik criticizes the conventional view of philosophical change in the late Koryŏ and early Chosŏn periods, arguing that there was a common academic trend between the Confucianism of the late Koryŏ and that of the sixteenth century (Kang Munsik, "Sŏngnihak ŭi suyong kwa kŭ sŏngkyŏk" (Introduction of Neo-Confucianism and its nature), in *Koryŏ esŏ Chosŏn ŭro: yŏmal sŏnch'o tanjŏrin'ga kyesŭngin'ga*, 2019, pp. 48–74). If further efforts are made to comprehensively explain how these academic trends influenced political behavior, how Confucian culture was disseminated in society, and how intellectual trends shaped people's daily lives, studies of fourteenth- and fifteenth-century Korea could provide valuable discussions on the "historical significance" of this period.

Bibliography

Barker, Francis, Peter Hulme, Margaret Iversen, and Diana Loxley. *Literature, Politics, and Theory*. London: Methuen, 1986.

Ch'oe, Idon. *Chungse rŭl nŏmŏ Kŭndae rul pumŭn Chosŏn* (Chosŏn, the beginning of the modern era after the medieval period). Seoul: Yŏksain, 2021.

Chŏng, TuHŭi. *Chosŏn ch'ogi chŏngch'i seryŏk yŏn'gu* (Studies on the political power of the early Chosŏn dynasty). Seoul: Ilchogak, 1983.

Chŏng, Yogŭn, ed. *Koryŏ esŏ Chosŏn ŭro: yŏmal sŏnch'o tanjŏrin'ga kyesŭngin'ga* (From Koryŏ to Chosŏn: Does the transitional period between the Koryŏ dynasty and the Chosŏn dynasty mean discontinuity or continuity?). Koyang: Yŏksa pip'yŏngsa, 2019.

Chosŏn T'ongsa (History of Korea), P'yŏngyang: Sahoe Kwahagwŏn, 1977.

Duncan, John B. *The Origins of the Chosŏn Dynasty*. Seattle: University of Washington Press, 2000.

Duncan, John B. "The Social Background to the Founding of the Chosŏn Dynasty: Change or Continuity?" *Journal of Korean Studies* 6 (1988-89).

Han, Honggu. "Miguk han'gukhak ŭi sŏn'guja James Palais: chŏngnyŏn kinyŏm taedam" (The pioneer of Korean studies in the United States, James Palais: A dialogue in honor of retirement). *Chŏngsin munhwa yŏn'gu* 24-2 (2001).

Han'guk Yŏksa Yŏn'guhoe (Korean History Research Society), ed. *Han'guk yŏksa immun 2. Chungse p'yŏn* (A guide to Korean history, part 2: the Middle Ages). Seoul: P'ulpit, 1995.

Hobsbawm, E. J. *On History*. New York: New Press, 1997.

Hong, Cheyŏn. "Yŏmal sŏnch'o Kŭmsan chiyŏk ŭi chaeji seryŏk kwa sinjin sadaebu ŭi chŏngch'ak" (The movement of the local noble family and the settlement of the new scholar-officials in the Kŭmsan area during from the late Koryŏ period to the early Chosŏn period). *Chŏnbuk sahak* 52 (2018).

Kang, Munsik. "Sŏngnihak ŭi suyong kwa kŭ sŏngkyŏk"(Introduction of Neo-Confucianism and its nature). In *Koryŏ esŏ Chosŏn ŭro: yŏmal sŏnch'o tanjŏrin'ga kyesŭngin'ga*, edited by Yogŭn Chŏng. Koyang:

Yŏksa pip'yŏngsa, 2019.

Kim, Kwangch'ŏl. *Koryŏ hugi sejokch'ŭng yŏn'gu* (Studies on late Koryŏ hereditary descent groups). Pusan: Tonga Taehakkyo, 1991.

_________. "Pokkop'ung sinjin sadaebu ŭi chaehyŏn–hyŏnhaeng chunghakkyo yŏksa kyokwasŏ ŭi 'sinjin sadaebu' sŏsul kŏmt'o" (The reappearance of the retro theory of the new scholar-officials–a survey on the description of the new scholar-officials in the current middle school history textbook). *Sŏktang nonch'ong* 62 (2015).

_________. *Yuan kansŏpki Koryŏ ŭi ch'ŭkkŭn chŏngch'i wa kaehyŏk chŏngch'i* (Politics of royal aides and politics of social reform in Koryŏ under the intervention of the Yuan empire). Kyŏnggi to: Kyŏngin munhwasa, 2018.

Kim, Tangt'aek. "Ch'ungnyŏl wang ŭi pongnip kwajŏng ŭl t'onghae pon ch'ŏn'gye ch'ulsin kwallyo wa 'sajok' chu'ulsin kwallyo ŭi chŏngch'i chŏk kaltŭng: 'sadaebu' kaenyŏm e taehan kŏmt'o" (Political conflict between officials of mean origins and officials of *sajok* origins as seen in the reenthronement of King Ch'ungnyŏl: An examination of the *sadaebu* concept). *Tonga yŏn'gu* 17 (1989).

_________. *Yi Sŏnggye wa Cho Chun·Chŏng Tojŏn ŭi Chosŏn kaech'ang* (The foundation of the Chosŏn dynasty by Yi Sŏnggye with Cho Chun and Chŏng Tojŏn). Kwangju: Chŏnnam tahakkyo ch'ulp'anbu, 2012.

Kim, Yunju. "Chosŏn T'aejo–T'aejong dae chŏngch'i wa chŏngch'i seryŏk" (The politics and political power in the reigns of King T'aejo and King T'aejong). PhD diss., Sŏul sirip tahakkyo, 2011.

Min, Hyŏn'gu. "Koryŏ hugi kwŏnmun sejok ŭi sŏnggnip" (The rise of the late Koryŏ powerful families). *Honam munhw yŏn'gu* 6 (1974).

_________. "Sin Ton ŭi chipkwŏn kwa kŭ chŏngch'ijŏk sŏnggyŏk" (The rule of Sin Ton and its political nature) Parts 1 and 2. *Yŏksa hakpo* 38, 40 (1968).

No, Yongp'il. "Hong Chabŏn ŭi 'p'yŏnmin sip'alsa' e taehan yŏn'gu" (Research on Hong Chabŏn's "The Eighteen Ways of Caring People"). *Yŏksa hakpo* 102, (1984).

Said, Edward W. *Orientalism*. New York: Pantheon Books, 1978.

_________. "Orientalism Reconsidered." In *Literature, Politics, and Theory*, edited by Francis Baker et al. London: Methuen, 1986.

Shin, Michael D. "Migungnae han'gukhak kyebo" (The genealogy of Korean studies in the United States). *Yŏksa pip'yŏng* 59 (2002).

Song, Ungsŏp. "Koryŏ mal–Chosŏn chŏn'gi chŏngch'i seryŏk ŭi ihae tasi pogi" (Reexamining the understanding of the political power in the late Koryŏ and early Chosŏn dynasties). *Yŏksa pip'yŏng* 120 (2017).

Yu, Sŭngwŏn. *Chosŏn ch'ogi sinbun yŏn'gu* (Studies on status strata in the early Chosŏn dynasty). Seoul: Ŭlyu Munhwasa, 1987.

Yi, Ikchu. "Koryŏ hugi sadaebu wa kwŏnmun sejok e taehan saeroun ihae: A book review of Kim Kwangch'ŏl, *Koryŏ hugi sejokch'ŭng yŏn'gu*" (A new understanding of the scholar–officials and the powerful families in late Koryŏ: A book rebiew of Kim Kwangch'ŏl, *Koryŏ hugi sejokch'ŭng yŏn'gu*). *Yŏksa wa hyŏnsil* 8 (1992).

_________. "Kwŏnmun sejok kwa sadaebu" (The powerful families and the scholar–officials) In *Han'guk yŏksa immun 2. Chungse p'yŏn* (A guide to Korean history, part 2: the Middle Ages) edited by Han'guk Yŏksa Yŏn'guhoe (Korean History Research Society). Seoul: P'ulpit, 1995.

Yi, Kinam. "Ch'ungsŏn wang ŭi kaehyŏk kwa Sarimwŏn ŭi sŏlch'i" (King Ch'ungsŏn's reforms and the establishment of the Sarimwŏn). *Yŏksa hakpo* 52, (1971).

Yi, T'aejin. "14·15 segi nongŏp kisul ŭi paltal kwa sinhŭng sajok" (Advances in agricultural technology and the new scholar–officials in the fourteenth and fifteenth centuries). *Tongyanghak* 9 (1978).

_________. *Han'guk sahoesa yŏn'gu: nongŏp kisul ŭi paltal kwa sahoe pyŏndong* (Studies in Korean social history: Advances in agricultural technology and social change). Seoul: Chisik Sanŏpsa, 1986:

_________. "Koryŏ mal·Chosŏn ch'o ŭi sahoe pyŏnhwa" (Social change between late Koryŏ and early Chosŏn). *Chindan hakpo* 55 (1983)

_________. *The Dynamics of Confucianism and Modernization in Korean History*. Ithaca, New York: Cornell University, 2007.

Yi, Usŏng. "Koryŏ ŭi 'i' e taehayŏ" (On the "clerks" of the Koryŏ dynasty). *Yŏksa hakpo* 63 (1964).

2

The Emergence of New Confucian Generations: A Critical Review of the *Sarim* Faction Theory in Early Chosŏn

Seung B. Kye

Sogang University

2 The Emergence of New Confucian Generations: A Critical Review of the *Sarim* Faction Theory in Early Chosŏn

Seung B. Kye (Sogang University)

1. Introduction

In explaining the political forces of early Chosŏn (15th–16th century), two significant theories stand out: the new Neo-Confucian scholar-officials (*sinjin sadaebu*) theory and the *sarim* faction theory. Involving some key figures, the former focuses on the transition from the Koryŏ to the Chosŏn dynasty in the late 1300s, while the latter explains the emergence of a new ruling class about a century later, as the dynasty's governance system solidified.

The *sarim* faction (*sarimp'a*) theory, which is based on the conflict between the *hun'gu* (established high-ranking officials and merit subjects) and the *sarim* (Confucian literati/gentry), can be summarized as follows: In the early Chosŏn dynasty in the 1400s, high-ranking officials of the central government were usually called *hun'gu*, which then consisted of merit subjects (*hun*) and established bureaucrats (*gu*). As for the concept of *sarim*, they were the academic descendants of those who opposed the founding of Chosŏn and thus retreated to the countryside. Following the scholarly lineage of Kil Chae (1353–1419), they were well-versed in Neo-Confucianism and emphasized classical studies (*kyŏnghak*) over literary composition (*sajang*). Based in rural areas as small and medium-sized landowners, they represented the interests of local gentry. From the late 1400s, they steadily advanced into the central political arena through the civil service examination system of the state. Occupying positions in the three remonstrance offices (*samsa*), they criticized contemporary politics and clashed with the established *hun'gu* faction. Despite suffering significant setbacks from successive literati purges (*sahwa*), they eventually ousted the *hun'gu* faction and seized power by the late 1500s.

However, this explanation lacks substantial evidence. Even the criteria distinguishing large estates from small or medium-sized ones were never clearly defined. Nevertheless, the theory first appeared as a hypothesis in domestic textbooks during the 1950s and 1960s and has since been perpetuated through education, rapidly gaining acceptance as an established theory without thorough argumentation. Continuous counter-evidence and criticism have led to its rejection, particularly among junior scholars, and new alternative explanations are emerging these days.

This chapter will first review the research trends related to the *sarim* faction in both domestic and international academia in chronological order. Additionally, it will reinterpret the political and social changes over the hundred years from the late 1400s to the early 1500s as the emergence of new younger generations armed with Confucian values and their decades-long "Confucianization movement" or "Confucian practice movement." By examining this movement, which spread among young Confucian students in the late 1400s, we aim to shed light on how Chosŏn evolved into a truly Confucian state over time.

2. A Critical Review of Existing Studies on the *Sarim* Faction

In describing the politico-intellectual history of early Chosŏn, the first scholar who used the term *sarimp'a* (*sarim* faction) was Yi Pyŏngdo. By specifically using the term "*Yŏngnam sarimp'a*," he portrayed *sarimp'a* as a newly rising power group from the province located in the southeast of the Korean peninsula. He also explained the series of literati purges as the result of conflicts between *hun'gu* and *sarim* factions.[1] But he did not mention the differences yet in socioeconomic foundations of the two factions. Yi Inyŏng shared Yi Pyŏngdo's view by emphasizing the confrontation between the old aristocracy (*hun'gu*, government officials) and the new aristocracy (*sarim*, Confucian literati). Particularly, Yi Inyŏng stressed the differences in land ownership bases, thereby adding a socioeconomic dimension to the distinction between the *hun'gu* and *sarim* factions.[2]

Criticism of the nascent *sarim* faction theory emerged promptly from abroad. In 1960, American scholar Edward W. Wagner examined the backgrounds of those who passed the recommendation examination (*hyŏllyangkwa*) and argued that it was difficult to distinguish the *hun'gu* and *sarim* factions as heterogeneous groups based on socioeconomic foundations.[3] Although written in English, this article was published in a Japanese journal, so Korean scholars of the time likely read it. However, there was no reaction. Instead, the trend of emphasizing the *sarim* faction theory intensified in Korea.

In fact, introductory survey books from the 1960s devoted substantial attention to explaining the newly rising *sarim* faction. Notably, in 1961, Yi Kibaek accepted the explanations of Yi Pyŏngdo and Yi Inyŏng, yet he further elaborated on the conflict between the *hun'gu* and *sarim* factions by emphasizing differences in their regional origins and landownership bases.[4] He highlighted their 'class-based' differences even more prominently. In a new introductory text published in 1967, Yi Kibaek included a new section titled "The rise of the sarim faction." In this section, he detailed the expansion of agricultural estates by the *hun'gu* faction, further emphasizing economic differences, such as land ownership, as the primary reasons for the series of conflicts between the *hun'gu* and *sarim* factions.[5]

In short, the framework for explaining early Chosŏn politics through the conflict between the *hun'gu* and *sarim* factions was firmly established in the 1960s. However, this framework was not the result of a substantial accumulation of scholarly research but rather remained a hypothesis at the conjectural stage.

The first domestic scholar to support the *sarim* faction hypothesis with a research paper was Yi T'aejin in 1972. According to him, the *sarim* faction, composed of small and medium landowners from Yöngnam Province, led by Kim Chongjik (1431–1492), opposed the central *hun'gu* faction through a movement to re-establish the *yuhyangso* (local yangban associations) and sought local autonomy against centralization. Yi consistently emphasized the conflict between the *sarim* and *hun'gu* factions, explaining their differences not only in attitudes towards Neo-Confucianism but also in terms of their socioeconomic bases. He even declared the rise of the *sarim* faction as a "victory of the small and medium landowners."[6] However, his work had a critical flaw in that it failed to demonstrate how land ownership differed in actuality between the *hun'gu* and *sarim* factions.

In 1974, Edward Wagner specifically pointed out the errors in the *sarim* faction theory in his study on *sahwa* (literati purges). He directly contradicted the prevailing theory in Korean academia that the literati purges occurred due to the conflict between the *hun'gu* and *sarim* factions. Instead, Wagner argued that the purges resulted from the unique system of the Chosön dynasty, particularly the censorate system.[7] Wagner's work did not merely refute the *sarim* faction theory but also proposed an alternative explanation, which was quite innovative at the time. However, there was little reaction from Korean academia. Perhaps the fact that the book was published in English in the United States meant that its existence was not widely known among Korean scholars of the time.

Despite Wagner's research, the study of the *sarim* faction in Korean academia continued to flourish. In 1979, Yi Sugŏn published a comprehensive study on the representative *sarim* figures from the Yŏngnam region. According to him, the *sarim* can be characterized as follows: They were local small and medium landowners whose status was elevated through positions such as honorary posts (*ch'ŏmsŏljik*).

They established a dominant base in rural society through their strong socioeconomic foundation and Neo-Confucian knowledge. They valued integrity and legitimacy, having retreated during the fall of Koryŏ and opposed Sejo's 'usurpation.' They preferred scholarly pursuits over official positions. Beyond literary composition, they emphasized personal cultivation and practical implementation based on Neo-Confucian ethics books. When they advanced to the central political arena, they were identified as a new political force opposing the established *hun'gu* faction.[8]

This study advanced the *sarim* faction hypothesis by understanding the *sarim* as a new political force dedicated to pursuing Neo-Confucian values and possessing a different socioeconomic base from the existing ruling class. This marked a significant step forward from the hypothesis stage, contributing to the historical understanding of the *sarim* faction's role and significance. According to the same book, however, leading figures of the *sarim* faction, such as Kim Keongp'il (1454-1504), Chŏng Yŏch'ang (1450-1504), Kim Ilson (1464-1498), Yi Hwang (1501-1570), and Yi I (1536-1584), were wealthy landowners who owned numerous slaves and farmlands across various regions of the country.[9] This indicates that they had the characteristics of large landowners and absentee landlords. Furthermore, YI's observation that the Yŏngnam *sarim* faction frequently formed marital ties with the central *hun'gu* families does not align well with his own definition of the *sarim* faction. In particular, the fact that many *sarim* lived in Seoul contradicts the understanding of the *sarim* faction as rural small and medium landowners. Despite uncovering significant facts about the *sarim* through empirical research, Yi Sugŏn ultimately adhered to the conventional notion of the *sarim* faction theory as rural small and medium landowners, leading to conclusions that conflicted with his own findings.

Wagner intervened again. In 1980, he published a paper in a Korean academic journal that addressed the *sarim* issue in depth. In this paper, he noted that many of the individuals who could be classified as prominent *sarim* figures—such as the twenty-four Confucian scholars from the Royal Academy (*Sŏnggyun'gwan*) who were punished for vehemently opposing

King Sŏngjong's Buddhist-style funeral in 1494, the eight individuals executed during the Literati Purge of 1519, and the twenty-eight successful candidates from the 1519 recommendation examination—were mostly from prestigious families in Seoul. Based on this, Wagner argued that the only distinguishing feature of the group called *sarim* at the time was their exceptional adherence to Neo-Confucian political principles and ethical norms. Therefore, he concluded that the term *sarim* was inappropriate to describe a distinct group or a new social class rising in opposition to the existing ruling elites (*hun'gu*).[10] Considering that there was no significant difference in land ownership between the *hun'gu* and *sarim* factions,[11] Wagner's view is quite persuasive. However, it has the drawback of underestimating the significance of the *sarim* as a political force or specific group, as frequently recorded in the dynastic annals. In other words, the term *sarim* encompassed not only individuals who were more faithful to Neo-Confucian values but also those who banded together and acted collectively to implement those values in practical politics.

However, Wagner's Korean-language paper was also ignored by domestic academia, eliciting no significant response. Instead, research explaining the distinction between the *hun'gu* and *sarim* factions based on socioeconomic differences continued to dominate, led by scholars like Yi T'aejin. From the late 1970s to the early 1980s, Yi published a series of papers that collectively contributed to this perspective.[12] He played a pivotal role in understanding the rise of the *sarim* faction in early Chosŏn (especially in the 16th century) through the lens of local societal development driven by the spread of agricultural technology. His work decisively contributed to the understanding of the *sarim* faction as a new class with a distinct socioeconomic foundation.

Based on this research, Yi T'aejin characterized the *sarim* faction as follows: They were from the small and medium landowner class in rural areas, whose status was elevated through positions like *ch'ŏmsŏljik*. Although they were initially concentrated in the southeast region of the Korean peninsula, they gradually spread to the central peninsula. They grew along with the development of the agricultural economy during the 15th and 16th centuries. They were firm believers in Neo-Confucian political ideals. They emerged as a new political force representing local interests against centralization.[13] Among these characteristics, the key themes emphasized by Yi were undoubtedly "rural areas" and "small and medium landowners." In essence, Yi's work reaffirmed the "formula" that the *sarim* faction consisted of the small and medium landowner class in rural areas. His research is significant in that it focused on the socioeconomic conditions necessary to explain the *sarim* faction as a new class or stratum.

However, Yi T'aejin did not adequately define the criteria for distinguishing between large and small landowners. He neither investigated nor compared the land ownership statuses of individuals from the *hun'gu* and *sarim* factions. Without substantial evidence, his arguments remained mere assertions. As revealed in Yi Sugŏn's 1979 study, prominent *sarim* figures were known to be wealthy individuals who owned extensive lands and slaves across various regions, which is a significant counterargument. In fact, in the numerous instances where the term "sarim" appears in the dynastic annals (*sillok*), there is no clear example of it being used specifically to refer to rural forces or small landowners. Even if some small landowners in rural areas were included among the *sarim* faction, this does not mean that the term "sarim" was used at the time to denote a specific class of small landowners residing in rural areas. Additionally, the sharp criticism pointed out that dividing the *hun'gu* and *sarim* factions based on their attitudes toward *yuhangso* (local yangban associations), *sach'ang* (village granaries), reclamation projects, and *sŏwŏn* (private academy) was never accurate.[14] Nevertheless, Yi T'aejin did not offer any rebuttal and continued to reiterate his claims without addressing these criticisms.

Around the same time, Yi Pyŏnghyu proposed a theory that slightly revised the existing understanding of the *sarim* faction, which garnered attention. He suggested that the term "*sarim*" originally referred to ordinary literati who could read books, but gradually became a concept specifically referring to Neo-Confucian students and scholars. By the time of King Sŏngjong (r. 1469-1494), it had solidified into a term denoting a political group opposing the *hun'gu* faction. Following several literati purges, it became a historical term specifically pointing to the victimized group.[15]

Based on his definition, Yi Pyŏnghyu investigated the backgrounds of 105 disciples of Kim Chongjik, Kim Keongp'il, and Chŏng Yŏch'ang, as well as 95 individuals known as the so-called *Kimyo sarim*, persecuted in the course of the literati purge of 1519. According to Yi, (1) the *sarim*p'a, formed in and after King Sŏngjong's reign, was primarily composed of individuals from the Kiho region rather than Yŏngnam. (2) Within the *sarim* faction, the proportion and political significance of members from prestigious *hun'gu* families were substantial. (3) External conditions such as social status or economic foundation were not sufficient to distinguish between the *hun'gu* and *sarim* factions. (4) Up until the literati purge of 1519, the *sarim* faction consisted of politically active and reform-minded individuals or those who shared a sense of solidarity with such figures.[16] Additionally, Yi Pyŏnghyu also asserted as follows: (5) his own findings did not significantly deviate from the general understanding that the *sarim* faction comprised local literti/gentry distinct from the *hun'gu* families. He also argued that (6) the political and social history of early Chosŏn was characterized by the interaction and development of central power (*hun'gu*) and local forces (*sarim*).[17]

While the newly uncovered facts about the sarim, as highlighted in points (1)-(4), are significant, Yi's adherence to the conventional understanding that *hun'gu* and *sarim* were heterogeneous social classes based on regional and economic foundations led to inconsistencies in his conclusions. The content of points (2) and (3) is incompatible with the assertions in points (5) and (6).

Aware of his own contradictions, Yi Pyŏnghyu attempted to downplay the proportion of individuals from prestigious families in Seoul among the twenty-eight successful candidates of the recommendation examination of 1519. He interpreted more than 50% of those from *hun'gu* families as having "switched" from *hun'gu* to *sarim*. Despite their clear status as members of prestigious families in Seoul, he categorized them as *sarim* whose power bases were in rural areas on the ground that their farms were located in Kyŏnggi or Ch'ungch'ŏng provinces.[18] Furthermore, Yi frequently used the term "converted *sarimp'a*" throughout his book to describe those who switched from the *hun'gu* faction to the *sarim* faction. While this term might make sense if it referred to a gradual ideological shift, it is questionable whether there has ever been a large-scale instance in human history, especially in a status-based society grounded in land ownership, where central large landowners voluntarily became rural small landowners. Although Yi intended to use the term "conversion" in the context of ideological changes, the term inevitably implies socioeconomic aspects due to his acceptance of the conventional notion of "*sarim* faction = rural small and medium landowners." In summary, the mere fact that a significant number of the twenty-eight *hyŏllyangkwa* candidates came from prestigious Seoul families undermines the conventional notion of the *sarim* faction as solely rural small and medium landowners.

In domestic academia, research efforts throughout the 1970s and 1980s aimed to empirically validate the existing conventional view that the *sarim* faction represented a new socioeconomic class and political force. Particularly during the 1980s, studies focusing on the actual activities of the *sarim* faction, such as remonstrance and impeachment, began to emerge. The distinctive feature of these studies was their utilization of the *sarim* faction theory while excluding the socio-economic foundation as a factor. In 1978, Song Ch'ansik viewed a series of literati purges from the reigns of King Sŏngjong to King Chungjong (1469-1544) as conflicts between the emerging *sarim* forces, who had taken control of the three censorial offices (*samsa*), and the established *hun'gu* forces, centered around the State Council and the six ministries.[19] This perspective interpreted the literati purges not as a result of economic differences between the *hun'gu* and *sarim* factions, but rather as conflicts arising from the unique political system of the Censorate (*taegan*) and the generational clash between the new (*sarim*) and the old (*hun'gu*). Overall, it can be seen as aligning with Wagner's view.

Following Song's research, studies in the 1980s by emerging domestic scholars significantly focused on understanding the *sarim* faction in relation to the activities of the Censorate. Notable scholars in this trend include Kim Ton, Nam Chidae, Kim Wugi, and Choi Idon, among others.[20] These studies, however, did not fundamentally question who the *sarim* were. Instead, they focused on the activities of those already classified as *sarim* on the political stage from the reigns of Sŏngjong to Chungjong and the resulting changes in the political structure and environment. Later, Kim Ton explicitly criticized the schematic distinction between *hun'gu* and *sarim*, particularly challenging the existing methods of distinguishing the two based on their origin (rural or not) and economic foundation (small landowners or not).[21] While these studies provided more detailed insights into the censorial activities of the *sarim* under the premise that the *sarim* were indeed rural small landowners, they did not challenge the existing *sarim* faction theory. The limitations were clear in that they adhered to the conventional notion of the *sarimp'a* as rural small landowners without reconsidering the fundamental concept or scope of the *sarim* faction.

In the 1990s, the dominant trend in domestic academia continued to follow the traditional *sarim* faction theory. However, significant criticisms of this conventional view began to emerge. For example, in 1994, Chŏng Tuhŭi investigated whether the officials of the three censorial offices (*samsa*), known as the stronghold of the *sarim* faction, actually matched the concept of the *sarim* faction as defined by the conventional theory. He conducted a comprehensive investigation of the family backgrounds of 373 individuals who served in the censorial offices during the reign of King Sŏngjong (1469–1494), a period known for the rise of the *sarim* faction on the political stage. The logic behind his research was that if the three censorial offices functioned as the power base of the *sarim* faction during King Sŏngjong's reign, as the conventional theory suggests, then the family backgrounds of those who served in the Censorate during this period should align with the conventional description of the *sarim* faction. His findings, however, demonstrated that most of the censorate officials during Sŏngjong's reign were actually from prestigious families of the capital city. This empirical evidence directly contradicted the conventional theory that viewed the sarim faction as composed of rural small landowners. Chŏng asserted that when there is a significant discrepancy between a theory and concrete facts, the theory must be cancelled.[22] Despite these findings, the academic response was surprisingly indifferent, with a strong tendency to ignore his work rather than engage in substantial debate.

Based on the research achievements of American scholars such as Wagner, in 1996, James Palais criticized the schema of "*sarim* faction = rural small landowners." He also criticized other criteria used by Yi T'aejin to differentiate between the *hun'gu* and *sarim* factions, such as attitudes towards local Confucian systems like *hyangyak* (community compact), *hyangsarye* (local archery rites), and *hyangŭmjurye* (local drinking rites). He argued that differences in views and positions on these issues did not necessarily align along the lines of the *hun'gu* and *sarim* factions.[23] This criticism was later inherited and elaborated by Kim Pŏm in Korean academia in 2003.[24] It is worth noting that this criticism was not part of a comprehensive investigation into the *sarim* faction debate but arose in the context of explaining the historical background of *hyangyak* as conceived by Yu Hyŏng-wŏn (1622-1673) in the 17th century. Consequently, it mainly served to critique the dominant theories in domestic academia without proposing a new explanatory framework.

Despite the criticisms of the conventional *sarim* faction theory from both domestic and international scholars, the mainstream view in domestic academia remained largely unchanged throughout the 1990s. This persistence is evident in the 1996 publication of *History of Korea 28: The Emergence and Activities of the Sarim Forces in Mid-Chos*ŏn by the National Institute of Korean History, which can be considered a definitive explanation of the *sarim* faction.[25] It is clear that this publication was entirely based on the existing conventional theory. Notably, despite serious counterarguments raised both domestically and internationally, the book simply repeated the existing theory without any defensive explanations or consideration of the criticisms.

Eventually, however, this academic atmosphere began to change in the 2000s. Research that challenged the conventional *sarim* faction theory emerged more prominently in domestic academia. For an instance, Song Ungsŏp conducted a study on the backgrounds of approximately 90 members of the so-called *Kimyo sarim* (ones punished in the Literati Purge of 1519) listed in several records, including the *Kimyodang chŏk*. (List of the *Kimyo* faction) According to him, approximately 70% of the *sarim* members resided in Seoul at the time they took the licentiate examination (*samasi*, preliminary exams). They had a variety of familial connections with meritorious subjects (*hunsin*, *kongsin*) and royal families (*wangjok*). They were also connected through marriage or mentorship with *hun'gu* families; for example, those of the meritorious subjects of King Chungjong's restoration such as Kim Anno (1495-1537) and Yi Haeng (1478-1534). Based on these findings, Song defined the *Kimyo sarim* as "a group of political figures who, alongside Cho Kwang-jo and others, rallied around sensitive political issues."[26] He refrained from making logically tenuous claims about differences in economic bases, thus avoiding the pitfalls of previous explanations. Later, he presented the same interpretation in his doctoral dissertation.[27] This research highlights the significant overlap in backgrounds between the *sarim* faction and the central ruling elite, challenging the traditional narrative of a fundamental conflict based on differing socioeconomic origins.

In this context, Yi T'aejin reiterated his claims in the preface of a book published in 2002. He acknowledged the criticism that demanded evidence for his theory, which classified the *sarim* faction as a class of small landowners, admitting that it was impossible to provide such evidence due to the absence of land registers of the time. He nevertheless insisted that dismissing such classifications just because they cannot be empirically proven would be a greater absurdity.[28] This stance, however, raises questions about the appropriate approach for a historian. If a hypothesis cannot be proven, it should remain a hypothesis and not be presented as fact. Furthermore, the problem with the claim that the "*sarim* faction = rural small landowners" goes beyond the difficulty of empirical proof. There is a bunch of significant counterevidence, such as the presence of wealthy *sarim* members who owned extensive lands and slaves across various regions of the country and *sarim* members who belonged to prestigious families residing in Seoul. Even if proving the hypothesis is challenging, a hypothesis must at least be defensible against counterevidence to maintain its validity. The persistence of Yi T'aejin's theory as a mainstream academic view despite these issues is puzzling. If a hypothesis cannot be proven and fails to address counterevidence adequately, it should be reconsidered. Common sense dictates that a hypothesis should be retracted when it clashes with established facts.

In 2003, Kim Pŏm published a significant critical paper on the *sarim* faction theory. This paper delved deeply into the inconsistencies between the binary opposition framework of *hun'gu* and *sarim* factions and the actual historical facts in explaining the political history of early Chosŏn. He pointed out that if the *hun'gu* and *sarim* factions were indeed so distinct, each would have shared consistent and well-defined characteristics, which was not the case. To substantiate this, he highlighted the inaccuracies in the commonly accepted academic concept of the *sarim* faction. He questioned the criteria used in previous studies to define the common characteristics of the *sarim* faction. These criteria included attitudes towards *hyangyak* (community compact), *sach'ang* (village granaries), the *Taedongpŏp* (Uniform Land Tax Law), economic bases such as wealth, land reclamation, and small landownership, as well as the credibility of the so-called genealogies of *sarim* faction members.[29] Kim's research demonstrated that it was impossible to schematically distinguish the *hun'gu* and *sarim* factions based on those conditions. This study is particularly significant as it synthesizes various individual research achievements in domestic academia to develop its argument.

Around the same time, Yi Hŭihwan investigated the actual usage of the term "*sarim*." According to his findings, "*sarim*" was not a term used to denote a specific class sharing academic connections, region, or economic base. Instead, it was used interchangeably with terms like "*sadaebu*" (scholar-officials) or "*saryu*" (literati), and was a general term similar to "*yusaeng*" (Confucian students) or "*yurim*" (society for Confucianism).

Therefore, Yi argued that the conventional understanding of the *sarim* faction as a specific socioeconomic class should be revised.[30]

In the 2010s, this trend of criticism grew even stronger. Among junior scholars, the critique of the *sarim* faction theory became an irreversible trend. The conventional theory that explained the *sarim* faction based on socioeconomic differences has now ended, at least among younger scholars. It is no exaggeration to say that we have now entered an era where new explanatory frameworks are being proposed to replace the traditional *sarim* faction theory. In fact, two doctoral dissertations examining the politics and nature of the ruling elites during the reigns of King Sŏngjong to King Chungjong, based on the rejection of the traditional *sarim* faction theory, were published in 2011.

In 2011, for example, Song Ungsŏp critically reviewed the debates related to the *hun'gu* and *sarim* factions and then conceptualized the politics after King Sŏngjong's reign as "*kongnon chŏngch'i*" (*kongnon* politics; politics based on Confucian opinion). He emphasized the need to focus not only on political factions but also on the expression of Confucian values pursued by these groups, centering on the Neo-Confucian values and justice shared by almost all officials and intellectuals, including the throne per se.[31] While the conclusion of "*kongnon* politics" seems to follow the research trends of the 1980s, it differs from previous studies by explicitly rejecting the conventional concept of the *sarim* faction. But it is regrettable that there is no thorough examination of whether the public opinion raised by the Censorate was genuinely *kongnon* (righteous opinion among Confucians) or if it had already effectively become *dangnon* (factional opinion).[32]

In 2011, Yun Insuk focused on the politico-intellectual significance of the book of *Elementary Learning* (*xiaoxue*, *sohak* in Ko.) rather than on political factions. She argued that the emerging political groups of the time formed multi-layered networks centered on the practice of *Elementary Learning*. She therefore suggested that the term "practitioners of *Elementary Learning*" would be more accurate than the socioeconomically loaded term "*sarim* faction."[33] This approach is significant as it not only critiques the existing *sarim* faction theory but also offers an alternative explanation. However, it lacks a diachronic explanation of why such a group of *Elementary Learning* practitioners emerged prominently during this specific period. Additionally, there were many individuals referred to as *sarim* who did not belong to these particular networks: a notable example is the Confucian students registered in public schools of the capital city. For this reason, a higher-level explanatory framework is needed to comprehensively encompass the term *sarim* as it frequently appears in the dynastic annals.

In 2014, Kim Tangt'aek criticized the existing *sarim* faction theory and defined the characteristics of politics from King Sŏngjong to King Chungjong as politics influenced by the *yŏron* (majority opinion) of yangban (hereditary ruling elites) who emphasized Confucian righteousness.[34] While he did not create and use a specific term like "*yŏron* politics," his work is significant for capturing the political atmosphere of the time as one driven by the expanding influence of the *sarim*'s opinion that valued righteousness, rather than the dichotomy of conflict between the *hun'gu* and *sarim* factions.

In the same year, Kye Sŭngbŏm criticized the existing *sarim* faction theory and proposed a new explanatory framework: a long-term "political reform movement" under the banner of practicing Confucian values. He defined the nature of this movement as the "*yugyohwa chŏngp'ung undong*" (rectification movement for Confucianization) and named it the "*sarim* movement" since its proponents were the *sarim*. According to him, in Chosŏn, where Confucianism was declared the state ideology, some Confucian scholars, having witnessed repeated power struggles like the usurpation by Great Prince Suyang, initiated a Confucianization movement. Over time, the number of supporters gradually increased, turning it into a kind of movement. Kye even drew an analogy between the "*sarim* movement" that carried out the rectification movement for Confucianization and the "student movement" in modern Korea that led the anti-dictatorship movement for democratization.[35]

In short, In the 2000s, the traditional view of the *sarim* faction receded into the background largely due to the inability of its proponents to effectively counter the continuous emergence of contradictory evidence. Nevertheless, there is still no definitive framework to replace the conventional understanding of the conflict between the *hun'gu* and *sarim* factions based on their differing socioeconomic foundations. Various interpretations are still competing for dominance. Among these, the most compelling approach reinterprets the political history from King Sŏngjong to King Chungjong through the lens of the Censorate system rather than the dichotomy of *hun'gu* and *sarim* factions. As previously discussed, the work of American scholar Edward Wagner is a prime example of this perspective. In recent times, although not overwhelmingly dominant, there has been a steady stream of research in Korea that aligns with Wagner's views.[36]

But if the literati purges (*sahwa*) indeed resulted from the Censorate system, which allowed for almost unlimited remonstrations and impeachments disregarding bureaucratic hierarchy, it raises the question of why such conflicts occurred only temporarily around the turn of the 16th century for about half a century. Logically, if the Censorate system persisted, such conflicts should have continued intermittently. However, despite the system lasting until the late 19th century, the literati purges were confined to a specific period around the early 1500s. Scholars who support Wagner's revised theory must provide a satisfactory explanation for this. This calls for a reevaluation of the term *sarim* and the context in which it was used. It might involve examining the socio-political and cultural dynamics of the period, the ideological conflicts, and the practical roles these scholars played within the bureaucracy. A nuanced understanding that goes beyond simplistic binary oppositions or rigid class distinctions is necessary to get closer to the historical reality.

Given this context, who were the numerous figures referred to as *sarim* in the *Annals of the Chosŏn Dynasty* (*Chosŏn wangjo sillok*) from the 15th to the 16th centuries? How should we understand the concept of *sarim*? What approach offers the most accurate explanation?

3. The Emergence of New Confucian Generations and the Sarim Movement

Based on the analysis so far, several points can be confirmed regarding *sarim*: The framework of distinguishing the *hun'gu* faction and the *sarim* faction based on socioeconomic foundations is invalid, as there are too many contradictory cases. The *sarim* was not a new socioeconomic force or class but rather part of the existing ruling elite. The core members of the *sarim* were predominantly from prestigious families based in Seoul. They sharply criticized the behavior of high-ranking officials, known as the *hun'gu*, during the process of applying Confucian values in reality. Despite this, they maintained close familial ties with these prestigious families.

These characteristics become even more evident when examining the usage of the term *sarim* in the dynastic annals. Since the usage is not highly varied, there is no need to create a table. Over the 150 years from King T'aejo (r. 1392–1398) to King Chungjong (r. 1506–1544), the term *sarim* appears nearly 700 times in the dynastic annals, but there are virtually no instances where it specifically refers to a particular political faction. Instead, it generally indicates literati with Confucian knowledge and virtues. The term *sarim* frequently appears in court discussions of significant political issues, comments (*saron*), or evaluations of officials, consistently conveying the idea of a Confucianism. This is similar to the terms *yurim* (society for Confucianism or Confucian intellectuals). Additionally, the usage of phrases like "Many *sarim* present in the court"[37] indicates that *sarim* was a broad concept encompassing all intellectuals who respected and pursued Neo-Confucian values, rather than being limited to either officials or Confucian students (*yusaeng*). In fact, the term *sarim* was often used interchangeably with *saryu* (Confucian literati) or *sadaebu* (scholar-officials). The primary criteria were not external conditions like academic lineage, family background, or economic base, but rather the extent to which one respected and practiced Neo-Confucian values. Key attributes included Confucian learning, rejection of Buddhism and superstition, criticism of Sejo's usurpation, righteousness, and moral character.[38]

Why were the *sarim*, from the ruling elite families of Seoul, so critical of contemporary politics? What was the political situation that led the *sarim* to become harsh critics? Despite being a new dynasty founded on Confucian values, the political reality of the new Chosŏn dynasty was far from Confucian ideals. Let's consider the succession of the throne before the Restoration of Chungjong (1506, *Chungjong panjŏng*). Out of the ten kings, four—T'aejo (r. 1392-1398), Chŏngjong (r. 1398-1400), Tanjong (r. 1452-1455), and Yŏnsan'gun (r. 1494-1506)—were forcibly removed from the throne. Among them, two died in exile or were murdered, and three did not even receive posthumous temple names (*myoho*). King Chŏngjong was posthumously known as Kongjŏngwang, while Tanjong and Yŏnsan'gun were simply referred to as princes (kun). Four kings who ascended as crown princes and eldest sons—Munjong (r. 1450-1452), Tanjong (r. 1452-1455), Yejong (r. 1468-1469), and Yŏnsangun (r. 1494-1506)—either had very short reigns or were deposed. There were constant palace coups and treason incidents, and successful coups typically resulted in usurpation. Reflecting this unstable political reality, there were nine instances of conferring titles to meritorious subjects (kongsin) in just over a century since the founding of the new dynasty. The last of these, resulting from the Restration of Chungjong in 1506, was the largest, with 104 individuals receiving titles. Even without considering Confucian values, such a political reality was far from normal and can be described as dysfunctional.

The ascension of King Sejo (r. 1455-1468) left a significant and lasting impact on the political landscape of the time. Unlike previous coups, which mostly occurred among princes in the early phase of the dynasty's establishment, Sejo's ascension was markedly different. This event occurred after the reigns of T'aejong (r. 1400-1418) and Sejong (r. 1418-1450), during a period when the state had already developed a Confucian identity. Sejo, an uncle, forcibly took the throne from his nephew, the reigning king, and eventually had him killed. Even to the non-Confucian eye, Sejo's actions were easily perceived as usurpation.

The roots of many subsequent political conflicts can be traced back to Sejo's usurpation. Terms like "Six Martyred Subjects" (*sayuksin*) and "Six Loyal Subjects" (*saengyuksin*) were already popular during this time. The Chosŏn dynasty's subsequent major and minor political incidents, including the Literati Purge of 1498 (*Muo sahwa*) triggered by the "Cho Ŭije mun" (condolence on the death of Ŭije), were directly connected to this issue. Even half a century later, during the reign of Chungjong, the court was frequently troubled by issues related to the rehabilitation of those wronged by Sejo's usurpation.[39] The aftereffects of the usurpation were not fully resolved until 1698, when Nosan'gun was posthumously restored and given the temple name Tanjong.[40] The persistent efforts of the *sarim* to rehabilitate those wronged during Sejo's usurpation over many years were directly linked to the issue of Sejo's legitimacy.

Even to those who were not die-hard Confucian scholars, the political realities of the first 100 years of the Chosŏn dynasty were enough to warrant criticism. Nonetheless, as is well known, the *sarim* faction consistently used Neo-Confucian values as their standard for critique. Why, then, did the *sarim* place such importance on Confucian values, and why did they use these values as the basis for their political actions?

Everyone agrees that the *sarim* placed exceptional importance on practicing Neo-Confucian values such as righteousness. In Korean history, however, these values had never been as contentious as they were during the reigns of Sŏngjong through Chungjong (1469-1544). If we were to cite a precedent, it would probably be the differing attitudes towards the transition from the Koryŏ to the Chosŏn dynasty in the last decade of the 1300s: the fact that those who sought to more strictly adhere to and practice Confucian values (Koryŏ loyalists) were defeated by those who were less stringent in their adherence suggests that, at that time, Neo-Confucian values were beginning to spread within the intellectual community but had not yet become the dominant criteria guiding political reality. During the reigns of Sŏngjong and Chungjong, however, a seismic shift occurred in this trend. From then on, the history of Chosŏn was conducted, perceived, educated, and recorded according to these standards.

This indicates that the political and intellectual currents of the Chosŏn dynasty shifted during this period. It was a transitional period when Confucianization became more pronounced. Why did the term *sarim*, which had been a common noun, appear so prominently on the political stage during the reigns of Sŏngjong through Chungjong in early Chosŏn? The emergence of the *sarim* can be understood in the context of the historical background, particularly in relation to the political reality of the time, which was contrary to the trend of Confucianization and Confucian political ideals that the Chosŏn dynasty aimed to pursue.

A hundred years after adopting Confucian values as its founding ideology, Confucian ideals continued to spread. The Royal Academy (*Sŏnggyun'gwan*) and the Four Schools (*sahak*) in Seoul served as the stronghold of Confucian political ideology and a stepping stone for entering officialdom. The civil service examination system was further strengthened, becoming a firmly established path to success. Not only official schools but also private academies (*sŏjae*) focused on preparing students for these exams flourished. Success in these endeavors required acquiring Confucian knowledge and virtues. From the beginning of the dynasty, the state diligently promoted books such as the *Zhouli* (Rites of Zhou), *Karye* (Family Rites), *Daxue yanyi* (Extended meaning of the Great Learning), and *Sohak* (Elementary Learning). These works, along with the classic Four Books and Five Classics, were widely disseminated as examination textbooks, guides for daily living, and educational materials. The Chosŏn government vigorously pursued Confucianization through the dissemination of these texts from the outset.[41] The Hall of Worthies (Chiphyŏnjŏn) gathered almost all necessary materials for the establishment of a new Confucian state, leading the knowledge efforts, and the promulgation of the final version of the Grand code for State Governance (*Kyŏngguk Taejŏn*) in 1484 marked the culmination of Confucian state model establishment. Every young person aspiring to success in Chosŏn studied Confucian texts and values from an early age, learning Chinese characters and the Confucian classics, and growing up believing that these values were the foundation of human ethics and the backbone of politics.

But the political reality of the time was marked by repeated coups, usurpations, and despotic tyranny, where the logic of power still prevailed. Confucian values and ethics did not effectively exert influence on the political stage. There was a persistent conflict between the political reality and Confucian values, creating a continuous sense of instability. Sejo's usurpation acted as a detonator in this context, providing intellectuals who critiqued reality through the lens of Confucian standards with a decisive reason for criticism and resistance.

Even if a young person came from a high-ranking official family, if he was a perceptive youth, he couldn't help but be troubled by the gap between the Confucian values he learned through school education and reading, and the bloody political reality before his eyes. A good example is the lengthy memorials submitted by Yi Simwŏn (1454–1594), a royal family member, and Nam Hyoon (1454–1492), from a prestigious family in Seoul, advocating for the reinstatement of Queen Hyŏndŏk (1418-1441), the mother of the deposed king Nosan'gun and wife of King Munjong, who had been deposed posthumously by Sejo. Sin Chongho (1456–1497), who triggered the criticism of Sejo's immorality issue that led to the Literati Purge of 1598 (*Muo sahwa*), was the grandson of Sin Sukchu (1417-1475), a notable figure of Sejo's meritorious subjects. Im Huijae (1472-1504), who associated with the *sarim* and was executed during the Literati Purge of 1506 (*Kapcha sahwa*), was the son of Im Sahong (1445-1506), a key figure in that purge and a member of the royal in-law family. Yu Pang, who called himself one of the *Chungnim ch'rhyŏn* (Seven sages of the bamboo grove) and associated with the *sarim*, was the son of Yu Chagwang (1439-1512), who led the Literati Purge of 1498 (Muo sahwa).[42] In short, regardless of whether their fathers were meritorious subjects or rural literati, the scholarly and political tendencies of the entire yangban intellectual class of Chosŏn, especially among younger generations of literati, had already shifted towards emphasizing Confucian values and their practical application. The *sarim*, a group that first emerged in Seoul, fostering *kongnon* on various current affairs, can be seen as a product of this trend of the time.

This phenomenon can also be observed through the activities of Confucian students registered in the Royal Academy (*Sŏnggyun'gwan*). During the reigns of Sŏngjong to Chungjong (1469-1544), *Sŏnggyun'gwan* students united with the students from public academies in Seoul and some regional students to play a central role in forming *kongnon*. Especially during Chungjong's reign (1506-1544), their activities became so influential that they, together with the Censorate, impacted national policy decisions.[43] This trend significantly contributed to the establishment of an independent status for the memorials submitted by Confucian students centered around *Sŏggyun'gwan*, separate from the activities of censorial officials, starting from the 16th century.[44]

Especially in the 200 years between the founding of the Chosŏn and the outbreak of the Imjin War (1592-1598), there were four instances of *Sŏnggyun'gwan* students engaging in what could be considered strike actions, known as *konggwan* (emptying the academy). All these actions aimed to reject Buddhist rituals and uphold Confucian values.[45] This demonstrates that the activities of *Sŏnggyun'gwan* students were closely related to the movement for Confucianization. From the early days of Chosŏn, the students admitted to *Sŏnggyun'gwan* were primarily the sons of high-ranking officials in the central government. Descendants of Seoul's prestigious families could enter *Sŏnggyun'gwan* without taking the preliminary exams, benefiting from various privileges.[46] Cho Kwangjo, the most famous leader of the *sarim* during King Chungjong's reign, was also a descendant of a meritorious subject residing in Seoul and a graduate of *Sŏnggyun'gwan*. In short, during the reigns of Sŏngjong through Chungjong, those who promoted Confucian values and stirred *kongnon* outside the court were mainly *Sŏnggyun'gwan* students from prestigious families in Seoul. This indicates that their thoughts and political stances were much more inclined toward Confucianism per se than those of their predecessors, such as their fathers or grandfathers.

The crucial point is that since the Chosŏn dynasty had established Neo-Confucianism as its founding ideology and declared Confucian values as the state doctrine, no one could openly oppose the fundamental assertion that Confucian values should be directly applied to political reality. Particularly, the heinous usurpation by Sejo, the anti-Confucian tyranny of King Yŏnsan'gun (r. 1494–1506), the inherent flaws of the Restoration of Chungjong (*Chungjong panjŏng*) that resolved issues through a military action rather than remonstrance, and the corruption of the meritorious subjects of the restoration remained unsolved: all of these contributed to the growing consensus that political reform was urgently needed in the turbulent political landscape of the time.

In response, the number of young intellectuals who believed that directly applying Confucian ideology to political reality was the key and the only solution to these issues naturally increased. Over time, the scope of the *sarim* continued to expand. While it is difficult to determine how purely each member of the *sarim* adhered to Neo-Confucian values, and there were likely differences in the intensity of their beliefs, it is important to note that they publicly advocated these values, and their critics could not fundamentally oppose them publicly. To draw a parallel, it is similar to how, in contemporary times, a politician may personally dislike democracy but must publicly proclaim respect for and adherence to democratic values. Cho Kwangjo was the most ardent activist who directly represented the *kongnon* of the *sarim* in the political arena amidst this prevailing atmosphere. He actively engaged in political reform movements, representing the *sarim*'s opinion and advocating for Confucian values in political reality.

As the leaders of these movements were the *sarim*, and their goal was the practical application of Confucian values without any compromise, this can be conceptualized as the "*Sarim* movement" or the "rectification movement for Confucianization" (*yugyohwa chŏngp'ung undong*) of the *sarim*. It is therefore natural that this movement arose in Seoul, the central hub of the country, and that its leaders were mostly intellectuals residing in Seoul, with many young individuals from prestigious families in Seoul participating. As previously mentioned, the absolute majority of the censors working in the Censorate during King Sŏngjong's reign, as well as many members of the *sarim* of 1519 (those who persecuted in the Literati Purge of 1519) including Cho Kwangjo, were from prominent families in Seoul. Furthermore, the movement to restore Cho Kwangjo's honor was also largely conducted in Seoul.

In response to this trend, some high officials and meritorious subjects (and even more so their descendants) joined the "Sarim movement," both openly and covertly. An Tang (1461-1521), who came from a prestigious family and himself became a meritorious subject during the early reign of King Chungjong, eventually serving as the Third State Councilor (Uŭijŏng), recommended many *sarim* members such as Cho Kwangjo and Kim An'guk (1478-1543) while serving as Minister of Personnel. Furthermore, he politically supported Cho Kwangjo to such an extent that he could be considered a *sarim* member himself, with all three of his sons being selected for the recommendation examination (*hyŏllyangkwa*) launched by Cho. Kim Sep'il (1473-1533), who also hailed from a prestigious family that had been prominent since the founding of Chosŏn, grew up in a typical *hun'gu* family but supported the movement led by Cho Kwangjo and his followers. He spoke out against the excessive punishment in the course of the Literati Purge of 1519, which led to his own exile.[47]

There were quite a few high-ranking officials who supported the Sarim movement even if they did not directly participate. One prominent example is Chŏng Kwangp'il (1462-1538), who served as Chief State Councilor during King Chungjong's reign. He showed a relatively favorable attitude towards the *sarim*'s remonstration activities and various reform proposals right before the Literati Purge of 1519 (*Kimyo sahwa*). Another example is Sim Ŭigyŏm (1535-1587), who played a role in the division of the *sarim* into the Easterners and Westerners. Interestingly enough, Sim was the brother of Queen Insun (1532-1563), King Myeongjong's queen, and thus he was a royal in-law. His grandfather, Sim Yŏnwŏn (1491-1558), was appointed as a meritorious subject right after the Literati Purge of 1545 (*Eŭlsa sahwa*),[48] and rose through the ranks during King Myŏngjong's reign (1545-1567). From the 6th year to the 13th year of Myeongjong's reign, he served as Chief State Councilor for seven years, solidifying his power as a royal in-law.[49] Sim Ŭigyŏm frequently associated with the *sarim*. For his tenure as the deputy official in the Ministry of Personnel (*Ijo chŏllang*), he was praised by Yi Hwang and Yi I for his efforts in recruiting many *sarim* members.[50] There are countless such examples. In short, after the Restoration of Chungjong in 1506, the distinction between the *hun'gu* and *sarim* became meaningless, as many intellectuals, including officials, increasingly supported the *sarim*'s ideals. Even among the high-ranking officials from the royal in-law families, there were quite a few who sympathized with the *sarim*'s cause.

Given these points, the process by which the *sarim* gradually took over political leadership offers significant insights into understanding the nature of the *sarim*. If the *sarim* had been a distinctly different socioeconomic class from the *hun'gu*, there would have been a decisive event leading to a regime change or revolutionary measures, such as land reforms targeting the large landowner *hun'gu* faction, in the course of this process of regime change. However, no such events occurred. Despite experiencing several major political defeats, such as the four literati purges, the *sarim* eventually took control of the government without bloodshed. In contrast, the *hun'gu* faction, which 'always won' in political conflicts with the *sarim*, quietly disappeared over time without any significant political defeat. How could this make sense? If they were heterogeneous social classes with different regional and economic bases (central large landowners vs. local small landowners), how could such a transition occur?

Let's examine an interesting piece of data. During the 75 years spanning the reigns of Sŏngjong through Chungjong (1469-1544), a total of 1,595 individuals passed the civil service examination (*munkwa*) in 89 sessions. Of these, 1,120 (70%) appear in the *Genealogy of the Munhwa Yu Clan*. (*Munhwa Yu ssi Kajŏng po*) Only 49 (3%) of the successful examinees belonged to the Munhwa Yu Clan itself. Even if we extend the period to include the entire early Chosŏn era (15th-16th centuries), approximately 60% of the successful examinees in the civil service examination are recorded in this single genealogy. For instance, figures such as Yi Jing-ok (?-1453) and Chŏng Yŏrip (1546-1589), who were executed for treason, as well as famous individuals like Yi Hwang (1501-1570) and Admiral Yi Sunsin (1545-1598), are all listed in this genealogy. This fact illustrates the high level of homogeneity through marriage and blood relations among the ruling elite in Chosŏn society at the time.[51]

In short, the numerous political conflicts that occurred during the reigns of Sŏngjong through Chungjong were not clashes between heterogeneous classes or groups with different socioeconomic power bases. Rather, these conflicts were part of a political rectification movement that naturally arose in Chosŏn society of the time, which was fraught with contradictions between Confucian ideology and political reality. From the time of King Sejo (r. 1455-1468) to Myŏngjong (r. 1545-1567), a span of about 100 years, these contradictions became increasingly evident. During this period, Chosŏn's Confucian orientation evolved continually, criticizing the political reality maintained by the logic of power and the sword, and emphasizing the practical application of Confucian values without any compromises.

Although many kings and high officials were displeased with this trend, no one could officially or theoretically condemn it, given that Confucian values were declared the founding justification of the new Chosŏn dynasty. Especially after experiencing the tyranny of King Yŏnsan'gun and the Restoration of Chungjong in 1506, the voice of the *sarim*, who were convinced that implementing Neo-Confucian values in reality was the only way to reform the corrupt political reality, grew even louder. Those who opposed this movement found their positions increasingly marginalized. Consequently, even high-ranking officials began to shift their stance to acknowledge the *sarim* movement. They either tacitly approved of it or offered passive support. Frankly, this is why, during this period (1455-1567), there were few significant differences in the background or economic bases of officials regardless of *hun'gu* or *sarim*, and no meaningful land reforms took place.

In the process of the *sarim* movement, the so-called *hun'gu* can be described as high-ranking officials who were relatively less aligned with *sarim* ideals. Their gradual disappearance from the scene can be explained as follows: In a society that proclaimed Confucianism as one of its founding ideologies, the anti-Confucian and violent politics practiced for over a century deepened the contradiction between ideology and reality. As a result, the rectification movement for Confucianization, initially led by a small number of Confucian intellectuals and students, spread to the entire ruling yangban society by the early 16th century. As it became increasingly difficult to resist this historical trend by force, some senior officials in the existing political establishment began to slowly shift their stance towards acknowledging the *sarim* movement. They went further by supporting the movement and appointing *sarim* members, thus becoming their political patrons. In the changing political landscape, the *hun'gu* transformed admirably. While the *hun'gu* disappeared from the political stage, the individuals (and families) who were once called the *hun'gu* did not vanish.

The disappearance of the *hun'gu* during the *sarim* movement is somewhat analogous to the disappearance of political soldiers during South Korea's democratization movement. In the Republic of Korea, which proclaimed democracy as one of its founding ideologies, over 30 years of anti-democratic military dictatorship deepened the contradiction between ideology and reality. As a result, the democratization movement, initially led by a small number of progressive intellectuals and students, spread to the general populace by the 1980s. As it became increasingly difficult to resist this historical trend by force, military politicians began to shift their stance towards acknowledging the democratization movement around 1987. After the Democratic Justice Party, composed of military figures, merged with the Democratic Party led by Kim Yŏngsam (1928-2015), a faction of the democratization movement, in 1989, political soldiers and their followers (from the Democratic Justice Party to the Democratic Liberal Party to the New Korea Party) started to advocate for democratization themselves. This allowed them to survive the major political transition from a military regime to a civilian government. These individuals and their political successors still form a significant part of South Korea's mainstream political landscape today. In short, while political soldiers disappeared from the political stage, the "individuals and their political successors" have remained influential.

Ultimately, the *sarim* who led Chosŏn politics in the 16th century were Confucian literati who firmly believed that the best way to reform the increasingly dysfunctional political reality was to uncompromisingly apply Neo-Confucian values directly to politics. Their collective and long-term actions manifested as an extended movement. They were not a new socioeconomic class or stratum but rather young people with critical views of the existing political reality—mostly those born in the mid to late 15th century and brainwashed with Neo-Confucianism, who studied primarily in Seoul and entered government service. This generation formed a group that conducted a prolonged Confucian rectification movement.

Yi I (1536–1584), one of their leaders during the early reign of King Sŏnjo, defined the *sarim* as follows: "Those who, in their hearts, yearn for the ancient way, strive for Confucian conduct in their actions, speak of righteous words, and support *kongnon* with these principles." Yi further diagnosed that if such *sarim* held positions in the court and executed their duties, the country would be well-governed; if not, the country would fall into disorder.[52] It is clear that terms such as ancient way, Confucian conduct, righteous words, and *kongnon* all relate to the pursuit and practice of Confucian values. Yi's diagnosis, as someone who lived through the tumultuous 16th century, is crucial for understanding the meaning of the *sarim*. He defined the *sarim* explicitly as those who uphold and practice Confucian norms and support *kongnon*, without any mention of being from local villages or small landowners. Therefore, the series of movements initiated by the *sarim* in the central government from King Sŏngjong's reign (1469–1494) onward for nearly 100 years naturally manifested as political reform movements or Confucian rectification movements.

To understand the political ruling elites and their political orientations in early Chosŏn from a diachronic perspective, therefore, it is necessary to adopt a new approach that incorporates the concept of generational differences arising inevitably from the long-term Confucianization process from the 14th to the 16th century. By doing so, we can go beyond simply criticizing the existing theories of the new scholarly class (*sinjin sadaebu*) and the *sarim* based on the fact that most of the noble families were descendants of the powerful aristocrats of Koryŏ and that the *hun'gu* and *sarim* factions were homogeneous noble groups with similar family backgrounds, regions, and socioeconomic statuses. This approach allows for a comprehensive and dynamic explanation of the evolution of the political history of early Chosŏn from a diachronic perspective. It posits that both the noble families and the *sarim*, even if they belonged to the same family, represented new generations with different political lines, ideologies, and philosophies from their fathers' and grandfathers' generations. The voices of these new Confucian generations, armed with Confucian values, grew increasingly prominent over time.

4. Epilogue

In light of the characteristics of the *sarim*, there is a need to reinterpret early Chosŏn political history through the lens of the center (central government) and the periphery (local regions). The rise of the *sarim* was not the result of a particular social class growing and taking the political stage, nor was it due to the deepening scholarship of the reclusive scholars in the provinces like Kil Chae (1353–1419). It was also not a case of local forces influencing the central government. Rather, the rise of the *sarim* and the spread of the *sarim* movement were academically and ideologically products of the Confucianization policies that had been enforced and promoted by the central government (the state) since the founding of the new Chosŏn dynasty, beginning in Seoul. Politically, it was a reaction by Confucian literati to the violent political reality, deviated from Confucian norms, that followed Sejo's usurpation.

Therefore, the rise of the *sarim* were essentially a phenomenon and movement that originated in the center. From a broader perspective, although the Sarim movement temporarily waned due to events like the literati purges (*sahwa*), it later spread to the provinces through systems such as the *hyangyak* (community compacts) and *sŏwŏn* (private academies in rural arears). In other words, while the traditional view emphasizes a flow "from the provinces to Seoul," a more accurate understanding of the historical reality is the reverse—"from Seoul to the provinces." Given that Chosŏn had achieved a significant level of centralization and that all knowledge and information related to Neo-Confucianism could not disseminate to the provinces without passing through Seoul, the issue of the center and the periphery offers new insights into understanding the historical significance of the *sarim* and the trends and nature of early Chosŏn political and intellectual history.

Note

1 See Yi Pyŏngdo, *Chosŏnsa taegwan* (The outline of Chosŏn History), Seoul: Tongjisa, 1948, pp. 358–360; Yi Pyŏngdo, *Sinsu kuksa taegwan* (The new outline of national history), Seoul: Pomungak, 1956, pp. 381–383. Yi continued to maintain this explanation in revised editions of his survey books. For an instance, see Yi Pyŏngdo, *Han'guksa taegwan* (The outline of Korean history), Pomungak, 1968, pp. 357–369.

2 See Yi Inyŏng, *Kuksa yoron* (Essential discussions on national history), Seoul: Min'gyosa, 1956, pp. 139–151.

3 See Edward Wagner, "The Recommendation Examination of 1519: Its Place in Early Yi Dynasty History," *Chosēn gkuhō,* Vol. 15, 1960.

4 See Yi Kibaek, *New Interpretation of National History*, Seoul: T'aesŏngsa, 1961, pp. 217–223.

5 See Yi Kibaek, *New Interpretation of Korean History*, Seoul: Ilchogak, 1967, pp. 234–238.

6 See Yi T'aejin, "Sarimp'a ŭi yuhyangso pongnip undong: Chosön ch'ogi söngnihak chöngch'ak ŭi sahoejök paegyöng" (The movement to re–establish *yuhyangso* by the sarim faction: the social background of the establishment of Neo–Confucianism in early Chosön) *Chindan hakpo*, Vol. 34·35, 1972·1973.

7 See Edward Willett Wagner, *The Literati Purges: Political Conflict in Early Yi Korea*, Cambridge: East Asian Research Center, Harvard University, 1974).

8 See Yi Sugŏn, *Yŏngnam sarimp'a ŭi hyŏngsŏng* (The formation of the Yŏngnam sarim faction), Taegu: Yŏngnam taehakkyo ch'ulp'anbu, 1979, pp. 18–22 and 277–280.

9 See Yi Sugŏn, *Yŏngnam sarimp'a ŭi hyŏngsŏng* (The formation of the Yŏngnam sarim faction), pp. 184–230.

10 See Edward W. Wagner, "Yijo sarim munje e taehan chae kŏmt'o" (Reexamination of the *sarim* Problem of the Chosŏn dynasty), *Chŏnbuk sahak,* Vol. 4, 1980, pp. 163–173.

11 For a review article on the *sarimp'a* theory, see Kim Pŏm, "Chosŏn chŏn'gi

hun'gu-sarim seryŏk ŭi chae kŏmt'o" (Reexamination of the *hun'gu-sarim* forces' in early Chosŏn), *Han'guk sahakpo*, Vol. 15, pp. 91-92.

12 These papers were later compiled in Yi T'aejin, *Han'guk sahoesa yŏn'gu: nongŏp kisul paltal kwa sahoe pyŏndong* (Research on Korean social history: development of agricultural technology and social change), Chisik sanŏpsa, 1986.

13 See Yi Tae-jin, *Han'guk sahoesa yŏn'gu* (Research on Korean social history), Seoul: Chisik sanŏpsa, 1986, pp. 125-185, 187-219, 253-288.

14 For a detailed review of related research, see Kim Pŏm, "Chosŏn chŏn'gi *hun'gu-sarim* seryŏk ŭi chae kŏmt'o" (Reexamination of the *hun'gu-sarim* forces' in early Chosŏn), *Han'guk sahakpo*, Vol. 15, pp. 85-94.

15 See Yi Pyŏnghyu, *Chosŏn chŏn'gi Kiho sarimp'a yŏn'gu* (Study of the *Kiho sarim* faction in early Chosŏn), Ilchogak, 1984, pp. 5-10. However, my investigation of the usage of "*sarim*" in the dynastic annals reveals problems with this understanding. Detailed discussions will follow in the next section.

16 See Yi Pyŏnghyu, *Chosŏn chŏn'gi Kiho sarimp'a yŏn'gu* (Study of the *Kiho sarim* faction in early Chosŏn), pp. 24-51 and 160-168.

17 See Yi Pyŏnghyu, *Chosŏn chŏn'gi sarimp'a ŭi hyŏnsil insik kwa taeŭng* (The *sarim* faction's perception of reality and response in early Chosŏn), Ilchogak, 1999, pp. 3-51, especially p. 47.

18 See Yi Pyŏnghyu, *Chosŏn chŏn'gi Kiho sarimp'a yŏn'gu* (Study of the *Kiho sarim* faction in early Chosŏn), pp. 25 and 243-247. Meanwhile, Chŏng Tuhŭi has already criticized Yi's criteria and methods for identifying Seoul residents among the 28 *hyŏllyangkwa* candidates. See Chŏng Tuhŭi, "Hoego wa chŏnmang: Chosŏn chŏn'gi" (Retrospect and Prospect: Early Joseon), *Yŏksa* hakpo, Vol. 104, 1984, pp. 201-224.

19 See Song Ch'ansik, "Chosŏn cho sarim chŏngch'i ŭi kyŏllyŏk kujo: chŏllang kwa samsa rŭl chungsom ŭro" (The Power structure of *sarim* politics in the Chosŏn dynasty: focusing on the *chŏllang* and the three censorial offices), *Kyŏngje sahak*, Vol. 2, 1978.

20 See Kim Ton, "Sŏngjong tae ŏn'gwan ŭi sŏngkyŏk pyŏnhwa wa sarim" (Changes in the character of the censorial officials and *sarim* during King Sŏngjong's reign), *Han'guk saron*, Vol. 10, 1984; Nam Chidae, "Chosŏn Sŏngjong tae ŭi taegan ŏllon" (The activities of the censorate during King

Sŏngjong's Reign), *Han'guk saron* Vol. 12, 1985; Kim Wugi, "Chosŏn chŏn'gi sarim ŭi chŏllangjik chinch'ul kwa kŭ yŏkhal" (The advancement and Role of *sarim* in the censorial office in Early Chosŏn," *Taegu sahak*, Vol. 29, 1986; Choi Idon, "16-segi nanggwankwŏn ŭi hyŏngsŏng kwajŏng" (The formation process of the *nanggwan*'s power in the 16th century), *Han'guk saron*, Vol. 14, 1986.

21 Later, Kim Ton explicitly criticized the schematic distinction between the *hun'gu* and *sarim* factions in a recent study. He pointed out the difficulties in categorizing these factions based on their origin (whether they were from rural areas) and economic foundation (whether they were small landowners). He argued that the existing method of distinguishing the two groups using these criteria was inadequate and problematic. See Kim Ton, *Chosŏn chunggi chŏngch'isa yŏn'gu* (Studies on the Political History of Mid-Chosŏn), Seoul: Kukhak chryowŏn, 2009, pp. 71-75.

22 See Chŏng Tuhŭi, *Chosŏn sidae ŭi taegan yŏn'gu* (Study of the censorate in the Chosŏn period), Seoul: Ilchogak, 1994, pp. 68-93 and 142-143.

23 See James B. Palais, *Confucian Statecraft and Korean Institutions: Yu Hyŏngwŏn and the Late Chosŏn Dynasty*, Seattle: University of Washington Press, 1996, pp. 709-717.

24 See Kim Pŏm, "Chosŏn chŏn'gi *hun'gu-sarim* seryŏk ŭi chae kŏmt'o" (Reexamination of the *hun'gu-sarim* forces' in early Chosŏn), *Han'guk sahakpo*, Vol. 15, 2003.

25 See Kuksa p'yŏnch'an wiwŏnhoe, ed., *Han'guksa 28: Chosŏn chunggi sarim seryŏk ŭi Tŭngjang kwa hwaltong* (History of Korea 28: The emergence and activities of the sarim forces in mMid-Chosŏn), Kwach'ōn: Kuksa p'yŏnch'an wiwŏnhoe, 1996). The contributors to this volume included Yi Sugŏn, Yi Pyŏnghyu, Yi Pŏmjik, Yi T'aejin, Yi Suhwan, and Kim T'aeyŏng.

26 See Song Ungsŏp, "Chungjong tae *Kimyo sarim* ŭi kusŏng kwa ch'ulsin paegyŏng" (The composition and background of the *Kimyo sarim* during King Chungjong's Reign), *Han'guk saron*, Vol. 45, 2001.

27 See Song Ungsŏp, "Chosŏn Sŏngjong tae kongnon chŏngch'I ŭi hyŏngsŏng" (The formation of *kongnon* politics in the reign of King Sŏngjong), PhD dissertation, Seoul taehakkyo, 2011, pp. 187-192.

28 See Yi Tae-jin, *Ŭisul kwa in'gu kŭrigo nongŏp kisul* (Medicine, population,

and pgricultural pechnology), T'aehaksa, 2002, pp. 9-10.

29 Kim Bŏm, "Chosŏn chŏn'gi *hun'gu-sarim* seryŏk ŭi chae kŏmt'o" (Reexamination of the *hun'gu-sarim* forces' in early Chosŏn), *Han'guk sahakpo*, Vol. 15, 2003.

30 See Yi Hŭihwan, "Chosŏn chŏn'gi sadaebu, saryu, sarim ŭi yongnye," (The usages of the terms *sadaebu*, *saryu*, and *sarim* in early Chosŏn), *Chŏnnam sahak* , Vol. 24, 2005.

31 See Song Wungsŏp, "Chosŏn Sŏngjong tae kongnon chŏngch'i ŭi hyŏngsŏng" (The formation of *kongnon* politics in the reign of King Sŏngjong), PhD dissertation, Seoul taehakkyo, 2011.

32 For reference, recent research examining the content of the remonstrations during the reigns of King Sŏngjong to King Chungjong (1469-1644), when the *sarim* faction supposedly grew and gained power, indicates that there were numerous instances of "fake news" in their remonstrations. Despite this, these discussions were recognized as *kongnon* due to their association with the three censorial offices and enjoyed authority similar to genuine *kongnon*. For further details, see Chŏng Tuhui and Kye Sŭngbŏm, *Yu Chagwang: Chosŏn ŭi yŏngwŏn han ibangin* (Yu Chagwang: the eternal outsider of the Chosŏn), Seoul: P'urŭn yŏksa, 2023.

33 See Yun In-suk, "Chosŏn chŏn'gi sarim ŭi sahoe kyŏngje chŏk kusang kwa sohak undong" (The socioeconomic ideas of the *sarim* and the *Sohak* movement in early Chosŏn), PhD dissertation, Sunggyungwan University, 2011.

34 See Kim Tangt'aek, "Chosŏn Sŏngjong-Chungjong tae chŏngch'isa ŭi ihae wa sarimp'a sŏl" (Understanding the political history from King Sŏngjong to King Chungjong and the *sarim* faction theory), *Yŏksahak yŏn'gu*, Vol. 54, 2014.

35 See Kye Sŭngbŏm, *Chungjong ŭi sidae: Chosŏn ŭi yugyohwa wa sarim undong* (The era of King Chungjong: Confucianization and the *sarim* movement in Chosŏn), Seoul: Yŏksa Pip'yŏngsa, 2014.

36 For instance, see Kim Pŏm, *Sahwa wa Panjŏng ŭi sidae* (The era of literati purges and restoration), Seoul: Yŏksa pip'yŏngsa, 2007.

37 See *Myŏnng sillok* (Annals of King Chungjong), Vol. 85, (32nd reign year. 10th month. 25th day) Same hereafter.

38 See Yi Hŭihwan, "Chosŏn chŏn'gi sadaebu, saryu, sarim ŭi yongnye," (The usages of the terms *sadaebu*, *saryu*, and *sarim* in early Chosŏn), *Chŏnnam sahak* , Vol. 24, 2005. pp. 176–186.

39 For example, the various rehabilitation movements led by Cho Kwangjo and his followers are detailed in Chŏng Tuhui, Cho Kwangjo (Cho Kwangjo), revised edition, Seoul: Akanet, 2000, pp. 271–294, as well as in Chŏng Tuhui and Kye Sŭngbŏm, *Yu Chagwang: Chosŏn ŭi yŏngwŏn han ibangin* (Yu Chagwang: the eternal outsider of Chosŏn), Seoul: P'urŭn yŏksa, 2023, pp. 161–176.

40 For a study on the long-term process of the restoration of Nosan'gun, see Kye Sŭngbŏm, "Yŏksa hwahae kwanchŏm esŏ pon Chosŏn Sukchong tae Nosan'dun pokkwŏn choch'i" (Rehabilitation of Nosan'gun during King Sukchong's reign from a Perspective of Historical Reconciliation), *Sŏgang inmun nonch'ong*, Vol. 57, 2020.

41 For more on this, see Martina Deuchler, *The Confucian Transformation of Korea: A Study of Society and Ideology*, Cambridge: Council on East Asian Studies, Harvard University, 1992, pp. 111–118; Choi Sŭnghui, *Chosŏn Ch'ogi chŏngch'i munhwa ŭi ihae* (Understanding the political culture of early Chosŏn), Seoul: Chisik sanŏpsa, 2005, pp. 89–151.

42 See Chŏng Tuhui and Kye Sŭngbŏm, *Yu Chagwang: Chosŏn ŭi yŏngwŏn han ibangin* (Yu Chagwang: the eternal outsider of Chosŏn), Seoul: P'urŭn yŏksa, 2023, pp. 161–169, 278–289, 305–308.

43 See P'i Chŏngnan, "Chosŏn chunggi Sŏnggyun'gwan yuseang ŭi ŏllon hwaltong ŭl t'onghan chŏngch'i ch'amyŏ e taehayŏ" (On the political participation of Sŏnggyun'gwan Students through public opinion activities in Mid-Chosŏn), *Sŏngdae sarim*, Vol. 12·13, 1997.

44 See Sŏl Sŏkkyu, *Chosŏn sidae yusaeng sangso wa kongnon chŏngch'i* (Memorials by Confucian Students and Public Opinion Politics in the Joseon Dynasty), Seoul: Sŏnin, 2002, pp. 34–44.

45 See Yi Huigwŏn, "Chosŏn chŏn'gi ŭi konggwan yŏn'gu" (A study on the konggwan in early Chosŏn), *Sahak yŏn'gu*, Vol. 28, 1978.

46 See Yi Sŏngmu, "Sŏn ch'o ŭi Sŏnggyun'gwan yŏn'gu" (A study of *Sŏnggyun'gwan* in the early Chosŏn period) *Yŏksa hakpo*, Vol. 35·36, 1967, pp. 254–257.

47 See Kim Hyŏnyŏng, "Hun'gu esŏ sarim ŭro: 15–16 segi Kyŏngju Kim ssi Sangch'on kagye rŭl chungsim ŭro" (From *hun'gu* to *sarim*: focusing on the Sangch'on lineage of the Kyŏngju Kim Clan in the 15th and 16th centuries) in *Chosŏn ŭi chŏngch'i wa sahoe* (Politics and society of Chosŏn), Seoul: Chimmundang, 2002.

48 See *Myŏnng sillok*, Vol. 32, 21.1.12.

49 See *Myŏnng sillok*, Vol. 1, 0.8.2. "0" means the year in which the new king ascended to the throne. For the political influence of Sim Ŭigyŏm's family, see Kim Wugi, *Chosŏn chunggi ch'ŏksin chŏngch'i yŏn'gu* (A study on the politics of royal In-laws in Mid-Chosŏn), Seoul: Chimmundang, 2001, p. 138.

50 See *Yŏlyŏsil kisul*, (Works of *Yŏlyŏsil*), Vol. 18, "Sim Ŭigyŏm" in Kugyŏk *Yŏlyŏsil kisul*, (Works of *Yŏlyŏsil*, trans.), Seoul: Minjok munhwa ch'ujinhoe, Vol. 4, p. 860. Also refer to Kim Ton, "Sŏnjo tae Sim Ŭigyŏm Kim Hyowŏn ŭi kaltŭng yoin kŏmt'o" (An examination of the conflict factors between Sim Ŭigyŏm and Kim Hyowŏn during King Sŏnjo's reign), *Yŏksa kyoyuk*, Vol. 79, 2001.

51 See Edward Wagner, "Two Early Genealogies and Women's Status in Early Yi Dynasty Korea," in Laurel Kendall & Mark Peterson, eds., *Korean Women: View from the Inner Room*, New Haven: East Rock Press, 1980; Edward Wagner, Yi Hunsang and Son Sukkyŏng, trans., *Chosŏn wangjo sahoe ŭi sŏngch'wi wa kwisok* (The achievements and belongings of Chosŏn dynasty society), Seoul: Ilchogak, 2007, pp. 227–244.

52 *Yulgok chŏnsŏ* (Complete works of Yulgok Yi I), Vol. 3, "Okdang chin sip'ye so" (Royal counsellors' memorials for eradicating current ills).

Bibliography

Primary Sources

Chungjong sillok (Annals of King Chungjong)
Myŏnng sillok (Annals of King Myŏngjong)
Yŏlyŏsil kisul, (Works of *Yŏlyŏsil*)
Yulgok chŏnsŏ (Complete works of Yulgok Yi I)

Secondary Sources

Choi, Idon, "16-segi nanggwankwŏn ŭi hyŏngsŏng kwajŏng" (The formation process of the *nanggwan*'s power in the 16th century), *Han'guk saron*, Vol. 14, 1986.

Choi, Sŭnghui, *Chosŏn Ch'ogi chŏngch'i munhwa ŭi ihae* (Understanding the political culture of early Chosŏn), Seoul: Chisik sanŏpsa, 2005.

Chŏng Tuhŭi, "Hoego wa chŏnmang: Chosŏn chŏn'gi" (Retrospect and Prospect: Early Joseon), *Yŏksa* hakpo, Vol. 104, 1984.

________, *Chosŏn sidae ŭi taegan yŏn'gu* (Study of the censorate in the Chosŏn period), Seoul: Ilchogak, 1994.

________, Cho Kwangjo (Cho Kwangjo), revised edition, Seoul: Akanet, 2000.

Chŏng, Tuhŭi and Kye, Sŭngbŏm, *Yu Chagwang: Chosŏn ŭi yŏngwŏn han ibangin* (Yu Chagwang: the eternal outsider of the Chosŏn), Seoul: P'urŭn yŏksa, 2023.

Deuchler, Martina, *The Confucian Transformation of Korea: A Study of Society and Ideology*, Cambridge: Council on East Asian Studies, Harvard University, 1992.

Kim, Hyŏnyŏng, "Hun'gu esŏ sarim ŭro: 15-16 segi Kyŏngju Kim ssi Sangch'on kagye rŭl chungsim ŭro" (From *hun'gu* to *sarim*: focusing on the Sangch'on lineage of the Kyŏngju Kim Clan in the 15th and 16th centuries) in *Chosŏn ŭi chŏngch'i wa sahoe* (Politics and society of Chosŏn), Seoul: Chimmundang, 2002.

Kim, Pŏm, "Chosŏn chŏn'gi *hun'gu-sarim* seryŏk ŭi chae kŏmt'o" (Reexamination of the *hun'gu-sarim* forces' in early Chosŏn), *Han'guk sahakpo*, Vol. 15, 2003.

________, *Sahwa wa Panjŏng ŭi sidae* (The era of literati purges and restoration), Seoul: Yŏksa pip'yŏngsa, 2007.

Kim, Tangt'aek, "Chosŏn Sŏngjong-Chungjong tae chŏngch'isa ŭi ihae wa sarimp'a sŏl" (Understanding the political history from King Sŏngjong to King Chungjong and the *sarim* faction theory), *Yŏksahak yŏn'gu*, Vol. 54, 2014.

Kim, Ton, "Sŏngjong tae ŏn'gwan ŭi sŏngkyŏk pyŏnhwa wa sarim" (Changes in the character of the censorial officials and *sarim* during King Sŏngjong's reign), *Han'guk saron*, Vol. 10, 1984.

________, "Sŏnjo tae Sim Ŭigyŏm Kim Hyowŏn ŭi kaltŭng yoin kŏmt'o" (An examination of the conflict factors between Sim Ŭigyŏm and Kim Hyowŏn during King Sŏnjo's reign), *Yŏksa kyoyuk*, Vol. 79, 2001.

________, *Chosŏn chunggi chŏngch'isa yŏn'gu* (Studies on the Political History of Mid-Chosŏn), Seoul: Kukhak chryowŏn, 2009.

Kim, Wugi, "Chosŏn chŏn'gi sarim ŭi chŏllangjik chinch'ul kwa kŭ yŏkhal" (The advancement and Role of *sarim* in the censorial office in Early Chosŏn," *Taegu sahak*, Vol. 29, 1986.

________, *Chosŏn chunggi ch'ŏksin chŏngch'i yŏn'gu* (A study on the politics of royal In-laws in Mid-Chosŏn), Seoul: Chimmundang, 2001.

Kuksa p'yŏnch'an wiwŏnhoe, ed., *Han'guksa 28: Chosŏn chunggi sarim seryŏk ŭi Tŭngjang kwa hwaltong* (History of Korea 28: The emergence and activities of the sarim forces in mMid-Chosŏn), Kwachŏn: Kuksa p'yŏnch'an wiwŏnhoe, 1996.

Kye, Sŭngbŏm, *Chungjong ŭi sidae: Chosŏn ŭi yugyohwa wa sarim undong* (The era of King Chungjong: Confucianization and the *sarim* movement in Chosŏn), Seoul: Yŏksa Pip'yŏngsa, 2014.

________, "Yŏksa hwahae kwanchŏm esŏ pon Chosŏn Sukchong tae Nosan'dun pokkwŏn choch'i" (Rehabilitation of Nosan'gun during King Sukchong's reign from a Perspective of Historical Reconciliation), *Sŏgang inmun nonch'ong*, Vol. 57, 2020.

Nam, Chidae, "Chosŏn Sŏngjong tae ŭi taegan ŏllon" (The activities of the censorate during King Sŏngjong's Reign), *Han'guk saron* Vol. 12, 1985.

Song, Ch'ansik, "Chosŏn cho sarim chŏngch'i ŭi kyŏllyŏk kujo: chŏllang kwa samsa rŭl chungsom ŭro" (The Power structure of *sarim* politics in the Chosŏn dynasty: focusing on the *chŏllang* and the three censorial offices), *Kyŏngje sahak*, Vol. 2, 1978.

Sŏl, Sŏkkyu, *Chosŏn sidae yusaeng sangso wa kongnon chŏngch'i* (Memorials by Confucian Students and Public Opinion Politics in the Joseon Dynasty), Seoul: Sŏnin, 2002.

Song, Ungsŏp, "Chungjong tae *Kimyo sarim* ŭi kusŏng kwa ch'ulsin paegyŏng" (The composition and background of the *Kimyo sarim* during King Chungjong's Reign), *Han'guk saron*, Vol. 45, 2001.

________, "Chosŏn Sŏngjong tae kongnon chŏngch'I ŭi hyŏngsŏng" (The formation of *kongnon* politics in the reign of King Sŏngjong), PhD dissertation, Seoul taehakkyo, 2011.

Palais, James B., *Confucian Statecraft and Korean Institutions: Yu Hyŏngwŏn and the Late Chosŏn Dynasty*, Seattle: University of Washington Press, 1996.

P'i, Chŏngnan, "Chosŏn chunggi Sŏnggyun'gwan yuseang ŭi ŏllon hwaltong ŭl t'onghan chŏngch'i ch'amyŏ e taehayŏ" (On the political participation of Sŏnggyun'gwan Students through public opinion activities in Mid-Chosŏn), *Sŏngdae sarim*, Vol. 12·13, 1997.

Wagner, Edward W., "The Recommendation Examination of 1519: Its Place in Early Yi Dynasty History," *Chosēn gkuhō,* Vol. 15, 1960.

________, *The Literati Purges: Political Conflict in Early Yi Korea*, Cambridge: East Asian Research Center, Harvard University, 1974.

________, "Yijo sarim munje e taehan chae kŏmt'o" (Reexamination of the *sarim* Problem of the Chosŏn dynasty), *Chŏnbuk sahak,* Vol. 4, 1980.

________, "Two Early Genealogies and Women's Status in Early Yi Dynasty Korea," in Laurel Kendall & Mark Peterson, eds., *Korean Women: View from the Inner Room*, New Haven: East Rock Press, 1980.

Wagner, Edward, Yi, Hunsang and Son, Sukkyŏng, trans., *Chosŏn wangjo sahoe ŭi sŏngch'wi wa kwisok* (The achievements and belongings of Chosŏn dynasty society), Seoul: Ilchogak, 2007.

Yi, Huigwŏn, "Chosŏn chŏn'gi ŭi konggwan yŏn'gu" (A study on the konggwan in early Chosŏn), *Sahak yŏn'gu*, Vol. 28, 1978.

Yi, Hŭihwan, "Chosŏn chŏn'gi sadaebu, saryu, sarim ŭi yongnye," (The usages of the terms *sadaebu*, *saryu*, and *sarim* in early Chosŏn), *Chŏnnam sahak*, Vol. 24, 2005.

Yi, Inyŏng, *Kuksa yoron* (Essential discussions on national history), Seoul:

Min'gyosa, 1956.

Yi, Kibaek, *New Interpretation of National History*, Seoul: T'aesŏngsa, 1961.

________, *New Interpretation of Korean History*, Seoul: Ilchogak, 1967.

Yi, Pyŏngdo, *Chosŏnsa taegwan* (The outline of Chosŏn History), Seoul: Tongjisa, 1948.

________, *Sinsu kuksa taegwan* (The new outline of national history), Seoul: Pomungak, 1956.

________, *Han'guksa taegwan* (The outline of Korean history), Pomungak, 1968.

Yi, Pyŏnghyu, *Chosŏn chŏn'gi Kiho sarimp'a yŏn'gu* (Study of the *Kiho sarim* faction in early Chosŏn), Ilchogak, 1984.

________, *Chosŏn chŏn'gi sarimp'a ŭi hyŏnsil insik kwa taeŭng* (The *sarim* faction's perception of reality and response in early Chosŏn), Ilchogak, 1999.

Yi, Sŏngmu, "Sŏn ch'o ŭi Sŏnggyun'gwan yŏn'gu" (A study of *Sŏnggyun'gwan* in the early Chosŏn period) *Yŏksa hakpo*, Vol.35·36, 1967.

Yi, Sugŏn, *Yŏngnam sarimp'a ŭi hyŏngsŏng* (The formation of the Yŏngnam sarim faction), Taegu: Yŏngnam taehakkyo ch'ulp'anbu, 1979.

Yi, T'aejin, "Sarimp'a ŭi yuhyangso pongnip undong: Chosön ch'ogi söngnihak chöngch'ak ŭi sahoejök paegyöng" (The movement to re-establish *yuhyangso* by the sarim faction: the social background of the establishment of Neo-Confucianism in early Chosön) *Chindan hakpo*, Vol.34·35, 1972·1973.

________, *Han'guk sahoesa yŏn'gu* (Research on Korean social history), Seoul: Chisiksanŏpsa, 1986,

________, *Ŭisul kwa in'gu kŭrigo nongŏp kisul* (Medicine, population, and pgricultural pechnology), T'aehaksa, 2002.

________, *Han'guk sahoesa yŏn'gu: nongŏp kisul paltal kwa sahoe pyŏndong* (Research on Korean social history: development of agricultural technology and social change), Chisik sanŏpsa, 1986.

Yun, In-suk, "Chosŏn chŏn'gi sarim ŭi sahoe kyŏngje chŏk kusang kwa sohak undong" (The socioeconomic ideas of the *sarim* and the *Sohak* movement in early Chosŏn), PhD dissertation, Sunggyungwan University, 2011.

3

The Scars of War Left in Chosŏn: A Study on the Perceptions of the Imjin War in Chosŏn

Hyunchae Lim

Sogang University

3 The Scars of War Left in Chosŏn: A Study on the Perceptions of the Imjin War in Chosŏn

Hyunchae Lim (Sogang University)

1. Introduction

Toyotomi Hideyoshi (豊臣秀吉), who unified Japan, mobilized an army of 130,000 to invade Chosŏn in April 1592. The Imjin War, which lasted for a staggering seven years, was an exceptionally large-scale conflict in the East Asian world. As such, the war drew significant attention from the three countries involved—China, Korea, and Japan. Chosŏn, in particular, suffered immense damage as the main battlefield during those seven years. In modern times, alongside Japan's colonial rule over Korea, this event is considered one of the most representative examples of the harm inflicted by Japan. Historically, the Imjin War (1592-1598), along with the Manchu invasion of 1636-1637, marked a turning point that distinguishes the early and late periods of the Chosŏn Dynasty. Specifically, the Imjin War was the only instance where Japan, as an external power, challenged the Sino-centric tributary system (the Huayi (華夷) order). In the 20th century, the war was primarily understood on the Korean peninsula as a story of overcoming foreign invasions and defending the nation. However, as we entered the 21st century, the perspective shifted, and the Imjin War came to be widely recognized as an

East Asian international war. As a result, the focus today has moved away from a national history perspective centered on Chosŏn to a more East Asia-centric approach, emphasizing mutual exchanges and interactions. This has led to the predominance of international research methodologies that analyze the war within the broader context of East Asian dynamics.

Meanwhile, as the perspective of the Imjin War as an international war emerged, studies focusing on perceptions of war, or the understanding of self and others, began to take shape in this field. War represents the most extreme form of conflict among political actors. Understanding and analyzing oneself and one's opponents provides key insights into the nature of a war. In particular, the Imjin War was an event that disrupted nearly 200 years of peace and forced Chosŏn, Japan, and even the Ming Dynasty to confront significant changes. Consequently, as Chosŏn experienced the changes brought about by the war, it was compelled to reassess its own value system.

While studies related to the Imjin War are predominantly focused on military history, this paper will concentrate on research related to perceptions of the war. Studies on perception have primarily been conducted within the framework of historical memory or personal memory. Up until the 20th century, research on Chosŏn's perceptions tended to align with Practical Learning (Silhak), emphasizing a search for empirical modernity. However, in the United States and Europe, historical memory emerged as a new academic focus in the late 20th century. Similarly, in Korea, the study of memory began to gain prominence in the 2000s.[1] Particularly in the field of modern and contemporary Korean history, scholars have actively adopted the concept of "memory" from Western academia, making it a widely recognized area of study by the 2020s.[2] Although premodern historical studies tend to be limited to examining records and commemorative forms produced after specific events, often lacking in theoretical depth, research on the Chosŏn Dynasty has shown signs of moving away from strictly positivist tendencies. Regarding the Imjin War specifically, studies on contemporary perceptions of the war were virtually nonexistent in the 20th century. However, in the 21st century, a notable number of studies have emerged under the themes of perception and memory.

This paper will explore various perceptions shaped by the Imjin War, focusing particularly on Chosŏn's self-perception and its perception of others (China and Japan). However, even within the narrowed scope of the Imjin War, it is not feasible to cover all aspects of perception studies related to the conflict. For instance, topics such as Japan's postwar self-perception or the perception of Toyotomi Hideyoshi connect to the larger discourses of the Edo bakufu, modern Japan's theory of conquering Korea (seikanron), Japanese imperialism, and contemporary disputes over history textbooks.[3] While such approaches may be valuable for examining internal perceptions within Japan, they are not suitable for tracing Chosŏn's perspective. Furthermore, this study seeks to limit its temporal scope to the period from the outbreak of the war to within the Chosŏn era (the 18th century). Expanding the timeframe to include modern history could enrich the discussion,[4] but it would lead the analysis beyond the framework of the Chosŏn Dynasty, which would fall outside the intended focus of this paper.

Furthermore, memory, perception, and information each exist on different levels. Information is knowledge constructed from experiences collected from various sources. Perception, on the other hand, operates on a higher level, encompassing universally held concepts. Memory, in contrast, is used in a broader sense than universal perception, referring to impressions or experiences that can resurface or fade as needed, depending on context. However, if the scope of analysis is limited to the Chosŏn Dynasty, the "memories" that remain from the premodern era tend to converge with studies addressing the perceptions of another premodern period. Therefore, this paper aims to include as comprehensively as possible studies that deal with the Imjin War in relation to memory or perception.[5]

In Chapter 2, this paper examines the research conducted on the perceptions Chosŏn had of itself and its internal constituents during the war. Since war prompts actors to reflect on themselves, the study aims to trace which values newly emerged and which remained within the realm of universal perception during the conflict. While most studies focus on the Chosŏn court, exceptional cases occasionally arise, which will be addressed in the relevant sections. In Chapter 3, the paper explores studies on how Chosŏn perceived foreign nations, specifically the Ming Dynasty and Japan, during the war. By examining the information Chosŏn internalized about other countries through its wartime interactions, the paper seeks to understand what became universally accepted knowledge. This analysis will conclude by summarizing the findings and suggesting future research directions.

2. Chosŏn's Self-Perception

1) The 2000s: Postwar Recovery and the Recall of Memory

The first scholar in Korea to present Chosŏn's own memory of the Imjin War was Roh, Young-Koo. He examined the compilation process of *Tongguk sinsok samgang haengsil to* (東國新續三綱行實圖, *Illustrated Conduct of the Three Bonds in Korea: New Supplement*) during the reign of King Kwanghae and the recording of meritorious officials in the late reign of King Sŏnjo to uncover the reasons why memories of the Imjin War were shaped around the limited events of its early stages.

Regarding records of meritorious subjects, the main point of contention was determining which military commanders had truly achieved notable accomplishments. King Sŏnjo maintained that the war could not have been overcome without the assistance of the Heavenly Soldiers (Ming army) and argued that, among domestic commanders, only Yi Sunsin, Wŏn Kyun, and Kwŏn Yul had made significant contributions. This perspective stemmed from Sŏnjo's tendency to place greater value on officials who accompanied Hosŏng kongsin (扈聖功臣, the royal court during its evacuation). However, the Office for Meritorious Subject Designation suggested that restricting recognition to Hosŏng kongsin could provoke widespread dissatisfaction, and therefore advocated for selecting as many individuals as possible. Despite these efforts, Sŏnmu kongsin (宣武功臣, Meritorious Subjects for Military Achievement) primarily recognized naval forces, while most members of the Righteous Army were excluded from the list. As a result, through the first half of the 17th century, the majority of regular army personnel (especially infantry) and the Righteous Army were largely overlooked in terms of recognition.

During the reign of King Kwanghaegun, efforts to investigate and reward loyal subjects and virtuous women were expanded. In the 5th year of King Kwanghaegun's reign (1613), the compilation of *Tongguk sinsok samgang haengsil to* began. During this process, much information about acts of integrity from the early stages of the Imjin War was restored. Through this, Chosŏn incorporated the activities of local officials and the Righteous Army into the narrative of those who played central roles in overcoming the Imjin War, thereby linking the memory of the war to the legitimacy of the ruling regime. In the late 17th century, as Chosŏn entered an international order centered around the Qing Dynasty, the theory of reverence for the Zhou gained prominence. This led to the large-scale commemoration of loyal subjects, martyrs, and members of the Righteous Army associated with the Imjin War. Such interpretations of the Imjin War suggest the possibility that they were not entirely based on historical realities but were influenced by political motives.[6] This study was the first to bring the memory of the Imjin War into focus and examines the use of that memory as a tool for legitimizing the ruling power.

The Imjin War also provided an opportunity to reevaluate the status of Buddhism within Chosŏn. Kyungsoon Lee traced the memory of Samyŏngdang Yuchŏng (四溟堂 惟政) to examine how an image of Samyŏngdang, distinct from historical facts, was constructed. While Samyŏngdang's participation in the war has largely been positively evaluated, within the Buddhist community, there were doubts and controversies surrounding the very act of participation due to religious issues. In reality, the faction led by Samyŏngdang did not dominate the Buddhist community, indicating significant resistance within the Buddhist order regarding involvement in the war. This suggests that there was considerable opposition to participation among Buddhist circles.

In the commemorative projects of the 18th century, Samyŏngdang also reemerged, but his contributions were reframed with a Confucian tone of loyalty and righteousness rather than as achievements rooted in Buddhism. On a popular level, the memory of Samyŏngdang extended to Japan, where he was recorded as a victor who subdued the Japanese king. Koreans used the figure of Samyŏngdang, with his marginal and shamanistic characteristics, to construct a memory of victory in the war. However, Samyŏngdang's identity as a Buddhist was erased, leaving him as a symbol of Patriotic Buddhism into modern times.[7] This study traced how the memory of Samyŏngdang, rejected by the Buddhist community, transformed in conjunction with shamanistic elements to survive in late Chosŏn society. In doing so, it focused on popular narratives outside the court and the yangban bureaucracy, contributing to the understanding of civilian perceptions and memories of the war.

In the process of overcoming the war, the Chosŏn court and intellectuals sought clues in historical precedent. Huh, Tae-Yong pointed out that the Imjin War played a significant role in strengthening the perception of ancient northern history in late Chosŏn historical consciousness and traced this process. Until the early Chosŏn period, Koguryŏ was primarily regarded as a cautionary tale—a state that revered martial strength, refused to conform to the Sinocentric order, and was ultimately destroyed by the emperor. However, after the Imjin War, Koguryŏ's victories came to be viewed not only as evidence of Koguryŏ's strength but also as a reflection of Chosŏn's potential strength. This shift in perception also validated the historical experience of fortifying defenses, particularly around mountain fortresses, as an effective wartime strategy.

During the war, King Sŏnjo devoted efforts to examining his country's history and ultimately ordered the compilation of records detailing the conflict with Japan from past to present. Around the same time, the Ming Dynasty, in its dealings with Chosŏn, expressed anxieties related to the memory of Koguryŏ—highlighting Chosŏn's lack of Koguryŏ's formidable strength and suggesting its current vulnerability. Against this backdrop, the strength of Koguryŏ gained prominence within Chosŏn's historical consciousness. The first figure to explicitly reference Koguryŏ's victories was King Kwanghaegun. He recalled the Battle of Yŏnan Fortress (延安城), in which Kuroda Nagamasa (黒田長政)'s forces were repelled, as a continuation of the triumphs of Ansi Fortress (安市城) during Koguryŏ's era.[8]

The memory of Koguryŏ's strength was intertwined with Chosŏn's confidence in its own resilience and was even cited as a reason to oppose peace negotiations with Japan. Shortly after the war, during conflicts with the Jurchens, Chosŏn figures positively referenced Yŏn Kaesomun (淵蓋蘇文), showing that the memory of Koguryŏ continued to resurface. This was also reflected in historical writings. In *Tongguk ch'anyo* (東國纂要, *Essentials of Korea*), Ansi Fortress and Ŭlchi Mundŏk (乙支文德) received special attention. Similarly, in *Tongguk chiriji* (東國地理志, *Geography of Korea*), the northern threat was associated with the loss of Koguryŏ's former territories.

This study highlights the significance of how the state of Chosŏn, which had originally regarded Koguryŏ's image with some taboo, positively re-evaluated it during the Imjin War, connecting this shift to the development of perceptions of northern ancient history in the late Chosŏn period. However, the precise reasons why Koguryŏ's history was emphasized remain unclear. One of the sources mentioned in this research, *Waebyŏnrok* (倭變錄, *Record of the Japanese Disturbances*), covers events from the 8th year of King Hyŏkkŏse of Silla to the Imjin War. Meanwhile, Sŏng Hon (成渾) emphasized the unification of Silla. Given that historical encounters with Japan predominantly involved Paekche and Silla rather than Koguryŏ, the focus on Koguryŏ inevitably shifts the narrative towards the memory of northern Korean ancient states engaging with Chinese dynasties. Therefore, careful consideration is needed to understand why Chosŏn directed its attention toward northern ancient history, particularly Koguryŏ, during this period.

Meanwhile, the scholar who introduced the modern concept of

“nation” in relation to Korea was John B. Duncan from the United States. He previously challenged the Korean academic position that the Korean nation had formed as early as Unified Silla and the early Koryŏ period. Drawing on Hobsbawm’s four elements of a nation—language, ethnicity, religion, and historical state—Duncan argued that it is difficult to identify a complete sense of unity in these aspects during that time.[9] Regarding the Imjin War, Duncan adopted the memory discourse that had emerged in Western academia to trace the influence of popular oral traditions, such as the *Imjinrok* (壬辰錄, *Record of the Imjin War*), on the formation of the concept of “nation” in late Chosŏn and modern Korea. He identified nationalist tendencies in the *Imjinrok*, particularly in the heroization of Chosŏn generals and the expression of hostility toward both Japan and China.

He pointed out that, regarding the popular memory of the Imjin War, there was already an awareness of an exclusive unity, as suggested by Hobsbawm. Another piece of evidence was the diversity of regions (localities) mentioned in the oral traditions, which indicated a sense of nationwide homogeneity. While the author used the example of the Chinese-origin Kwanwangmyo (關王廟, Temple of Lord Guan) to argue against the formation of a modern concept of nation in Chosŏn, it was still possible to trace the emergence of a shared sense of solidarity among Koreans. This was further exemplified by the consistent portrayal of Chosŏn figures across these traditions. However, the author also noted that several versions of the *Imjinrok* contain expressions of hostility toward the state—specifically, the royal court. Based on this, the author expressed skepticism about whether the “state tradition” described by Hobsbawm truly existed in Chosŏn.[10] Duncan’s study is significant as it was the first to attempt to trace the presence of the concept of “nation” in premodern Chosŏn using Western theoretical frameworks, particularly those of Hobsbawm. However, the study did not address whether the sense of solidarity among Chosŏn people was limited to the memory of the Imjin War or whether it extended to other universal forms of shared identity.

Based on the research outcomes reviewed thus far, the trends up to the 2000s in Korean scholarship largely focus on discussing ways to overcome the aftermath of the Imjin War. These studies examine how past events were distorted in memory or revived in ways aligned with contemporary contexts. However, this research trend did not completely move away from the narrative of Chosŏn overcoming its national crisis. While dealing with the theme of memory, much of the research remained tied to a nationalist framework. In the American academic sphere, Duncan attempted an exploratory approach to the concept of "nation," but no studies in Korea appear to have been directly influenced by his work. In the 2000s, American research on the Imjin War was primarily in the stage of confirming basic historical facts through book-based studies. However, during this period,[11] it would be difficult to claim that there was active scholarly exchange between Korea and the United States in the field of perceptions surrounding the Imjin War.

2) Post-2010s: Virtuous Women and Nation

In the 2010s, in-depth studies on how the state remembers specific groups were actively conducted. Research emerged that sought to trace newly emphasized concepts in Chosŏn society through the relationship between *Tongguk sinsok samgang haengsil to* and the Imjin War, with particular focus on studies related to women in Chosŏn. Jung, Ji-young examined changes in the gendered composition of filial piety (孝), loyalty (忠), and virtue (烈) in the process of recording and commemorating women who died during the Imjin War. One notable case involved a sabi (私婢, privately-owned female slave) being included in the 'Ch'ungsindo' (忠臣圖, Portraits of Loyal Subjects). This was unusual, as such a figure did not fit within the traditionally male-centered kunshin (君臣, lord-vassal) relationships defined by earlier *Samgang haengsil to* (三綱行實圖). The deaths of these sabi were attributed to actions by Japanese invaders, and in the exceptional circumstances of war, they were recognized as loyal subjects for having died protecting their masters—who symbolized the king. This expansion of the concept of loyalty to include even slaves reflected a broader redefinition of loyalty during the Imjin War. It demonstrated how the unique context of the war led to an evolution in the understanding of loyalty itself.

Another case, the kisaeng Nongae, while not included in *Tongguk sinsok samgang haengsil to*, emerged in Chosŏn society as a figure embodying loyalty (ch'ung, 忠). The reason Nongae was not recognized as a virtuous woman (烈女) lay in the unique circumstances of her actions—being associated with multiple men and killing them. Traditionally, women were not seen as capable of directly performing acts of loyalty. However, as demonstrated by Nongae's case, her act of killing Japanese enemies was acknowledged as loyal, and she was recognized as a ŭigi (義妓, righteous courtesan). By the 18th century, debates surrounding Nongae centered on whether the story of her death was factual, with her status as a courtesan becoming a less significant issue. This shift aligns with the broader context of post-Manchu invasions in the 17th century, when the necessity of protecting Chosŏn from "barbarians" (Japan and the Manchurian) became firmly established. This development reflects the emergence of a national consciousness in Chosŏn, which created a practical need to recognize and elevate the contributions of lower social classes within Chosŏn society. Nongae's story thus connects to the broader reality of accommodating various social groups in the evolving perception of Chosŏn as a nation-state.[12]

Michael J. Pettid examined the concept of the virtuous woman that emerged in late Chosŏn as a result of the Imjin War. In the process of reviving the collapsing Neo-Confucian order during the war, the ruling elite sought to elevate the values of loyalty, filial piety, and virtue. This effort culminated in the compilation of *Tongguk sinsok samgang haengsil to*, which prominently featured women who suffered at the hands of the Japanese invaders. Most of the women included in this work were those who chose martyrdom, reflecting an educational intent to valorize heroic death over survival after external assault, particularly rape by the enemy. This emphasis served as a moral and didactic tool for reinforcing Confucian values in a time of social and cultural upheaval.

In unofficial narratives, different perspectives emerge. In *Chibong yusŏl* (芝峰類說, *Topical Discourses of Chibong*), an extreme case is described in which a woman chooses martyrdom, simply because she held another man's hand while fleeing, even if the story is fictional. Similarly, *Ŏu yadam* (於于野談, *Unofficial Stories from Ŏu*) includes a depiction of the loyalty and chastity of the kisaeng Nongae. However, such depictions did not represent the full reality of women during the war. In practice, there were women who could not endure starvation and were abandoned by their husbands, women taken captive by Japanese forces who never returned, and women who chose vengeance over martyrdom. These diverse cases reflect a more complex reality. Nonetheless, these realities did not align with the idealized image desired by the court and the ruling elite. As the central government sought to control the image of virtuous women, obtaining detailed information about the broader experiences of women during the war became increasingly difficult.[13]

Jeong, Ho Hun also focused on *Tongguk sinsok samgang haengsil to*, as it represents Chosŏn's official efforts to process and organize the aftermath of the war. The Chosŏn court sought to embrace and mourn the deaths that occurred within the Chosŏn community while simultaneously engaging in the work of judging human actions, lives, and deaths. The compilation of this book was actively pursued during the reign of King Kwanghaegun, with the first draft completed in the 5th year of his reign (1613). This version included 1,123 individuals categorized as filial sons (hyoja, 孝子), loyal subjects (ch'ungsin, 忠臣), and virtuous women. In 1615, the scope was expanded to include not only postwar figures but also individuals from before the war. Figures listed in *Sinjŭng yŏji sŭngnam* (新增輿地勝覽, *Newly Expanded Geographic Survey*) were incorporated, extending the coverage from ancient times to the period of compilation. Further revisions to the 'Ch'ungsindo' (忠臣圖, Portraits of Loyal Subjects) were undertaken, and by 1616, the book was finalized. It ultimately took on a character that encompassed not only the war but also Chosŏn's broader historical traditions.

The book consists of eight volumes of 'Hyojado' (孝子圖, Portraits of

Filial Sons), one volume of 'Ch'ungsindo', and eight volumes of 'Yŏllyŏdo' (烈女圖, Portraits of Virtuous Women). Among the individuals included, those associated with the Imjin War accounted for 38% of the total. However, only 14% of the Hyojado entries were related to the Imjin War, while the proportions for Ch'ungsindo and Yŏllyŏdo exceeded 60%. In addition, by the late Chosŏn period, 97% of honorific plaques (chŏngmun, 旌門) were dedicated to virtuous women, reflecting the emphasis Chosŏn society placed on this category. Cases of individuals commended for resisting foreign invaders were specifically associated with the Imjin War, and their deaths were described as unimaginably brutal. The Chosŏn court, under King Kwanghaegun and the Northern Faction (Pugin, 北人), sought to strongly memorialize the horrors of wartime deaths. This reflected their hope to suppress future wars and maintain nationwide peace.[14]

The three studies discussed above all focus on *Tongguk sinsok samgang haengsil to* and the women (yŏllyŏ, 烈女) included within it, but their areas of focus differ significantly. Chŏng Chi-yŏng highlights the inclusion of lower-class individuals, such as slaves and women, by the court. Michael J. Pettid, in addition, examines how the memories of the extensive suffering endured by women during the war were gradually forgotten. Meanwhile, Chŏng Ho-hun emphasizes how the court remembered the war and used these memories to pray for national stability and peace. The first two studies, in particular, represent an expansion in memory research by focusing on the recall of Chosŏn's subjugated classes. However, all three studies share a common methodological approach in that their focus is not on the war itself but on uncovering the intentions of the power holders who compiled these records. Although some research has explored the memories of marginalized groups in Chosŏn society, much of the focus remains on individuals officially commemorated by the state, reflecting the limitations of the sources available for analysis.

In a different context, Jahyun Haboush Kim, in her posthumously published work, explored the possibility that the concept of "nation" in Chosŏn may have originated from the Imjin War. The concept of nation is inherently Eurocentric, and previous studies on the formation of modern

East Asian nations have predominantly relied on European theoretical frameworks. However, since the historical trajectory of East Asia differs, applying the same concept directly is challenging. Despite this, Kim argued that by tracing similarities, it is possible to reveal how Chosŏn, under foreign invasion, exhibited characteristics of a coherent and unified community.

Kyŏngmun (Proclamations), t'ongmun (Circulars), ch'oyumun (Exhortations) issued by the Righteous Army often emphasized the atrocities of the invaders, awareness of their homeland, and Chosŏn's position as a civilized state opposed to barbarism. The Chosŏn dynasty traditionally prohibited private armies, and individuals were not permitted to assert independent voices. However, leaders of the Righteous Army, such as Ko Kyŏng-myŏng, independently issued proclamations to encourage the recruitment of militias. This development allowed individuals from the subjugated classes to emerge as protectors of the dynasty's legitimacy, embodying a form of popular sovereignty. At the same time, the militia leaders, who were often members of the local yangban, positioned themselves on equal footing with the state, perceiving their loyalty (ch'ung, 忠) to the state as aligning with their actions. As these dynamics progressed with a certain degree of horizontality, the Righteous Army movement evolved into a form of "national" movement.

In terms of language, the war exhibited characteristics akin to a "national war." The Japanese army primarily relied on the Chinese writing of monks to produce documents, using classical Chinese (hanmun, 漢文) to communicate information in the occupied territories of Chosŏn and even attempting to introduce the Japanese language. After the Ming forces joined the war, they also used classical Chinese to disseminate information and convey the emperor's will. In response, the Chosŏn court utilized hangŭl (한글, Korean script) when communicating its intentions to the people, thereby distinguishing Chosŏn from external entities. By leveraging the exclusivity of hangŭl, the court aimed to foster the unity of the Chosŏn "nation."

The author analyzed the postwar perceptions of Chosŏn people through the genre of *mongyurok* (夢遊錄, *Records of Dream Journeys*). The study focused on three works: *Talch'ŏn mongyurok* (達川夢遊錄), *P'isaeng mongyurok* (皮生夢遊錄), and *Kangdo mongyurok* (江都夢遊錄). *Talch'ŏn mongyurok* highlighted wartime heroes while criticizing the collapse of the state's moral order. *P'isaeng mongyurok* sought to liberate the nameless commoners who died in the war from tragedy, employing Taoist rather than Confucian values. *Kangdo mongyurok*, though rooted in the memory of the Manchu invasions (Pyŏngja horan), used the voices of women to criticize the collapse of Chosŏn's patriarchal system. However, these attempts stopped short of overturning Chosŏn's Confucian order, merely pointing out its imperfections. At the same time, by commemorating the victory of the Imjin War, Chosŏn, which had suffered devastating blows during the two invasions (particularly Pyŏngja Horan), sought to integrate the memory of war and lay the foundation for modern nationalist discourse.[15]

Haboush's approach is significant in that it expanded the analysis of collective identity, which Duncan had previously explored on an experimental level, to include broader dimensions of worldview and language. Starting from the emergence of the people's voices during the Imjin War, the study sheds light on ideological and linguistic characteristics that could be shared within Chosŏn.

However, perhaps due to the limitations of the work being posthumously compiled, the focus from Chapter 3 (Language) onward shifts heavily toward explaining the Ming and Japan rather than Chosŏn. In Chapter 5 (Mongyurok), the Imjin War and the Manchu invasions are mixed together, and the term "nation" (minjok, 民族) is only used in the final paragraph, making it somewhat misaligned with the title of the book.[16] Even setting aside these structural weaknesses, it remains conventional wisdom that shared Korean sentiment and identity began at least as early as the Unified Silla period. While Duncan and others have challenged this view, whether a distinct nationalist consciousness emerged specifically during the Imjin War remains a question that requires further detailed exploration.[17] Moreover, the "people" that Haboush presents are ultimately the local yangban, and those who used hangŭl were limited to the ruling classes of Chosŏn and Japan. Consequently, it is difficult to discern the dynamics of the subjugated classes, which are critical to understanding true national cohesion and identity. J. Marshall Craig reconstructed the Imjin War based on the records of five individuals: Xŭ Yí Hòu (許儀後), Yoshino JIngozaemon (吉野甚五左衛門), O Hŭimun (吳希文), Hwang Sin (黃愼), and Keinen (慶念). Structurally, this book does not develop a single argument throughout its chapters but rather traces various perspectives of the war as witnessed by these individuals.[18] The main text, divided into nine chapters including a Prologue and Epilogue, devotes six chapters to thoroughly analyzing the records left by each of these figures. Chapter 7 briefly addresses how the Ming and Japan each remembered the war as a victory for their respective nations. While the content itself may not seem groundbreaking, this study holds significant value as it is the first analysis of primary sources on the Imjin War within English-speaking academia. Based on his analysis in the main text, the author tackles the issue of "nation" during the Imjin War in the Epilogue, a section that will be the focus of analysis in this study.

In the Epilogue, the author articulated his views on nationalism and proto-nationalism in premodern East Asia. To define the issue of "nation", he analyzed three key aspects: cultural identity (culture as identity), imagined communities, and mass participation. First, regarding cultural identity, the author argued that Chosŏn shared a fundamental sense of civility with China. However, during the war, Chosŏn also emphasized its unique characteristics, such as linguistic homogeneity, to distinguish itself. On the topic of community, the author highlighted three points. First, the three countries involved in the war (Chosŏn, Ming, and Japan) emphasized their current political structures, cultural achievements, and territorial claims linked to ancient kingdoms. Second, these nations prioritized the state (state) and territory (territory) over the people (people) as their defining elements. Third, while the "othering" of groups such as the Wa (倭, Japanese) and the Yi (夷, "barbarians") was relatively clear, the fluid and expandable notion of "self-identity" centered on Sinocentrism (chunghwa, 中華) meant that the "other" was not perceived as a distinct ethnic group.

For mass participation, the author focused on the ch'angŭimun (倡義文, "Proclamations of Righteous Uprising") previously analyzed by Haboush. These proclamations successfully encouraged the participation of scholars and bureaucratic elites but left unclear whether they were effective in mobilizing the lowest classes. According to contemporary records, widespread rumors of betrayal and duplicity hindered people's ability to imagine a shared past, present, and future. Instead, the author suggested that national memory of the "silent" classes might be more effectively found in temples and monuments erected in Jinju to commemorate the war.

Ultimately, the author assessed the issue of "nation" as presenting both congruities and incongruities with Western patterns of nation formation. On the one hand, there is evidence of shared historical memory and unified thought across social strata. On the other hand, certain aspects diverge significantly from the Western experience of nation-building. The author cautioned that labeling the phenomenon as "national" risks overlooking nuances within the sources, while dismissing it as "non-national" leads to the problematic tendency of viewing it as less nationalistic or as merely exhibiting proto-nationalist characteristics in comparison to the West. To resolve this dilemma, the author argued for redefining "nation" beyond a Eurocentric framework, adopting a broader and more inclusive perspective.[19]

Craig's approach can be seen as a critique of the ambitious application of modern concepts, such as those used by Haboush. In this regard, Craig effectively identified the inherent issues with the concept of "nation". However, the strength of this argument is not particularly compelling. As Haboush also pointed out, the concept of nation is fundamentally Eurocentric, making it difficult to apply directly to East Asian societies—a premise that had already been acknowledged. Thus, the task that this book needed to undertake was to move beyond merely declaring the need for a new interpretation suited to the East Asian context and to explore methodologies or new conceptual frameworks. Unfortunately, the book falls short of offering alternatives to advance the "nation" debate in East Asia to the next stage, leaving room for further exploration.

In Korea, Hur, Joon also focused on the issue of Chosŏn's "nation" (minjok, 民族). He emphasized that the emergence of the Chosŏn nation was neither solely rooted in historical origins nor a product of the modern era by examining the identity of hangwae (降倭, surrendered Japanese soldiers). The hangwae actively sought to adopt a Chosŏn identity and, in doing so, displayed hostility toward the Japanese army. While it may not be entirely accurate to interpret this behavior as reflecting their genuine intentions, their statements provide evidence that their affiliation with Japan did not rely on the strong sense of solidarity associated with modern national consciousness. This illustrates that the hangwae's detachment from Japan was not rooted in the cohesive ties of modern nationalism.

On the other hand, the Chosŏn court adopted a stance of actively integrating the hangwae. This contrasted with the widespread distrust toward the hangwae at the local level. The court emphasized the fact that the hangwae had participated in the war as subjects and servants of the king, ensuring that they were not regarded as outsiders or threats within Chosŏn society. The hangwae themselves were acutely aware of their precarious position and strongly expressed their determination to live as Chosŏn people after the war. Through this process, the hangwae became included within the category of Chosŏn citizens, and the memory of them as part of the "invaders" gradually faded.[20]

Hur, Joon's study critically builds upon Haboush's perspective, aiming to demonstrate that the identity of being Chosŏn people was not rooted in modern concepts. This research highlights the fluidity of the concept of "nation" as it pertains to Chosŏn. The fading memory of the hangwae as part of the invaders must also be examined alongside the broader shifts in the collective memory of the Imjin War. However, Hŏ's study focuses on the Chosŏn court's stance on integrating the hangwae and interpretations based on the statements made by the hangwae themselves. Given that not all memories of Japan pertain to the Imjin War, and not all Japanese individuals were involved in the conflict, this issue leaves room for more complex interpretations.

Kim Kyong-tae addressed the issue of memory regarding the Imjin War but approached it from a perspective somewhat different from studies focusing on the subjugated classes or shared consciousness. He revisited Chosŏn's perceptions during the war itself with a more empirical approach. Modern memories of the Imjin War, as seen in *Tongguk saryak* (東國史略, *Concise History of Korea*) and the earlier *Chōsen Kinse shi* (朝鮮近世史, *Early Modern History of Chosŏn*), often emphasize factional strife and criticize the incompetence of the king and his officials. Notably, narratives frequently begin with depictions of King Sŏnjo indulging in leisure or neglecting state affairs, coupled with factional struggles. Kim's primary goal was to investigate whether such perceptions existed in Chosŏn during the Imjin War itself and to trace how they differed from later interpretations.

During the war, rhetorical expressions within Chosŏn often criticized King Sŏnjo and Crown Prince Kwanghaegun for failing to govern effectively, but these claims remained largely political rhetoric without substantial evidence. Instead, it was the Ming generals who solidified their positions by criticizing Chosŏn's ministers and monarch for their perceived incompetence. They even repurposed Chosŏn court rhetoric, which lamented its own lack of preparedness due to complacency during peacetime. Ultimately, Ming criticism of Chosŏn found its way into the emperor's edicts, which included statements such as, "The king indulges in leisure, neglects his people, and fails to maintain military supplies." While Chosŏn refuted these allegations, tensions between Chosŏn and the Ming escalated, and these criticisms were reiterated, reaching their peak in Ding Yingtai's (丁应泰) vehement denunciations of Chosŏn.

After the war, reflections on the conflict occasionally surfaced in Chosŏn. However, the level of introspection varied. In *Chingbirok* (懲毖錄, *The Book of Corrections*), Yu Sŏngnyong emphasized that Chosŏn had not reached a state of "decadence" and refrained from making significant criticisms of King Sŏnjo. Yi Su-gwang's *Chibong yusŏl* (芝峯類說)

attributed responsibility for the war to Toyotomi Hideyoshi rather than Chosŏn. Similarly, retrospectives by Yi Hang-bok, An Pang-jun's *Ŭnbong yasa pyŏllok* (隱峯野史別錄), and Yi Ik's *Sŏngho sasŏl* (星湖僿說) acknowledged factional strife but avoided criticizing the dynasty itself. Thus, from Chosŏn's official perspective, criticism of the court was absent.[21] This image of an "incompetent Chosŏn" was instead actively propagated in postwar China and Japan. The author examined this official stance, which included the yangban class along with the court, reaffirming that criticism of the court was inconceivable within yangban society. However, unofficial perspectives within Chosŏn, such as those found in popular tales like *Imjinrok* (壬辰錄), frequently featured criticisms of the court, as established in previous studies. Does this mean that criticisms of the Chosŏn court were imported from China or Japan?

In summary, Chosŏn employed various methods to remember the scars of war and sought internal cohesion through this process. As research on memory and perception gained momentum, scholars have moved beyond taking Chosŏn's "nationalism" for granted, instead focusing on the processes through which self-identity and the Chosŏn "nation" were formed. Both Korean and US studies have predominantly analyzed *Tongguk sinsok samgang haengsil to* from the perspective of Confucianization in the postwar period, highlighting how the court expanded its acceptance of women and the subjugated classes. Although many studies have moved away from the nationalist narrative of overcoming a national crisis, the understanding of Chosŏn often remains centered on the court. Consequently, expressions and perceptions from the time of the war have often been overlooked in domestic scholarship. Yet, shifts in perception began occurring as early as the outbreak of the conflict. In the United States, Haboush explored various utterances from the wartime period, and Craig focused on analyzing primary sources. Moving forward, it is hoped that more studies will delve into the perceptions that arose during the war itself.

3. Chosŏn's Perception of Others

1) Perception of the Ming: The Grace of Rebuilding (再造之恩) and Reverence for the Zhou and Great Righteousness (尊周大義)

While various studies have explored Chosŏn's self-perception in relation to the Imjin War, research on its external perceptions has been comparatively less active. Issues surrounding Chosŏn-Ming and Chosŏn-Japan relations are typically studied within the realm of relational history, which often leans heavily toward political and diplomatic history. As a result, these studies tend to prioritize political and diplomatic interests and judgments tied to contemporary circumstances over a more "universal" understanding of the other. At the same time, Chosŏn's perception of the Ming is more significantly shaped by the Ming-Qing transition, making the Imjin War a less central focus in such studies. Nonetheless, there are works that examine Chosŏn's perception of the Ming in the context of the Imjin War, and these deserve attention as part of this discussion.

Han Myung-gi analyzed how the concept of chaejo chi ŭn (再造之恩, "the grace of rebuilding") from the Ming toward Chosŏn was formed and what it signified. During the Imjin War, the Ming approached Chosŏn with the logic of sunmang ch'i han (脣亡齒寒, "the lips are gone, the teeth are cold"), viewing Chosŏn's stability as critical to its own. However, the influence of the Ming army on Chosŏn was not entirely positive. Despite this, Chosŏn began to emphasize chaejo chi ŭn—the "grace of reviving a collapsing Chosŏn court"—toward the end of the war. The author attributes this to the court's dire circumstances; early in the war, the Chosŏn court was on the run from the Japanese army and losing the support of its people. In this context, the Ming army's intervention and victories represented a beacon of hope. Even though the Ming army dominated the peace negotiations and intervened in Chosŏn's military operations, King Sŏnjo demonstrated an attitude of absolute dependence on the Ming. While commoners were not entirely ungrateful toward the

Ming, their appreciation was less intense compared to the ruling elite, as they directly suffered from the Ming army's actions.

Within this dynamic, Chosŏn's ruling elite, particularly King Sŏnjo, understood the presence of the Ming army as directly tied to their own authority. The king believed that if the Ming forces were to leave, public sentiment would immediately turn against him, potentially leading to rebellion. Although he acknowledged the existence of the Righteous Army in the early stages of the war, he found them difficult to control. Thus, the more the court emphasized "the grace of rebuilding", the stronger its position became. By highlighting their role in summoning the Ming forces, King Sŏnjo and the Loyal Subjects Who Escorted the King could recover from their failures during the early war. On the other hand, the Ming also used the concept of the grace of rebuilding as a tool to exert control over Chosŏn. After the rise of the Later Jin (後金), the Ming leveraged the "grace of rebuilding" to dictate Chosŏn's actions. As a result, the grace of rebuilding became a key issue not only in Chosŏn's perception of the Ming but also in its overall relationship with the Ming.[22] Han Myung-gi's account of the grace of rebuilding has largely been carried forward without significant changes in subsequent studies. Accordingly, later researchers have sought to explore Ming-related perceptions in areas other than the grace of rebuilding itself.

Kuwano Eiji focused on state rituals in late Chosŏn, particularly those surrounding Kwanwangmyo (關王廟, Temple of Lord Guan), Muyŏlsa (武烈祠, Shrine of Martial Valor), Sŏnmusa (宣武祠, Shrine of Military Merits), and Minch'ungdan (愍忠壇, Altar of Loyal Martyrs), to examine Chosŏn's perception of the Ming. Kwanwangmyo was a shrine dedicated to the Chinese military deity Guan Yu (關羽), which the Ming forces actively promoted for establishment in Chosŏn. King Sŏnjo of Chosŏn was compelled to participate in worship alongside Ming generals, and in 1598 he personally visited one of these shrines. However, King Sŏnjo only visited once, and the Chosŏn court opposed not only the southern Kwanwangmyo but also the establishment of an eastern Kwanwangmyo. *The Veritable Records of the Chosŏn Dynasty* (朝鮮王朝實錄) also reveals

King Kwanghaegun's skeptical stance toward Kwanwangmyo.

Muyŏlsa (武烈祠) was a shrine dedicated to figures such as Shi Xing (石星) and Li Rusong (李如松), established around 1595–1596. Among them, Li Rusong, a prominent figure, was later enshrined at Taebodan (大報壇, Great Gratitude Altar) during the reign of King Yŏngjo. Meanwhile, Sŏnmusa (宣武祠) was a shrine established in 1599 to honor Xing Jie (邢玠) and Yang Hao (楊鎬). Although both Muyŏlsa and Sŏnmusa were fundamentally meant to venerate the Ming forces, their management waned during King Kwanghaegun's reign. By the time of the Chŏngmyo Invasion (1627), the shrines had fallen into disrepair, with their portraits burned. Only after replacing the destroyed portraits could the rituals be barely maintained.

Minch'ungdan (愍忠壇) was not a shrine dedicated to specific Ming generals but was instead established in 1593 to commemorate the entire Ming army that had participated in the war in Chosŏn. It was initially managed by the Ming Ministry of Rites (禮部尙書) under the orders of the Wanli Emperor, but the shrine fell into neglect with the Ming–Qing transition. In 1668, the rituals at Minch'ungdan were revived, but this was unrelated to the Ming; the revival was prompted by famines and droughts in Chosŏn. The author interprets this as evidence that the renewal of Minch'ungdan rituals was difficult to connect with a broader trend of venerating the Ming.[23] Kuwano's study emphasizes that in the early 17th century, before Chosŏn felt the influence of the Qing, the grace of rebuilding and the commemoration of Ming figures were not strongly upheld in Chosŏn. However, this does not necessarily indicate that the grace of rebuilding was weak in Chosŏn. A more comprehensive interpretation would need to consider Chosŏn's financial constraints and its Confucian character.

Woo Kyungsup approached the topic from a slightly different perspective than Kuwano, focusing not only on symbolic sites like Minch'ungdan, Muyŏlsa, and Sŏnmusa but also on the lives of Ming soldiers who settled in Chosŏn and their descendants. Through this, he traced how the memory of the Imjin War and the practical discourse surrounding the grace of rebuilding evolved over time. While Minch'ungdan, Muyŏlsa, and Sŏnmusa were altars dedicated to Ming generals and soldiers, U's research aligns with Kuwano's conclusion that active rituals at these sites were not consistently performed during the 17th–century Ming–Qing transition.

In the late 17th century, as Wu Sangui's rebellion was suppressed and the Qing stabilized, Chosŏn established Mandongmyo (萬東廟) and Taepodan (大報壇) to conduct rituals in honor of the Wanli Emperor. During this period, Chosŏn began to incorporate the descendants of Ming soldiers and immigrant Chinese who had been neglected until then. At the same time, Chosŏn's ideological framework shifted, with the grace of rebuilding diminishing in significance and reverence for the Zhou and great righteousness (chonju taeŭi, 尊周大義) emerging as a central theme. The author attributes the weakening of the grace of rebuilding logic to three factors: first, The Qing's appropriation of the grace of rebuilding narrative. Second, the corruption and failures demonstrated by the Ming army during the Imjin War. Third, the diminished memory of the Manchu invasions and the Ming–Qing transition.

From this point onward, rituals at Minch'ungdan, Sŏnmusa, and Muyŏlsa were revived. However, these rituals were likely subsumed within the broader framework of reverence for the Zhou and great righteousness. This is evidenced by their being treated on par with shrines like Hyŏnjŏlsa (顯節祠) and Ch'ungnyŏlsa (忠烈祠), which commemorated Chosŏn individuals who died in martyrdom at Namhansansŏng and Kanghwa Island. Meanwhile, the descendants of Ming soldiers who participated in the Imjin War were marginalized within naturalized Chinese communities in Chosŏn. Instead, the descendants of Ming literati who sought refuge in Chosŏn during the Ming–Qing transition took on a more central role in these communities.[24]

Prior to Woo Kyungsup's work, Yun Hye–min also examined how Chosŏn's perception of the grace of rebuilding evolved, focusing on changing views of Shi Xing, the Ming Minister of War. During the war, evaluations of Shi Xing were divided into two phases: an initial positive response to his apparent willingness to attack Japan, and later negative reactions to his shift toward advocating peace during the negotiation period. However, after the war ended and Shi Xing died in prison, Chosŏn began to honor him with rituals and regard him as a benefactor. This shift can be understood as part of King Sŏnjo's broader efforts to reinforce the grace of rebuilding as a central narrative.

Starting from King Injo's reign, Chosŏn's interest in the broader concept of civilization grew, moving beyond the framework of the grace of rebuilding to an aspiration for the universal civilization represented by the Ming as Chunghwa. Shi Xing was also revived under the principle of reverence for the Zhou and great righteousness, as a protector of civilization. From 1709, rituals honoring Shi Xing were formally conducted at Muyŏlsa (武烈祠). His case became a model for ceremonial practices honoring the achievements of loyalists and martyrs in Chosŏn. This commemoration effort by the court not only influenced Chosŏn scholars but also transformed Shi Xing into a figure of integrity in the popular imagination. The author concludes that late Chosŏn's perception of Chunghwa was not one of blind veneration for the Ming but rather an appreciation for the values embodied by Chunghwa civilization itself.[25]

Studies on commemorative projects related to the Imjin War in late Chosŏn have focused on tracing how Chosŏn's perception of the Ming evolved in response to changes in Chosŏn society. Rather than examining Chosŏn's perceptions of the Ming during and immediately after the Imjin War, these studies have centered on how the grace of rebuilding transitioned into reverence for the Zhou and righteous principles within the framework of Chosŏn Sinocentrism. While these research trends can be seen as part of the broader understanding of perceptions of the Imjin War, they do not directly analyze the war's immediate impact. This is because such studies primarily focus on the transformation of Chosŏn-China(not Ming) relations rather than the specific influence of the Imjin War itself.

Kim Kyong-tae investigated the possibility that the Imjin War served as a turning point in Chosŏn's perception of Jizi (箕子), whom Chosŏn regarded as its historical progenitor. While Jizi was held in high regard after Chosŏn's founding, he received less attention compared to figures like Confucius, the founder of Koryŏ, or Tan'gun. However, Ming general Li Rusong, upon entering P'yŏngyang, performed rituals at Jizi's shrine and restored Jizi's tomb, which had been damaged during the war. In response, Chosŏn elevated its treatment of Jizi, formally initiating rituals for him in 1602. From this point onward, Jizi's status rose significantly, and King Sŏnjo, who endured the hardships of the war, was seen as upholding the same righteous principles as Jizi, who had left China for Chosŏn to preserve his integrity. Subsequently, various relics and writings about Jizi emerged, reinforcing the perception—regardless of historical accuracy—that Chosŏn was preserving Confucian universality.

Furthermore, even before the Imjin War, Koreans emphasized their identity as a state of propriety, nearly equal in standing to the Ming, by highlighting the belief that Jizi had introduced propriety to their land. This sentiment was amplified when the Imjin War broke out and the Ming forces came eastward to assist Chosŏn. During the war, references to restoring the state of Jizi, increased in Chosŏn, and the Ming similarly used the phrase to claim they were helping restore the land of Jizi. Although the urgency of wartime politics left little room for formalities, this discourse fostered a sense of shared identity between the Ming and Chosŏn through their mutual connection to Jizi.[26] This study supports the existing view that Chosŏn's longstanding So Chunghwa (小中華, Little China) consciousness, which had been highly regarded even before the war, was further concretized through the Ming's tangible presence and actions. In summary, Chosŏn's perception of the Ming resulting from the Imjin War can be encapsulated in the concept of the grace of rebuilding. Although impressions of the Ming forces during the war were not entirely positive, the Chosŏn court recognized the Ming as having granted the grace of reviving the nation. However, the process of venerating the Ming's intervention was not smooth immediately after the war. Instead, the resurgence of veneration occurred in the late 17th to 18th centuries, coinciding with the revival of reverence for the Zhou and righteous. During this period, the meaning of the Ming forces' participation shifted, with less focus on the Ming as a state and more on their actions being representative of universal Civilization. The Ming's role, therefore, aligned with Chosŏn's evolving So Chunghwa (小中華, "Little China") consciousness, demonstrating how Chosŏn's memory and perception adapted to broader trends. Nevertheless, the memory of the Imjin War and Chosŏn's late-period perceptions of the Ming or China are overshadowed by the presence of the Qing and the profound impact of the Chŏngch'uk haseong (丁丑下城, 1637 surrender to the Qing), making this a more fitting evaluation of Chosŏn's historical narrative.

2) Perception of Japan: The Substance of Hostility

Chosŏn's perception of Japan can be summarized as originating from the Sinocentric worldview of civilized (hua, 華) versus barbarian (yi, 夷) distinction, which placed Chosŏn in a superior position to Japan.[27] While Chosŏn's subordinate status as a tributary state was more prominent in its relationship with the Ming, its Little China consciousness became more pronounced in relation to Japan. As a result, the majority of Chosŏn people regarded Japan as barbarians and viewed them as entities outside the realm of civilization, thereby perceiving them with disdain. This perspective was prevalent not only before the Imjin War but also persisted after the war had ended. Therefore, to analyze the impact of the Imjin War as a unique event on Chosŏn's perception of Japan, a more specific and nuanced approach is needed beyond the framework of Hua-Yi perspective.

Ki-Cheol Bang published a diachronic study on Chosŏn's perception of Japan. This book examines perceptions of Japan before and after the Imjin War (Chosŏn-Japan War), using the war as a pivotal point. It begins with a general overview of prewar perceptions. From the Three Kingdoms period through the Chosŏn dynasty, Chosŏn regarded Tsushima (對馬) as a den of Japanese pirates (倭寇. K: waegu, J: Wakō) and engaged with the island primarily to control these raiders. The book then focuses on the responses of 16th-century intellectuals, particularly Yi Hwang (李滉), Cho Sik (曺植), and Yi I (李珥). Yi Hwang viewed Japan as a realm of beasts and advocated granting trade permits over military intervention. Cho Sik emphasized the need to suppress Japanese raids through military force. Yi I shared Cho Sik's perspective on severing trade ties and preparing militarily but aligned with Yi Hwang in believing that Japan should also be governed through virtue (德). While all three regarded Japan as a barbarian entity, their views diverged on the role of military action versus virtuous governance.

On the eve of the war, two primary views on Japan existed within the Chosŏn court. One, based on the Hua-Yi perspective, held by figures like Kim Sŏng-il, argued that barbarians could not attack a civilized nation like Chosŏn. The other view acknowledged the possibility of a Japanese invasion but regarded it as being on the scale of border raids by the Japanese pirates. When the war broke out, Chosŏn intellectuals attributed the defeat to Japan's challenge to the Hua-Yi order, blaming the incompetence of officials while refraining from criticizing the king. Chosŏn's perception of Japan during the war was examined through the perspectives of central official Yu Sŏngnyong (柳成龍), local official Kwŏn Tumun (權斗文), and scholar-official O Hŭimun (吳希文). Yu Sŏngnyong initially assessed Japanese military power highly, but as the tide of the war turned in Chosŏn's favor, he dismissed their techniques. Kwŏn Tumun recognized the Japanese forces as strong but characterized them as uncivilized barbarians due to their brutality and acts of rape. Nevertheless, he recorded aspects such as dietary habits, sleeping arrangements, and funeral customs in a relatively objective manner. O Hŭimun labeled Japan as barbarians that must be swiftly suppressed and even supported an expedition to Tsushima to address the issue. All three figures shared a deeply rooted Hua-Yi perspective, distinguishing between Chosŏn (civilization) and Japan (barbarians).

After the war, the author first examined perceptions of Japan among Confucian scholars who had been taken captive. These scholars uniformly attributed the cause of Chosŏn's invasion to Tsushima and Toyotomi Hideyoshi. Kang Hang (姜沆) and Chŏng Hŭidŭk (鄭希得), both former captives, harshly criticized Tsushima for enticing Hideyoshi to attack

Chosŏn. Regarding Hideyoshi, they shared a common view, labeling him as cruel and incompetent in governance. However, opinions among the captives differed on the likelihood of Japan's reinvasion. By 1603, a consensus had emerged, advocating for preventing war through diplomatic engagement. Evaluations of Tokugawa Ieyasu (徳川家康) were similarly divided. The Border Defense Council (Pibyŏnsa, 備邊司) emphasized that Ieyasu had not been involved in Chosŏn's invasion, while the Office of the Inspector General (Sahŏnbu, 司憲府) criticized him, arguing that today's Ieyasu could become tomorrow's Hideyoshi. Ultimately, trade relations were restored, but Chosŏn's vigilance toward Japan remained.[28]

Ki-Cheol Bang's study is significant as the first diachronic research examining Chosŏn's perception of Japan with the Imjin War as a central framework. However, several limitations can be noted. First, the study relies excessively on the narrative framework of the Hua-Yi perspective. While it is undeniable that Chosŏn's relations with Japan were influenced by this perspective, the author seems to interpret Chosŏn's critical stance as representing a barbarian viewpoint, while positive or objective assessments are framed as shocks to or overcoming of the Hua-Yi perspective. Although the preface raises the question of whether the Imjin War intensified the Hua-Yi perspective, the analysis of the concept of barbarian itself is not sufficiently in-depth, giving the impression of a somewhat convenient narrative.

Second, the study heavily enumerates the thoughts of specific individuals, making Chosŏn's general perception of Japan appear fragmented and scattered. Third, the study does not provide a clear answer to how the hostile anti-Japanese sentiment triggered by the Imjin War was resolved. Instead, based on this research alone, one might conclude that the war's most significant issue—hostility toward Japan—persisted until the end of the studied period(1615).

Yi Kyubae pointed out that previous studies on Chosŏn's hostile perception of Japan failed to clearly articulate its specific nature. His research focuses on analyzing the state of hostility toward Japan after the Imjin War and the factors contributing to this perception.

Yi Kyu-bae pointed out that previous studies on Chosŏn's hostile perception of Japan failed to clearly articulate its specific nature. His research focuses on analyzing the state of hostility toward Japan after the Imjin War and the factors contributing to this perception. In the early 17th century, immediately after the war, Chosŏn treated the Imjin War as an unforgettable event for generations to come and expressed the stance that Japan was an irreconcilable enemy. The acceptance of peace requests and the exchange of diplomatic missions, such as the communication envoys (通信使, K: t'ongsinsa, J: tsūshinshi), were fundamentally aimed at placating Japan rather than reflecting genuine trust in their intentions.

This hostility toward Japan in the aftermath of the Imjin War solidified in the 18th century as a form of vigilance regarding matters related to the war. By this period, while Chosŏn acknowledged the long-standing kyorin (交隣, "neighborly relations") and the impracticality of retribution, sentiments of enmity lingered. Yi Ik's *Sŏngho sasŏl*, a work by one of the most well-informed scholars about Japan, still described the Imjin War as a grudge that must eventually be repaid. This cautionary attitude toward Japan is also evident in the continued commemoration of Yi Sunsin and in various *P'yohaerok* (漂海錄, *records of drift voyages*), which emphasized Chosŏn's military achievements and maintained awareness of Japan's past actions. Similarly, in the 19th century, works such as *Kyŏngse yup'yo* (經世遺表, *Design for Good Governance*) and *Haedong yŏksa* (海東歷史, *History of the Eastern Sea*) continued to express concerns about Japanese aggression.[29] However, this study selectively highlights instances of anti-Japanese hostility, seemingly overlooking the diverse perspectives on Japan in late Chosŏn. Additionally, even before the war, Chosŏn harbored distrust not only toward Japanese pirates but also toward the Japanese state itself, a bias that is not adequately addressed here.

Han Myung-gi offered a more detailed account of theory of irreconcilable enmity during the Imjin War. He noted that while Chosŏn distrusted Japan in the 15th century, by the 16th century, it regarded Japan as a manageable diplomatic neighbor. However, after the Imjin War, Chosŏn officially designated Japan as a "perpetual, irreconcilable enemy", a target for revenge that required washin sangdam (臥薪嘗膽, "lying on firewood and tasting gall") to achieve eventual retaliation. Chosŏn also came to fear Japan's military capabilities, perceiving Japan as a force difficult for the world to confront.

While this hostility remained largely unchanged over time, the 1637 Treaty of Surrender by Qing prompted discussions about revising Chosŏn's perception of Japan. Jo Kyŏng argued that while hostility toward Japan should be maintained, Tokugawa Ieyasu and his regime were not enemies. Instead, he proposed an alliance with Japan to counter the new enemy: the Qing.[30] This perspective, although reflective of Chosŏn's pragmatic stance, suggests that perceptions could shift in accordance with changing realities, offering valuable insights for further consideration.

Lim Hyunchae narrowed the focus on the specific targets of Chosŏn's contempt during the Imjin War by analyzing the naming conventions employed by Japan at the time. Toyotomi Hideyoshi's Toyotomi (豊臣) was a uji (氏, clan) bestowed upon him by the emperor when he assumed the title of kampaku (關白, regent). Hideyoshi himself actively propagated the Toyotomi name to establish a new clan-based power structure. As a result, many Japanese generals who participated in the Imjin War also adopted the Toyotomi name, and this aspect is well-documented in Chosŏn records. Moreover, the Toyotomi name even appeared in the imperial edict of investiture issued by the Wanli Emperor, reflecting how Hideyoshi's utilization of the name was acknowledged at the Ming court as well.

However, despite being aware of Hideyoshi's use of the Toyotomi name, Chosŏn intentionally avoided acknowledging it. Instead, Chosŏn referred to him using the Taira (平) clan name. While Hideyoshi had indeed used this name at some point, making it seem like a simple misunderstanding from a historical perspective, Chosŏn deliberately adhered to the Taira name even when the Ming recognized the Toyotomi name in their official documents. At the time, Chosŏn believed that the original rulers of Japan, the Minamoto clan (Gen-ji, 源氏), had been eradicated and replaced by the Taira clan (Hei-shi, 平氏). Drawing on the portrayal of the Taira clan as immoral in the *Haedong chegukki*

(海東諸國紀, *Record of Countries East of the Sea*), Chosŏn linked this image to Hideyoshi, framing him as an illegitimate ruler. This perspective also helps explain why Chosŏn found it relatively easy to negotiate with Tokugawa Ieyasu, who emphasized his ties to the Minamoto clan. Chosŏn justified Japan as a country belonging to the Minamoto clan, providing a framework for a more conciliatory stance.[31]

This methodology goes beyond broadly demonizing Japan as a whole or viewing it solely as an adversary. Instead, it highlights Chosŏn's targeted hostility toward specific groups within Japan. The study is significant in examining this nuanced approach. However, it remains unclear whether this methodology can be extended beyond the Imjin War, such as to postwar perceptions of Japan, as further research has yet to be conducted.

In summary, perceptions and memories related to the Imjin War and Japan largely focus on analyzing the war's direct impacts. While the concept of hostility is acknowledged as a somewhat ambiguous phenomenon, there has yet to be a clear and comprehensive analysis of its nature. This gap stems from the lack of a multi-layered approach to the Imjin War and the prevailing assumption that it is impossible to maintain good relations with a nation that initiated such a conflict.

However, Chosŏn itself officially dispatched envoys to Japan as early as 1607, swiftly working to restore previous relations with the aggressor. Therefore, it is essential to undertake a more nuanced, multi-dimensional analysis of the hostility associated with the Imjin War. Above all, descriptions of the period before and after the war remain insufficient, making it crucial to uncover the connections between these phases to provide a more comprehensive understanding.

4. Conclusion

Studies on the Imjin War often face criticism for their disproportionate emphasis on narratives of national crisis and recovery, particularly focusing on righteous armies and military history. This paper examines research stemming from such critiques, particularly those exploring Chosŏn's self-perception and views of the other. Unsurprisingly, the most active field of study has been the exploration of Chosŏn's self-identity. Within Chosŏn's internal memory and perception, the Imjin War is largely framed as an ordeal to be overcome. Consequently, research tends to focus on commemorative and recognition projects that emerged after the war rather than during the war itself. Among Korean scholars, *Tongguk sinsok samgang haengsil to* has attracted the most attention, revealing how the war sought to incorporate or exclude women from Chosŏn society in the late period. Meanwhile, American researchers have concentrated more on records produced during the war itself, often challenging concepts like "nation". This approach, while raising questions about the reliability of sources, provides a strategy to move beyond the power-centered narratives that dominate Chosŏn studies. It is hoped that domestic research will also delve deeper into the immediacy of the war itself, exploring perspectives formed during the conflict rather than focusing predominantly on its aftermath.

Compared to the active research on Chosŏn's self-perception, studies on Chosŏn's perception of the Ming have generally begun with the firmly established framework of the grace of rebuilding. Subsequent research has therefore focused on examining the implementation and evolution of "The grace of rebuilding". As with studies on Chosŏn's self-perception, research on its perception of the Ming has also centered on commemorative monuments and recognition projects. However, in the process, the immediacy of the Imjin War has gradually faded, and Chosŏn's perception of the Ming has transformed into a broader theory of Chosŏn as the inheritor of Chinese civilization. While this transformation represents a meaningful way of remembering and understanding the Imjin War, it also reveals a limitation: the war itself often becomes a peripheral issue when examined within the context of broader Sinocentric ideologies.

On the other hand, research specifically focused on Chosŏn's perception of Japan, particularly in the context of the Imjin War, remains relatively limited. This is because Chosŏn's perception of Japan was largely framed within the grand narrative of the Hua-Yi perspective, and the Imjin War is often regarded as merely one of many events that stimulated this worldview. Nevertheless, some studies have analyzed the nature of Chosŏn's hostility toward Japan. Among these are works that reveal postwar discussions advocating for Japan to be recruited as an ally when necessary or that highlight Chosŏn's hostility and vigilance toward specific groups within Japan rather than toward Japan as a whole. These exploratory studies provide a nuanced view of Chosŏn's perceptions of Japan beyond broad generalizations.

In summary, while the Imjin War was a conflict involving Chosŏn, the Ming, and Japan, research on the perception of self and others revealed through the war remains relatively underdeveloped. In particular, despite hostility toward Japan being one of the most fundamental concepts in constructing a sense of "nation" or national identity, concrete studies on the nature of this hostility are still lacking. It remains unclear whether Chosŏn's postwar hostility targeted all Japanese, how this hostility differed from the existing Hua-Yi perspective, or whether it was specifically directed at Hideyoshi and the Toyotomi family. Furthermore, since the Imjin War was followed by a relatively swift return to the prewar international order, it is challenging to determine the war's long-term impact with clarity.

Furthermore, research on the Imjin War in Korea has yet to produce many comprehensive works authored by a single researcher based on a cohesive framework. This is particularly evident in the relatively new fields of memory and perception studies, which emerged as research areas in the 21st century and remain without any single-author monographs in Korea. As a result, the research landscape has primarily been shaped by shorter, fragmented articles, which face the critical issue of lacking cohesion across various subfields. While the absence of independent research monographs is pronounced in Korea, even in the United States—where research monographs are more common—there has only been one posthumous collection of essays attempting a unified perspective on the topic. This indicates that research on memory and perception related to the Imjin War has not yet reached a stage where long-term, comprehensive interpretations can be achieved. Future research must move beyond piecing together isolated arguments from disparate fields. Instead, there is a need to create a unified narrative that draws a comprehensive picture of the Imjin War. Most importantly, as perceptions of the war differ significantly from those of the prewar and postwar periods, it will be essential to conduct studies that examine the Imjin War in relation to its preceding and subsequent contexts for a holistic understanding.

Note

1 Particularly in the field of modern and contemporary Korean history, academia in Korea has actively embraced Western scholarship on "memory" studies, making it a widely recognized and established area of research by the 2020s. Ahn Byung-Jik, "Han'guk Sahoe esŏ ŭi 'Kiŏk' kwa 'Yŏksa'"(On Memory and History in the Korean context), *YOKSA HAKBO* 193, 2007, pp. 275–276; Jeong Il Yeong, "2000-nyŏn ihu Han'guksa Pun'ya ŭi Kiŏk Yŏn'gu Kyŏnghyang" (Trends in Memory Research in Korean History Studies Since 2000: Focusing on Research Achievements and Collective Memory Research Projects), *Sahakchi* 64, 2024, pp. 40–41.

2 *Ibid.*, p.42.

3 Ike Susumu, "Sengokuki Shakai no Kioku: Toyotomi Hideyoshi-zō no Sōshutsu" (The Memory of Sengoku Society: The Creation of the Toyotomi Hideyoshi Image), *Muromachi Sengokuki no Shakai Kōzō (The Social Structure of the Muromachi and Sengoku Periods)*, Tōkyō: Yoshikawa Kōbunkan, 2010.

4 Heroes like Yi Sunsin (李舜臣) continue to be revered as objects of admiration even in modern times, with their memory enduring to the present day. The scope of analysis in the paper also extends to modernity, including the 20th century. Chung, Doo-Hee, "Yi Sunsin e Taehan Kiŏk ŭi Yŏksa wa Yŏksahwa" (History and Historicization of Memories of Admiral Yi Sunshin), *Han'guk Sahaksa Hakpo* 14, 2006.

5 Recently, a significant number of studies in the United States have been conducted from the perspective of "The Imjin War as Seen from the West" (AFTERMATH OF THE EAST ASIAN WAR OF 1592–1598: A European Research Council project investigating the legacy of the Imjin War, https://aftermath.uab.cat/, accessed on October 29, 2024). However, among these studies, those focusing on Chosŏn as the subject are limited to the field of Japanese captives, which falls outside the scope of analysis for this paper.

6 Roh, Young-Koo, "Kongshin Sŏnjŏng kwa Chŏnjaeng Pyŏngga rŭl Tonghan Imjin Waeran Kiŏk ŭi Hyŏngsŏng" (The Appointments of Meritorious Retainers and the Forming of Memories of the Imjin War), *Yŏksa wa Hyŏnsil* 51, 2004.

7 Kyungsoon Lee, "Kiŏk ŭrosŏ ŭi 'Imjin Waeran kwa Pulgyo'" (Imjin War and

Buddhism as Memories), *Maŭm Sasang* 3, 2005.

8 Huh, Tae-Yong, "Imjin Waeran ŭi Kyŏnghŏm kwa Koguryŏsa Insik ŭi Kanghwa" (The Changing Historical Notion of Koguryŏ after the Japan Invasion of Imjin), *YOKSA HAKBO* 190, 2006.

9 John B. Duncan, "Proto-nationalism in Premodern Korea", Lee, Sang Oak and Park, Duk Soo eds., *Perspectives on Korea*, Sydney: Wild Peony, 1998.

10 John B. Duncan, "Imjin Waeran ŭi Kiŏk kwa Minjok Ŭisik Hyŏngsŏng (The Memory of the Imjin War and the Formation of National Consciousness), Chung, Doo-Hee and Lee, Kyungsoon eds., *Imjin Waeran: Tongasia Samguk Chŏnjaeng (A Transnational History of the 'Imjin Waeran' 1592~1598: The East Asian Dimension)*, Seoul: Humanist, 2007.

11 In the 2000s, several books were published in the United States introducing the Imjin War(Stephen Turnbull, *Samurai Invasion: Japan's Korean War 1592~1598*, London: Cassell, 2002; Samuel Hawley, *The Imjin War: Japan's Sixteenth Century Invasion of Korea and Attempt to Conquer China*, Seoul: Royal Asiatic Society Korea Branch, 2005; Kenneth Swope, *A Dragon's Head and a Serpent's Tail: Ming China and the First Great East Asian War, 1592~1598*, Norman: University of Oklahoma Press, 2009). These works have also been introduced in Korea. KYE, Seung-Bum, "Imjin Waeran ŭl Ponŭn Se Kaji Sigak (Three Perspectives of the Imjin War(1592~1598))", *Han'guk Sahaksa Hakpo* 34, 2016.

12 Jung, Ji-young, "Imjin Waeran Ihu Yŏsŏng Kyoyuk kwa Saeroun 'Chung' ŭi Tŭngjang" (Education of Women and the Appearance of New "Loyalty" after Imjin War), *Kung'hak Yŏn'gu* 18, 2011.

13 Michael J. Pettid, "Fashioning womanly Confucian virtue: The virtuous woman in post-war literary discourse", James B. Lewis ed., *The East Asian War, 1592-1598*, London and New York: Routledge, 2015.

14 Jeong, Ho Hun, "Chŏnjaeng ŭi Kiŏk kwa Chŏngch'iron, *Tongguk Sinsok Samgang Haengsil To*" (*Tongguk Sinsok Samgang Haengsil To*: Memory of War and Political Theory), *Han'guk Sasang Yŏn'gu* 58, 2018.

15 JaHyun Haboush Kim, *The Great East Asian War and the Birth of the Korean Nation*, New York: Columbia University Press, 2016.

16 Chaeyoung Choo pointed out that while Chapter 5 acknowledges criticism of Confucian society or an awareness of its imperfections, it does not address how these aspects connect to the formation of national consciousness. Chaeyoung Choo, "Imjin Chŏnjaeng kwa Han'guk Minjok Tamnon ŭi

Ch'ulhyŏn" (The Imjin War and the emergence of the discours of Korean nation), *Han'guk Sahaksa Hakpo* 35, 2017.

17 James B. Lewis stated that Haboush's frame must be examined to see whether it can apply not only to wartime but also to peacetime. See James B. Lewis, "Book Review: *The Great East Asian War and the Birth of the Korean Nation* by JaHyun Kim Haboush, William J. Haboush, Jisoo M. Kim", *Monumenta Nipponica* 72-2, 2017, p. 313.

18 Adam C. Bohnet, "BOOK REVIEWS: *J. Marshall Craig, China, Korea, and Japan at War, 1592~1598: Eyewitness Accounts (Asian States & Empires)*", London: Routledge, 2020, *Journal of Chinese Military History* 12, 2023.

19 J. Marshall Craig, "Epilogue: The war of 1592-1598 and national identity", *China, Korea, and Japan at War, 1592~1598: Eyewitness Accounts*, London: Routledge, 2020.

20 Hur, Joon, "Imjin Waeran kwa Minjok Kosŏngwŏn ŭi Hwakt'ae" (The Imjin War and Expansion of the Concept of the Koreans), *CHIYEOK KWA YEOKSA* 49, 2021.

21 Kim, Kyong-tae, "Imjin Waeran'gi Chosŏn ŭi Imiji e Taehan Insik kwa Kŭ Pyŏnhwa" (Origins of the Image of "Lazy and Dissipated Chosŏn" during the Japanese Invasion of Korea in 1592), *Yŏksahak Yŏn'gu* 87, 2022.

22 Han, Myung-gi, "Imjin Waeran Sigi 'Chaejo chi Ŭn' ŭi Hyŏngsŏng kwa Kŭ Ŭimi" (The Formation and Significance of Chaejo chi Ŭn During the Imjin War), *Tongyanghak* 29, 1999.

23 Kuwano Eiji, "Chosŏn Korea and Ming China after the Imjin Waeran: state rituals in the Later Chosŏn period", James B. Lewis ed., *The East Asian War, 1592-1598*, London and New York: Routledge, 2015.

24 WOO KYUNGSUP, "17-18 Segi Imjin Waeran Ch'amjŏn Myŏnggun e Taehan Kiŏk" (The Memories of Ming Dynasty's Army in Imjin War during the 17-18th Century), *Han'gukhak Yŏn'gu* 46, 2017.

25 Yun, Hye-min, "Chosŏn Hugi Sŏksŏng e Taehan Insik Pyŏnhwa wa Kŭ Ŭimi" (Shifting Perceptions of Shi Xing in the Late Chosŏn Period and Its Historical Significance), *Chosŏn Sidaesa Hakpo* 70, 2014.

26 Kim, Kyong-Tae, "Imjin Waeran Sigi Chosŏn-Myŏng Kwangye wa Kija Insik ŭi Yangsang" (The Diplomatic Relations between Chosŏn and Ming during Imjin War and the Aspects of Understanding on JIzi), *Han'guk Sa Hakpo* 65, 2016.

27 Ha Woo Bong, *Chosŏn sidae Han'gugin ŭi Ilbon Insik(Korean Perceptions of*

the Japanese During the Chosŏn Dynasty), Seoul: Hyean, 2006, pp. 17~25; pp. 27~30.

28 Ki-Cheol Bang, *Chosŏnil Chŏnjaeng kwa Chosŏnin ŭi Ilbon Insik (The Chosŏn -Japanese War and Chosŏn People's Perception of Japan)*, Seoul: Kung'hak Charyo Wŏn, 2010.

29 Lee Kyu-bae, "Chosŏn Sidae Chŏktaejŏk Taeil Insik e Kwanhan Koch'al " (A Study on Koreans' hostile view of Japan during the Chosŏn Period), *Kunsa* 84, 2012.

30 Han, Myung-gi, "Chosŏn Sidae Han-Chung-Il Kwangye wa Sangho Insik ŭi Ch'ui" (The Relationship Between Korea, China, and Japan in the Era of Chosŏn Dynasty and Transistions of Their Mutual Perceptions), *Han'gukhak Yŏn'gu* 57, 2020.

31 Lim Hyunchae, "Imjin Waeran'gi Chosŏn kwa Ilbon ŭi Toyotomi-shi Hwalyong kwa Kŭ Insik" (The Use and Recognition of Toyotomi Uji(Clan) in Choson and Japan, during the Imjin War), *Han-Il Kwangyesa Yŏn'gu* 71, 2021.

Bibliography

Ahn, Byung-Jik, "Han'guk Sahoe esŏ ŭi 'Kiŏk' kwa 'Yŏksa'"(On Memory and History in the Korean context), YOKSA HAKBO 193, 2007.

Bang, Ki-Cheol, *Chosŏnil Chŏnjaeng kwa Chosŏnin ŭi Ilbon Insik (The Chosŏn -Japanese War and Chosŏn People's Perception of Japan)*, Seoul: Kung'hak Charyo Wŏn, 2010.

Bohnet, Adam C., "BOOK REVIEWS: *J. Marshall Craig, China, Korea, and Japan at War, 1592~1598: Eyewitness Accounts (Asian States & Empires)*", London: Routledge, 2020, *Journal of Chinese Military History* 12, 2023.

Choo, Chaeyoung, "Imjin Chŏnjaeng kwa Han'guk Minjok Tamnon ŭi Ch'ulhyŏn" (The Imjin War and the emergence of the discours of Korean nation), *Han'guk Sahaksa Hakpo* 35, 2017.

Chung, Doo-Hee, "Yi Sunsin e Taehan Kiŏk ŭi Yŏksa wa Yŏksahwa" (History and Historicization of Memories of Admiral Yi Sunshin), *Han'guk Sahaksa Hakpo* 14, 2006.

Craig, J. Marshall, "Epilogue: The war of 1592-1598 and national identity", *China, Korea, and Japan at War, 1592~1598: Eyewitness Accounts*, London: Routledge, 2020.

Duncan, John B., "Proto-nationalism in Premodern Korea", Lee, Sang Oak and Park, Duk Soo eds., *Perspectives on Korea*, Sydney: Wild Peony, 1998.

Duncan, John B., "Imjin Waeran ŭi Kiŏk kwa Minjok Ŭisik Hyŏngsŏng (The Memory of the Imjin War and the Formation of National Consciousness), Chung, Doo-Hee and Lee, Kyungsoon eds., *Imjin Waeran: Tongasia Samguk Chŏnjaeng (A Transnational History of the 'Imjin Waeran' 1592~1598: The East Asian Dimension)*, Seoul: Humanist, 2007.

Kuwano, Eiji, "Chosŏn Korea and Ming China after the Imjin Waeran: state rituals in the Later Chosŏn period", James B. Lewis ed., *The East Asian War, 1592-1598*, London and New York: Routledge, 2015.

Ike, Susumu, "Sengokuki Shakai no Kioku: Toyotomi Hideyoshi-zō no Sōshutsu" (The Memory of Sengoku Society: The Creation of the Toyotomi Hideyoshi Image), *Muromachi Sengokuki no Shakai Kōzō*

(The Social Structure of the Muromachi and Sengoku Periods), Tōkyō: Yoshikawa Kōbunkan, 2010.

Ha, Woo Bong, *Chosŏn sidae Han'gugin ŭi Ilbon Insik(Korean Perceptions of the Japanese During the Chosŏn Dynasty)*, Seoul: Hyean, 2006.

Han, Myung-gi, "Imjin Waeran Sigi 'Chaejo chi Ŭn' ŭi Hyŏngsŏng kwa Kŭ Ŭimi" (The Formation and Significance of Chaejo chi Ŭn During the Imjin War), *Tongyanghak* 29, 1999.

Han, Myung-gi, "Chosŏn Sidae Han-Chung-Il Kwangye wa Sangho Insik ŭi Ch'ui" (The Relationship Between Korea, China, and Japan in the Era of Chosŏn Dynasty and Transistions of Their Mutual Perceptions), *Han'gukhak Yŏn'gu* 57, 2020.

Hawley, Samuel, *The Imjin War: Japan's Sixteenth Century Invasion of Korea and Attempt to Conquer China*, Seoul: Royal Asiatic Society Korea Branch, 2005.

Huh, Tae-Yong, "Imjin Waeran ŭi Kyŏnghŏm kwa Koguryŏsa Insik ŭi Kanghwa" (The Changing Historical Notion of Koguryŏ after the Japan Invasion of Imjin), *YOKSA HAKBO* 190, 2006.

Hur, Joon, "Imjin Waeran kwa Minjok Kosŏngwŏn ŭi Hwakt'ae" (The Imjin War and Expansion of the Concept of the Koreans), *CHIYEOK KWA YEOKSA* 49, 2021.

Jeong, Ho Hun, "Chŏnjaeng ŭi Kiŏk kwa Chŏngch'iron, *Tongguk Sinsok Samgang Haengsil To*" (*Tongguk Sinsok Samgang Haengsil To*: Memory of War and Political Theory), *Han'guk Sasang Yŏn'gu* 58, 2018.

Jeong, Il Yeong, "2000-nyŏn ihu Han'guksa Pun'ya ŭi Kiŏk Yŏn'gu Kyŏnghyang" (Trends in Memory Research in Korean History Studies Since 2000: Focusing on Research Achievements and Collective Memory Research Projects), *Sahakchi* 64, 2024.

Jung, Ji-young, "Imjin Waeran Ihu Yŏsŏng Kyoyuk kwa Saeroun 'Chung' ŭi Tŭngjang" (Education of Women and the Appearance of New "Loyalty" after Imjin War), *Kung'hak Yŏn'gu* 18, 2011.

Kim, JaHyun Haboush, *The Great East Asian War and the Birth of the Korean Nation*, New York: Columbia University Press, 2016.

Kim, Kyong-Tae, "Imjin Waeran Sigi Chosŏn-Myŏng Kwangye wa Kija Insik ŭi Yangsang" (The Diplomatic Relations between Chosŏn and Ming during Imjin War and the Aspects of Understanding on JIzi), *Han'guk Sa*

Hakpo 65, 2016.

Kim, Kyong-tae, "Imjin Waeran'gi Chosŏn ŭi Imiji e Taehan Insik kwa Kŭ Pyŏnhwa" (Origins of the Image of "Lazy and Dissipated Chosŏn" during the Japanese Invasion of Korea in 1592), *Yŏksahak Yŏn'gu* 87, 2022.

KYE, Seung-Bum, "Imjin Waeran ŭl Ponŭn Se Kaji Sigak (Three Perspectives of the Imjin War(1592~1598))", *Han'guk Sahaksa Hakpo* 34, 2016.

Lee, Kyu-bae, "Chosŏn Sidae Chŏktaejŏk Taeil Insik e Kwanhan Koch'al" (A Study on Koreans' hostile view of Japan during the Chosŏn Period), *Kunsa* 84, 2012.

Lee, Kyungsoon, "Kiŏk ŭrosŏ ŭi 'Imjin Waeran kwa Pulgyo'" (Imjin War and Buddhism as Memories), *Maŭm Sasang* 3, 2005.

Lewis, James B., "Book Review: *The Great East Asian War and the Birth of the Korean Nation* by JaHyun Kim Haboush, William J. Haboush, Jisoo M. Kim", *Monumenta Nipponica* 72-2, 2017.

Pettid, Michael J., "Fashioning womanly Confucian virtue: The virtuous woman in post-war literary discourse", James B. Lewis ed., *The East Asian War, 1592-1598*, London and New York: Routledge, 2015.

Lim, Hyunchae, "Imjin Waeran'gi Chosŏn kwa Ilbon ŭi Toyotomi-shi Hwalyong kwa Kŭ Insik" (The Use and Recognition of Toyotomi Uji(Clan) in Choson and Japan, during the Imjin War), *Han-Il Kwangyesa Yŏn'gu* 71, 2021.

Roh, Young-Koo, "Kongshin Sŏnjŏng kwa Chŏnjaeng Pyŏngga rŭl Tonghan Imjin Waeran Kiŏk ŭi Hyŏngsŏng" (The Appointments of Meritorious Retainers and the Forming of Memories of the Imjin War), *Yŏksa wa Hyŏnsil*51, 2004.

Swope, Kenneth, *A Dragon's Head and a Serpent's Tail: Ming China and the First Great East Asian War, 1592~1598*, Norman: University of Oklahoma Press, 2009.

Turnbull, Stephen, *Samurai Invasion: Japan's Korean War 1592~1598*, London: Cassell, 2002.

WOO, KYUNGSUP, "17-18 Segi Imjin Waeran Ch'amjŏn Myŏnggun e Taehan Kiŏk" (The Memories of Ming Dynasty's Army in Imjin War during the 17-18th Century), *Han'gukhak Yŏn'gu* 46, 2017.

Yun, Hye-min, "Chosŏn Hugi Sŏksŏng e Taehan Insik Pyŏnhwa wa Kŭ

Ŭimi" (Shifting Perceptions of Shi Xing in the Late Chosŏn Period and Its Historical Significance) *Chosŏn Sidaesa Hakpo* 70, 2014.

4

Kingship of Two Chosŏn Kings in the 18th Century: A Review of Studies on the Governance Theories of King Yŏngjo and King Chŏngjo

Chaeyoung Choo

Sogang University

4 Kingship of Two Chosŏn Kings in the 18th Century: A Review of Studies on the Governance Theories of King Yŏngjo and King Chŏngjo

Chaeyoung Choo (Sogang University)

1. Introduction

The 18th century marked a globally transformative era. In the West, revolutionary movements facilitated the transition into modern nation-states, accompanied by the intensification of imperialist expansion. Simultaneously, in East Asia, the Qing reached its zenith during the Kangxi-Yongzheng-Qianlong Prosperous Era, while Japan's Edo Shogunate experienced a prolonged period of stability, fostering growth in both domestic and international capacities.

During this period, Chosŏn faced a significant identity crisis following the fall of the Ming dynasty, a Han Chinese regime that had served as a Confucian political and ritual suzerain, and the subsequent rise of the Manchu-led Qing. This crisis became particularly evident during the accession and reign of King Hyojong (r. 1649–1659), whose succession deviated from the principle of primogeniture. Disputes over royal legitimacy among political factions escalated into the *Ritual Controversy*, which lacked an overarching authority to mediate and thereby undermined the authority of the king and the royal family.[1]

In response, King Sukchong (r.1674–1720) sought to restore royal authority through the implementation of divide-and-conquer policy. However, the repeated shifts in factional power, initially rooted in differences in scholarly traditions and political ideologies, devolved into catastrophic conflicts centered on royal succession, further destabilizing the Chosŏn political system.

The detrimental effects of factional strife exerted immense pressure on King Kyŏngjong (r. 1720–1724), King Yŏngjo (r. 1724–1776), and King Chŏngjo (r. 1776–1800). Despite their royal lineage, these monarchs were forced to prove their legitimacy during the succession process. King Yŏngjo ascended the throne amid suspicions of involvement in his predecessor's death, which motivated his profound desire to resolve factional disputes and restore both the legitimacy of his reign and the diminished authority of the royal family.

Throughout his reign, Yŏngjo focused on eradicating factionalism and implemented significant political and social reforms to strengthen both royal authority and improve the welfare of his subjects. However, the temporarily suppressed factional conflicts culminated in the tragic event of Yŏngjo was compelled to execute his own son and heir with his own hands. This act, intended to secure the legitimacy of his grandson, King Chŏngjo, left a lasting mark on the latter's claim to rightful authority.

King Chŏngjo inherited both the strengths and weaknesses of his predecessors, striving to overcome these challenges throughout his reign. Early on, he faced assassination threats and persistent disputes stemming from the circumstances surrounding his father's death. Nevertheless, Chŏngjo sought to elevate his status to that of *kunsa* (a Philosopher-King 君師) by leveraging his intellectual superiority and striving to subdue Confucian scholar-officials who resisted royal authority.

To achieve this, Chŏngjo imparted his political philosophy to promising young officials while persistently engaging in rigorous debates with seasoned Confucian ministers, seeking their acquiescence. Through these ideologically aligned young bureaucrats, he aimed to establish a new political order. However, Chŏngjo's aspirations remained unfulfilled, as his untimely death left his vision incomplete. He passed away, leaving behind a young crown prince and an unfinished legacy.

Both monarchs endured destructive factional conflicts that undermined their legitimacy. Despite this, each strived to assert their qualifications as sovereigns and dedicated themselves to revitalizing Chosŏn throughout the 18th century. However, following King Chŏngjo's death, Chosŏn experienced a rapid collapse of its political and administrative systems, ultimately entering a period of decline that culminated in its disappearance from history.

Scholars seeking to understand the causes of contrasting fortunes in the Chosŏn dynasty—the aspirations for revival in the 18th century and the sudden collapse in the 19th century—have frequently turned to the reigns of Kings Yŏngjo and Chŏngjo for answers. Consequently, these two monarchs have received considerable attention in Korean historiography. In particular, *Tangp'yŏng* 蕩平, the policy they advocated to resolve factional conflicts and political strife, has emerged as a defining concept of this period.[2]

Moreover, the rise of the theory of internal development during the 1980s and 1990s, spurred by efforts to transcend colonial historiography,[3] further underscored the significance of Yŏngjo and Chŏngjo as reformist rulers. Despite the increasing focus their reigns, however, discussions surrounding their governance methods and theories of monarchy remain relatively underexplored.

In a dynastic state, the monarch was inherently synonymous with the state. Understanding the history of such a nation necessitates a thorough examination of the reigns and governing methods of its monarchs. Even a seemingly powerless king can exert considerable influence over the fate of the nation. The ineffective rule of monarchs who succeeded King Chŏngjo serves as a compelling example, as their failures led Chosŏn into political and social disarray.

This connection between monarchical governance and national outcomes holds even greater significance for Kings Yŏngjo and Chŏngjo, who are widely credited with leading the revival of 18th-century Chosŏn. Thus, any effort to uncover the factors behind Chosŏn's 18th-century revival, as well as the critical turning points that led to its eventual decline, must begin with a close analysis of their governance theories and practices.

This study examines the theories of governance and monarchy concerning Kings Yŏngjo and Chŏngjo as explored in Korean historical scholarship. While a substantial body of research has emphasized their scholarly and philosophical pursuits or analyzed specific policies and initiatives—such as *Kyunyŏkpŏp* (the Equalized Military Tax Law 均役法), the establishment of *Kyujanggak* (the royal library 奎章閣), the organization of the *Changyŏngyŏng* (The King's Royal Guard 壯勇營), and the loosening of restrictions on Chosŏn's expanding commercial trade through *Sinhae T'onggong* (the Commercial Equalization Law[4] 辛亥通共)—comprehensive analyses of their overall governance remain relatively scarce.

This paper seeks to address this gap by exploring their governance through a focus on political behavior, including the management of state affairs and strategic political actions, with an emphasis on coherence and comprehensiveness. Additionally, this study critically engages with existing discourses on these two monarchs to provide a nuanced and in-depth analysis of their rule.

The structure of this paper is as follows. Chapter II analyzes studies that comprehensively examine King Yŏngjo's governance. These studies commonly portray King Yŏngjo as a "sage king," and this chapter seeks to elucidate the context behind the emergence of this characterization while exploring its implications within academic discourse.

Chapter III focuses on writings that analyze King Chŏngjo's governance, with particular attention to the ongoing discourse in Korean scholarship framing King Chŏngjo as a "reformist monarch." Since the 1990s, Korean academia has increasingly defined King Chŏngjo and his era using terms such as reform, development, and revival. This chapter investigates the origins of this perspective and traces its evolution into the dominant narrative observed today.

Through this analysis, it will be possible to gain a deeper understanding of the Korean academic perspective on the two monarchs who stood at the crossroads of revival and decline in Chosŏn. Furthermore, this study aims to reflect on potential directions for future research concerning the historical roles and legacies of Kings Yŏngjo and Chŏngjo.

2. King Yŏngjo -The Neo-Confucian Sage Kingship

Despite the extensive volume of discussions on the 18th century and the *Tangpyeong*-centered reign of King Yŏngjo, comprehensive studies on Yŏngjo's governance theories and state management remain scarce in Korean academia. Remarkably, efforts to understand "King Yŏngjo" and " Yŏngjo as a politician" from the perspective of monarchic theory first emerged in American academia. Jahyun Kim Haboush garnered significant attention for her analysis of Yeongjo's monarchical philosophy, portraying him as a ruler who devoted his life to realizing the ideal of "Confucian kingship."

According to her, in Confucianism, which ideologically dominated East Asia, the monarch was regarded as a being endowed with *Heaven's Mandate* 天命, tasked with embodying the moral order of the universe in the human world. This mandate provided the monarch with the legitimacy of power. However, unlike the Chinese emperor, the king of Chosŏn, as a vassal state ruler, could not receive *Heaven's Mandate*. In Chosŏn, where mechanisms were meticulously designed to regulate the qualities and governance of hereditary monarchs, the king had to compete for power with scholar-officials. Moreover, the king of Chosŏn lacked even a personal guard or loyal military organization.

King Yŏngjo ascended to the throne during a period of intense factional strife, with his legitimacy heavily scrutinized, further exacerbated by accusations of involvement in the death of his predecessor. Confronted with these challenges, he focused on Neo-Confucian virtues, which inherently constrained his authority. By emphasizing the rhetoric of moral governance, King Yŏngjo sought to secure political stability and ensure his survival as a ruler.

Throughout his reign, King Yŏngjo maintained a posture of humility before Heaven, adhered strictly to Zhu Xi's Neo-Confucian principles, and expressed deep empathy for the suffering of the people. Positioned in an ambiguous role as neither a fully sovereign *Son of Heaven 天子* nor a subordinate ruler, he carefully crafted a narrative highlighting "*the grace of Ming in saving Chosŏn 再造之恩*." This rhetorical strategy enabled him to position himself as the guardian of Confucian civilization, portraying Chosŏn as the legitimate heir to the cultural and ideological legacy of the Ming dynasty.

To embody moral governance, the king was required to actively participate in Royal lectures alongside scholar-officials. King Yŏngjo, known for his enthusiasm for learning, quickly established intellectual dominance over his officials through these sessions, thereby reinforcing his position as the ultimate decision-maker. By emphasizing moral governance, he not only confronted his officials but also secured moral authority, which he skillfully translated into practical politics.

Aspiring to be a monarch who would lead a revival, King Yŏngjo identified the heavy burden of military service on the populace as the most pressing issue requiring reform. A significant obstacle to these reforms, however, was the widespread avoidance of military service by the yangban class. The yangban, whose social identity was deeply tied to scholarly pursuits, regarded exemption from military service as an inherent right.

The tension between alleviating the burdens placed on the common people and preserving the privileges of the yangban class had long been a contentious issue in Chosŏn society. Despite King Yŏngjo's strong desire for reform, achieving meaningful changes without the consent or approval of the yangban class was virtually impossible.

Since the debate was deeply rooted in Confucian ideology, any proposed solution needed to be articulated within a Confucian framework. King Yŏngjo employed the Confucian narrative of the monarch as both ruler and father to legitimize his reforms. By personally engaging with the populace and appealing directly for their support, he successfully garnered public backing for his reform initiatives, enabling him to achieve his objectives.

Ascending the throne amidst factional strife that threatened the lives of both the king and his successor, King Yŏngjo implemented the Tangp'yŏng policy to dismantle factionalism. Despite these efforts, *the Noron* (The Old Doctrine Faction, 老論) and *the Soron* (The Young Doctrine Faction, 小論) factions persisted in their relentless conflicts, often centered on debates over loyalty and treachery.

To establish himself as the guardian of Confucian civilization and the protector of the people's welfare, King Yŏngjo devoted himself to various ceremonial practices and rigorous self-cultivation. Holding himself accountable for the shortcomings in governance, he engaged in extreme acts of self-discipline and applied moral pressure on his officials, including the dramatic gesture of offering to abdicate the throne.

However, King Yŏngjo's use of Confucian rhetoric to reinforce his authority inadvertently strained his relationship with his successor. His excessive emphasis on filial piety intensified tensions with the crown prince, further complicating the delicate balance of power between them. This discord ultimately escalated into an unprecedented tragedy, culminating in the death of the crown prince at the hands of his father.

While King Yŏngjo sought to project an image of a compassionate ruler to the public, to his son, he revealed a contrasting image—that of a ruthless and uncompromising father.[5]

Haboush characterized King Yŏngjo's method of consolidating dominance over state affairs as the "use of rhetoric." According to her analysis, King Yŏngjo strategically employed rhetoric rooted in the principles of Neo-Confucianism—values deeply ingrained in Chosŏn society and therefore difficult to contest—to check the power of officials and reinforce monarchical authority.

Haboush's study emerged as a seminal work in a scholarly context where comprehensive research on monarchical theory or King Yŏngjo's governance was virtually nonexistent. Its significance lies particularly in its evaluation of Chosŏn history within the broader frameworks of global historical trends and East Asian history, as well as its detailed elucidation of the operational principles of Neo-Confucian governance in Chosŏn.

By employing the rhetoric of the "Confucian sage king," Haboush's work made a substantial contribution to establishing the global relevance of Chosŏn's monarchical theories. Furthermore, it opened a new chapter in the study of monarchy within Korean academia, providing a foundational framework for subsequent research.

In American academia, Chosŏn was a relatively unfamiliar subject and often difficult to distinguish from China. Nevertheless, Haboush effectively demonstrated, through the shared political ideology of Confucianism in East Asia, how the king of Chosŏn—while not an emperor—secured authority and took control of state affairs as the monarch of the Chosŏn people.

She portrayed King Yŏngjo, celebrated in Korean scholarship as a monarch of reform and Tangp'yŏng policies, as a political figure actively striving to acquire and wield power in practice. This perspective offered a refreshing and novel approach, departing from conventional views in Korean academia and shedding new light on his reign.

Lee Hee-hwan analyzed King Yŏngjo's governance following the *Imo* tragedy[6] to elucidate the practical implementation of *the Tangp'yŏng policy* during his reign. According to his analysis, for King Yŏngjo, the pursuit of *Tangp'yŏng*, the ideals of Yao and Shun, Royal lectures, ancestor worship, and ascetic Neo-Confucian values functioned not only as ideological justifications but also as instruments to consolidate and strengthen his authority.

King Sukchong's repeated *Hwanguk Chŏngch'i* (shifts in power shifts in factional power 換局政治) distorted the original identities of these groups. The conflict between the *Noron* and the *Soron* eventually escalated into a struggle over royal succession, posing a direct threat to the lives of both King Kyŏngjong and King Yŏngjo.

The radical Soron faction, opposing the Noron-backed Prince *Yŏning* (The future King Yŏngjo) as Kyŏngjong's successor, launched a series of attacks against both *the Noron factio*n and Prince Yŏning himself. After the Noron were removed from power, it was the moderate *Soron* faction that ultimately offered protection to Prince *Yŏning*.

Upon King Yŏngjo's accession, the *Noron* faction demanded retribution against the *Soron*. However, Yŏngjo faced the dual challenge of eliminating radical elements while protecting the moderate Soron faction. In response, he advocated for *Tangp'yŏng*, but his approach was met with dissatisfaction from both factions.

Early in his reign, Yŏngjo struggled to address these grievances. He structured his administration around moderate members of both factions while resorting to extreme measures—such as fasting, strikes, and even declarations of abdication—to suppress officials who opposed *Tangp'yŏng*. These dramatic actions were ultimately aimed at stabilizing the volatile political landscape.

Simultaneously, Yŏngjo significantly increased his participation in royal lectures achieving intellectual dominance over his officials by the mid-period of his reign. He also performed elaborate rituals centered on filial piety, presenting himself as an ideal Confucian monarch. This self-presentation functioned as a strategic tool to demand loyalty and filial obedience from those obstructing *Tangp'yŏng*.

Yŏngjo dismantled institutional mechanisms designed to check royal authority, consolidating power through loyal officials collectively known as the *Tangp'yŏng* faction. In a dramatic and controversial move, he even orchestrated the death of his own son, who had served as regent, for opposing his policies, underscoring the lengths to which he was willing to go to maintain control.

After the death of the crown prince, King Yŏngjo began to unilaterally manage state affairs, disregarding even the authority of high-ranking officials. Upon resuming direct governance, and despite his advanced age, he significantly increased the frequency of royal lectures. He also personally performed rituals and frequently undertook visits to royal tombs.

Yŏngjo demonstrated a pronounced preoccupation with the formality and frequency of these rituals, using them as a means to exemplify the Confucian virtue of filial piety. Through these actions, he sought to set a moral example for his officials and reinforce his image as a model Confucian monarch.

Lee Hee-hwan observed that King Yŏngjo's practice of filial piety was marked more by performative actions than by ideological depth. He concluded that Yŏngjo's behavior was intended to project the image of a morally exemplary monarch. Furthermore, Lee argued that Yŏngjo's emphasis on frugality, self-discipline rituals, and the prohibition of alcohol exemplified ascetic practices. These practices were strategically employed both as a justification for and a means of implementing *Tangp'yŏng* while consolidating royal authority.

Evidence supporting this interpretation is found in King Yŏngjo's governance style during the latter part of his reign, which tolerated neither opposition nor institutional checks on his authority. He frequently replaced and punished senior officials who formed the core of state administration. The average tenure of key administrative posts was significantly reduced compared to the regency period, and the tenure of officials in the Three Offices also declined markedly.

This environment weakened the activities of the censors, as Yŏngjo increasingly dismissed or replaced officials at will if they failed to align with his preferences. Over time, he abandoned established personnel practices in favor of unilateral decision-making, further consolidating his authority.

Lee argued that Yŏngjo's policies of *Tangp'yŏng*, asceticism, and extreme filial piety were strategically employed as tools to facilitate his unilateral control over state affairs. For Yŏngjo, *Tangp'yŏng* served as a mechanism to dispel accusations against him and consolidate his authority, while royal lectures, ancestor worship, and ascetic practices functioned as instruments and pretexts to justify his autocratic governance.[7]

Lee Hee-hwan provided a rare, pragmatic critique of King Yŏngjo's *Tangp'yŏng* policy, which has traditionally been praised as a stabilizing strategy for state affairs. While previous studies largely approached the *Tangp'yŏng* policy as an "ideological" concept or a form of political logic, Lee focused on the nature of the power Yŏngjo acquired through the rhetoric of *Tangp'yŏng*.

Lee further interpreted Yŏngjo's practices of asceticism and filial piety as integral components of a broader political strategy designed to maintain dominance over state affairs.

The most significant contribution of Lee's study lies in its interpretation of Yŏngjo's governance not as an abstract or ideological endeavor, but as tangible and pragmatic political behavior. This perspective aligns with Haboush's observation regarding Yŏngjo's strategic use of rhetoric, reflecting a shared understanding of his practical approach to consolidating and exercising power.

Meanwhile, another scholar of King Yŏngjo, Kim Paek-ch'ŏl, evaluated Yŏngjo's governance from a contrasting perspective. Kim focused on Yŏngjo's consistent adherence to *Sŏnggun Chŏngch'iron* (the theory of sage-king politics 聖君政治論). According to Kim, Yŏngjo's approach to sage-king politics was rooted in the aspiration to emulate the governance of Yao 堯 and Shun 舜 while striving to realize the principles of the *Zhouli* (The rites of Zhou 周禮).

Kim argued that during the process of appointing a crown prince, King Yŏngjo's authority was undermined by factional conflicts, leading to his stigmatization as "the king chosen by the Noron." To transcend these challenges, Yŏngjo sought to embody the governance ideals of Yao and Shun. He established the ideal societies of the Three Dynasties (Xia 夏, Shang 商, and Zhou 周) as *Hwanggŭk Tangp'yŏngnon* (concrete models for his theory of political equilibrium under imperial authority 皇極蕩平論).

As a practical means of realizing this vision, Yŏngjo adopted the Zhouli. He framed *Tangp'yŏng* as the logical successor to and embodiment of the political ideals of the Three Dynasties, deriving its justification from the governance principles of Yao and Shun.

Yŏngjo extended this logic further by applying the principles of *Tangp'yŏng* not only to politics but also as a foundational rationale across various domains. To assert his legitimacy, he aligned his impartiality and governance with the ideals of Yao and Shun, framing his ascension to the throne as a continuation of their virtuous rule.

Additionally, Yŏngjo equated the authority of his ancestors with that of Yao and Shun, positioning himself as their rightful successor. For the reform of national institutions, he adopted the Zhouli as his model, viewing it as a concrete manifestation of the virtuous governance exemplified by Yao and Shun.

Meanwhile, Kim Paek-ch'ŏl observed that King Yŏngjo proclaimed the banner of "restoration" and concentrated on reforming cultural and institutional systems. As part of this process, Yŏngjo developed a renewed perception of the populace. This re-evaluation, rooted in the Confucian principle of "*Aemin* (Loving the people 愛民)", took into account two key factors: changes in the socio-economic structure and the growing influence of the common people.

Initiatives such as *Sok Taejŏn* (the compilation of legal codes 續大典), reforms to the military tax system, and adjustments to the status system reflected this shift in Yŏngjo's understanding of the role and significance of the people in governance.

In the latter part of his reign, Yŏngjo increasingly consolidated autocratic authority and transcendent legitimacy. By leveraging this transcendent authority, he projected himself as an absolute monarch while simultaneously portraying himself as the "father of the people." Through his emphasis on " *Aemin* " and "*Wimin* (Dedicated to the People 爲民)", he sought to solidify his image as a benevolent ruler.[8]

Additionally, Yŏngjo positioned himself as the implementer of the Zhouli, further highlighting his commitment to the well-being of his subjects and his dedication to virtuous governance.

Kim Baek-chul also highlighted King Yŏngjo's aspiration to embody the image of a Confucian sage king. The "theory of sage-king politics" and the pursuit of the ideals of Yao and Shun, as proposed by Kim, represent the quintessential model of kingship within Confucian political philosophy. For Yŏngjo, this was the ultimate political goal he sought to achieve throughout his life.

However, unlike earlier scholars who interpreted Yŏngjo's sage-king orientation as a justification or tool for consolidating political dominance, Kim regarded it as a genuine, lifelong objective of King Yŏngjo, shaping his governance and legacy.

Furthermore, Kim argued that the power King Yŏngjo attained extended beyond the elite yangban and bureaucratic circles, ultimately benefiting the general populace. According to Kim's assessment, Yŏngjo ascended to the status of a sage king who actively promoted Tangp'yŏng and implemented reforms aimed at improving the well-being of the people, earning him the title of a "compassionate father of the people."

Kim Baek-chul's writings are notable for their exceptionally detailed reviews of previous research, serving as an excellent guide for emerging scholars new to the field. These comprehensive reviews provide a solid foundation for understanding the existing academic discourse. Furthermore, through his introductory discussions, Kim clearly outlines the direction and focus of his own research.

For instance, in The Two Faces of King Yŏngjo, Kim not only offers an extensive review of prior studies but also articulates his perspectives and research approach, particularly emphasizing the significance of synchronicity and comparative history in understanding King Yŏngjo's reign.

However, this raises certain questions. While the author references prominent Western thinkers such as Max Weber, Karl Marx, and Hegel, along with the histories of China, Japan, and Mongolia, advocating for the comparison of Chosŏn history within these broader contexts, such a comparative historical methodology is scarcely evident in the main body of his work.

His analysis of Yŏngjo's governance remains largely confined within the boundaries of Chosŏn itself, with limited application of the comparative framework that he emphasizes in his introductory discussions.

Despite Kim Baek-chul's extensive examination of historical records and studies, his portrayal of King Yŏngjo as a politician remains somewhat one-dimensional. Kim characterizes the latter part of Yŏngjo's reign in terms of "autocratic authority" and "transcendent legitimacy." However, this depiction appears inconsistent with the discourse of "sage-king politics" through which Kim defines Yŏngjo.

The idea that Yŏngjo, who should have embodied Collaborative Governance between Sovereign and Officials to achieve the status of an ideal Confucian monarch, instead exercised autocratic power seems contradictory and raises questions about the coherence of Kim's interpretation.

Moreover, Kim's argument that Yŏngjo wielded autocratic authority for the benefit of "the people" contains certain flaws. What, then, does "the people" signify? It appears that Kim's definition of Yŏngjo's people excludes the yangban and bureaucratic class. This interpretation is particularly questionable when considering Yŏngjo's reforms, such as his adjustments to the military tax system.

Ultimately, Yŏngjo abandoned *Hop'opŏp* (the Household Military Tax Reform 戶布法) and reverted to *Kampil* (a reduction in the number of taxable rolls 減匹). This decision was not solely due to intense opposition but also reflected the reality that the economic struggles of the yangban and officials, who were themselves largely considered part of the populace, could not be ignored.[9] King Yŏngjo's eventual abandonment of the Household Tax System in favor of reducing the number of taxable rolls during his military tax reform was not solely due to strong opposition. Another significant reason was his inability to disregard the economic hardships faced by the *yangban* and bureaucratic class, who were also effectively regarded as part of the broader populace.[10] However, the use of such expressions without a clear definition of "the people" risks significant misunderstandings. The ambiguity surrounding this term creates interpretative challenges, especially when analyzing policies that claim to address the populace as a whole.

King Yŏngjo articulated his thoughts and aspirations directly through various royal writings. Notably, he expressed positive evaluations of historical figures such as the Hongwu Emperor of the Ming dynasty and the First Emperor of Qin. This stance is particularly striking given their generally negative reception among Confucian scholars, who criticized these rulers for actions that were seen as contradicting Confucian values.[11] King Yŏngjo's admiration for these historical figures stemmed from his fascination with their overwhelming authority, which enabled them to dominate their officials. Furthermore, Yŏngjo redefined *the Sŏnghak Chip'yo* 聖學輯要,[12] traditionally regarded as a guide for the monarch's self-cultivation, as a symbol of loyalty and cooperation from officials in governance.[13] Such examples illustrate that Yŏngjo's ultimate goal was the establishment of a strong and centralized royal authority.

Similar examples abound. Nevertheless, Kim Baek-chul argued that Yŏngjo pursued the governance ideals of Yao and Shun and regarded the realization of "loving the people" and "protecting the people" as the ultimate goal of his political life. While it is true that Yŏngjo repeatedly declared and openly promoted such ideals, one must ask: would any ruler not make similar claims? Since the dawn of history, all regimes and holders of power have invoked Heaven's Mandate and the will of the people to legitimize their rule. This was particularly true in Northeast Asia, where Confucian political ideals were deeply entrenched. Even Yŏnsan'gun (r. 1494–1506), often regarded as a symbol of tyranny, did not deny the concepts of Heaven's Mandate and the will of the people.

When evaluating the governance of a ruler, a historian must go beyond analyzing the slogans and justifications presented by that ruler. Instead, the researcher must rigorously scrutinize the ruler's intentions and actions to uncover the underlying motivations and actual impact of their policies.

Comprehensively evaluating the life of an individual or the reign of a monarch is an exceedingly challenging task. For a ruler like King Yŏngjo, whose reign spanned over half a century, a superficial evaluation would fail to provide a holistic understanding of his character and governance.

While human actions are rarely driven solely by intentions, it is equally true that no one—unless they are a saint—can lead a life guided purely by altruism. This reality is especially pronounced for a politician responsible for governing an entire nation, where decisions often involve navigating complex and competing interests.

Just as Yŏngjo endeavored to embody the role of a sage king, analyses of his intentions and the outcomes of his efforts must not be overlooked.

As previously noted, King Yŏngjo faced persistent controversies and disputes surrounding his legitimacy, beginning with his appointment as crown prince. The *Noron* and *Soron* factions clashed over issues of his legitimacy, pressuring Yŏngjo to deliver conflicting judgments on questions of loyalty and treachery. These circumstances not only undermined his authority but also posed significant challenges to his governance, complicating his efforts to achieve stability.

Earlier studies primarily focused on Yŏngjo's use of Confucian values to establish himself as a sage king who flawlessly embodied Neo-Confucian ideals, emphasizing this as a means to overcome political crises. While these works highlighted the significance of ideological justifications in Yŏngjo's governance, they paid relatively little attention to the political strategies and actions he employed to navigate crises or resolve political deadlocks before solidifying his ideological foundation.

Choo Chae-young's research addressed this gap by analyzing Yŏngjo's governance theory along two axes: the controversy surrounding his legitimacy and the resolution of public welfare issues. Ju argued that Yŏngjo's strategies, including the Royal demonstrations of authority and *Taemin Sunmun* (consultations with the populace 對民詢問), were key methods through which he navigated challenges to his legitimacy and tackled pressing public welfare concerns.

According to Choo Chae-young, the controversy surrounding King Yŏngjo's legitimacy originated during the reign of King Kyŏngjong, when the *Noron* faction hastily advocated for the appointment of the Crown Prince and pushed for the transfer of regency powers. As a result, Yŏngjo faced doubts about his legitimacy from the very moment he was appointed as Crown Prince.

This controversy culminated in the *Noron* faction's expulsion from the political arena, following accusations of treason leveled against them by King Kyŏngjong and the *Soron* faction. Deprived of the *Noron*'s support, the Crown Prince was compelled to seek independent means of survival in the politically volatile environment.

To turn the tide, the Crown Prince actively defended himself by publicizing allegations that eunuchs had conspired against him, bringing the matter to the attention of the court. In the face of a political crisis, he staged his first significant political demonstration by declaring his intention to abdicate—a bold move aimed at reversing the precarious situation. This marked Yŏngjo's first act of political demonstration.

This act of defiance against King Kyŏngjong and the court allowed the Crown Prince to regain King Kyŏngjong's trust and secure allies within the court who could protect his position.

After ascending the throne, King Yŏngjo's use of protest actions to achieve his objectives became more pronounced. The *Noron* and *Soron* factions, locked in a fierce dispute over his legitimacy, refused to yield any ground. As a directly involved party, Yŏngjo's authority to mediate was inherently constrained. In this polarized environment, persuasion and earnest appeals proved ineffective, and the relentless conflicts and opposition began to exhaust Yŏngjo's patience.

Faced with political deadlock, Yŏngjo devised a unique method to break through the impasse: a form of demonstrating bordering on self-harm. By leveraging the symbolic authority of the king's position, he applied moral and political pressure on his officials to force resolutions.

Yŏngjo frequently showcased his efforts to embody the image of a diligent and virtuous ruler committed to enacting good governance, ensuring that his actions were visible to the public. In doing so, he accentuated the disloyalty of officials who failed to support their king, thereby making their opposition conspicuous to the nation. This strategic maneuver enabled Yŏngjo to apply psychological pressure on his officials, compelling them to conform to his will.

Yŏngjo astutely identified situations in which defiance was untenable and capitalized on them. As a result, while officials may have understood Yŏngjo's underlying intentions, they found themselves unable to withstand the stigma of disloyalty. To harm the health of their sovereign or oppose the will of their lord and father would bring dishonor and jeopardize their reputations. Confronted with the risk of such disgrace, the officials ultimately capitulated to Yŏngjo's demands.

King Yŏngjo's demonstration actions gradually evolved into a definitive tool for governance, exhibiting a consistent pattern in terms of their form, target, and location. Through these calculated actions, he implemented his intentions step by step, ultimately securing dominance over state affairs.

However, Yŏngjo did not rely on such protests to address pressing public welfare issues. Instead, he sought solutions by directly engaging in communication with the populace, demonstrating his commitment to resolving their concerns through active dialogue.

King Yŏngjo actively encouraged petitions and the striking of a gong as a means for the populace to present grievances. He expanded the scope of consultations, which had traditionally been limited to officials, to include the general populace. Through repeated direct inquiries, Yŏngjo went beyond merely listening to public opinion, actively involving the people in the policy-making process.

For example, he sought the people's views on the feasibility of reforms to the military tax system. Based on their feedback, he declared a tax reduction, which facilitated the successful implementation of the Equalized Military Tax Law This event marked a significant moment in which the previously abstract concept of "the people" was concretely engaged in governance.

Yŏngjo continued to incorporate public opinion into state affairs, extending his direct inquiries to include merchants and artisans. This practice reflected the societal changes of the 18th century and demonstrated Yŏngjo's responsiveness to evolving economic and social dynamics.

Yŏngjo's activities in direct public consultations hold substantial significance as a novel governance tool. By involving the populace in the decision-making process, he redefined their role, positioning them as active partners in governance. His acknowledgment of societal changes and their integration into governance practices exemplified his adaptability and responsiveness to the evolving dynamics of 18th-century society.

Through these actions, Yŏngjo cultivated the image of a monarch deeply committed to serving the people. His protests and direct public consultations functioned as strategic tools to resolve political conflicts and address urgent issues of public welfare. Both practices, however, emerged as responses to mistrust rooted in his conflicts with officials. Yŏngjo skillfully leveraged the performative aspects of these actions to achieve his desired objectives, blending practicality with symbolism in his governance.[14]

Choo Chae-young's study holds historiographical significance for its emphasis on the tangible actions of a practical politician in the political field, rather than abstract ideals or lofty rhetoric, to illuminate King Yŏngjo's governance theory. In politics, actions themselves often serve as powerful messages. This is particularly true for a Chosŏn monarch, whose every action—due to the absence of a private sphere—must be interpreted within the framework of governance.

Choo's work identifies King Yŏngjo's methods of governance by closely examining his actions, a perspective largely overlooked in previous studies. However, a notable shortcoming of the study is its limited discussion of the Imo Tragedy, arguably one of the most critical events of Yŏngjo's reign. Yŏngjo, who more than anyone sought to demonstrate his adherence to Confucian values to solidify his legitimacy, committed the unprecedented act of killing his own son, the Crown Prince and designated political successor, without any formal procedural justification.

The absence of an analysis of this extraordinary event leaves a significant gap in the understanding of Yŏngjo's monarchical philosophy. Addressing and rectifying this omission remains an important task for future research.

This study has reviewed four major works that comprehensively analyze King Yŏngjo's governance. All of these studies emphasize Yŏngjo's aspiration to embody the role of a sage king. The sage-king framework employed in these works refers to "a monarch who diligently adhered to Confucian political ideals, such as self-cultivation, asceticism, filial piety, and the continuation of virtuous governance, while striving to emulate the governance of Yao and Shun."

However, the concept of the "sage king" highlighted in these studies does not serve as an evaluation of Yŏngjo but rather as a rhetorical construct that reflects his self-proclaimed ideal of kingship. By adopting Yŏngjo's own self-assessment in their analyses of his monarchical philosophy, these four studies implicitly acknowledge that he successfully achieved the status of a sage king.

Nevertheless, Haboush, Lee Hee-hwan, and Choo Chae-young do not concur that Yŏngjo succeeded in sustaining his authority in the long term. In contrast, Kim Baek-chul recognizes Yŏngjo as a sage king, arguing that he attained transcendent authority and exercised it benevolently for the benefit of the people.

3. King Chŏngjo - The Reformist Monarch

While studies on King Yŏngjo's monarchical philosophy were published in the United States relatively early, American academic interest in King Chŏngjo has emerged only recently. The first major contribution to this field was Christopher Lovins's 2019 study.[15] Lovins characterizes King Chŏngjo as an "Enlightened Despot," a perspective that aligns with Yi T'ae-jin's 1993 essay, which described Chŏngjo as a "Confucian Enlightened Despot." Lovins's work thus revives Yi T'ae-jin's thesis, which had largely been overlooked for the past three decades.

Academic interest in King Chŏngjo's governance began to emerge gradually in the 1980s. Yi T'ae-jin published a paper on factional politics, in which he defined King Chŏngjo as a reformist monarch.[16] Furthermore, in his 1993 article titled "King Chŏngjo—*Yugyojŏk Kyemong Chŏldaegunjoo* (a Confucian Enlightened Absolute Monarch)," published in the Korean History Civic Lecture, Yi compared King Chŏngjo to Frederick II of Prussia and characterized him as an "enlightened absolute monarch."

Yi regarded the era of King Chŏngjo as a period of burgeoning commercial capitalism and argued that Chŏngjo's reformist politics represented the potential for indigenous modernization in Korea.

According to Yi T'ae-jin, King Chŏngjo was a benevolent monarch who frequently engaged with his people and a scholarly ruler who established the *Kyujanggak* to promote academic advancement and cultivate officials capable of supporting royal authority. At the same time, Chŏngjo sought to balance civil and military affairs by compiling martial arts manuals and founding the royal guard unit, the *Changyŏngyŏng* (Royal Guards).

Through the *Changyŏngyŏng*, Chŏngjo achieved notable success in suppressing factions that opposed his policies of impartiality and reform, both militarily and economically. The construction of *Hwasŏng* 華城 *new town* marked the culmination of the inner and outer divisions of the *Changyŏngyŏng*, symbolizing the pinnacle of royal authority. This act represented King Chŏngjo's confidence as a ruler who embodied the teachings of sages since the time of Yao and Shun and demonstrated the alignment between the monarch and the people.

It also reflected his political philosophy, which aimed to dismantle factionalism and establish monarch-centered governance. Yi T'ae-jin referred to this as the "Absolute Monarchy of the Virtuous King", drawing parallels to the ideology of European enlightened monarchs.[17]

Although this study remained at the level of a preliminary essay, it holds significant historical value in academic discourse as one of the first attempts to comprehensively outline King Chŏngjo's governance and to define the Chŏngjo era through comparisons with contemporary Western contexts. However, the study made somewhat overreaching claims by employing terms such as "enlightenment" and "absolutism" without providing clear conceptual definitions or robust academic justifications, relying primarily on situational similarities.

Furthermore, while evaluating the late Chosŏn period, particularly the 18th century, as a time of "developing commercial capitalism," the study failed to present substantial historical or logical evidence to support this assertion. Yi T'ae-jin used specialized historical terms such as "commercial capitalism," "enlightenment," and "absolute monarchy," which originated in European historical contexts, in a largely declarative manner without adequate contextual reinterpretation or detailed argumentation.

Even considering the nature of the publication—a journal aimed at public enlightenment rather than an academic journal—such an approach can be deemed precarious. Non-specialists are likely to accept the claims of a renowned scholar like Yi T'ae-jin without critical scrutiny, which risks fostering significant misconceptions.

Public-oriented historical scholarship should not compromise the rigor of its argumentation. Instead, it should aim for accessible narrative construction—writing history that is considerate and easy to read while maintaining scholarly accuracy and methodological integrity.

Following Yi T'ae-jin, more comprehensive studies on King Chŏngjo's politics and philosophy were conducted by Park Hyun-mo. Park approached Chŏngjo's era and governance from a political science perspective, utilizing the Veritable Records of King Chŏngjo as his primary source and *the Hongjae Chŏnsŏ* 弘齋全書[18] as a supplementary resource. By tracing political events documented in these historical records, Park articulated King Chŏngjo's theory of governance.

Park's work is structured into two parts. The first part focuses on Chŏngjo's politics and scholarship, presenting the theories of *Kwŏndo* (expediental means, 權道) and *Sŏngwang* (a sage king, 聖王). The second part examines Chŏngjo's various reform policies. Park emphasized Chŏngjo's proactive and dynamic approach to governance.

According to Park, Chŏngjo reinterpreted the "politics of Yao and Shun" as active, monarch-centered governance aimed at bestowing five blessings upon his subjects. Through this framework, Chŏngjo reestablished himself as a reformist monarch and Sŏngwang.

The core of King Chŏngjo's ideology and statecraft, as analyzed by Park Hyun-mo, lay in several key principles. First, the theory of expediental means emphasized the discretionary use of power within the boundaries of the law. Second, the *Tangp'yŏng* positioned the king as a mediator of "righteousness and talent," balancing political factions. Third, the theory of orthodox Neo-Confucianism underscored Chŏngjo's efforts to educate and transform officials into royal confidants aligned with his vision.

Park portrayed Chŏngjo as a proactive *Sŏngwang* who placed himself at the center of governance. Through the strategic application of expediental means, Chŏngjo maintained balance among political factions, pursued reforms, and wielded power for the benefit of the people, embodying his philosophy of monarch-centered statecraft.

At the same time, Park Hyun-mo portrayed King Chŏngjo as a practitioner of history—an inconsistent and anxious figure who repeatedly questioned the meaning of history and made decisions amidst uncertainty. According to Park, Chŏngjo's failures stemmed from several key factors:

Failure to completely relinquish self-interest: Despite advocating public-mindedness, Chŏngjo could not fully overcome his private inclinations. His trusted aides succumbed to personal greed, and Chŏngjo himself failed to transcend self-interest in matters such as his conflict with his half-brother.

Lack of delegation and fostering responsibility: Chŏngjo's deep distrust of his officials led him to micromanage and excessively intervene in governance, preventing his subordinates from developing a sense of responsibility or exercising independent judgment.

Inability to seize opportunities due to indecision: Chŏngjo's characteristic indecisiveness and hypersensitivity to political dynamics inhibited his ability to effectively initiate significant reforms.

Excessive pursuit of centralized command: His efforts to unify the chain of command weakened the bureaucratic system's checks and balances, neutralizing the critical oversight functions of officials.

Poor selection of officials: Despite emphasizing the importance of appointing "individuals well-versed in governance," Chŏngjo frequently placed incompetent officials in administrative positions, resulting in the paralysis of military and local governance. Abuses by local clerks became rampant, but although Chŏngjo acknowledged their misconduct, his reforms were limited to urging magistrates to act with integrity and diligence, leaving systemic issues unaddressed.

Through this analysis, Park argued that Chŏngjo ultimately fell short of becoming the Sŏngwang he aspired to be. Moreover, Park held Chŏngjo accountable for contributing to the eventual tragedy of the regent-dominated political system that followed.[19]

While many researchers of this period focused on King Chŏngjo's *Sŏnghak* (Study of Sage Governance 聖學), Park Hyun-mo introduced his own framework, *Sŏngwangnon* (the theory of the virtuous monarch 聖王論). Notably, Park's emphasis on the proactive role of the monarch in clarifying Chŏngjo's politics is particularly striking. Furthermore, by extending his analysis of Chŏngjo's royal ideology to the post-Chŏngjo era and the regent-dominated political system, Park provided valuable insights into the causes of Chosŏn's rapid decline following Chŏngjo's reign.

However, Park's work also has certain limitations. First, apart from its emphasis on the monarch's proactivity, the concept of the "theory of the virtuous monarch lacks clarity. To systematically explain his framework, Park presented a comparative table centered on the literati, contrasting Discourse on the Study of Sage Governance with Theory of the virtuous monarch.[20] Yet, the substantive differences between these two frameworks remain insufficiently pronounced, leaving the distinctions between them vague.

Second, the book dedicates a significant portion of its second part to a critical analysis of King Chŏngjo's failures, ultimately concluding that he did not achieve the status of a of the virtuous monarch. In the first part, Park meticulously demonstrated how Chŏngjo exercised discretion and employed expediental means to position himself at the center of state governance, pursuing innovations in factional politics and cultural reforms.

However, in the second part, Park shifted focus to Chŏngjo's shortcomings in implementing reforms, wielding *Kwŏndo*, and leading state governance. Park argued that these failures ultimately prevented Chŏngjo from attaining the ideal status of a virtuous monarch.

If the book's central theme is "King Chŏngjo as a virtuous monarch," its heavy emphasis on his failures risks creating a somewhat deflating narrative structure. A more balanced exploration of both his successes and shortcomings might have provided a more compelling and cohesive analysis.

Despite its limitations, Park Hyun-mo's unwavering determination to clearly define King Chŏngjo's statecraft as practiced on the actual political stage, while holding him accountable for the subsequent rise of the regent-dominated political system, represents a bold and uncommon endeavor.[21] Perhaps it was Park's foundation in political science, rather than in historical studies, that enabled such a distinctive approach.

After Park Hyun-mo, comprehensive discussions on King Chŏngjo's royal ideology and statecraft in Korean academia entered a period of stagnation. In contrast, in the United States, Christopher Lovins published a scholarly work addressing Chŏngjo's royal philosophy. Lovins defined Chŏngjo as an "Enlightened Despot."

Unlike Yi T'ae-jin, Lovins devoted significant attention to justifying the application of the academic term "Enlightened Despot" to the context of the Chosŏn dynasty, providing a detailed rationale for its relevance and adaptability to Korean history.

Lovins drew upon the research of Peter H. Wilson and Victor Lieberman to define the early modern period (15th to 19th centuries) through several key indicators: centralization, the development of bureaucracy, and the existence of a monarch recognized as the sole legitimate ruler within a shared political culture. He argued that absolutist systems emerged within such political climates.[22] According to Lovins, the political entities of East Asia, including the Korean Peninsula, fulfilled these conditions of early modernity during their transition from ancient states. For instance, even in the Koryŏ Dynasty, Korea already exhibited centralization, bureaucracy, and monarchs acknowledged as legitimate and unique rulers.

However, the tendency to schematically apply criteria derived from European history to Korean history warrants reconsideration, as such critiques have become repetitive and predictable in academic discourse.

According to Lovins, monarchs sought the cooperation of the aristocracy as a supportive base for their governance, while the aristocracy relied on monarchs to mediate internal conflicts. This mutual dependence created an agreement in which monarchs upheld aristocratic privileges, and aristocrats, in turn, recognized and supported the monarch's transcendent authority.

Within this framework, the absolute monarch, as defined by Lovins, was constrained by the need for aristocratic recognition of legitimacy but exercised maximum discretionary power within those boundaries.

Lovins projected his concepts of early modernity and absolutism onto Chosŏn and King Chŏngjo. According to his analysis, Chŏngjo sought to secure discretionary power within his relationship with the yangban class, who served as both hereditary aristocrats and bureaucrats in Chosŏn.

By surpassing the yangban in their core domain of Neo-Confucian scholarship, Chŏngjo established himself as their intellectual superior, positioning himself as the Philosopher-King. This intellectual dominance allowed him to transcend the constraints imposed by the yangban class and assert greater autonomy in governance.

Through an active reinterpretation of the *Five Classics* 五經, ancient Confucianism preceding Neo-Confucianism, and the teachings of Yao and Shun, King Chŏngjo emphasized monarch-centered governance. By employing strategic governance tailored to the circumstances, he expanded the scope of his political maneuverability, demonstrating a flexible yet authoritative approach to statecraft.

King Chŏngjo also sought to strengthen the permanence of royal authority through institutional reforms. He established the *Kyujanggak*, implemented *Ch'okye Munch'in* (the special training program for young scholars 抄啓文臣), appointed individuals from marginalized groups such as the offspring of secondary status and northwesterners, and engaged directly with the populace. These efforts were aimed at broadening his support base and expanding the operational scope of the monarchy.

Furthermore, Chŏngjo sought to enhance his military foundation by constructing *Hwasŏng Fortress* and organizing the *Changyŏngyŏng*, thereby consolidating royal authority and ensuring the security of his rule.

Movements opposing King Chŏngjo's reforms were neutralized by his strategic invocation of filial piety, enabling him to maintain direct control over military power and pose a tangible threat to the yangban. Lovins argued that while Chŏngjo's reforms sought to expand royal authority, they did not fundamentally infringe upon the core interests of the yangban, thereby occasionally securing their support.

Based on this analysis, Lovins concluded that Chŏngjo's governance aligned with the concept of an absolute monarch.

In the final chapter of his book, Lovins compared King Chŏngjo to the Qianlong Emperor of Qing China and Louis XIV of France. While it may initially seem intuitive to draw parallels between King Chŏngjo and the Qianlong Emperor due to their shared foundation in Confucian political ideology, Lovins argued that significant distinctions arose from differences in territorial and population scales, as well as the contrasting presence or absence of hereditary ruling classes within their respective political systems.

Conversely, Lovins posited that King Chŏngjo bore greater resemblance to Louis XIV of France, primarily due to analogous geographical and cultural conditions. He outlined the following grounds for this comparison:

The process of consolidating royal authority through both negotiation and confrontation with a powerful hereditary aristocracy.

A pronounced emphasis on ceremonial practices.

The regression of reforms following their deaths, driven by resistance from adversaries.

This analytical framework supported Lovins' argument that King Chŏngjo and Louis XIV were more closely aligned in their political and cultural contexts.

Lovins criticized the prevailing perspective in Korean academia that regards King Chŏngjo as a "reformist monarch with modern aspirations." Instead, he attempted to evaluate Chŏngjo from an objective standpoint. Furthermore, Lovins sought to analyze 18th-century Chosŏn and its monarchy within a broader framework of global historical universality. His effort to situate Chŏngjo and 18th-century Chosŏn in a comparative and universal historical context underscores the scholarly significance of his work.

However, certain aspects of Lovins' work are challenging to accept. First, the book's title prominently employs the term "Enlightened Despot." Despite this, the author devotes most of the text to discussing "absolutism" and "absolute monarchs," offering minimal engagement with concepts such as the social contract or enlightenment. Considering that the book's stated objective was to critique the tendency within Korean academia to attribute modernist aspirations to King Chŏngjo, the concept of "enlightenment" appears to occupy a peripheral role. This discrepancy raises a critical question: why was the term "enlightened" included in the title? The author's reasoning behind this decision requires further clarification.

Moreover, it is questionable whether the "conditions of absolute monarchy" as outlined by Lovins are consistent with those commonly accepted in historical studies. Lovins defined an absolute monarch as a ruler who possesses and exercises legislative authority without requiring consent. He further argued that when such a monarch is appropriately influenced by enlightenment ideals, they may be regarded as an enlightened despot. Lovins' interpretation of an enlightened despot has already been subject to substantial criticism, which will not be reiterated here.[23]

Lovins' assertion that an "absolute monarch" legislates without consent is problematic when applied to the three figures he identified as enlightened despots—King Chŏngjo, Louis XIV, and the Qianlong Emperor—none of whom possessed such authority. Specifically, Lovins argued that the commonality between King Chŏngjo and Louis XIV lay in their "collaborative relationship with hereditary aristocrats" and their "reforms limited to areas that did not infringe upon aristocratic interests." These characterizations are inconsistent with the idea of unilateral legislative authority. Such contradictions between Lovins' conceptual definitions and his actual arguments indicate that either his definitions, his reasoning, or both, are insufficient.

Second, Lovins advanced various arguments to characterize King Chŏngjo as an absolute monarch. However, many of the features he highlighted are commonly observed in the reigns of earlier monarchs, including King Yŏngjo. Lovins sought to differentiate Chŏngjo's governance by emphasizing specific contrasts, such as Chŏngjo's refusal to adopt rituals like meal abstention or the use of abdication threats, practices associated with Yŏngjo. Nevertheless, Yŏngjo also employed strategies involving both checks and negotiations with his officials to expand royal authority, demonstrating governance methods similar to those attributed to Chŏngjo.

Moreover, many aspects of Chŏngjo's statecraft—such as military policies, frequent visits to royal tombs, interactions with the populace, Neo-Confucian justifications for diplomacy with the Ming dynasty, the lifting of status restrictions on *Sŏŏl* (child of a concubine 庶孼), and he loosening of restrictions on Chosŏn's expanding commercial trade through the Commercial Equalization Law—were continuations of Yŏngjo's initiatives. The consolidation of royal authority through the embodiment of Neo-Confucian values was a strategic objective and fundamental duty for all Chosŏn kings, differing primarily in the methods of execution and the rulers' individual capacities.

Lovins, however, treated these practices as if they were unique to King Chŏngjo. If his logic were applied consistently, a significant number of Chosŏn monarchs would need to be re-evaluated as absolute monarchs, which would undermine the distinctiveness of Chŏngjo's reign within this framework.

Finally, Lovins' study does not appear to diverge significantly from the arguments advanced by Yi T'ae-jin. Even the reasoning offered by Lovins closely parallels Yi's earlier work. While there are differences in the conceptual background and framework of absolutism employed by Lovins, the similarities are difficult to ignore, particularly given that Yi's research had a preliminary and exploratory nature.

Moreover, given that Lovins completed his academic training and conducts research in Korea, it is highly probable that he was significantly influenced by Yi T'ae-jin's scholarship. It is unfortunate that the sole English-language study on this subject remains largely restricted to reiterating arguments presented in Korean academia over three decades ago, without offering significant new insights or advancements.

In 2020, a group of researchers from Seoul National University specializing in the study of King Chŏngjo and the 18th century published a comprehensive volume on Chŏngjo. These scholars adopted a critical perspective, emphasizing that Chŏngjo must be understood within the historical context of his time. Accordingly, they established a clear objective for their work: to reevaluate the interpretation of the 18th century as the dawn of modernity and of Chŏngjo as an "enlightened monarch who overcame Neo-Confucianism and initiated a new era through Practical Learning."

Instead, they sought to situate Chŏngjo within the context of his time, emphasizing his pursuit of "the study of restoring correctness" as central to their interpretation. This intent and objective were explicitly articulated at the outset of the publication.

The compendium consists of four volumes, each addressing a specific aspect of King Chŏngjo's governance: *Munch'i* (civil governance 文治) by Paek Sŭng-ho, *Much'i* (chmilitary governance 武治) by Hŏ T'ae-gu, *Yech'i* (ritual governance 禮治) by Kim Chi-yŏng, and *Pŏpch'i* (legal governance 法治) by Kim Ho.

The first volume, authored by Paek Sŭng-ho, explores Chŏngjo's theory of literature. According to Paek, "literature" as conceived by Chŏngjo encompassed all forms of everyday writing. Paek analyzes Chŏngjo's literary activities across three stages: during his time as Crown Prince, following his ascension to the throne and his direct governance of the state, and within the literary endeavors of officials who were educated under Chŏngjo's guidance.

The first section illustrates how Chŏngjo utilized writing to correspond with palace officials, thereby consolidating loyalist factions and reinforcing his legitimacy as the rightful successor. Additionally, it examines how he documented the misconduct of factions opposing his ascension in the *Chŏnhaenggak ilgi* 尊賢閣日記,[24] a record intended to prepare for his future reign.

The second section, which examines the period following Chŏngjo's enthronement, reveals that his writings functioned as a tool for generating political discourse and reinforcing the legitimacy of his reign. According to Paek, Chŏngjo employed his extensive writings to embody a Neo-Confucian worldview, assert royal authority, and strengthen communication with his officials. Additionally, he initiated large-scale compilation projects centered on the *Kyujanggak* library, aiming to construct a collective memory of the state. These efforts glorified three generations of sage kings: his grandfather King Yŏngjo, himself, and his anticipated successor.

The third section explores Chŏngjo's efforts to advance Neo-Confucian ideals through *Munch'e Panjŏng* (the Rectification of Literary Styles 文體反正) movement and the revitalization of the Six Classics and classical prose. Paek concludes that, for Chŏngjo, literature served as a crucial medium for embodying and disseminating Neo-Confucian principles.[25]

The second study examines King Chŏngjo's military governance, which Hŏ T'ae-gu defines as the "restoration of ancient systems." Hŏ characterizes Chŏngjo's era as a period of relative stability in East Asia, reducing the necessity for extensive military fortification. To analyze Chŏngjo's military governance, the study focuses on three key elements: *Chinha Oegyo* (Tributary Congratulations 進賀外交), the Changyongyŏng and Hwasŏng Fortress, and the concept of the integration of civil and military virtues.

First, the central premise of Chŏngjo's Tributary Congratulations was the idea that performing meticulous rituals of tribute to Qing was a matter of "ritual propriety" rather than an adherence to Ming loyalism. Chŏngjo recognized serving the greater power as an obligation for a small state and positively evaluated the Qianlong Emperor. He also regarded diplomacy with Qing as a expediental means essential for securing peace and protecting the people, which could be separated from Ming loyalist ideology.

Second, Hŏ asserts that Chŏngjo's military activities, including the establishment of the *Changyongyŏng*, the construction of *Hwasŏng* Fortress, and the compilation of military manuals, were aimed at restoring ancient rites and systems rather than bolstering military capacity. To support this argument, he cites the stability of East Asia during Chŏngjo's reign and the limited military and defensive functionality of *Hwasŏng*.

Third, in the section discussing Chŏngjo's integration of civil and military virtues, Hŏ examines Chŏngjo's reevaluation of *Yi Sunsin* (1545 ~ 1598) as the ideal figure embodying both qualities. The author contends that this was not an effort to enhance national defense or elevate the status of military affairs. Instead, it was Chŏngjo's attempt to move beyond excessive civil governance and return to the Neo-Confucian principle of harmony and balance between civil and military domains.[26]

Ji-yŏng Kim has written about governance through rites, arguing that King Chŏngjo elevated the concept from a simple observance of rituals to a comprehensive principle encompassing state administration, governance, integration, and diplomacy. Kim categorized Chŏngjo's Ritual Governance into five types, noting that the scope of ritual propriety expanded progressively from the family to the village, the school, the state, and ultimately to the world.

In the first part of the paper, the author examines family rites within the contexts of private reverence for father and governance through filial piety. Chŏngjo adhered to the public-mindedness central to propriety and opposed excessive posthumous honors. This principle is encapsulated in the *Kungwŏnŭi* 宮園儀, which demonstrates Chŏngjo's effort to uphold royal succession while respecting personal affections.

The second part discusses the compilation of the *Hyangnye Hapbyŏn* 鄉禮合編, which aimed to promote voluntary moral cultivation among the populace and to establish a mutually supportive community through the *Hyangŭmchurye* (village drinking ceremony 鄉飮酒禮).

The third part analyzes the *T'aehakchi* 太學志, which reflects Chŏngjo's aspirations for normalizing the operations of the National Academy. This work underscores his broader vision for institutional and educational reforms.

This represented one aspect of King Chŏngjo's proactive strategy for cultivating talent. The fourth section examines state rites as a mechanism for actualizing the "order of virtue." Chŏngjo institutionalized Confucian virtues such as loyalty and filial piety through rituals and historical records, thereby transforming these values into national ideologies. To this end, he revised the *Rituals of the Martial Temple* and re-evaluated historical figures who either promoted peace with the Qing or advocated for northern campaigns, portraying both groups as individuals who upheld righteousness.

Additionally, Chŏngjo oversaw the compilation of the *Chŏngni T'onggo* 整理通考, elevating his filial piety toward his father, Crown Prince Sado, from a private virtue to a public standard, thereby establishing a model for his subjects and future generations. For Chŏngjo, the proper practice of filial piety began with personal devotion and extended to the realization of governance through filial principles, embodying a vision of universal public harmony.

The fifth section analyzes *Sadaeryesŏl* 事大禮說 to elucidate Chŏngjo's theory of Confucian moral principles toward the Ming and the significance of serving the Qing. A debate emerged in 1799 following the death of Emperor Qianlong over the appropriate mourning attire for Chosŏn officials. Chŏngjo actively led the discussion, focusing not merely on the attire itself but on the underlying principles of orthodoxy and righteousness.

According to the author, Chŏngjo attributed symbolic meaning to wearing the proper mourning attire, framing it as an effort to avoid falling into barbarity like the Qing. He argued that this act aligned with the concept of universal harmony, wherein multiple states coexist in balance.[27]

Ho Kim asserts that the core of King Chŏngjo's legal governance lay in achieving the "harmony of precision and principle." His book examines Chŏngjo's theories on criminal justice and moral cultivation through an analysis of texts such as the *Muwŏnrok* (Records of No Grievances 無冤錄), the *Iltŭngnok* (Daily Gleanings 日得錄), and the *Simnirok* (Records of Judicial Review 審理錄).

The book also delves into posthumous evaluations of Chŏngjo's criminal justice theories by figures such as *Chŏng Wŏn-yong* (1783~1873) and *Chŏng Yak-yong* (1762~1836). In the introduction, Ho Kim dedicates significant attention to Chosŏn's legal culture, aiming to challenge the prevailing tendency to disparage East Asian legal traditions from the standpoint of Western modernity, which often labels them as irrational, non-legalistic, and highly arbitrary.

This book focuses on how King Chŏngjo's rulings harmonized the unique circumstances of individual cases, human morality, and societal values with the law. Through this analysis, the author demonstrates that Chŏngjo regarded criminal justice as an auxiliary tool for moral cultivation. In administering justice, Chŏngjo embraced the Confucian ideal of balanced action and was unafraid of suspicions that he might be bending the law to reconcile it with principles and moral governance.

To realize the Neo-Confucian ideal of constructing a voluntary moral community, Chŏngjo encouraged righteous valor and issued rulings that stimulated the sense of honor even among the common people. When his decisions faced opposition or criticism, Chŏngjo rationalized them by invoking expedient means or the Confucian ideal of balanced action Later generations have evaluated Chŏngjo's approach to criminal justice as "the official penal theory of the virtue of valuing life" or, more critically, as an excess of morality.[28]

The four volumes on King Chŏngjo collectively analyze the core pillars of his governance—civil administration, military strategy, ritual governance, and legal governance —from multiple perspectives, offering a comprehensive understanding of Chŏngjo's political philosophy. As stated in the purpose of these works, the volumes clarify that Chŏngjo's ideology and statecraft aimed at realizing a Neo-Confucian ideal society.

The series evaluates Chŏngjo as a monarch striving to transform Chosŏn into such a Neo-Confucian utopia. His reforms were fundamentally a return to the roots of Neo-Confucianism. Nonetheless, much of Korean scholarship continues to interpret Chŏngjo within the framework of a reformist monarch who supported heterodox Neo-Confucianism, Practical

Learning, and Northern Learning.

Thus, efforts to move beyond this conventional framework represent not only a significant academic attempt but perhaps an inevitable development in reassessing Chŏngjo's legacy.

However, several issues warrant further discussion. First, the interpretation of Chŏngjo's theory on serving the Qing presented by Hŏ T'ae-gu and Kim Chi-yŏng is perhaps the most intriguing and contentious aspect of the series. They argue that Chŏngjo was able to avoid contradictions by approaching Ming loyalism and Qing tribute separately through the use of expediential means.

However, one must question whether it is possible to separate, righteousness from ritual within the Neo-Confucian worldview. If righteousness is removed from *ritual*, what remains is mere "formality." This notion does not align with the vision of governance by Chŏngjo as explained and clarified in the four volumes. The same can be said of expediential means. Ming loyalism symbolized Chosŏn's identity, while Qing tribute was a matter of the kingdom's survival. Neither the king nor his officials could afford to neglect or deny Ming loyalism without risking their positions. The deposition of King Kwanghaegun (r.1608~1623) and the Restoration of King Injo (r.1623~1649) attest to this.

For these reasons, the claim that Chŏngjo resolved the apparent contradictions between these two issues through a simple invocation of expediential means is difficult to accept.

Second, Hŏ T'ae-gu's assessment of Chŏngjo's military governance as measures to restore ancient rites and systems is refreshing, and the argumentation supporting this perspective is persuasive. Notably, Hŏ's critique of the deficiencies in military and defensive capabilities and his interpretation of Hwasŏng as a symbolic space of Chŏngjo's governance distinguish his work from other studies.

However, actions such as the removal of powerful officials who controlled military authority, the unification of the command system under the Minister of War, the reorganization of the Five Military Commands, and the establishment of the Royal Guards are often seen as efforts not merely to strengthen national defense but also to consolidate Chŏngjo's control over military authority and to bolster his personal loyalist faction. In reality, Chŏngjo did not initially have full control over military authority; during the early years of his reign, his power was precarious, and he faced threats of assassination. Measures such as the elimination of military power held by influential officials and the creation of the *Changyongyŏng* stabilized Chŏngjo's position.

Moreover, the completion of the inner and outer units of the *Changyongyŏng* and the construction of *Hwasŏng* marked the zenith of his reign. Taken together, the *Changyongyŏng* appears to be better interpreted as a means to enhance Chŏngjo's power and authority rather than as a restoration of ancient rites. Additionally, if *Hwasŏng* remains merely a symbolic space, it raises the question of how to evaluate a monarch like Chŏngjo, who emphasized principles and aspired to be a sage king, for expending vast national resources and efforts on such a monumental project.

For a king, especially one like Chŏngjo, who prioritized ideals and sought to embody the virtues of a Confucian ruler, there must have been a clear sense of purpose if he were to ignore the fiscal constraints of a financially strained nation and spearhead such a large-scale initiative. Even if it remains speculative and difficult to fully substantiate, presenting a discourse on this issue could have been a meaningful alternative.

In 2023, Paek-ch'ŏl Kim published a new book compiling his previous articles to offer a fresh perspective on King Chŏngjo's image as a monarch. The book begins with an introductory chapter that provides the research background, reviews prior studies, and outlines the central research questions, followed by three main sections.

Kim's central research question critiques earlier studies that emphasize the fragility of Chŏngjo's royal authority. He challenges the prevailing view of Chŏngjo as a ruler who struggled with weak kingship during the early years of his reign and failed to complete his reforms, arguing that this perspective is a misconception. The stated purpose of his study is to illuminate the true nature of Chŏngjo's kingship.

In Part 1, Kim examines Chŏngjo's role as a successor to *t'angp'yŏng*. According to Kim, the notion of Chŏngjo's unstable kingship during the early years of his reign—widely assumed in most studies—was intentionally fabricated by Chŏngjo himself. The claims of assassination threats described in the *Chonhyŏn'gak Ilgi* were, Kim argues, a deliberate move to expose the threats posed by opposing factions during his time as Crown Prince, thereby providing justification for suppressing rebellion. Kim questions whether a ruler with truly fragile authority would openly reveal such vulnerabilities.

According to Kim, within six months of ascending to the throne, Chŏngjo had decisively removed all close relatives, including maternal and paternal in-laws. He also exposed the conspiracy of criminal plots against the palace and annihilated the remaining adversaries. These actions, carried out with resolute and bold determination, would have been impossible for a ruler with weak authority. After quelling minor rebellions in the subsequent period, Chŏngjo reached the pinnacle of his power and positioned himself as a strong arbiter of disputes.

Kim argues that during this phase, Chŏngjo returned to the principle of *Hwanggŭk T'angp'yŏng* based on the factional dissolution policies of his predecessors.

Part 2 defines Chŏngjo as a "guardian of national law." By analyzing the legal code *Taejŏn T'ongp'yŏn* (The legal code published during King Jeongjo's reign 大典通編), compiled during Chŏngjo's reign, Paek-ch'ŏl Kim examines the king's reform policies and state administration. Kim argues that the compilation of the *Taejŏn T'ongp'yŏn* represents the culmination of the legislative reforms initiated by the *t'angp'yŏng* monarchs, including Kings Sukchong and Yŏngjo, and embodies the political aspirations of the *t'angp'yŏng* era. In this context, the *Taejŏn T'ongp'yŏn* adhered to the general direction established by the earlier *Soktaejŏn*.

However, while *Soktaejŏn* focused primarily on the Penal Code, *Taejŏn T'ongp'yŏn* centered on the Military Code, reflecting Chŏngjo's military reforms. With a strong commitment to military affairs, Chŏngjo frequently utilized royal excursions as opportunities to conduct military training. He also boosted military morale by appointing talented individuals from the northwestern provinces, known for their martial vigor. All these efforts were part of Chŏngjo's strategy to cultivate a loyal and capable personal military force.

Part 3, titled "The Memory Wars of the *T'angp'yŏng* Era," emphasizes that the discourse on *Silhak* (Practical Learning 實學) was shaped by biases against Neo-Confucianism and the logic of civilization propagated by Imperial Japan. According to Kim, during the modernization efforts following the opening of Korea's ports, the reigns of Kings Yŏngjo and Chŏngjo, along with Practical Learning, were reinterpreted as models of tradition. This trend persisted beyond the Korean Empire and into the period of forced annexation by Japan. Ultimately, lingering regret over unfulfilled reforms was projected onto this reinterpretation, giving rise to a "memory war."

Kim argues that the image of Chŏngjo as a reformist monarch who left his reforms incomplete due to fragile royal authority is an illusion crafted by later generations. In reality, Chŏngjo was a powerful *t'angp'yŏng* monarch and a steadfast guardian of national law from the very beginning of his reign.[29]

Kim Paek-ch'ŏl's research effectively captures one of the most crucial aspects of history: the continuity of time. The 18th century in Chosŏn was a period when the reigns of Yŏngjo and Chŏngjo overlapped, and the keyword continuation and transmission is indispensable in defining their kingships. Nevertheless, much of the existing scholarship neglects not only the preceding era but also the continuity between Yŏngjo and Chŏngjo.

In contrast, Kim Paek-ch'ŏl explains Chŏngjo's *t'angp'yŏng* and policies on the premise of succession from Yŏngjo. This approach allows for a comparative understanding of the two monarchs' responses to the political challenges and characteristics of 18th-century Chosŏn politics. During this era, the raison d'être of political factions transformed into a mechanism for determining royal legitimacy. Both Yŏngjo and Chŏngjo struggled to prove their legitimacy, and this struggle manifested in the form of *t'angp'yŏng* policies.

However, the two monarchs approached *t'angp'yŏng* governance in markedly different ways. Yŏngjo structured his *t'angp'yŏng* policies around moderate and adopted methods that suppressed debates on factional disputes altogether. In contrast, Chŏngjo's governance focused on more rigid figures, strictly adjudicating factional disputes and emphasizing clear distinctions between right and wrong.

Highlighting these differences can provide deeper insight into Chŏngjo's statecraft and governance strategies. However, this does not necessarily suggest that Yŏngjo failed in his *t'angp'yŏng* efforts or that Chŏngjo successfully established a balanced governance system. The determination of success depends on the criteria applied. As Paek-ch'ŏl Kim argues, Chŏngjo's reforms were not a completed endeavor.

As Hyŏn-mo Park has pointed out, King Chŏngjo could not be entirely absolved of responsibility for the rise of politics dominated by powerful aristocratic families. Chŏngjo's monarch-centered theories of *t'angp'yŏng* and military governance ultimately dismantled mechanisms of public discourse and checks and balances. Furthermore, *Kim Cho-sun* (1765~1832), to whom Chŏngjo delegated considerable power, marked the beginning of the politics dominated by powerful aristocratic families dominance of the Andong Kim clan.

Many of the reforms initiated by Chŏngjo were either discontinued or abolished after his death, leaving them with little lasting impact.

On the other hand, the nature of Chŏngjo's "reforms" must also be considered. Alongside the Chŏngjo series, Sŏng-hwan Ch'oe has interpreted Chŏngjo's reforms as a "restoration of Neo-Confucian order." Ch'oe argues that the portrayal of Chŏngjo as an enlightened despot or absolutist monarch, as suggested in some quarters, stems from traditions similar to those underpinning the militaristic state-building efforts of the *Meiji Restoration*.

Chŏngjo's reforms, as Kim Paek-ch'ŏl contended, were not focused on resolving the challenges of the era or improving the lives of the people. Considering that most of Chŏngjo's reforms ended in incompletion or failure, it is difficult to agree with Kim's evaluation that they represented a completed or fully realized reform agenda.[30]

The author challenges the prevailing academic consensus that Chŏngjo struggled with an unstable position and weakened royal authority during the early years of his reign. Notably, the author makes the striking claim that the "assassination threat" narrative was a fabrication orchestrated by Chŏngjo himself to justify campaigns against his enemies. While this is undoubtedly an intriguing perspective, it cannot rest on circumstantial evidence alone.

The majority of studies and historical records accept the "assassination threat" as fact. Articles from the *Chonhyŏn'gak Ilgi* claim that Chŏngjo's royal authority was firmly established from the beginning of his reign is also difficult to accept. The image of the Crown Prince under duress, as portrayed in the *Chonhyŏn'gak Ilgi* was already widely shared among officials at court. Moreover, the veritable records of the Yŏngjo contains accounts illustrating the precarious position of the Crown Prince.[31]

Given the substantial evidence supporting Chŏngjo's tenuous position, any attempt to refute it requires stronger evidence and sharper reasoning. The disclosure of assassination threats by Chŏngjo was likely not a reflection of strong royal authority but rather an effort to strengthen the justification for eliminating his political rivals. This becomes particularly evident when considering the unique nature of the individuals targeted for suppression.

The majority of studies and historical records accept the "assassination threat" as fact. Articles from the *Chonhyŏn'gak Ilgi* and the veritable records of the Chŏngjo substantiate this narrative. To refute it, one would need either new historical sources or a compelling alternative argument. However, the author's assertions remain speculative, supported only by minimal evidence bolstering his claims. Based on this limited foundation, dismissing the "assassination threat" as a fabrication appears premature.

Punishing close relatives would have been far more challenging than dealing with other officials of similar rank. For instance, non-relatives like Kim Sang-no were swiftly punished shortly after Chŏngjo's ascension. His lack of familial ties to Chŏngjo made such an action feasible.[32]

In contrast, punishing royal relatives required stronger evidence and justification. Chŏngjo may have documented confidential incidents occurring within the royal palace to serve as evidence for such actions. Consequently, the issue at hand is not the strength or weakness of royal authority but rather the unique circumstances surrounding the individuals targeted for punishment.

The overarching theme in discussions about Chŏngjo's monarchic philosophy has centered on his reforms, particularly their direction and intent. T'ae-jin Yi interprets Chŏngjo's reign as a period marked by monarch-led reform efforts amid the early development of commercial capitalism. Yi characterizes Chŏngjo as a "Confucian enlightened absolutist monarch," a figure perceived as a savior capable of rescuing Chosŏn on the brink of decline.

For Hyŏn-mo Park, Chŏngjo was a politician who pursued reforms but ultimately failed to achieve them. Despite his abilities and efforts, Park argues, Chŏngjo could not overcome his inherent limitations. Nevertheless, to Pak, Chŏngjo remains a reformist monarch who strove toward change.

Lovins offers a contrasting perspective. Lovins interprets many of Chŏngjo's reform initiatives as measures to expand royal prerogatives. Based on this premise, Lovins also defines him as an "enlightened absolutist monarch." Policies often labeled as "reforms" by many Korean scholars were, in Lovins' view, less about societal change and more about transactions with the yangban elite aimed at strengthening royal authority.

The Chŏngjo portrayed in the collected series on his reign emerges as a guardian of orthodoxy and Neo-Confucianism. Nonetheless, even within this framework, Chŏngjo remains a reformist monarch. The distinction lies in the direction of his reforms, which were oriented toward restoring ancient systems and rituals.

For Paek-ch'ŏl Kim, Chŏngjo was an assertive and strong monarch who actively led the political arena. He was a reformist king who carried forward the policies of his predecessors and completed his reforms. Kim argues that depicting Chŏngjo as a weak ruler or characterizing his reforms as incomplete are distortions introduced by later generations.

King Chŏngjo aspired to embody the ideal ruler who stood at the center of military and state governance while realizing Neo-Confucian ideals. He followed the path laid by his grandfather, King Yŏngjo, a point acknowledged by all studies on the subject. Chŏngjo's dominance in political affairs and the stability of his royal authority were made possible by his presentation of himself as an exemplary monarch who pursued both military strength and moral governance.

However, there are clear differences in how Yŏngjo and Chŏngjo are evaluated. While Yŏngjo's theory of kingship focused on the image of a ruler striving to reach the ideal of a "Neo-Confucian sage king," Chŏngjo's theory emphasized the "reform politics" of an ideal monarch. While interpretations of the direction and outcomes of these reforms vary, much of the existing research focuses more on the results of Chŏngjo's reforms rather than the process. This is why this section is titled "The Reformist Monarch."

One term that appears repeatedly in discussions of Chŏngjo's governance—far more frequently than in evaluations of Yŏngjo—is expediental means. With the exception of T'ae-jin Yi's exploratory study, works by Hyŏn-mo Park, Lovins, the Chŏngjo Series, and Paek-ch'ŏl Kim all frequently reference *kwŏndo* when describing Chŏngjo's governance. This consistent emphasis makes it reasonable to characterize Chŏngjo's rule as "the politics of expediency."

The lack of in-depth analyses on Chŏngjo's kwŏndo theory is somewhat surprising, especially given its centrality in existing studies. As discussions of Chŏngjo's theory of governance evolve, future research clarifying the relationship between his governance and the concept of *expediental means* would be highly valuable.

4. Conclusion

The study thus far has conducted a comprehensive analysis of the governance of Kings Yŏngjo and Chŏngjo, examining the flow of time to contextualize their reigns. A joint review of their theories of kingship reveals a shared keyword that encapsulates both monarchs: the "Neo-Confucian ideal monarch." Given that Chosŏn was founded on Neo-Confucianism as its state ideology and that its principles shaped the governance of state and society, this designation might appear natural. However, one might question why this label is uniquely associated with Yŏngjo and Chŏngjo. Is it because they were monarchs who, for a brief period, managed to sustain the declining Chosŏn dynasty during the 18th century?

Another significant similarity between the two monarchs emerges: both faced doubts about their legitimacy as rulers and had to actively demonstrate the justness of their succession to the throne. Unlike the early Chosŏn kings, whose legitimacy was inherently secured by their royal bloodline, Yŏngjo and Chŏngjo operated under very different circumstances.

Following the *Imjin* and *Chŏngmyo* Wars, the Injo Restoration, and the Ritual Controversies, the authority of the royal family had significantly diminished. Kings could no longer rely solely on their lineage to be seen as unquestionable rulers; instead, they had to actively demonstrate their capabilities and justify their authority to govern.

The inability of a king to stand at the center of governance represented a fundamental disruption to the foundations of the dynasty, and the crisis of late Chosŏn may have originated from this shift. This was the challenge of the era that both Yŏngjo and Chŏngjo had to confront. Yŏngjo sought to meet this challenge and establish his legitimacy by embodying the Neo-Confucian ideal monarch, a strategy that allowed him to secure a certain degree of dominance over political affairs. However, he ultimately failed to resolve the broader systemic issues of the time, leaving the burden of addressing these unresolved challenges to his successor, Chŏngjo.

Chŏngjo inherited Yŏngjo's methods, adopting a similar approach to position himself at the center of governance. He then sought to address the challenges he identified as defining his era, an endeavor referred to as "reform." This may explain why Yŏngjo is often associated with the "theory of the sage king," while Chŏngjo is described through the "theory of the reformist monarch."

A growing trend in scholarship seeks to analyze the governance of Yŏngjo and Chŏngjo within the context of their respective times. As exemplified in the *Chŏngjo Series*, this perspective underscores the importance of understanding these monarchs through the lens of contemporary values, rather than projecting later desires or intentions onto them. In Chosŏn, kings were posthumously granted honorific titles and additional honorifics by their successors. These titles reflected evaluations made within the historical context of their own time, addressing the needs and values of that era.

Both Yŏngjo and Chŏngjo likely established their political goals and pursued them in alignment with the demands of their respective periods. Their efforts corresponded with the conditions expected of monarchs in the late Chosŏn dynasty. The authority they sought as rulers was shaped by the expectations and requirements of their time.

Ultimately, the theories of governance developed by Yŏngjo and Chŏngjo may provide answers to questions about the origins of a monarch's authority and the qualities demanded of rulers by their era. Therefore, it is worth considering their theories of kingship more deeply within their historical context. Are sage kings a product of their contemporary circumstances, or are they creations of history?

While examining the theories of kingship of Yŏngjo and Chŏngjo, certain limitations become apparent. As discussed, the two rulers share significant continuity and similarity in their governance. Nevertheless, there is a noticeable lack of studies that examine their theories of governance in a sequential and interconnected manner.

Although studies by scholars such as Pak Kwang-yong and Kim Sŏng-yun compare Yŏngjo and Chŏngjo's *t'angp'yŏng* policies, these works approach the two rulers primarily from the perspective of *t'angp'yŏng*.[33] From the perspective of theories of kingship, no substantial comparative research exists to date.

However, Paek-ch'ŏl Kim's book employs a somewhat similar methodological approach, demonstrating a degree of continuity between the two monarchs' theories of governance. Even so, his work treats Yŏngjo and Chŏngjo as separate research subjects, which limits its ability to capture the response of Chosŏn monarchs to the 18th century's challenges in a comprehensive and interconnected way.

History is a discipline rooted in the concept of temporality. Building upon the research accumulated thus far, it is now necessary to seek new perspectives that allow us to view the theories of governance of these two monarchs as part of a unified historical continuum.

The most frequently encountered terms in introductory or general narratives of Korean history are likely "centralization" and "strengthening royal authority". From the early state period characterized by confederated kingdoms to the Three Kingdoms and South-North States eras, and through Koryŏ and Chosŏn, political developments have consistently been described as the "progression of centralization and the strengthening of royal authority."

But has Korean history truly been a continuous trajectory of centralization and the enhancement of royal authority? Is it not possible to explain the evolution of political history without relying on this framework?

The keyword "strengthening royal authority" also prominently features in the theories of kingship of Yŏngjo and Chŏngjo. As discussed in the preceding studies, both monarchs struggled to secure strong royal authority. After arduous efforts, they reached the point where they could declare, "I alone am the state," thereby attaining transcendent authority and unilaterally steering political affairs. By invoking expediental means, they overcame opposition from their ministers and reached the zenith of their reigns.

Most studies interpret this as evidence of strengthened royal authority and regard it as a form of "success." But is this interpretation truly valid? In the context of the Chosŏn dynasty, ideal governance was characterized by *Collaborative Governance between Sovereign and Officials*, or "joint rule by the king and his ministers." The strengthening of royal authority and unilateral rule by the monarch diverge significantly from the ideal political vision of Chosŏn. Such an evaluation seems misaligned with two rulers who spent their lives striving to become Neo-Confucian sage kings.

It is time to move away from analyzing the strength or weakness of royal authority when discussing their governance and theories of kingship. Instead, we should evaluate how closely their rule aligned with their intentions and goals, how they sought to address the challenges of their era, and what lessons their governance offers us today. Such approaches could provide a more meaningful lens through which to examine their theories of kingship.

Note

1 JaHyun Kim Haboush discusses these developments in "Constructing the Center: The Ritual Controversy and the Search for a New Identity in Seventeenth-Century Korea," in JaHyun Kim Haboush and Martina Deuchlereds. *Culture and the State in Late Chosŏn Korea*, Cambridge, MA: Harvard University Asia Center, 1999, pp. 46–70.

2 Toshio Ishii, "Kōki Richō Tōsōshi ni Tsuite no Ichikōsatsu—*Kōki Richō Rigaku Jōshūshugi Kokka Shakai no Shōchō Yori Mitai"*(A Study on the History of Factional Struggles in the Late Joseon Dynasty—From the Perspective of the Rise and Fall of the Neo-Confucian Supremacist State and Society in the Late Joseon Dynasty), *Shakai Keizaishi Gaku* Vol. 10, 1940, pp. 6–7 ; Seong Nak-hun, *Han'guktangjaengsa*(History of Factional Struggles in Korea), Seoul:KoreaUniversity Institute of Korean Culture, 1965 ; Lee Jae-ho, t'angp'yŏngjŏngch'aegŭi ponjilgo(sang)(A Study on the Nature of Tangpyeong Policy (Part I)), *Pusan National University Journal*, Vol. 1, 1981, pp. 45–72 ; Park Kwang-yong, "Chosŏnhugi t'angp'yŏngjŏngch'aek yŏn'gu"(A Study on Tangpyeong in the Late Joseon Period), PhD diss., Department of Korean History, Seoul National University, 1994 ; Kim Sung-yoon, *Cosŏnhugi t'angp'yŏngjŏngch'i yŏn'gu*(A Study on Tangpyeong Politics in the Late Joseon Perio), Seoul:Jisik Sanupsa, 1997 ; Lee Geun-ho, *Chosŏnhugi t'angp'yŏngp'aŭi kukchŏngunyŏng*(The Governance of the Tangpyeong Faction in the Late Joseon Period) , Seoul:Minsokwon, 2016.

3 Among the critiques of the *theory of internal development*, relatively balanced perspectives can be found in the following works: Park Chan-seung, *"Han'gukhak yŏn'gu p'aerŏdaimŭl tullŏssan nonŭi: naejaejŏk paljŏllonŭl chungsimŭro"*(Discussions on the Paradigm of Korean Studies: Focusing on the Theory of Internal Development), *Han'gukhangnonjip*, Vol. 35, 2007; Lee Young-ho, "Naejaejŏk paljŏllon' yŏksainsigŭi kwejŏkkwa chŏnmang"(The Trajectory and Prospects of Historical Perceptions of the 'Theory of Internal Development', *Han'guksayŏn'gu* Vol. 152, 2011; Kwon Nae-hyun, Naejaejŏk paljŏllon'gwa Chosŏn hugisa insik(The Theory of Internal Development and Perceptions of Late Joseon History), *Yŏksabip'yŏng,* Vol. 111, 2015; Ch'oejongsŏk, "Naejaejŏk paljŏllon 'ihu'e taehan myŏt kaji komin"(Reflections on the Post-Theory of Internal Development), *Yŏksawa hyŏnsil,* Vol. 100, 2016.

4 Chŏng Yŏn-sik, *Yŏngjo dae ŭi Yangyŏk Chŏngch'aek kwa Kyunyŏkpŏp* (Taxation Policies and the Kyunyŏk Law during the Reign of King Yŏngjo), Seongnam: *Han'gukhakchungangyŏn'guwŏnch'ulp'anbu*, 2015 ; Chŏng Ok-cha, *Chŏngjoŭi Munye Sasangkwa Kyujanggak*(King Chŏngjo's Literary Thought and Kyujanggak), Seoul:Hyohyŏng, 2001 ; Kim Chŏng-ja, "Chosŏn Hugi Chŏngjo dae ŭi Chŏngguk kwa Sijŏn Chŏngch'aek: Kongsinin Sunmak ŭl Chungsim ŭro"(Political Situations and Market Policies during King Chŏngjo's Reign in the Late Joseon Dynasty: Focusing on the Investigation of Market Merchants' Hardships), *Han'gukhangnonch'ong* Vol. 147, 2013; Kim Chun-hyŏk, (*Chŏngjo ka Mandŭn Chosŏn ŭi Ch'oegang Kundae) Changyongyŏng* ((The Strongest Army of Joseon Created by King Chŏngjo) The Changyŏngyŏng), Seoul:Tŏbom, 2018.

5 JaHyun Kim Haboush, *A HERITAGE OF KINGS : One Man's Monarchy in the Confucian World*, New York : Columbia University Press, 1988 ; *The Confucian Kingship in Korea : Yŏngjo and the Politics of Sagacity*, New York : Columbia University Press, 2001.

6 In 1762, King Yŏngjo had his son, Crown Prince Sado, confined in a rice chest, leading to his death. The exact circumstances surrounding this tragic event remain unclear, as records related to the incident in the *Sŭngjŏngwŏn ilgi* (Daily Records of the Royal Secretariat) were erased at the request of Sado's son, King Chŏngjo, prior to his ascension to the throne. However, historical accounts suggest that the political climate of the time, Sado's history of mental illness, and the resulting conflicts between Yŏngjo and Sado played significant roles. There are also speculations that Crown Prince Sado may have been plotting a rebellion.

7 Yi Hee-hwan, "Yŏngjodae t'angp'yŏngch'aegŭi silsang(sang)"(Tangp'yŏng and the Politics of King Yŏngjo*) Chŏnbuk sahak* Vol. 16,1993 *;* " Yŏngjodae t'angp'yŏngch'aegŭi silsang(ha)"*, Chŏnbuk sahak,* Vol. 17, 1994.

8 Kim Baek-chul, "Chosŏnhugi *Y*ŏngjodae t'angp'yŏngjŏngch'iŭi inyŏmgwa Churye"(The Ideology of Tangpyeong Politics during King Yŏngjo's Reign and the Zhouli), *Han'guksaron* Vol. 51, 2005 : *Chosŏnhugi Yŏngjoŭi t'angp'yŏngjŏngch'i : 『soktaejŏn』ŭi p'yŏnch'an'gwa paeksŏngŭi chaeinsik*(Tangpyeong Politics of King Yŏngjo in the Late Chosŏn Period: Compilation of the Sok Daejeon and the Re-evaluation of the People), Seoul: Taehaksa, 2010 ; *Tuŏlgurŭi yŏngjo : 18segi t'angp'yŏnggunjusangŭi chaegŏmt'o*(The Two Faces of King Yŏngjo: A Reappraisal of the 18th-Century Tangpyeong Monarch*)*, Seoul: Taehaksa, 2014.

9 Kim, Baek-chul. *Tuŏlgurŭi yŏngjo : 18segi t'angp'yŏnggunjusangŭi chaegŏmt'o*(The Two Faces of King Yŏngjo: A Reappraisal of the 18th-Century Tangpyeong Monarch*),* Seoul: Taehaksa, 2014, pp. 137-141.

10 Choo Chae-young," Yŏngjoŭi kukchŏngunyŏng pangsik yŏn'gu"(A Study on King Yŏngjo's Governance Method), PhD diss., Sogang University, 2022, pp. 94–98.

11 Yŏngjo expanded the Daebodan Shrine and, despite opposition from his officials, strongly pursued the enshrinement of Emperor Hongwu. He also expressed admiration for the absolute authority wielded by Emperor Qin Shi Huang. See, Seung B. Kye, *Chŏngjidoen sigan : Chosŏnŭi taebodan'gwa kŭndaeŭi munt'ŏk*(Frozen Time: Chosŏn's Daebodan and the Threshold of Modernity*),* Seoul: Sogang University Press, 2011, pp. 132-134 ; Chŏng Kyung-hee, "Yŏngjohuban'gi(1749-177) kyŏngyŏn'gwa yŏngjoŭi ŭiriron kanghwa"(The Strengthening of Ethical Principles during King Yŏngjo's Later Years (1749-1776) and Royal Lectures), *Yŏksahakpo* Vol. 162 ,1999, p. 54.

12 The *Seonghak Jibyo* (聖學輯要, *Essentials of the Learning of the Sages*) is a book written in 1575 by Yi I, a Chosŏn scholar and statesman, to guide the academic and moral development of monarchs. Yi I compiled this work by extracting the core principles of *Dao* from the *Four Books* and *Six Classics*. He described it as a guide intended to help kings adhere to the path of righteousness in governance.

13 Yoon Jung, "Yŏngjoŭi sŏnghakchipyo chin'ganggwa chŏngch'aekchŏk hwaryong"(King Yŏngjo's Royal Lectures on The Seonghak Jibyo (聖學輯要, *Essentials of the Learning of the Sages*) and Its Policy Applications), *Han'gungmunhwa*, Vol. 38, 2006, p. 305.

14 Choo Chae-young, "Yŏngjoŭi kukchŏngunyŏng pangsik yŏn'gu"(A Study on King Yŏngjo's Governance Method*),* PhD diss., Sogang University, 2022.

15 Christopher Lovins*, King Chŏngjo, An Enlightened Despot in Early Modern Korea,* Albany, NY: State University of New York, 2019.

16 Yi, Tae-jin. Tangjaengŭl ŏttŏk'e pol kŏsin'ga (How Should We Understand Factional Struggles?), *Dansu* Vol. 14, 1985.

17 Yi, Tae-jin. Chŏngjo - yugyojŏk kyemongjŏldaegunju(King Chŏngjo —A Confucian Enlightened Absolute Monarch), Seoul:*Han'guksa simin'gangjwa* Vol. 13, 1993.

18 Collected Writings of King Chŏngjo.

19 Park Hyun-mo, *Chŏngch'iga Chŏngjo* (The Politician Chŏngjo*),* Seoul: P'urŭnyŏksa, 2001.

20 Park Hyun-mo*, Chŏngch'iga Chŏngjo* (The Politician Chŏngjo*),* Seoul: P'urŭnyŏksa, 2001, p. 25.

21 Park Hyun-mo, *Chŏngjo sahu 63nyŏn : sedo chŏngch'igiŭi kungnaeoe chŏngch'iyŏn'gu*(63 Years After Chŏngjo: A Study of Domestic and Foreign Politics During the Sedo Period). Seoul: Changbi, 2011.

22 The political systems of East Asia, including the Korean Peninsula, fulfilled the conditions of early modernity as outlined by Lovins during the stage of ancient states. Even within the Korean dynastic context, as early as the Koryŏ period, there existed centralization, a bureaucratic structure, and monarchs recognized as unique and legitimate rulers. However, the tendency to schematically apply criteria derived from European historical contexts to Korean history is an approach that should now be reconsidered. Such critiques themselves have become repetitive and somewhat overused in academic discussions.

23 Christopher Lovins, *King Chŏngjo, An Enlightened Despot in Early Modern Korea*, Albany, NY: State University of New York Press, 2019, pp. 5–6.

24 The *Chŏnhaenggak ilgi* is a diary in which Chŏngjo documented the political environment surrounding him prior to his ascension to the throne, vividly recording the threats posed by opposing factions.

25 Paek Sŭng-ho. *Chŏngjoŭi munch'i-kŭlssŭgiro inŭiŭi chŏngch'irŭl p'yŏda*(The Civil Governance of Chŏngjo: Establishing Politics of Benevolence through Writing), Seoul: Humanist, 2020.

26 Hŏ T'ae-gu. *Chŏngjoŭi much'i - munmurŭl katch'un wanjŏnhan nararŭl kkumkkuda*(The Military Governance of Chŏngjo: Dreaming of a Nation Perfectly Balanced in Civil and Military Virtues), Seoul: Humanist, 2020.

27 Kim Chi-yŏng. *Chŏngjoŭi yech'i - yerŭl parojapa paeksŏngŭi maŭmŭl kirŭda*(Chŏngjo's Ritual Governance: Rectifying Rites to Cultivate the Hearts of the People), Seoul: Humanist, 2020.

28 Kim Ho. *Chŏngjo ŭi Pŏpch'i: Pŏp ŭi Chŏulro Seŭi Barŭm ŭl Salp'ida* (Chŏngjo's Legal Governance: Examining Righteousness in the World Through the Scales of Law), Seoul: Humanist, 2020.

29 See Pak Kwang-yong, "Chosŏn Hugi "T'angp'yŏng" Yŏn'gu", PhD diss., Seoul National University, 1994 ; Kim Sŏng-yun, *Chosŏn Hugi T'angp'yŏng Chŏngch'i Yŏn'gu*, Seoul: Chisik Sanŏpsa, 1997.

30 Ch'oe Sŏng-hwan. Chosŏn Hugi Chŏngch'i ŭi Maeknak esŏ T'angp'yŏng Kunju Chŏngjo Ilgi(Reading King Chŏngjo as a *T'angp'yŏng* Monarch in the Context of Late Chosŏn Politics),*Yŏksa Pip'yŏng* Vol. 115, 2016, pp. 143-144.

31 One prominent example is found in *Yŏngjo sillok* (The veritable records of the Yŏngjo), Vol. 125, 51st year, 11th month, 20th day. On this occasion, Hong In-han declared, "The Crown Prince has no need to know about Noron or Soron, no need to know the Ministers of Personnel or War, and no need to know the affairs of the court at all (東宮不必知老論少論 不必知吏判兵判尤不必知朝事矣)." Other high officials present that day agreed with Hong's remarks.

32 According to *Chŏngjo sillok*(The veritable records of the Chŏngjo), Vol. 1, Accession Year, 3rd month, 30th day, Chŏngjo used King Yŏngjo's will as a pretext to punish Kim Sang-No.

33 See Pak Kwang-yong, "Chosŏn Hugi "T'angp'yŏng" Yŏn'gu", PhD diss., Seoul National University, 1994; Kim Sŏng-yun, *Chosŏn Hugi T'angp'yŏng Chŏngch'i Yŏn'gu*, Seoul: Chisik Sanŏpsa, 1997.

Bibliography

Primary Sources

Yŏngjo sillok (The veritable records of the Yŏngjo)
Chŏngjo sillok (The veritable records of the Chŏngjo)

Secondary Sources

Ch'oe, Jongsŏk, "Naejaejŏk paljŏllon 'ihu'e taehan myŏt kaji komin" (Reflections on the Post-Theory of Internal Development), *Yŏksawa hyŏnsil,* Vol. 100, 2016.

Ch'oe, Sŏng–hwan, "Chosŏn Hugi Chŏngch'i ŭi Maeknakesŏ T'angp'yŏng Kunju Chŏngjo Ilgi"(Reading King Chŏngjo as a *T'angp'yŏng* Monarch in the Context of Late Chosŏn Politics), *Yŏksa Pip'yŏng* Vol. 115, 2016.

Chŏng, Kyung–hee, "Yŏngjohuban'gi(1749~177) kyŏngyŏn'gwa Yŏngjoŭi ŭiriron kanghwa"(The Strengthening of Ethical Principles during King Yŏngjo's Later Years (1749-1776) and Royal Lectures), *Yŏksahakpo* Vol. 162, 1999.

Chŏng, Ok–cha, *Chŏngjoŭi Munye Sasangkwa Kyujanggak* (KingChŏngjo's Literary Thought and Kyujanggak), Seoul: Hyohyŏng, 2001.

Chŏng, Yŏn–sik, *Yŏngjodaeŭi Yangyŏk Chŏngch'aekkwa Kyunyŏkpŏp* (Taxation Policies and the Kyunyŏk Law during the Reign of King Yŏngjo),Seongnam: *Han'gukhakchungangyŏn'guwŏnch'ulp'anbu*, 2015.

Choo, Chae–young, "Yŏngjoŭi kukchŏngunyŏng pangsik yŏn'gu"(A Study on King Yŏngjo's Governance Method), PhD diss., Sogang University, 2022.

Haboush, JaHyun Kim, "Constructing the Center: The Ritual Controversy and the Search for a New Identity in Seventeenth-Century Korea", in JaHyun Kim Haboush and Martina Deuchler eds. *Culture and the State in Late Chosŏn Korea*, Cambridge, MA: Harvard University Asia Center, 1999.

________, *A HERITAGE OF KINGS: One Man's Monarchy in the Confucian World*, New York: Columbia University Press, 1988; *The Confucian Kingship in Korea: Yŏngjo and the Politics of Sagacity*, New York: Columbia University Press, 2001.

Hŏ, T'ae-gu. *Chŏngjoŭi much'i - munmurŭl katch'un wanjŏnhan nararŭl kkumkkuda*(The Military Governance of Chŏngjo: Dreaming of a Nation Perfectly Balanced in Civil and Military Virtues), Seoul: Humanist, 2020.

Kim, Baek–chul, "Chosŏnhugi Yŏngjodae t'angp'yŏngjŏngch'iŭi inyŏmgwa Churye"(The Ideology of Tangpyeong Politics during King Yŏngjo's Reign and the Zhouli), *Han'guksaron* Vol. 51, 2005.

________, *Chosŏnhugi Yŏngjoŭi t'angp'yŏngjŏngch'i: 『Soktaejŏn』 ŭi p'yŏnch'an'gwa paeksŏngŭi chaeinsik*(Tangpyeong Politics of King Yŏngjo in the Late Chosŏn Period: Compilation of the Sok Daejeon and the Re–evaluation of the People), Seoul: Taehaksa, 2010.

________, *Tuŏlgurŭi Yŏngjo : 18segi t'angp'yŏnggunjusangŭi chaegŏmt'o* (The Two Faces of King Yŏngjo: A Reappraisal of the 18th–Century Tangpyeong Monarch*)*, Seoul: Taehaksa, 2014.

Kim, Chi–yŏng. *Chŏngjoŭi yech'i - yerŭl parojapa paeksŏngŭi maŭmŭl kirŭda*(Chŏngjo's Ritual Governance: Rectifying Rites to Cultivate the Hearts of the People), Seoul: Humanist, 2020.

Kim, Chŏng–ja, "Chosŏn Hugi Chŏngjodaeŭi Chŏnggukkwa Sijŏn Chŏngch'aek: Kongsinin Sunmakŭl Chungsimŭro"(Political Situations and Market Policies during King Chŏngjo's Reign in the Late Chosŏn Dynasty: Focusing on the Investigation of Market Merchants' Hardships), *Han'gukhangnonch'ong,* Vol. 147, 2013.

Kim, Chun–hyŏk, (*Chŏngjo ka Mandŭn Chosŏn ŭi Ch'oegang Kundae) Changyongyŏng* (The Strongest Army of Chosŏn Created by King Chŏngjo) The Changyŏngyŏng, Seoul: Tŏbom, 2018.

Kim, Ho, *Chŏngjo ŭi Pŏpch'i: Pŏp ŭi Chŏulro Seŭi Barŭm ŭl Salp'ida* (Chŏngjo's Legal Governance: Examining Righteousness in the World Through the Scales of Law), Seoul: Humanist, 2020.

Kim, Sung–yoon, *Cosŏnhugi t'angp'yŏngjŏngch'i yŏn'gu*(A Study on Tangpyeong Politics in the Late Joseon Perio), Seoul:Jisik Sanupsa, 1997.

Kwon, Nae–hyun, "Naejaejŏk paljŏllon'gwa Chosŏn hugisa insik"(The Theory of Internal Development and Perceptions of Late Chosŏn History), *Yŏksabip'yŏng* Vol. 111, 2015.

Kye, Seung B., *Chŏngjidoen sigan : Chosŏnŭi taebodan'gwa kŭndaeŭi munt'ŏk*(Frozen Time: Joseon's Daebodan and the Threshold of Modernity*)*, Seoul: Sogang University Press, 2011.

Lee, Geun–ho, *Chosŏnhugi t'angp'yŏngp'aŭi kukchŏngunyŏng*(The Governance of the Tangpyeong Faction in the Late Chosŏn Period), Seoul:Minsokwon, 2016.

Lee, Hee–hwan, "Yŏngjodae t'angp'yŏngch'aegŭi silsang(sang)"(Tangp'yŏng and the Politics of King Yŏngjo*) Chŏnbuk sahak,* Vol. 16, 1993.

________, Yŏngjodae t'angp'yŏngch'aegŭi silsang(ha)*, Chŏnbuk sahak,* Vol. 17, 1994.

Lee, Jae-ho, "T'angp'yŏngjŏngch'aegŭi ponjilgo(sang)"(A Study on the Nature of Tangpyeong Policy (Part I)), *Pusan National University Journal* Vol. 1, 1981.

Lee, Young-ho, Naejaejŏk paljŏllon' yŏksainsigŭi kwejŏkkwa chŏnmang(The Trajectory and Prospects of Historical Perceptions of the 'Theory of Internal Development', Seoul: *Han'guksayŏn'gu* Vol. 152, 2011.

Lovins, Christopher, *King Chŏngjo, An Enlightened Despot in Early Modern Korea,* Albany, NY: State University of New York, 2019.

Park, Chan-seung, "Han'gukhak yŏn'gu p'aerŏdaimŭl tullŏssan nonŭi: naejaejŏk paljŏllonŭl chungsimŭro"(Discussions on the Paradigm of Korean Studies: Focusing on the Theory of Internal Development), Seoul:*Han'gukhangnonjip* Vol. 35, 2007.

Park, Hyun-mo, *Chŏngch'iga Chŏngjo* (The Politician Chŏngjo*),* Seoul: P'urŭnyŏksa, 2001.

Park, Kwang–yong, "Chosŏnhugi t'angp'yŏngjŏngch'aek yŏn'gu*"*(Study on Tangpyeong in the Late Chosŏn Period), PhD diss., Department of Korean History, Seoul National University, 1994.

Paek, Sŭng-ho, *Chŏngjoŭi munch'i-kŭlssŭgiro inŭiŭi chŏngch'irŭl p'yŏda*(The Civil Governance of Chŏngjo: Establishing Politics of Benevolence through Writing), Seoul: Humanist, 2020.

Seong, Nak-hun, *Han'guktangjaengsa*(History of Factional Struggles in Korea), Seoul:Korea University Institute of Korean Culture, 1965.

Toshio Ishii, "Kōki Richō Tōsōshi ni Tsuite no Ichikōsatsu—Kōki Richō Rigaku Jōshūshugi Kokka Shakai no Shōchō Yori Mitai"(A Study on the History of Factional Struggles in the Late Joseon Dynasty—From the Perspective of the Rise and Fall of the Neo-Confucian Supremacist State and Society in the Late Joseon Dynasty), *Shakai Keizaishi Gaku* Vol. 10, 1940.

Yi, Tae-jin. "Tangjaengŭl ŏttŏk'e pol kŏsin'ga"(How Should We Understand Factional Struggles?), *Dansu* Vol. 14, 1985.

_______, Chŏngjo - yugyojŏk kyemongjŏldaegunju(King Chŏngjo —A Confucian Enlightened Absolute Monarch), *Han'guksa simin'gangjwa* Vol. 13, 1993.

Yoon, Jung, "Yŏngjoŭi Sŏnghakchipyo chin'ganggwa chŏngch'aekchŏk hwaryong"(King Yŏngjo's Royal Lectures on The Seonghak Jibyo (聖學輯要, Essentials of the Learning of the Sages) and Its Policy Applications), *Han'gungmunhwa*, Vol. 38, 2006.

5

Establishment of the Confucian Family System and Changes in Women's Status in Chosŏn: A Focus on Existing Studies from Korean and American Academia

Karam Kim

Sogang University

5 Establishment of the Confucian Family System and Changes in Women's Status in Chosŏn: A Focus on Existing Studies from Korean and American Academia

Karam Kim (Sogang University)

1. Introduction

In 1392, Chosŏn was established with the goal of becoming a Confucian state, but it took considerable time to fully embody the characteristics of a Confucian society. This was due to the challenge of transitioning from the Buddhist ideology that had been deeply ingrained in the Korean Peninsula for over a millennium to Confucian principles. Even the royal court, expected to serve as a role model, established a Buddhist shrine (*Naebultang*, 內佛堂) in Kyŏngbok Palace and constructed temples near royal tombs during the early Chosŏn period. The number of people practicing Confucian mourning rites, such as the three-year mourning ritual, was also limited. In other words, the image of Chosŏn as a Confucian society, as we envision today, only emerged well after its founding. Despite this, Korean historiography for a long time viewed Chosŏn through the lens of its identity as a Confucian society, paying little attention to how it underwent this transformation into a Confucian state. Particularly in the 20th century, Korean historians focused on breaking away from colonial historiography, interpreting Chosŏn's changes mainly in terms of political, social, and economic developments toward modernization. Consequently, research on Confucianism as a framework for understanding Chosŏn was largely limited to studies of Confucian classics (*kyŏnghak*, 經學) and Confucian rituals (*yehak*, 禮學).

English-language scholarship posed new questions to this traditional perspective. In 1992, Martina Deuchler published *The Confucian Transformation of Korea: A Study of Society and Ideology*[1] (Cambridge, Mass: Council on East Asian Studies, Harvard University), which explored the transformation of Chosŏn society. This work examined the establishment of Confucian patriarchal order in Chosŏn through the introduction of Neo-Confucianism and changes in family systems. Deuchler's research generated significant impact both domestically and internationally.

Prior to Deuchler, Western academia tended to approach Chosŏn from a perspective of long-term continuity, asserting that Korean society showed little substantial change as it transitioned from Koryŏ to Chosŏn. This contrasted with Korean historiography, which interpreted the founding of Chosŏn as a significant societal transformation. Deuchler argued that while Korean society underwent gradual change overall, the transition to a Confucian society following Chosŏn's establishment marked a distinct shift. Her work offered a new interpretation that balanced the Western perspective of continuity and the Korean emphasis on transformation.

Building on this influence, Korean historians in the 21st century began to view Chosŏn not as a fully realized Confucian society but as one in the process of Confucianization, initiating research to explore this transition. Notably, studies focusing on changes in family systems and women's lives have become prominent, examining the process of internalizing and institutionalizing Confucian ethics.

The family, as both an individual's everyday space and the most basic social unit, became a focal point of state intervention in Chosŏn through legal and institutional measures. By reorganizing family hierarchy and marriage customs, Chosŏn sought to transform into a patriarchal society based on Confucian principles.

This transformation brought significant changes to women's lives. The traditional practice of *namgwi yŏgahŏn* (男歸女家婚), where the husband temporarily resided in the wife's family after marriage, was replaced by patrilocal residence. Ritual inheritance and equal division of property were reorganized around a primary heir (*sŭngjungja*, 承重者) responsible for ancestral rites. Women's roles within the family increasingly emphasized those of wives and daughters-in-law over daughters. The increasing number of women who became virtuous widows (*yŏllyŏ*, 烈女) through acts of suicide during late Chosŏn highlights the intensification of Confucian values of chastity and loyalty. These changes illustrate how family systems and women's roles reflected the Confucianization of Chosŏn society and Confucian ideology's characteristics.

This study examines how Korean and Western historians have interpreted changes in women's roles in Chosŏn through the lens of family systems. Early research on the Confucianization of Chosŏn primarily focused on political and ideological debates as well as the establishment of Confucian rituals. These studies clarified the envisioned model of Chosŏn as a Confucian state and contributed to defining its foundational structure, thereby offering a comprehensive understanding of Chosŏn as a nation. However, these macro-level studies, which explored Confucianization primarily through the lens of state and society, often overlooked the impacts on individual lives. Research focusing on changes in family systems and women's roles in Chosŏn sought to address this limitation by providing more detailed insights into these macro-level themes. Notably, by focusing on women—who constituted half of Chosŏn society but received limited attention in macro-level studies—it becomes possible to investigate how Confucian ideology was adapted and appropriated.

To achieve this, this study will first review existing research from both English-speaking and Korean academic traditions. Both academic spheres agree that the process of Confucianization in Chosŏn led to a decline in women's status and a narrowing of their spheres of activity. However, their methodologies differ. English-speaking scholars tend to approach the study of Chosŏn women from a comparative and diachronic perspective, often situating Chosŏn within broader contexts that include China and

Japan, employing interdisciplinary methodologies, or examining the entire Chosŏn period. These approaches effectively highlight the unique characteristics of Chosŏn women or the processes of change in their roles. In contrast, Korean academia focuses intensively on Chosŏn, offering detailed analyses of diverse cases. This focus enables Korean scholars to explore nuanced aspects of Chosŏn women's experiences that might otherwise be overlooked or generalized in broader comparative studies. The relative accessibility of primary sources in the Korean language and the active networks of scholars specializing in women's history further strengthen the capacity for such in-depth research in Korea.

Given these differences, collaboration and exchanges between English-speaking and Korean academic circles are essential for diversifying research on Chosŏn women and generating more comprehensive discourse. To facilitate this, it is first necessary to identify the research trends and characteristics of each academic tradition. Unfortunately, there are few studies that have explicitly compared the research approaches of these two traditions. However, several articles provide overviews of the research trends within each field.[2] Considering the overwhelming volume of research produced in Korean academia compared to English-speaking academia, a comprehensive comparison of the two fields remains challenging. Consequently, this paper will focus on the themes of family systems and changes in women's status, which have been central to both Korean and English-language research.

This endeavor is particularly significant in an era of globalization in historical studies, as it seeks to establish points of convergence between the two academic traditions through comparative analysis. By integrating the strengths of both approaches, this study can broaden the scope of Chosŏn research through the examination of diverse cases. Additionally, comparisons with other nations during the same period can further illuminate the unique characteristics of Chosŏn women and its family systems. This approach also helps clarify the Confucian social structure of Chosŏn.

Accordingly, this study will focus on changes in women's status within families as examined in English-speaking and Korean academic research on Chosŏn women's history. It will also trace shifts in research trends and the mutual influence of both academic traditions over time, culminating in a detailed discussion of the characteristics of 21st-century research.

2. Women's Studies in the Chosŏn Dynasty in English-Speaking Academia

1) 20th-Century Research: Constructing Discourses on the Confucianization of Chosŏn and Women

With the women's movement in full swing in the mid-20th century, Western academia began to take an interest in women's history. In response to this trend, North American academics also began to study women in pre-modern East Asian history, focusing on Chinese history, and in the process expanding the scope of their research to include the Confucian state of Chosŏn.

One of the most representative works in this context was The Virtues of Conflict, edited by Sandra Mattielli in 1977.[3] This book examines the status and roles of Korean women from the Chosŏn Dynasty to the present day, covering history, anthropology, sociology, psychology, and linguistics.[4] In particular, the work of Martina Deuchler, who would later become one of the foremost scholars of Chosŏn history, is included to showcase her early work. Through her analysis of Chinese, Japanese, and Korean sources and comparisons with Goryeo, Deuchler identified changes in the status of women in Chosŏn, particularly as Chosŏn bureaucrats formalized the distinction between women and men based on Confucian scriptures, which led to a decline in women's status.[5]

Focusing on papers presented at a symposium on Korean women at the annual meeting of the Asian Studies Association in Los Angeles in 1979.[6] In 1983, Laurel Kendall and Mark Peterson published Women in Korea.[7] In this symposium, Edward Wagner, through his analysis of the genealogies of two families from early Chosŏn, confirmed two key points: first, that there was little difference in status between men and women within the family; and second, that when a woman remarried, both of her husbands were recorded in the genealogies. He noted that this was a stark departure from later Chosŏn society, where Confucianization was more prevalent.[8] Mark Peterson agrees with Wagner's view, arguing that daughters and sons had nearly equal status through institutions such as rituals, inheritance of property, and adoption, which is a significant difference compared to the fact that women rarely inherited in late Chosŏn.[9]

The above studies focus on the changing status of women in Chosŏn and show that, unlike in the late Chosŏn period, women's status within the family was significantly different from that of men in the early Chosŏn period. The subsequent decline of women's status was analyzed in detail by Martina Deuchler in her 1992 work, *The Confucian Transformation of Korean Society*.[10] The book traces the social changes in Chosŏn to the introduction of Neo-Confucianism and focuses on the emergence of a patriarchal tribal society amid the gradual Confucianization of Chosŏn, including changes in hierarchical relationships within the family and the roles of family members, changes in public ceremonies and property inheritance, and changes in the status of women. In particular, She regarded the introduction and reform of Neo-Confucianism as the most significant since the reforms of Wang Anshi during the Song dynasty. In other words, early Chosŏn Confucian scholars sought to realize a far-reaching reform through the ideology of Neo-Confucianism. In the process, a highly developed patrilineal, lineage-centered society emerged.

The book caused quite a stir in Korean academia. Two to three critical reviews were published before the 2003 translation was published,[11] and four to five reviews were published after the 2003 translation was published[12]. In addition to these full-scale reviews, many Korean scholarly works on family and women in Korea published in the 21st century have also taken the book's arguments seriously. Previously, women in Korea had been portrayed as victims of a Confucian patriarchal society that diminished their status within the family. After the publication of this book, however, women in Korea were portrayed as conforming to Confucian society by practicing Confucian ethics in fulfilling their respective roles as daughters, wives, daughters-in-law, and even servants.

In 1996, Mark Peterson also published *The Creation of Confucian Society: Adoption and the Transformation of the Inheritance System in the Middle Chosŏn Dynasty*, which synthesized his research.[13] In this book, Peterson uses adoption and inheritance documents and case studies from the middle Chosŏn Dynasty to illustrate the transition to a patrilineal society centered on the firstborn. He also argues that the status of daughters declined as the inheritance and reincarnation services, which had been divided between sons and daughters, were concentrated on the firstborn son. His arguments are not very different from the works of Deuchler and other earlier scholars. However, it differs from previous studies in that it does not focus solely on Confucianism as a driver of social change in Chosŏn, but also considers various other factors in society.[14] In particular, whereas Deuchler sought to clarify the process of Confucianization of Chosŏn through neo-Confucianism by excluding political and social factors as much as possible, Peterson sought to explain the changes in Chosŏn society in a complex manner through various political and social changes.

Although there are several other individual studies, most of them follow the same line of argument as the research discussed above. Prior to 2000, Anglo-American scholarship on Chosŏn family systems and women was characterized by a focus on the changes in family systems and women's status with the advent of Confucianism. This was influenced by Western scholarship's focus on the long-term continuity of Chosŏn history. As a result, it has had a significant impact on Korean scholarship in that it has revealed a process of change that has been overlooked by Korean scholars. It clearly shows that the family and women's roles changed over time, and that Confucian understandings underlie these changes. It is also characteristic that studies of this period have tended to focus on the formation of large-scale discourses. However, there is also a danger that this may lead to a rather simplistic schematization of the Confucianization process in Chosŏn society. In short, while studies from this period effectively highlight the Confucianization of Chosŏn and its impact on family institutions and women's status, it is regrettable that they do not adequately capture the complex interplay between the Confucianizing state and the customary practices that resisted such reforms. This has led to a portrayal in which women in Chosŏn appear solely as passive subjects conforming to the established order.

2) 21st-Century Research: Examining Women's Responses within Confucian Society

In the 21st century, the study of family systems and women's history in the Chosŏn Dynasty in Anglo-American academia has undergone a transformation. First of all, while studies before the 2000s focused on creating a discourse on the family system and women in Confucianization, studies since the 2000s have attempted to diversify their research based on more sources and cases. This is a result of the development of the Internet, which has made it easier to secure data from Korea than in the past. Second, while studies before the 21st century focused on women in family relationships, studies in the 21st century focus on women alone. In this process, the study of family relationships has not progressed much compared to the past, which is a major difference from the process of Korean scholars identifying various aspects of the family based on various archival documents. Finally, while before the 21st century, research was centered on foreign scholars, the number of Korean scholars active in Anglo-American academia has increased in the 21st century. Because Korean scholars have a deep understanding of Korea, they are able to detect subtle nuances in sources and case materials, while at the same time interpreting them from a global perspective. As a result, scholarship on Chosŏn women's history in the twenty-first century has become more diverse and analytically sharper.

This change was recognized in the book *Women and Confucian Culture in Premodern China and Japan*, published in 2003.[15] Martina Deuchler and JaHyun Kim Haboush focus on Confucian female representations and language as mediators of women's inclusion in Confucian society, respectively. Deuchler points out that Confucian models of female virtue were particularly enforced upon women from elite yangban families.[16] She also emphasizes that while patriarchy was clearly a system that was unfavorable to women, women in Chosŏn Korea had historical power as essential actors in the maintenance and survival of Confucianism and the social system.[17] However, while Deuchler evaluated Chosŏn women as possessing historical power, she nevertheless interpreted them as passive rather than active agents, conforming to the social order. In other words, they are seen as attempting to secure a more advantageous position within their given circumstances in order to consolidate their own status. This becomes clearer when we compare her to Kim Jahyun Habush.

Through a comparative analysis of texts about Queen Inhyeon, Haboush argues that women who were excluded from social activities participated in shaping social discourse through writing.[18] She argues that the Korean script, a female script rather than a male script, shapes discourse outside of established male society, but in the process mobilizes the literary imagination to present an idealized image of women who practice Confucian values such as loyalty and modesty. In addition, Haboush argued that palace women, though remaining anonymous, should be regarded as cultural producers, based on sources such as the Kyech'uk ilgi (癸丑日記; Diary of the Year Kyech'uk), written by court ladies in the mid-Chosŏn period, and records of courtly material usage from the late Chosŏn dynasty.[19] Haboush, who is of Korean descent, is keenly aware of the subtleties of the Hangul language and reads its gendered elements. She also argues that even if they were excluded from social activities, women in the Chosŏn Dynasty participated in social activities as discourse shapers and culture creators.

Both Deuchler and Haboush emphasize the active role of women in Chosŏn society. Even though the advent of Confucianism made it virtuous for women to support men rather than speak up for themselves, they did speak up for themselves. Despite these commonalities, the two scholars differ fundamentally in their perspectives on women's roles and activities in Chosŏn Korea. While Deuchler's Chosŏn women were passive in that they spoke out to maintain their position, Haboush's Chosŏn women were active in that they wrote down the situation they were in and revealed their feelings and thoughts to overthrow it. Another difference is that while Deuchler's women spoke out primarily in the private space of the family, Haboush's women left their mark in the public space as well.

It is worth examining the work of John Duncan, a scholar who extended research on women from the family to society. Based on Queen Sohye's *Naehun* 內訓; Instructions for Women, Duncan participated in these debates by focusing on the agency of women within Confucian society.[20] He critiqued both the perspective that emphasizes women as victims of Confucianism and the view that acknowledges a certain degree of authority women held within the household. Instead, he highlighted Queen Sohye's active role in shaping her life by practicing Confucian virtues and promoting women's education as demanded by society. Duncan argued that *Naehun* should be viewed not merely as a vehicle for promoting Confucian norms, but as an active process by which women carried out the roles demanded by their social context. However, it remains questionable whether the activities of individuals in unique positions, such as Queen Sohye, can be used to assert the agency of women in the Chosŏn dynasty. One might question whether it is necessary to deny *Naehun*'s role in reinforcing Confucian norms, given that it ultimately led to the formation of another set of norms that regulated women's behavior.

In 2007, Jungwon Kim's doctoral dissertation focused on chastity and women's lives in late Chosŏn.[21] Kim examines women in the Chosŏn Dynasty through official Korean documents, but noted two key limitations in such research: that these documents were authored by men, and that the surviving records primarily concern women from elite yangban families. Kim pointed out that women's chastity needs to be approached through various factors such as the state, the family, the women themselves, and their personal status, rather than as a result of Confucianism. His argument is distinguished from previous studies in that it reveals various stances on chastity through various cases. It also highlights a distinctive aspect of late Chosŏn society, how the collectivization of emotion into public discourse served to justify extreme acts of violence, including the suicide of women committed in the name of chastity.

In 2011, Michael J. Pitted and Youngmin Kim published *Women and Confucianism in Chosŏn: A New Perspective*, suggesting that the existing research on women's relationship with Confucianism should move beyond the one-dimensional view.[22] Their work is indicative of the direction of 21st-century research. It argues for a shift in perspective, moving beyond the view of Confucianism solely as a system of female subjugation to an understanding of how women actively responded within and against Confucian constraints by drawing on a wide range of historical sources. Moreover, they noted that women's Confucianization varied according to their status, and it was necessary to move away from the view of Confucianism and women as a single unit.

Jisoo Kim's work is also in line with the previous studies in that it emphasizes the importance of emotions and the active response of women. In her 2015 book, *The emotions of justice*, Kim identified women who use legal action to maximize their personal sense of injustice by strategically using Confucian language and values to achieve their own advantage.[23] Rather than merely tracing institutional changes through legislation and court rulings, the active use of formal complaints and other legal documents represents an attempt to listen more directly to the voices of women in Chosŏn society. It not only broadened the scope of the study, but also revealed the activism of women in terms of being women who utilized the system rather than women who created the system.

As we have seen, 21st-century Anglo-American studies of Chosŏn women has increasingly focused on their diverse activities, drawing on a wide range of historical sources. While studies up to the 20th century were based on keywords such as Confucianization, the family system, and the status of women, studies in the 21st century are actively utilizing keywords such as responses to Confucianization and women's activities within the categories of law, literature, and culture. This is an attempt to move away from a compassionate view of women as unconditional victims and to reveal the various aspects of women's oppression and responses to it. Although the status of women within the family is not significantly different from research conducted in the 20th century. However it is noteworthy that the study attempts to reveal the existence of diverse lives of women, rather than generalizing women as a single element of the system established by Confucian society.

3. Women's Studies in the Chosŏn Dynasty in Korean Academia

1) 20th-Century Research: The Victim Narrative and Uniformity in Studies on Chosŏn Women

The 21st century has brought both qualitative and quantitative growth to Korean academia. From 2000 to 2022, more than 140 books and 540 articles were published on women's history in the Chosŏn Dynasty.[24] On average, 6 to 7 monographs and 24 to 25 articles are published each year. This increase in research is based on the growing interest in women, the development of postmodern historiography, and the ease of excavating and accessing archives. By comparison, research on women's history in the 20th century in Korea has been considerably slower. After independence in 1945, interest in women's history was hampered by the establishment of a historiography outside of the colonial perspective, the rightward turn of national history in the 1960s and 1970s in the midst of the confrontation with North Korea, and the overthrow of the dictatorship.

In the 1970s, two groundbreaking works on Korean women's history were published: *Korean Women's History* (*Hanguk Yŏsŏngsa*)[25], Korea's first comprehensive history of women, and *History of Chosŏn Women* (*Ijo*

Yŏsŏngsa), which focused specifically on the Chosŏn period.[26]

Korean Women's History offered an extensive overview of research available at the time, dividing its narrative into distinct periods from prehistoric times to Koryŏ, Chosŏn, the Enlightenment era, and up to 1945. The work begins with an examination of women's subordination to men during the Paleolithic era and proceeds to explore in depth the status and everyday lives of women during the Three Kingdoms, Koryŏ, Chosŏn, and Japanese colonial periods. However, the work devoted considerable space to specific groups, such as royal women, shamans, and kisaengs, which may be considered a limitation. This focus likely reflects the challenges of the time, as the scarcity of sources on women and the prevailing research environment, which prioritized macrohistorical themes like politics and institutions, left few alternatives for scholars.

History of Chosŏn Women, on the other hand, examined the mechanisms of women's oppression during the Chosŏn period, such as the enforcement of monogamy and the prohibition of remarriage for women. It also analyzed the decline of Confucian views on women during late Chosŏn and explored women's autonomous activities during the Japanese colonial period. One notable achievement of this work was its identification of figures such as Kang Wansuk, uncovered through research on ideological shifts, including the spread of Catholicism during late Chosŏn.

Nevertheless, due to the limited availability of source materials, both works necessarily focused on women who operated within systems established by men. This emphasis highlights the broader constraints of women's history research during this period, shaped by the scarcity of sources and the dominance of macrohistorical perspectives in historiography.

The 1980s were characterized by the study of women's history through family systems and customs. A representative study is Ch'oe Chaesŏk, *A Study of the Korean Family System*, which deals with the family system from ancient times to the Chosŏn Dynasty.[27] In particular, the study points out that from the mid-17th century, the inheritance system changed from equal inheritance for men and women to favoring the firstborn son, and the adoption system was activated for family succession. In addition, he made use of various punjaegi (分財記; documents recording the division of property) and genealogies, thereby opening the door to later studies on family systems and women's history.

During this period, research on women in Chosŏn focused on demonstrating the decline in the status of women in the Chosŏn Dynasty. To this end, they pointed to changes in the inheritance system, as well as a shift in the marriage system from male-returning female family marriages to *chinyeong* (親迎). At the same time, it emphasized that the Confucian view of women and Confucian ideology oppressed women, in which women's responses were interpreted as conformity to Confucian society, thus portraying them as passive. This is a result of traditional views of women in the Chosŏn Dynasty that viewed them only in terms of discrimination and oppression.

Serious research on women in the Chosŏn Dynasty began in the 1990s. This was a time of new cultural currents. The democratization of Korean society and the end of the Cold War in the world allowed for the diversification of research topics and the introduction of new research methods that were difficult to accommodate in the old rigid system. In this social climate, the need for women's history came to the fore with the expanding interest in women. Researchers moved away from studying women as part of the family system and expanded their research to include other institutions and customs related to women. Pak Chu examined records of chŏngnyŏ (旌閭; honorific memorial gates awarded for virtuous women) based on the Annals of the Chosŏn Dynasty (Chosŏn Wangjo Sillok), through which he identified the Confucian ethical standards imposed on women and traced the process of Confucianization in Chosŏn society.[28] Yi Sugŏn pointed out that the principle of equal inheritance between sons and daughters in the Chosŏn period, as evidenced in punjaegi (inheritance division documents) and genealogies, reflects non-patrilineal aspects of Chosŏn society.[29] This was different from China, where inheritance was centered on the firstborn or son. Jang Byung-in, *A Study of Marriage in Early Chosŏn,* examines attempts to establish monogamy through the institutionalization of marriage rituals, remarriage and divorce, and adultery.[30] Yi Sunggu, *The Acceptance of Species Law and Changes in the Status of Women in Early Chosŏn*, examines the impact of the introduction of the Confucian patrilineal order on the status of women.[31]

The study of women's history in the Chosŏn Dynasty by Korean academics in the 20th century showed both its potential and its limitations. It is encouraging that interest in women's history has increased in response to the new research climate. At the same time, attempts were made to interpret history centered on women, which is an advance compared to the previous period.

However, it is regrettable that the studies remained fragmentary and attempted to interpret women only as agents of oppression and discrimination. At the same time, Anglo-American scholars demonstrated the decline of women's status along with changes in the family system through diachronic studies. In particular, the process of politicizing the changes in various relationships within the family and the process of establishing the Confucian patrilineal order was outstanding. In contrast, Korean scholarship, despite having access to a wide range of sources, tended to interpret women solely through the singular lens of victimhood. This is a result of being overwhelmed by the Korean society's prism of female obedience and sacrifice.

2) 21st-Century Research: Unearthing New Cases and Diversifying Research

With the advent of the 21st century, research on the history of women in the Chosŏn dynasty underwent significant changes. First, the conditions for actively incorporating research from English-speaking academia were established. Active exchanges between Korean and Western academia began to flourish, supported by a sharp increase in the number of Korean scholars studying abroad in English-speaking countries and the creation of social conditions that allowed for the systematic import of English-speaking academic studies. A representative example is the Korean translation of Martina Deuchler's *The Confucian Transformation of Korea*, originally published in 1992, which finally appeared in 2003. As noted in the preface, this work brought about a major breakthrough in Korean studies on women and family systems in the Chosŏn dynasty. While many researchers had already accessed the English version, the Korean translation became a catalyst for a broader audience of scholars, including those in adjacent fields, to engage with Deuchler's arguments about the introduction of Neo-Confucianism, the emergence of a highly structured patrilineal society, and the consequent decline in the status of women.

The enthusiastic response of Korean academia to *The Confucian Transformation of Korea*, coupled with societal changes in 21st-century Korea and the rapid development of the internet, accelerated the incorporation of English-speaking academic research.[32] In the 20th century, Korean academia was slow to accept trends in English-speaking research due to the insularity of the academic environment shaped by ideological debates. However, 21st-century Korean society moved toward openness and diversity, becoming rapidly globalized. Various studies conducted by English-speaking scholars, many of whom had benefited from South Korean government initiatives in the late 20th century, provided Korean scholars with access to a wide range of foreign research. Moreover, the rapid proliferation of the internet enabled scholars to access foreign studies without direct contact with international researchers. This societal shift played a pivotal role in facilitating the integration of Western research into Korean academia.

Another significant development was the diversification of historical sources and the improved accessibility to them. Beginning in the late 1990s, Korean academia embraced postmodernist historiography from the West, which heightened interest in microhistory and everyday history. This methodological shift led to the diversification of research topics, the active discovery of new sources, and a deeper understanding of society through micro-level studies. Research on women in the Chosŏn dynasty actively adopted these methodological changes, achieving considerable results. Previously, state records such as official documents and public archives, which predominantly centered on men, were the main sources for research. Similarly, personal writings like literary collections were primarily produced by men who could write in classical Chinese. Aside from the records of royal women or a few elite yangban women, written materials produced by women were almost nonexistent. However, sources such as diaries, property division documents, and genealogies included records related to women as family members, providing valuable clues for tracing their lives. Furthermore, active database projects on these materials significantly improved access for researchers, leading to an increase in related studies.

Finally, there was a notable shift in the perception of women in the Chosŏn dynasty. Previously, women were not recognized as central members of society but rather as peripheral figures. This perception stemmed from the fact that women at the time were confined to the domestic sphere and did not form official groups capable of exerting societal influence. As a result, they were not regarded as social beings, and academic interest in women was naturally limited. However, with the emergence of methodologies like microhistory in the 21st century, it became possible to examine society through individuals rather than groups. Consequently, research began to focus on women as individuals rather than solely as members of royal or familial groups. This shift in perspective also led to efforts to uncover individual female historical figures.

In response to these changes, the number of specialists in the history of women in the Chosŏn dynasty increased, producing studies on a variety of topics such as inheritance, family succession, the rights of principal wives, economic activities, regency politics, concubinage, childbirth culture, women's norms and instructional texts, and female household heads.[33] Given the limited scope of this study, it is not feasible to examine all of these diverse topics in detail. Moreover, the purpose of this research is to investigate how the Confucianization of Chosŏn and the resulting changes in women's status have been studied. Thus, this chapter will focus on the characteristics of 21st-century Korean research by comparing it with English-speaking academic studies, particularly those of Deuchler.

Since the publication of Deuchler's *Confucian Transformation of Korean Society* (2003) in Korea, Deuchler's work has operated as a discourse for understanding women within the kinship and servile order of the Chosŏn Dynasty, both domestically and internationally. This was due to the deepening understanding of Neo-Confucianism, which legitimized the claim that the status of women in the Chosŏn Dynasty was declining due to changes in inheritance, marriage, etc. Since then, Korean scholars have tended to attempt to prove or disprove Deuchler's discourse through various cases based on Deuchler's discourse. In particular, they have focused on proving the status of women in the early Chosŏn Dynasty through various documents, or proving the inheritance of property and the authority of daughters-in-law in the late Chosŏn Dynasty. This has led to the view that it is difficult to view late Chosŏn society as a period when the status of women declined or when a Confucian patriarchal society was established. However, this view is based on individual cases. While there are cases of split inheritance and reincarnation service after the 18th century, it is hard to see this as a major trend.

It is worth noting, however, that the criticism of Deuchler began to gain considerable strength. In *Under the Eyes of the Ancestors* (2018), Deuchler strengthens her case studies to illustrate what she argues is the long-term Confucianization of Chosŏn. However, she still maintains the same position as before in terms of the static attitude of women in Chosŏn and their conformity to preserve their status.

In contrast, Korean scholars have begun to focus on women's activism. First of all, there are studies that approach the process of women's conformity to Confucian society from the perspective of voluntary conformity as well as coercion by the dominant group. For example, Kang Myeong-kwan, in *The Birth of Virtuous Women*, describes the process of women's transformation of the *Samgang haengsilto* (三綱行實圖; llustrated Guide to the Conduct of the Three Bonds) into chastity, i.e., the process of accepting and practicing male Confucian language. In doing so, he reveals that women voluntarily participated in Confucian society.[34] This trend of research has become more prominent in recent years, focusing on the process of maintaining the family fortune through lawsuits, or using chastity to consolidate one's position. In other words, women did not just lose their positions and gains through Confucianization, but actively sought to gain them by adapting to the changed society.

Moreover, domestic academia has begun to focus on women's agency and circumstances that deviate from Deuchler's discourse by analyzing various cases. Notably, through diverse examples, scholars have demonstrated that marriage in the Chosŏn dynasty, even into the late period, was typically conducted in a semi-chinyŏng (半親迎; pan-chinyŏng) form, which was an intermediate stage between chinyŏng (親迎, groom's procession to the bride's home) and namgwi-yŏgahŏn (男歸女家婚). Additionally, studies have shown that rituals and inheritance practices were not always executed according to the provisions of the *Kyŏngguk taejŏn* (The National Code), but rather varied depending on the family and circumstances. These findings challenge Deuchler's discourse that the Confucianization of Chosŏn led to a decline in women's status within the family.

Furthermore, research into the recording practices of women in household registers and genealogies has gained attention, introducing cases such as female household heads and non-patrilineal elements operating within marriage practices. These studies provide valuable insights into understanding the complexities of gender and family dynamics in the Chosŏn dynasty.

In this respect, Deuchler has been criticized for portraying women in Chosŏn as passive. However, the decline of women's status and the preservation of their position should not be regarded as equivalent. Rather, women's active behavior may be understood as a strategy of position preservation, aimed at resisting the accelerating decline of their status within the constrained social environment of Chosŏn. That is, women were not necessarily asserting their position through overt resistance, but rather struggling to maintain or safeguard it in order to survive.

The above is a review of research on women in the Chosŏn Dynasty in the 21st century. Although there have been many qualitative and quantitative advancements in the study of Chosŏn women, notable gaps remain. One persistent issue is the tendency to interpret women solely through their relationships within the husband's household. In particular, the figure of the "daughter" has been largely overlooked in favor of examining women's roles as "daughters-in-law." This relational framing limits a more comprehensive understanding of women's historical experiences. A more nuanced approach would consider women as independent actors or collective subjects beyond relational categories such as "father-in-law and daughter-in-law" or "mother and daughter." Although recent research has begun to explore women as autonomous figures, these efforts have predominantly focused on female intellectuals and women of the royal court, leaving a broader spectrum of women's lives underexplored.

In this regard, there are also fragmented studies that focus on cases. It is necessary to consider whether the selected cases are representative. For example, the emergence of an exceptional figure such as Yŏjung kunja (女中君子) cannot be presented as a general trend of the time. However, many books published in the 21st century that study individual women in the Chosŏn Dynasty claim to examine the lives of women in the Chosŏn Dynasty by referring to these special women, which may have the effect of emphasizing the oppression of ordinary women.

The last limitation is the lack of discourse generation by focusing on individual studies. This is a result of the failure to create a framework for interpreting the representation of women in the Chosŏn Dynasty that can be seen in various cases. Rather, the current research seems to focus on overcoming the discourse of the doi healer. However, it is worth noting that, unlike previous studies, recent research emphasizes that women were not passive conformists in Confucian society.

4. Conclusion

This paper has examined the research on women in the Chosŏn Dynasty from both Anglo-American and Korean scholars. Both approaches to the study of women in Chosŏn began with an examination of the family system. Confucianization of the Chosŏn Dynasty led to changes in customs, including the institution of arranged marriages, as well as changes in rituals and property inheritance, which led to a decline in the status of women. Indeed, Confucianization in Chosŏn relegated married women's space to the marketplace and excluded them from rituals and property inheritance.

While these studies were common in both Korean and Anglo-American scholarship in the 1980s, it was not until the 1990s that they were synthesized. This synthesis culminated in Martina Deuchler's *The Confucian Transformation of Korean Society*. This book argues that the introduction of Neo-Confucianism spurred a transformation of Chosŏn society, in which women's status declined as the country attempted to establish a highly patriarchal society. To arrive at this conclusion, the book examines various family and kinship ties, including the understanding of Neo-Confucianism among early Chosŏn scholars. The book has since had an enormous impact on both Korean and Anglo-American scholarship. Korean scholars have supplemented Deuchler's arguments with a variety of sources, and Western researchers studying pre-modern East Asian Confucian societies have used the book to understand East Asian Confucianism.

In the 21st century, however, the landscape of research has gradually changed. Critics began to criticize Deuchler's work for its passive view of women in the Chosŏn Dynasty. At the opposite end of the spectrum was Haboush, who took a more proactive approach to portraying women in Chosŏn by emphasizing their role in shaping public opinion and creating culture through the written language of Hangul and literature. This trend has also begun to emerge in Korean scholarship, with a growing number of studies suggesting that women's actions, such as the defense of their in-laws' property through their authority and legal acts as servants, and the Confucian attitudes of Yŏjung kunja (女中君子) were various responses to Confucian society. Anglo-American studies have also pointed out that existing studies have viewed the relationship between Confucian society and women in the Chosŏn Dynasty in a flat way. They pointed out that women's Confucianization varied depending on their situation and status, and that women sometimes actively used their Confucian virtues to resolve their feelings of injustice.

The exchange between the Western academia, which is strong in diachronic and non-diachronic research, and the Korean academia, which is strong in utilizing various sources, will be a process of expanding the scope of women's history research in the Chosŏn Dynasty. However, it is quite regrettable that Korean history research in Western academia is concentrated on the modern period. Although the number of Korean researchers is increasing and they are conducting research on women in the Chosŏn Dynasty in a variety of topics, without new external stimuli, they may end up reproducing past research. In addition, the majority of Korean academic research has focused in the late Chosŏn period which has led to a time bias. Of course, it can be said that this is an inevitable result because the number of types and amounts of sources is much larger than in the early Chosŏn period, but it is also worth noting that research limited to the late Chosŏn period can lead to the result of looking only at the surface phenomena. In short, in order to better characterize Confucianism or women in Chosŏn, we need a study that can trace the process of change over time and that can be compared with neighboring countries.

Note

1 Deuchler, Martina, *The confucian Transformation of Korea: A study of Society and Ideology,* Cambridge, Mass: Council on East Asin Studies, Harvard University, 1992.

2 Kim Chŏngwŏn(Kim Jungwon), "Pukmiesŏüi Chosŏn Sidae Yŏsŏngsa Yŏn'gu Tonghyang" (Historical Studies on Choson Women in North America), *Yŏksawa Hyŏnsil* Vol. 94, 2014; Chang Pyŏngin(Chang Byung-inn), "Chosŏn Sidae Yŏsŏngsa Yŏn'gu ŭi Hyŏnhwang kwa Kwaje," (The Current and Assignment for Women's History of Chosŏn Period), *Yŏsŏngkwa Yŏksa* Vol. 6, 2007; Chŏng Haeŭn(Chung Hae-eun), "Chosŏn Sidae Yŏsŏngsa Yŏn'gu, Ŏdiro KakoIn'nŭn'ga?" (Historical Studies of the Chosŏn Females: future prospects), *Yŏksawa Hyŏnsil* Vol. 91, 2014.

Chŏng Haeŭn(Chung Hae-eun), "Chosŏn Sidae Yŏsŏngsa Yŏn'gue Taehan Myŏt Kajŭ Chilmŭn: 2000 Nyŏnhu Yŏn'gu Sŏngkwa rŭl Chungsim ŭro," (A Few Questions about the Study of Women's History in the Chosŏn Dynasty in the 21st Century), *Chosŏnsidae Sahakbo* Vol. 105, 2023.

3 Sandra Mattielli ed., *Virtues in Conflict: Tradition and the Korean Woman Today*, Seoul: Samhwa (for The Royal Asiatic Society, Korea Branch), 1977.

4 Kim Chŏngwŏn(Kim Jungwon), *Ibid*, 343.

5 Deuchler, Martina, "The tradition: Women during the Yi Dynasty", in Sandra mattielli (ed), *op. cit.*

6 Katayama, Takahiro, "Korean women: view from the inner room", *Asian Folklore Studies 46(1),* 1987.

7 Laurel Kendall and Mark Peterson, eds. *Korean Women: view from the Inner Room,* New Haven, CT: East Rock Press, 1983.

8 Wagner, Edward W, "Two Early Genealogies and Women's Status in Early Yi Dynasty Korea", in Laurel Kendall and Mark Peterson (eds.), *op. cit.*

9 Peterson, Mark, "Women without Sons: A Measure of social change in Yi Dynasty Korea", in Laurel Kendall and Mark Peterson (eds.), *op. cit.*

10 Martina Deuchler, *The confucian Transformation of Korea: A study of Society and Ideology,* Cambridge, Mass: Council on East Asin Studies, Harvard University, 1992. In Korea, the book was published in 2003 and went out of print, but was republished in 2013 at the request of scholars.

11 Paek Seung-jong, "Book Review: Martina Deuchler, *The Confucian Transformation of Korea: A Study of Society and Ideology*", *The Yŏksahakbo 141*, 1994 Chŏng Du-hŭi, "Chŏkchangja Chungshim ŭi Kabujangjŏk Chosŏn Sahoe ŭi Sŏngnip kwa Kŭ Sŏnggyŏk" (The Establishment and Characteristics of the Primogeniture-Based Patriarchal Society in Chosŏn Korea), Korean History Studies in America, Seoul: Kukhak Charyowŏn, 1999.

12 Ham Han-hŭi, "Han'guk ŭi Yugyojŏk Pyŏnhwa—Isang kwa Silche Sai ŭi Kaldŭng Sŏlmyŏng Mothae" (Book Review: *The Confucian Transformation of Korea—Unable to Explain the Conflict Between Ideals and Reality*), *Kyosusinhŭn,* February 23, 2004; Kwŏn Yŏngung, "Sŏp'yŏng: Sup ŭro Chomanghan Chosŏn ŭi Ch'injok Sahoe" (Book Review: *The Confucian Transformation of Korea*—A Bird's-Eye View of the Kinship Society in Chosŏn Korea), *Kyosusinhŭn*, February 23, 2004 Kim Hŭn-sik (Kim Hun-sik), "Sŏp'yŏng: Martina Deuchler 'Han'guk Sahoe ŭi Yugyojŏk Pyŏnhwan'" (Book Review: Martina Deuchler, Translated by Hun-sang Lee, *The Confucian Transformation of Korea*), *Yŏksawa Kyŏnggye* Vol. 52, 2004; Kye Sŭngbŏm, "Han'gukŭi Yugyohwawa 17-segi: Deuchlerŭi 『Han'guk Sahoe ŭi Yugyojŏk Pyŏnhwan』kwa Kŭ Haesŏk," (The Korean Version of Confucianization and the Significance ot the Seventeeth Century: A Riview of Martina Deuchler's *The Confucian Tranformation of Korea*) *Han'guk Sahaksahakbo* Vol. 20, 2009.

13 Mark Peterson, *Korean Adoption and Inheritance: Case Studies in the Creation of a Classic Confusion society,* Ithaca: Comell University East Asia Series, 1996.

14 Kim Chŏngwŏn(Kim Jungwon), *Ibid*., 346.

15 Dorothy Ko, JaHyun Kim Haboush, and Joan R. Piggott, eds., *Women and Confusian cultures in Premodern China, Korea, and Japan,* Berkeley: University of California Press, 2003.

16 Martina Deuchler, "Propagating Female Virtues in Choson Korea", in idem. *Women and Confusian cultures in Premodern China, Korea, and Japan.*

17 Kim Chŏngwŏn(Kim Jungwon), *Ibid*., 347.

18 JaHyun Kim Haboush, "Versions of Subversions: Patriarchy and Polygamy in Korean Narratives", in idem, *Women and Confusian cultures in Premodern China, Korea, and Japan.*

19 JaHyun Kim Haboush, "The Vanished Women of Korea: The Anonymity of Texts and the Historicity of Subjects", *In servants of the Dynasty: Palace*

Women in World History, ed. Anne Walthall, Berkeley: University of California Press, 2008.

20 John Duncan, "The Nashun and Politics of Gender in Fifteenth-Century Korea", in Yong-key Kim-Renaud, ed. *Creative Women of Korea: The Fifteenth through Twentieth Centuries,* New York: M. E. Sharp, 2004.

21 Kim Chŏngwŏn(Kim Jungwon), "Negotiating Virtue and the Lives of Women in Late Choson Korea", Ph. D. dissertation, Harvard University, 2007.

22 Youngmin Kim and Michael J. Pitted eds. *Confucianism and Women in Chosŏn Korea: New perspectives,* Albany: SUNY Press, 2011.

23 Jisoo Kim, *The emotions of justice: gender, status, and legal performance in Chosŏn Korea,* Seattle: University of Washington, 2015.

24 Chŏng Haeŭn (Chung Hae-eun), "Chosŏn Sidae Yŏsŏngsa Yŏn'gue Taehan Myŏt Kajŭ Chilmŭn: 2000 Nyŏnhu Yŏn'gu Sŏngkwa rŭl Chungsim ŭro," (A Few Questions about the Study of Women's History in the Chosŏn Dynasty in the 21st Century), *Chosŏnsidae Sahakbo* Vol. 105, 2023.

25 Kim Yŏngdŏk, *Han'guk Yŏsŏngsa* (Korean Women's History), Ewha Womans University, 1972.

26 Pak Yongok (Park Yongok), "Ijoyŏsŏngsa" (History of Women), Han'gukilbosa, 1975.

27 Ch'oe Chaesŏk, "Han'guk Kajok Yŏn'gu" (Korean Family in Historical Perspective), Iljisa, 1983.

28 Pak Chu (Park Joo), "Chosŏn Sidae ŭi Chŏngp'yo Chŏngch'aek" (Chŏngp'yo Policy in the Chosŏn Dynasty), Ilchogak, 1990.

29 Yi Sugŏn (Lee, Soo-gun), "Chosŏn Chŏn'gi Sahoe Pyŏndong kwa Sangsokjedo" (Social Change and the Inheritance System in the Chosŏn Dynasty), *Yŏksahakbo* Vol. 129, 1991.

30 Chang Pyŏngin (Chang Byung-inn), "Chosŏn Ch'ogi Honinje Yŏn'gu," (A Study of the Early Chosŏn Marriage System), Ph.D. dissertation, Seoul National University, 1993.

31 Yi Sunggu (Lee, Soon-Koo), "Chosŏn Ch'ogi Chongbŏp ŭi Suyong kwa Yŏsŏng Chiwie ŭi Pyŏnhwa" ("The Acceptance of Bell Law and the Changes in Women's Status in Early Chosŏn), Ph.D. dissertation, Korea Institute of Spiritual Culture, 1995.

32 Yi Hunsang (Lee Hunsang), "Sŏgu Han'gukhak Yŏn'gu Sŏngkwaŭi Han'gŭl Pŏnyŏkkwa Kŭ Ŭimi," (A Study on Hangŭl Translation of the Western

Korean Studies), *K'ok'ito* (Cogito) Vol. 87, 2019.

33 Chŏng Haeŭn (Chung Hae-eun), *Ibid*, 146.

34 Kang Myung-kwan, *Yŏlnyŏŭi T'ansaeng* (The Birth of Virtuous Women), Dolbaegae, 2009.

Bibliography

Chang, Pyŏngin (Chang Byung-inn), "Chosŏn Ch'ogi Honinje Yŏn'gu," (A Study of the Early Chosŏn Marriage System), Ph.D. dissertation, Seoul National University, 1993.

________, "Chosŏn Sidae Yŏsŏngsa Yŏn'gu ŭi Hyŏnhwang kwa Kwaje," (The Current and Assignment for Women's History of Chosŏn Period), *Yŏsŏngkwa Yŏksa* Vol. 6, 2007.

Ch'oe, Chaesŏk, "Han'guk Kajok Yŏn'gu" (Korean Family in Historical Perspective), Iljisa, 1983.

Chŏng, Du-hŭi, "Chŏkchangja Chungshim ŭi Kabujangjŏk Chosŏn Sahoe ŭi Sŏngnip kwa Kŭ Sŏnggyŏk" (The Establishment and Characteristics of the Primogeniture-Based Patriarchal Society in Chosŏn Korea), Korean History Studies in America, Seoul: Kukhak Charyowŏn, 1999.

________, "Chosŏn Sidae Yŏsŏngsa Yŏn'gu, Ŏdiro KakoIn'nŭn'ga?" (Historical Studies of the Chosŏn Females: Future Prospects), *Yŏksawa Hyŏnsil* Vol. 91, 2014.

Chŏng Haeŭn (Chung Hae-eun), "Chosŏn Sidae Yŏsŏngsa Yŏn'gue Taehan Myŏt Kajŭ Chilmŭn: 2000 Nyŏnhu Yŏn'gu Sŏngkwa rŭl Chungsim ŭro," (A Few Questions about the Study of Women's History in the Chosŏn Dynasty in the 21st Century), *Chosŏnsidae Sahakbo* Vol. 105, 2023.

Deuchler, Martina, "Chosang ŭi Nun Arae Sŏ," Nŏmŏbooks, 2018.

________, *The Confucian Transformation of Korea: A Study of Society and Ideology*, Cambridge, Mass: Council on East Asian Studies, Harvard University, 1992.

Dix, Griffin, "Virtues in Conflict: Tradition and the Korean Woman Today. Sandra Mattielli," *The Journal of Asian Studies* 40(3), 1981.

Duncan, John, "The Nashun and Politics of Gender in Fifteenth-Century Korea," in Yong-key Kim-Renaud, ed., *Creative Women of Korea: The Fifteenth through Twentieth Centuries*, New York: M. E. Sharp, 2004.

Ham, Han-hŭi, "Han'guk ŭi Yugyojŏk Pyŏnhwa—Isang kwa Silche Sai ŭi Kaldŭng Sŏlmyŏng Mothae" (Book Review: *The Confucian Transformation of Korea—Unable to Explain the Conflict Between Ideals and Reality*), *Kyosusinhŭn,* February 23, 2004.

Katayama, Takahiro, "Korean Women: View from the Inner Room," *Asian Folklore Studies* 46(1), 1987.

Kang, Myung-kwan, *Yŏlnyŏŭi T'ansaeng* (The Birth of Virtuous Women), Dolbaegae, 2009.

Kendall, Laurel, and Peterson, Mark, eds., *Korean Women: View from the Inner Room*, New Haven, CT: East Rock Press, 1983.

Kim, Chŏngwŏn (Kim Jungwon), "Pukmiesŏŭi Chosŏn Sidae Yŏsŏngsa Yŏn'gu Tonghyang" (Historical Studies on Chosŏn Women in North America), *Yŏksawa Hyŏnsil* Vol. 94, 2014.

________, "Negotiating Virtue and the Lives of Women in Late Chosŏn Korea," Ph.D. dissertation, Harvard University, 2007.

Kim, Hŭn-sik (Kim Hun-sik), "Sŏp'yŏng: Martina Deuchler 'Han'guk Sahoe ŭi Yugyojŏk Pyŏnhwan'" (Book Review: Martina Deuchler, Translated by Hun-sang Lee, *The Confucian Transformation of Korea*), *Yŏksawa Kyŏnggye* Vol. 52, 2004.

Kim, JaHyun Haboush, "The Vanished Women of Korea: The Anonymity of Texts and the Historicity of Subjects," in Anne Walthall, ed., *Servants of the Dynasty: Palace Women in World History*, Berkeley: University of California Press, 2008.

________, "Versions of Subversions: Patriarchy and Polygamy in Korean Narratives," in *Women and Confucian Cultures in Premodern China, Korea, and Japan*.

Kim, Yŏngdŏk, *Han'guk Yŏsŏngsa* (Korean Women's History), Ewha Womans University, 1972.

Kim Youngmin and Michael Pitted, eds., *Confucianism and Women in Chosŏn Korea: New Perspectives*, Albany: SUNY Press, 2011.

Ko Dorothy, Kim JaHyun Haboush and Joan Piggott, eds., *Women and Confucian Cultures in Premodern China, Korea, and Japan*, Berkeley: University of California Press, 2003.

Kwŏn, Yŏngung, "Sŏp'yŏng: Sup ŭro Chomanghan Chosŏn ŭi Ch'injok Sahoe" (Book Review: *The Confucian Transformation of Korea*—A Bird's-Eye View of the Kinship Society in Chosŏn Korea), *Kyosusinhŭn*, February 23, 2004.

Kye, Sŭngbŏm, "Han'gukŭi Yugyohwawa 17-segi: Deuchlerŭi 『Han'guk Sahoe ŭi Yugyojŏk Pyŏnhwan』kwa Kŭ Haesŏk," (The Korean Version of Confucianization and the Significance ot the Seventeeth Century: A Riview of Martina Deuchler's *The Confucian Tranformation of Korea*) *Han'guk Sahaksahakbo* Vol. 20, 2009.

Mattielli, Sandra (ed), *Virtue in Conflict: Tradition and Korean Women Today*, Seoul: The Royal Asiatic Society, Korea Branch, 1977.

Pak, Chu (Park Joo), "Chosŏn Sidae ŭi Chŏngp'yo Chŏngch'aek" (Chŏngp'yo Policy in the Chosŏn Dynasty), Ilchogak, 1990.

Pak, Yongok (Park Yongok), "Ijoyŏsŏngsa" (History of Women), Han'gukilbosa, 1975.

Paek, Sŭngjong, "Book Review: Martina Deuchler, *The Confucian Transformation of Korea: A Study of Society and Ideology*," *Yŏksahakbo* Vol. 141, 1994.

Peterson, Mark, *Korean Adoption and Inheritance: Case Studies in the Creation of a Classic Confucian Society*, Ithaca: Cornell University East Asia Series, 1996.

Wagner, Edward, "Two Early Genealogies and Women's Status in Early Yi Dynasty Korea," in Laurel Kendall and Mark Peterson (eds.), *op. cit.*

Yi, Hunsang (Lee Hunsang), "Sŏgu Han'gukhak Yŏn'gu Sŏngkwaŭi Han'gŭl Pŏnyŏkkwa Kŭ Ŭimi," (A Study on Hangŭl Translation of the Western Korean Studies), *K'ok'ito* (Cogito) Vol. 87, 2019.

Yi, Sugŏn (Lee, Soo-gun), "Chosŏn Chŏn'gi Sahoe Pyŏndong kwa Sangsokjedo" (Social Change and the Inheritance System in the Chosŏn Dynasty), *Yŏksahakbo* Vol. 129, 1991.

Yi, Sunggu (Lee, Soon-Koo), "Chosŏn Ch'ogi Chongbŏp ŭi Suyong kwa Yŏsŏng Chiwie ŭi Pyŏnhwa" ("The Acceptance of Bell Law and the Changes in Women's Status in Early Chosŏn), Ph.D. dissertation, Korea Institute of Spiritual Culture, 1995.

6

The Military Revolution in Late Chosŏn: Interpretations and Reflections

Kunha Kim

Sogang University

6 The Military Revolution in Late Chosŏn: Interpretations and Reflections

Kunha Kim (Sogang University)

1. Introduction

The military system of late Chosŏn underwent significant changes compared to the early Chosŏn period. The Imjin War and the Manchu invasions of Korea became pivotal turning points for Chosŏn's military structure. Through these two major conflicts, Chosŏn's military system experienced extensive reforms.[1]

Despite the changes in military operation, organization, defense systems, military administration, weaponry, and tactics, there is no comprehensive term to describe these changes collectively. This may be because military history is a highly diverse and specialized field, compelling researchers to focus on specific areas. Consequently, high-quality research results have accumulated across various fields of military history. However, there is no appropriate framework to explain the military changes in late Chosŏn other than listing individual changes in each sector. This situation contrasts with other academic disciplines, where numerous discourses exist to describe the late Chosŏn period. On the other hand, in the field of military history, there are specific frameworks to explain certain aspects—such as the Five Military Divisions system or the Capital

Defense System—there is no overarching framework to describe the changes in the military system of late Chosŏn.

Nonetheless, there have been attempts to explain the military changes in late Chosŏn through a unified discourse: the attempt to apply the Military Revolution Thesis of Europe to late Chosŏn. Such efforts originated in Korean academia, which subsequently prompted scholars in the Anglophone academia to investigate the applicability of the Military Revolution theory in greater detail. The Military Revolution Thesis is already a subject of significant debate within Anglophone academia. Despite this, there have been diverse attempts to apply the concept of a military revolution to regions outside Europe, particularly in Asian history. The effort to apply the Military Revolution theory to Chosŏn emerges from such scholarly trends.

Therefore, examining the discourse on Chosŏn's Military Revolution is meaningful on two levels: first, on a domestic level, it provides an alternative perspective for understanding the military history of late Chosŏn as a unified discourse; and second, on a global level, it enables the comparison of the general and unique aspects of Korean military history with those of other countries using a common theoretical framework.[2]

The objective of this study is to comprehensively introduce and compare the debates surrounding the Military Revolution of late Chosŏn in both Anglophone and Korean academia. To this end, the study focuses particularly on two aspects: first, understanding how Anglophone and Korean scholars analyze the Military Revolution in Chosŏn. By doing so, the study aims to compare the perspectives and approaches taken by these two scholarly communities in examining the military revolution of late Chosŏn. Second, it aims to identify key commonalities and differences between the two academic circles. Through this, the study seeks a comprehensive understanding of the discourse on Chosŏn's Military Revolution from both global and Korean perspectives.

This study utilizes literature analysis to compare major studies on Chosŏn's Military Revolution in Anglophone and Korean academia. In the Anglophone academia, the study examines two key articles: Hyeok

Hweon Kang's "Big Heads and Buddhist Demons: The Korean Musketry Revolution and the Northern Expeditions of 1654 and 1658" in *Journal of Chinese Military History* 2 (2013), and Tonio Andrade, Hyeok Hweon Kang, and Kirsten Cooper's "A Korean Military Revolution? Parallel Military Innovations in East Asia and Europe" in *Journal of World History* 25-1 (2014). These two studies are the only specialized research on Chosŏn's Military Revolution in the Anglophone academia, and thus are essential for understanding how Anglophone scholars perceive the Military Revolution of Chosŏn and the military system of late Chosŏn.

In Korean academia, this study analyzes two papers: No, Yŏnggu (Young-koo Roh). "'Military Revolution' and Chosŏn Dynasty's Military Reforms in the 17th and 18th Centuries." in *Journal of Western History 36* (2007), and Kim Yeong-joon's "Training Methods and Military Discipline of Chosun Musketeer Around the 17th Century" in *Journal of Military History* 92 (2014). No Yŏnggu's work is of great academic significance as the first study to suggest the possibility of a Military Revolution in Chosŏn. Notably, on the first page of Tonio Andrade's article, there is a special acknowledgment indicating that the research was supported by No Yŏnggu. This fact reveals that No Yŏnggu's research directly influenced the study in Anglophone academia. Kim Yeong-joon's work is also worthy of introduction as it explicitly aims to understand military changes in late Chosŏn from the perspective of the Military Revolution. Kim Yeong-joon emphasizes the importance of military training, which is also a point of focus in Anglophone academia, making his study a valuable reference for comparing perspectives between the two academic communities.

This paper is organized as follows. Chapter 2 introduces the two studies in Anglophone academia on the Military Revolution of Chosŏn. Through the works of Hyeok Hweon Kang, Tonio Andrade, and Kirsten Cooper, the study examines how Anglophone scholars explain the Military Revolution in Chosŏn, particularly focusing on what military changes in late Chosŏn drew their attention.

Chapter 3 introduces the discussion in Korean academia, focusing on the studies by No Yŏnggu and Kim Yeong-joon, with particular attention to what aspects of the 'Military Revolution' are highlighted in these studies.

Chapter 4 draws out the commonalities and differences between the Anglophone and Korean academic communities. There are clear features of the Military Revolution that both academic circles commonly highlight. However, subtle differences also exist in the ways they validate the Military Revolution, which are examined in detail. This study aims to present a detailed introduction to the Military Revolution in Chosŏn while exploring the possibility of a new discourse for explaining the military history of late Chosŏn. It aims to contribute to promoting a public debate on establishing a more comprehensive and systematic framework for the study of late Chosŏn military history.

2. The Military Revolution of Chosŏn in the Anglophone Academia

Interest in the Asian Military Revolution Thesis is considerable in Anglophone academia, but it is generally focused on China, Japan, or cases of conflict between Asia and maritime empires like Portugal and Spain. It is necessary to first point out that interest in Chosŏn's Military Revolution is very limited, even within the broader interest in the Asian Military Revolution. Only two studies have dealt with the Military Revolution of Chosŏn seriously, and notably, Hyeok Hweon Kang is an author on both studies. As a result, the content of these two studies overlaps significantly. Nevertheless, there are differences in the aspects of Chosŏn's military innovations that each study emphasizes, which justifies a separate and detailed introduction of each. The paper co-authored by Tonio Andrade, Hyeok Hweon Kang, and Kirsten Cooper in 2014 offers a more comprehensive exploration of the Military Revolution of Chosŏn. However, in this paper, the discussion will proceed in chronological order of publication, starting with the solo-authored paper by Hyeok Hweon Kang in 2013.

1) Kang, Hyeok Hweon, 'Big Heads and Buddhist Demons: The Korean Musketry Revolution and the Northern Expeditions of 1654 and 1658.', *Journal of Chinese Military History* 2, No. 2 (2013)

The military revolution thesis highlights the military and technological changes in Europe during the 16th and 17th centuries and argues that it prompted the birth of modern war-making and eventually the modern state system. Some recent studies suggest that similar revolutions occurred in Asia, particularly in Korean peninsula under Chosŏn dynasty, as explored by Hyeok Hweon Kang in his study on the Korean Musketry Revolution and Northern Expeditions of 1654 and 1658. By applying the theory of European military revolution to Chosŏn Korea, Kang attempts to connect Chosŏn's military innovations to global history.

His paper explores how Chosŏn's military revolution, though resembling Europe's, took a unique path. Focusing on Chosŏn's northern expeditions of 1654 and 1658 against Russian Cossacks at the Qing's request, Chosŏn successfully used firearms to repel Cossack forces. According to Kang, this event, so called 'Nashin Expedition', demonstrated Chosŏn's military advancements, particularly in gunpowder weapons.[3]

Kang argues that Chosŏn's military innovations are significant in three ways: (1) The number of musketeers increased rapidly after the Imjin War, with musketeers replacing archers in military units by 1708. (2) Chosŏn improved training methods, introducing advanced tactics like volley and rotating fire. (3) Chosŏn expanded its military budget to maintain these innovations, shifting from unpaid conscripts to salaried soldiers, implying that Chosŏn government somehow following the similar path to contemporary European 'fiscal-military states'.

These changes align with Peter Lorge's definition of a revolution as a "permanent change." Chosŏn restructured its military around infantry firearms, making lasting institutional changes. However, compared to

Europe, Chosŏn's revolution remained incomplete, largely confined to musketry. The momentum for reform declined under Qing hegemony after the Manchu invasions.

Despite the success of the northern expeditions, Chosŏn lost the drive to continue military innovations, as the stabilization of the Qing borders removed external pressures. Consequently, Chosŏn did not complete the financial reforms needed to sustain its military revolution.

2) Tonio Andrade, Hyeok Hweon Kang, and Kirsten Cooper. 'A Korean Military Revolution? Parallel Military Innovations in East Asia and Europe.', *Journal of World History* 25, No. 1 (2014).

The next paper to examine is "A Korean Military Revolution? Parallel Military Innovations in East Asia and Europe" co-authored by Tonio Andrade, Hyeok Hweon Kang, and Kirsten Cooper (Journal of World History, 2014). This paper highlights how East Asian military innovations, particularly in Chosŏn, parallel developments in Europe, challenging the Eurocentric view of the military revolution. Tonio Andrade, the lead author, has extensively studied military revolutions in Asia, while Hyeok Hweon Kang focuses on Chosŏn's military changes, and Kirsten Cooper studies early modern European transnational interactions. Together, they offer a comprehensive analysis of the military revolution from Asian, Korean, and European perspectives.

The paper emphasizes the importance of East Asia in the global discourse on the military revolution, particularly focusing on the "Revolution in Drill" in Chosŏn. This concept refers to the introduction of disciplined, coordinated military units, essential for the effective use of gunpowder weapons. In Europe, leaders like William Louis of Nassau developed tactics such as volley fire, which allowed continuous shooting. Similarly, in Asia, China and Japan also adapted to gunpowder weapons, developing infantry tactics, as seen in Qi Jiguang's *"Ji xiao xin shu"* and

Japan's use of gunpowder in the Sengoku period.

According to the authors. the Imjin War played a particularly significant role in introducing these changes to Chosŏn. After the war, Chosŏn rapidly transformed its military system by adopting Japanese gunpowder weapons and also Chinese training methods. The establishment of the Military Training Agency (Hullyŏn Togam), a standing army of salaried full-time soldiers, marked a significant shift from Chosŏn's traditional conscription system, relying on peasant militia. The focus on musketeers and the adoption of advanced training methods, such as volley fire, allowed Chosŏn to modernize its military system.

The key argument of the paper is that Chosŏn's innovations in infantry tactics, particularly the use of musketeers and coordinated firing methods, paralleled developments in Europe. For example, the deployment and training of musketeers described in Chosŏn's *"Orientation to the Military Arts"* (The *Pyŏnghak chinam,* 兵學指南) closely resembles European manuals like William Barriffe's *"Military Discipline"*.[4] Both emphasized strict discipline, sequential firing, and the use of signals like drums to coordinate movements.

Even more, according to the authors, Chosŏn's these military innovations were not just a theoretical practice, but also successfully tested in the field, especially from the skirmishes with Russian Cossack forces during the Northern Expeditions of 1654 and 1658. Chosŏn's musketeers played a decisive role in these engagements, demonstrating the effectiveness of their training and tactics.

The paper concludes by questioning the Eurocentric perspective of the military revolution, arguing that similar developments occurred in East Asia. The authors call for further research and global data to support the idea that the military revolution was not confined to Europe.

3. The Military Revolution of Chosŏn in Korean Academia

Next, we will examine how the Military Revolution of Chosŏn is understood within Korean academia. In Anglophone academia, the Military Revolution Thesis is a substantial discourse, with its influence extending to the emergence of the Asian Military Revolution Thesis. The two papers discussed earlier from Anglophone academia also explored the Military Innovations of Late Chosŏn from the perspective of the Asian Military Revolution. In contrast, the Military Revolution Thesis itself is not a familiar concept within Korean academia, let alone discussions of Chosŏn's Military Revolution. There are occasional studies dealing with the Military Revolution Thesis, but these studies have largely been the domain of Western history researchers, with Korean history researchers showing little interest. Despite this, a small number of researchers have taken an interest in the Military Revolution of Chosŏn, and notably, No Yŏnggu was the first to suggest the possibility of a Military Revolution in Chosŏn, even preceding Anglophone academia. Therefore, this study will review No Yŏnggu's pioneering work and the research of Kim Yeong-joon, which explicitly examines Chosŏn's Military Revolution Thesis.

1) No Yŏnggu (Young-koo Roh). "Military Revolution' and Chosŏn Dynasty's Military Reforms in the 17th and 18th Centuries.' *Journal of Western History* 36 (2007)

No Yŏnggu's paper, "'Military Revolution' and Chosŏn Dynasty`s Military Reforms in the 17th and 18th Centuies" (2007), explores the possibility of linking Chosŏn's military changes with the theory of the military revolution. He challenges traditional explanations of Chosŏn's post-Imjin War changes based on internal development theories, arguing that these changes align more with the military transformations seen in Europe after large-scale wars.

The paper examines three main areas: changes in battle tactics, the expansion of military forces, and the establishment of a centralized fiscal structure. The main arguments are as below.

First, the battle tactics: Chosŏn's shift from cavalry-based to infantry-based tactics after the Imjin War parallels changes in 16th-century Europe. Chosŏn adopted Qi Jiguang's *Zhe School tactics* and muskets, replacing bows. Infantry, equipped with swords for close combat, became the primary military force, supported by cavalry. This resembled Europe's transition from medieval tactics dominated by cavarly to early modern tactics of musket and pike formations.

Second, military expansion: The size of Chosŏn's military grew significantly after the Imjin War, with an army of over 1 million by the early 18th century. The central army became dominant, and Chosŏn included lower social classes in its ranks. This expansion was driven by concerns over potential conflicts with the Qing and was part of King Hyojong's northern campaign policy.

Third, centralized fiscal structure: To support its expanded military, Chosŏn reformed its fiscal system, exemplified by the *Law of Great Equity*, which replaced tribute with rice and cloth, better suited for provisioning soldiers. Centralized taxation under the Seonhyecheong allowed for efficient resource management, like Europe's adoption of mercantilism to fund large-scale wars.

No Yŏnggu argues that the changes in Chosŏn reflect elements of a military revolution, as seen in Europe. While not identical, Chosŏn's military reforms, increased war expenditures, and centralized governance align with the global trends of military revolutions. The paper suggests that applying the military revolution theory offers a new perspective on late Chosŏn's historical significance within a global context, but it also acknowledges key differences between Chosŏn and Europe.

2) Kim Yeong-joon, "The Training Methods for Musketeers and Military Discipline in 17th Century Chosŏn"

Kim Yeong-joon's paper, "Training Methods and Military Discipline of Chosun Musketeer Around the 17th Century." (2014), is one of the few studies that explicitly review the military revolution theory in Chosŏn after No Yŏnggu. The paper criticizes the focus on military organization in late Chosŏn research while neglecting aspects such as training and tactics. It aims to explore the unique features of Chosŏn's military revolution compared to Europe, particularly focusing on musketeer training and discipline.

Kim examines Chosŏn's military innovations through two key aspects: musketeer training and military discipline. Musketeer training is divided into individual firearms training and formation training. Chosŏn emphasized accuracy in firearm handling, using techniques like cheek-firing, like those introduced in Japan by Portuguese traders. For formation training, Chosŏn adopted systems like European tactics, such as volley fire and rotating fire, documented in manuals like the *"New Artillery Manual"* and the *"Orientation to the Military Arts"*. However, historical records reveal that Chosŏn's musketeers often adapted their tactics in response to cavalry-centric opponents like the Manchus, sometimes abandoning volley fire in favor of individual shooting from cover.

Military discipline is examined through two systems: the Reward System for Enemy Heads and Collective Punishment. In contrast to Europe's focus on strict discipline, Chosŏn motivated soldiers by offering rewards for successful marksmanship, encouraging individual accuracy. The Collective Punishment system helped maintain unit cohesion, especially in mixed-rank units like the Sog'o Army, where lower social classes dominated. This system allowed commanders to maintain control and accountability, stabilizing the military from the mid-17th century.

The paper concludes that while Chosŏn's military innovations paralleled those in Europe, such as the emphasis on gunpowder weapons and new training methods, significant differences existed in how musketeers operated and the cultural values surrounding military discipline. Thus, mechanically applying the European military revolution theory to Chosŏn is problematic, as the cultural motivations and practices were distinct.

4. Comparison and Prospects Between Anglophone and Korean Academia

We have thus far explored how Anglophone and Korean academia explain the Military Revolution of Chosŏn. This chapter will examine the commonalities and differences between the two scholarly communities.

1) Similarities and Differences in Studies on the Military Revolution Thesis

First, the shared focus between Anglophone and Korean academia is clear: both highlight that a "Gunpowder Revolution" occurred in Chosŏn. China and Japan had already used firearms, and Chosŏn also employed large cannons. However, following the Imjin War, Chosŏn shifted its attention to individual firearms and rapidly replaced its weapon systems with personal firearms, notably muskets. Scholars from both traditions also agree not only on the increase in the number of musketeers but also on the development of new tactics and training methods for deploying these musketeers. In short, Chosŏn achieved both quantitative expansion and qualitative growth in its infantry armed with gunpowder weapons.

However, each researcher presents slightly different evidence. Hyeok Hweon Kang emphasizes the success of musketeer units during the Nashin Expedition, illustrating the success of the Gunpowder Revolution. Meanwhile, Tonio Andrade focuses more on the training methods of the musketeer units. He emphasizes that Chosŏn's musketeer units adopted volley fire and sequential fire tactics, similar to contemporary European musketeer units, and underwent strict training based on manuals to master these tactics. He thus pays more attention to the "Revolution in Drill" necessary for the Gunpowder Revolution to function effectively. In contrast, No Yŏnggu highlights the rapid expansion of musketeer numbers and the formation of a large-scale military, while Kim Yeong-joon points out that Chosŏn's musketeers were influenced by a military culture that emphasized individual capabilities rather than strict adherence to training manuals. These nuanced perspectives reveal that while scholars agree on the Gunpowder Revolution, they differ on its impact and contents.

Interest beyond the Gunpowder Revolution and Revolution in Drill varies among scholars. No Yŏnggu, the first to propose the possibility of a Military Revolution in Chosŏn, also mentions other aspects such as large-scale army operations and centralized financial restructuring to support military expenses. Hyeok Hweon Kang summarizes this but concludes that "Yet, although Korean military reforms were radical by local standards, ... the Korean Military Revolution was largely confined to a "musketry revolution" and, ... was limited in other areas such as fiscal mobilization and social reform."[5] Tonio Andrade also focuses on the contents of the Revolution in Drill, without addressing the relationship between military innovation and social change in Chosŏn. He even points out that despite the Gunpowder Revolution, the cultural tradition of archery remained strong in Chosŏn. Kim Yeong-joon does not elaborate on other aspects of the Military Revolution Thesis beyond changes in training techniques. In other words, except for No Yŏnggu, other scholars have taken a passive stance regarding the Military Revolution beyond the Gunpowder and Revolution in Drill.

There are also characteristics unique to Anglophone scholars. They tend to focus on the points of contact between Europe and Chosŏn, giving these connections significant meaning. Hyeok Hweon Kang views the two Northern Expeditions (Nashin Expeditions) as a clash between the European Military Revolution and the Chosŏn Military Revolution. He argues that the European Military Revolution failed in East Asia, while the Chosŏn Military Revolution proved its validity. Tonio Andrade, for his part, pays attention to Jan Janse Weltevree (Pak Yŏn, 朴淵), a Dutchman who drifted to Chosŏn. Andrade attaches great significance to the fact that Weltevree arrived during the period when Chosŏn was undergoing a Gunpowder Revolution. Weltevree hailed from the Netherlands, one of the most advanced countries in terms of military innovation in Europe. Andrade suggests that with Weltevree's assistance, Chosŏn improved its gunpowder weapons. Consequently, Andrade finds a link between Chosŏn and European military innovations through Weltevree.[6] Such findings show that Anglophone scholars actively seek to interpret historical meanings in even the smallest connections between European and Chosŏn military innovations.

2) Critique and Prospects of Research

How can we understand the lack of consistent assessments of the Military Revolution in Chosŏn beyond the Gunpowder Revolution? Ultimately, this suggests that military innovation in Chosŏn, aside from the advent of firearms, was highly limited and did not constitute a revolution worth being called a "Military Revolution". Several reasons can be considered.

First, it is difficult to argue that the quantitative expansion of musketeer units led to qualitative growth in Chosŏn. Instead, Chosŏn was unable to bear the costs of operating its expanded musketeer units, ultimately reverting to older practices. Rather than maintaining a large standing army with salaried soldiers, Chosŏn revived the relationship between regular soldiers (正軍) and support personnel (保人) and rotated soldiers through shifts (輪番). This system resembled the early Chosŏn military system, which operated based on a local conscription system (兵農一致制).[7] The Gunpowder Revolution did not lead to a fundamental reform of the conscription system. Instead, reforms in the conscription system effectively reversed the progress made by the Gunpowder Revolution.

Moreover, as Hyeok Hweon Kang emphasized, it is questionable whether the Nashin Expedition truly demonstrated the effectiveness of the

Gunpowder Revolution. Approximately 200 musketeers participated in the Nashin Expedition, and, as previous studies have pointed out, all were musketeers. However, more detailed verification is needed to determine whether they used volley fire and sequential fire during the campaign and how effective their combat performance was. While it is true that the Chosŏn army gained fame as "Big Heads" and successfully completed the Nashin Expedition, the precise impact of firearms in the actual battle has not been thoroughly investigated. Thus, drawing the conclusion that the Gunpowder Revolution was successful based solely on the use of gunpowder weapons and the expedition's success is logically weak.[8]

Furthermore, even the fundamental idea that Chosŏn swiftly reorganized its infantry around musketeers can be questioned in a different way. If Chosŏn truly had extensive combat experience, it would not have been possible to replace its forces entirely with musketeers. In Europe, while musketeers emerged, armies continued to integrate pikemen, cavalry, and other formations depending on combat situations, using them organically. After the Military Revolution, European forces improved their combat capabilities by restraining the rapid expansion of musketeer formations.[9] By contrast, as researchers have pointed out, Chosŏn drastically increased its musketeer formations to an almost disproportionate level. This suggests that Chosŏn lacked the opportunity to gain real combat experience and failed to adapt its military innovations to practical situations.

Above all, it is doubtful whether the logic of military innovation leading to societal reform could have worked under the Qing-dominated stable diplomatic order in East Asia. Although it is true that Chosŏn clashed militarily with the Qing and paid attention to military issues out of concern for further conflict, it is difficult to argue that Chosŏn aimed to become a military state. Fundamentally, Chosŏn faced diplomatic pressure from the Qing. Consequently, expanding armaments openly was nearly impossible, and indeed, under the Jŏngch'uk Treaty (丁丑約條) concluded immediately after the Second Manchu Invasion, Chosŏn was forbidden from building fortresses and strongholds without permission.

Additionally, while Hyojong used the Northern Campaign (北伐論) as a pretext, it was almost impossible for Chosŏn to expand its military to a level capable of confronting the Qing. In other words, as long as the Qing, a powerful empire, dominated the international order in East Asia, an independent Military Revolution in Chosŏn was unlikely to occur.

5. Conclusion

In this paper, we have examined the discussions surrounding the Military Revolution of Chosŏn in both Anglophone and Korean academia and compared the commonalities and differences between the two. The Military Revolution of Chosŏn represents an attempt to adapt the European Military Revolution Thesis to the context of Chosŏn. This theory was not influential enough to create a major ripple effect in academic circles. However, it is also true that it remains almost the only theory that attempts to explain the diverse military changes in late Chosŏn within a single discourse. This is precisely why the Military Revolution of Chosŏn deserves serious consideration.

The Military Revolution Thesis posits that the military innovations that occurred in Europe around the 16th century triggered social innovation, influencing the establishment of modern states. Initially, this theory garnered attention by focusing on the Gunpowder Revolution in Europe. However, it has faced criticism for its strong technological determinism and for glorifying the expansion of European colonies through force. Despite these criticisms, efforts were made to apply this theory to Asian history, resulting in the so-called Asian Military Revolution Thesis. According to this thesis, similar developments to those seen in Europe occurred in Asia as well. However, the Asian Military Revolution Thesis was also criticized for mechanically applying a European theory to Asia.

The Military Revolution of Chosŏn is, in the broader context, one case study of the Asian Military Revolution Thesis. In Anglophone academia, scholars like Tonio Andrade and Hyeok Hweon Kang have seriously explored this topic, while in Korean academia, No Yŏnggu and Kim

Yeong-joon have also delved into it. Tonio Andrade paid attention to the rapid increase in the proportion of musketeers in late Chosŏn, particularly emphasizing the standardization of musketeer training. Hyeok Hweon Kang focused on the case of the Nashin Expedition, which was an actual battle involving musketeers. Both scholars argued that the Gunpowder Revolution and Revolution in Drill, seen in Europe, also existed in Chosŏn, thus mentioning the possibility of a Military Revolution in Chosŏn.

Korean academia also applied the European Military Revolution Thesis to Chosŏn, but their points of interest differed somewhat from those of Anglophone academia. No Yŏnggu focused on how the rapid transition to a musketeer-centric army led to structural changes throughout society in late Chosŏn. He argued that to operate the rapidly expanding musketeer units, there were concurrent changes in the military service system and military financial management. Kim Yeong-joon, meanwhile, focused particularly on examples of training and discipline. He found that the manualization of training, especially the application of tactics like sequential fire, bore similarities to military innovations in Europe.

Scholars focusing on the Military Revolution of Chosŏn generally agree that a "Gunpowder Revolution" took place and use this as the basis for their discussion. However, they diverge in their interpretations of the contents of the Military Revolution. Hyeok Hweon Kang focused on the performance of musketeers during the Nashin Expedition, while Tonio Andrade emphasized the similarities between European and Chosŏn musketeer training manuals. No Yŏnggu focused on the changes in social structure triggered by the Military Revolution, while Kim Yeong-joon concentrated on the similarities between training manuals and tactics. This suggests that while the Gunpowder Revolution in Chosŏn is accepted, whether a Military Revolution took place remains a point of contention among scholars. Indeed, to varying degrees, the studies express skepticism regarding the Military Revolution Thesis of Chosŏn.

Ultimately, applying the Military Revolution Thesis to Chosŏn must be approached with caution. Not only does the theory itself have flaws, but, more importantly, the changes observed in Chosŏn are difficult to compare directly to those seen in Europe. Could we perhaps express it as Hyeok Hweon Kang did, saying, "The Military Revolution of Chosŏn was limited to a musketry revolution, and its impact in other areas was limited"? Such an expression may be valid. However, if the revolution was truly limited to muskets, we must question whether it is appropriate to call it a "revolution" at all. It may be that, for Chosŏn, the case holds more value as an example of failed military innovation rather than a successful one. Examining how Chosŏn overcame the shocks that arose from failing in military innovation might align more closely with historical reality.

Another point to consider is that it may not be important whether a Military Revolution took place in Chosŏn. The Military Revolution Thesis presupposes that military change is the starting point of social change. The core idea of the Military Revolution Thesis is that military change serves as the initial spark for all other changes. If we are to apply the Military Revolution Thesis to Chosŏn, we must actively consider whether this core idea is applicable.

Did late Chosŏn experience the Gunpowder Revolution, Revolution in Drill, or Military Revolution? As we have seen, each scholar has a different answer to this question. This difference arises because each scholar has their own understanding of the superficial changes that occurred. Thus, what impact did the military changes in late Chosŏn have on society? Regarding this question, both Anglophone and Korean academia, including the military history discourse, offer few meaningful answers. Rather, the traditional explanation often assumes that politics and diplomacy influence military policy. For example, conflicts between political factions led to various military commands being closely tied to political powers, or the diplomatic situation after the Manchu invasions prompted Hyojong's Northern Campaign and the establishment of a capital defense system. Conversely, it is challenging to find studies that understand the military history of late Chosŏn from the perspective that military changes were the starting point of societal changes.

Recently, scholars have proposed replacing the term "Revolution" with

"Evolution" when discussing the European Military Revolution Thesis.[10] The essence of evolution lies in adaptation. Chosŏn also succeeded in rapidly replacing its weapon system with gunpowder weapons through military innovation, but we can understand it as having adapted to the ensuing shock in its own unique way. The distinctiveness of Chosŏn in its method of adaptation may provide a clue to understanding the impact of military changes on Chosŏn society. In other words, instead of simply looking for cases of military innovation like those of Europe in Chosŏn, we still have the task of identifying Chosŏn's unique features—how it started military innovation in a form like Europe, but subsequently transformed its military system in a manner different from Europe. This is a task we plan to address in subsequent research.

Note

1 This article is a revised version of the presentation given at the Fall 2024 Symposium of the Institute of Humanities at Sogang University and the paper published in the JNAH 21-1(Journal of North-east Asia History), 2025, titled "Was There a Military Revolution in Late Chosŏn Korea? - A Comparative Analysis of the Recent Discussions on Late Chosŏn Military History in Korean and Anglo-American Academic Society-" by Dukhee Yun and Kunha Kim.

2 In this paper, the term "Chosŏn Military Revolution Thesis" is used. This is because all of the studies on the Military Revolution introduced in this paper focus on the context of Late Chosŏn. However, the formal academic term used in Anglophone academia is "Korean Military Revolution (Thesis)." A literal translation would be "Korean Military Revolution," but this translation fails to convey the specificity of the Late Chosŏn period. Moreover, there is a risk of confusion with the term "military revolution" from modern Korean history, which carries different connotations and potential controversy. Considering these factors, and to reflect both the historical context and meaning, the term is translated as "Chosŏn Military Revolution Thesis."

3 Representative studies on the "Nashin Expedition" in Korean academia include Pak T'aegŭn. "Chosŏn-gun ŭi Hŭngnyonggang Ch'ulbyŏn."(The Chosŏn Army's Expedition to the Heilongjiang River) Han'guksaron, Vol. 9, 1983, Pan Yunhong. "Pibyŏnsa ŭi Nasŏn Chŏngbŏl Chuhwek e Taehayŏ: Hyojongjo Yŏnggot'ap P'ab'yŏng Chŏlmok ŭl Chungsim ŭro."(On the Planning of the Naseon Expedition by the Border Defense Council: Focusing on the Military Dispatch Provisions of Yeonggotap during King Hyojong's Reign), Han'guksahakbo, Vol. 11, 2001, Yi Kangch'il. "Chosŏn Hyojong-jo Nasŏn Chŏngbŏl kwa P'ia Choch'ong e Taehan Sogo."(A Study on Rifles Used in Korean Expedition to Russia in the Reign of King Hyojong(1650-1659), Komunhwa, Vol. 20, 1982, Kye Sŭngbŏm. "Nasŏn Chŏngbŏl kwa Sin Yu ŭi 'Pukchŏngnok'."(The Naseon Expedition and Sin Yu's 'Record of the Northern Campaign'), Kunsasa Yŏn'gu Ch'ongsŏ, Vol. 5, 2008, Kye Sŭngbŏm. "17-segi Chungban Nasŏn Chŏngbŏl ŭi Ch'ui wa Kŭ Tongasiajŏk ŭimi."(The Mid-17th Century Naseon Expedition: Its Progress and East Asian Significance), Sahak Yŏn'gu, Vol. 110 (2013), Pak Chibae. "17-segi Chungban Rŏsia ŭi Tongbuk'a Chin'ul kwa 'Nasŏn

Chŏngbŏl' ŭi ŭimi."(The Expansion of Russia into Northeast Asia and the Significance of Manchu-Korean Expeditions during 1650s), Yŏksahakpo, Vol. 240, 2018. Among these, Hyeok Hweon Kang has stated that he referenced Kye Sŭngbŏm's study (2013).

4 The *Pyŏnghak chinam (兵學指南)* is a military manual compiled by Yu Sŏngnyong under the order of King Sŏnjo, summarizing key contents from *Ji xiao xin shu (紀效新書)*. It consists of five volumes in one book. Although the exact date of its initial publication is unclear, it was widely used as a representative combat training manual in the late Chosŏn period.

5 Hyeok Hweon Kang, *op. cit.*, p. 148.

6 However, this claim is not generally accepted in Korean academia. Rather, it is believed that while Chosŏn showed interest in the superior firearms and ships of the Netherlands, it maintained a defensive attitude toward adopting and improving its weapons system through Dutch influence.

7 In fact, except for the Military Training Agency (Hullyŏn Togam), the other military divisions—including the Chongyungchong, Sueochong, Oyongchong, and Kumwiyong—retained the structure of regular soldiers (chŏnggun) and support personnel (boin), similar to the early Chosŏn period. However, unlike in the early Chosŏn period, the boin did not directly provide the military service costs of the chŏnggun; instead, military finances were managed under the supervision of each military division.

8 In fact, when examining the details of the Nashin Expedition, it was not a pitched battle fought on an open plain with a well-formed battle line. Most of the combat took place on boats on the river or at positions near the riverbank, making it a type of riverine warfare and siege warfare. In such forms of combat as riverine battles and sieges, the use of tactics like volley fire or sequential firing was highly limited.

9 Recently, there has been a perspective that battles during the Military Revolution era were not based solely on musketry tactics but were conducted using composite tactics that organically integrated pike formations and other units. For related discussions, see Dukhee Yun, "The 'Push of Pike' in Seventeenth-Century English Infantry Combat," *Journal of Military History* 86, No. 4, 2022.

10 Frank Jacob and Gilmar Visoni-Alonzo, *The Military Revolution in Early Modern Europe: A Revision* (London: Palgrave Macmillan, 2016). These two researchers assert, in an extreme view, that the "Military Revolution" did not actually exist. Instead, they argue that military tactics and technologies

evolved and adapted to fit the specific conditions of each country or region around the world.

Bibliography

Books:

Andrade, Tonio. *The Gunpowder Age: China, Military Innovation, and the Rise of the West in World History.* Princeton, NJ: Princeton University Press, 2016.

Black, Jeremy. *Beyond the Military Revolution: War in the Seventeenth-Century World.* Basingstoke: Palgrave Macmillan, 2011.

Brewer, John. *The Sinews of Power: War, Money and the English State 1688-1783.* Cambridge, MA: Harvard University Press, 1989.

Cha, Moonseop. *Research on the Military System of the Chosŏn Dynasty.* Dankook University Press, 1973.

Cha, Moonseop. *Research on Military Affairs in the Chosŏn Dynasty.* Dankook University Press, 1995.

Choi, Hyosik. *Studies on the History of Military System in the Late Period of the Yi Dynasty.* PhD diss., Sungshin Women's University, 1991.

Jacob, Frank, and Gilmar Visioni-Alonze. *The Military Revolution in Early Modern Europe: A Revision.* London: Palgrave Macmillan, 2016.

Lorge, Peter A. *The Asian Military Revolution: From Gunpowder to the Bomb.* Cambridge: Cambridge University Press, 2008.

Lynn, John A. *Giant of the Grand Siècle: The French Army, 1610-1715.* Cambridge: Cambridge University Press, 1997.

Parker, Geoffrey. *The Military Revolution: Military Innovation and the Rise of the West, 1500-1800.* 2nd ed. Cambridge: Cambridge University Press, 1996.

Phillips, Gervase. *The Anglo-Scots Wars 1513-1550.* Woodbridge: Boydell Press, 1999.

Raymond, James. *Henry VIII's Military Revolution: The Armies of Sixteenth-Century Britain and Europe.* London: I.B. Tauris, 2007.

Showalter, Dennis E., and William J. Astore. *Soldiers' Lives Through History: The Early Modern World.* Westport, Conn.: Westview Press, 2007.

Starkey, Armstrong. *War in the Age of Enlightenment, 1700-1789.* Westport, Conn.: Praeger, 2003.

Weigley, Russel F. *The Age of Battles: The Quest for Decisive Warfare from*

Breitenfeld to Waterloo. Bloomington, IN: Indiana University Press, 1991.

Wilson, Peter. *Iron and Blood: A Military History of German-Speaking People since 1500*. London: Allan Lane, 2022.

Wilson, Peter. *The Thirty Years' War: Europe's Tragedy*. Cambridge: Cambridge University Press, 2009.

Journal Articles:

Andrade, Tonio, Hyeok Hweon Kang, and Kirsten Cooper. "A Korean Military Revolution? Parallel Military Innovations in East Asia and Europe.", *Journal of World History* 25, No. 1, 2014.

Black, Jeremy. "'A Military Revolution?'" In *The Military Revolution Debate: Readings on the Military Transformation of Early Modern Europe*, edited by Clifford J. Rogers, Boulder, CO: Westview Press, 1995.

Black, Jeremy. "Was There a Military Revolution in Early Modern Europe?", *History Today* 58, No. 7, 2008.

France, John. "Close Order and Close Quarter: The Culture of Combat in the West.", *The International History Review* 27, No. 3, 2005.

Geoffrey Parker. "The Limits of Revolutions in Military Affairs: Maurice of Nassau, The Battle of Niuwpoort (1600), and the Legacy.", *The Journal of Military History* 71, No. 2, 2007.

Kang, Hyeok Hweon. "Big Heads and Buddhist Demons: The Korean Musketry Revolution and the Northern Expeditions of 1654 and 1658.", *Journal of Chinese Military History* 2, No. 2, 2013.

Kim, Hyundong. "17-segi Ŏyŏngch'ŏng Ch'angsŏl kwa Pŏnsang Kŭpryoje ŭi Sŏngnip"(Inception of Eoyeong-Cheong and Establishment of On-duty Salary Payment System in the 17th century), *Korean Historical Studies,* Vol. 192, 2021.

Kim, Kunha. "Chŏngch'ung Yakcho ŭi Sŏnggyŏk kwa Hyŏnjongdae Anch'uwŏn Sagŏn"(The Peace Treaty of 1637 and the An Ch'uwon Case in 1666), *Journal of Chosŏn Dynasty History,* Vol. 78, 2016.

Kim, Moonsik. "18-segi Chosŏn Chisik'in ŭi Nedŏlland ŭi Hae"(Choson intellectual`s understanding of Holland in the 18th Century), J*ournal of Historical Studies,* Vol. 39, Dankook University, 2007.

Kim, Yeong-joon. "17-segi Chosŏn ŭi Posu Hullyŏn Pangsik kwa Kunyul."

(Training Methods and Military Discipline of Chosun Musketeer Around the 17th Century), *Journal of Military History*, Vol. 92, 2014.

Kye, Seung-bum. "17-segi Chungban Nasŏn Chŏngbŏl ŭi Ch'ui wa Kŭ Tongasiajŏk ŭimi." (Manchu-Korean Expeditions to the Amur of the 1650s in Russian Sources), *Yeolsang Gojon Yeongu,* Vol. 65, 2018.

No, Yŏnggu (Young-koo Roh). "Kunsahyŏngmyŏngnon kwa 17~18-segi Chosŏn ŭi Kunsajŏk Pyŏnhwa." ('Military Revolution' and Chosŏn Dynasty's Military Reforms in the 17th and 18th Centuries), *Journal of Western History,* Vol. 36, 2007.

Parrott, David A. "Strategy and Tactics in the Thirty Years' War: The 'Military Revolution'." In *The Military Revolution Debate: Readings on the Military Transformation of Early Modern Europe*, edited by Clifford J. Rogers, Boulder, CO: Westview Press, 1995.

Parker, Geoffrey. "The 'Military Revolution, 1560–1660' - A Myth?" In *The Military Revolution Debate: Readings on the Military Transformation of Early Modern Europe*, edited by Clifford J. Rogers, Boulder, CO: Westview Press, 1995.

Rogers, Clifford J. "The Military Revolution in History and Historiography." In *The Military Revolution Debate: Readings on the Military Transformation of Early Modern Europe*, edited by Clifford J. Rogers, Boulder, CO: Westview Press, 1995.

Yun, Dukhee. "The 'Push of Pike' in Seventeenth-Century English Infantry Combat", *Journal of Military History,* Vol. 86, No. 4, 2022.

7

"Unique" Positioning of a Universal Religion: The Origins of the Korean Catholic Church and Recent Debates

Hohyun Nam

Republic of Korea Air Force Academy

7 "Unique" Positioning of a Universal Religion: The Origins of the Korean Catholic Church and Recent Debates

Hohyun Nam (Republic of Korea Air Force Academy)

1. Introduction

> *"The Korean Church, which originated from the lay apostolate and was made fertile by the blood of martyrs, has been reborn, absorbing the evangelical zeal of the witnesses of faith and the recognition of the role and vocation of the laity as precious."*
>
> _Pope Francis (September 16, 2023)

On September 16, 2023, a statue of Father Kim Taegŏn 金大建 was erected on the outer wall of St. Peter's Basilica in the Vatican. Father Kim Taegŏn, known as the "first Korean priest," traveled throughout China, Manchuria, Mongolia, and Chosŏn, ministering while also seeking ways for Western missionaries to enter Chosŏn. He also served as an interpreter for the French military stationed in China. During one such endeavor to open a path for missionaries, he was captured on the west coast of Chosŏn and beheaded at the age of 25. His life and martyrdom illustrate the condition of Catholic believers under the Chosŏn dynasty and the efforts made beyond the boundaries of the Chosŏn court to improve their situation. Until now, the outer wall of St. Peter's Basilica has only featured statues of the founders of major religious orders. It is the first time that a statue representing a local church, rather than an order, has been erected. Archbishop Paul Gallagher of the Vatican emphasized that the presence of Father Kim Taegŏn's statue alongside the saints and blesseds on the outer wall of St. Peter's Basilica would not only enrich this line of saints but also express the universality of the Catholic Church.[1]

However, the process by which the "Chosŏn Catholic Church" was established as a local church was not universal. According to Catholic doctrine, a "Local Church" represents the "Universal Church" through a unified liturgy, but in Chosŏn, the Catholic Church emerged as a local church even before the presence of a priest to celebrate such liturgies. This uniqueness is well demonstrated by the fact that, while we recognize the origin of the Korean Catholic Church as dating back to 1784, the establishment of the Chosŏn Vicariate was only possible in 1831. Unlike in most regions of the world, where Catholicism was introduced by the arrival of priests, in Chosŏn, Chinese Catholic texts—often referred to as "*Sŏhak*" (Western Learning, 西學)—were transmitted before any missionaries arrived. On this basis, a spontaneous faith community emerged. Those who embraced Catholicism in Chosŏn made efforts to invite priests to conduct proper liturgies and even attempted direct contact with foreign nations. As a result, Yi Sŭnghun 李承薰, who participated as a member of the diplomatic mission to Beijing, received baptism at the Beijing Catholic Church and returned to baptize his fellow believers, thereby forming a group of Chosŏn Catholic believers mediated by baptism—thus giving birth to the Chosŏn Catholic Church.

The Chosŏn Catholic Church faced severe "persecution" immediately following its establishment. This was not only because the establishment of the Chosŏn Catholic Church occurred beyond the control of the state, but also because Catholic doctrine fundamentally differed from the Neo-Confucianism that had firmly taken root in Chosŏn society. Initially, these differences led only to criticism of Catholicism on an academic level, but by the 19th century, as the Chosŏn Catholic Church expanded its influence and as changes in the political situation of the Chosŏn

Dynasty and international affairs intersected with Catholicism, numerous believers were executed. The Chosŏn Dynasty began executing Catholic believers not merely because they adhered to a foreign religion, but because they were considered "criminals" who disobeyed the state's mandate to uphold Confucian values.[2] Socially, Catholic believers in Chosŏn were discriminated against, often subjected to arbitrary searches or expelled from their villages. As a result, for over a century following the establishment of the Chosŏn Catholic Church, until the latter half of the 19th century when religious freedom was permitted, the Chosŏn Catholic Church produced hundreds of martyrs. Pope Francis' reference to the Korean Church as "The Korean Church, which originated from the lay apostolate and was made fertile by the blood of martyrs" emphasizes this uniqueness of the Korean Catholic Church.

Thus, the history of the Chosŏn Catholic Church, beginning with the writings of missionaries and adorned with a history of martyrdom, has garnered attention both domestically and in Western academia. This is because the development of the Chosŏn Catholic Church's history was unique, and it also offers interpretative possibilities from the perspectives of East-West cultural exchange or East Asia as a whole. However, the study of the history of the Chosŏn Catholic Church in Korea is often regarded as a minor subfield of "Church History" within the broader field of Korean history. The significance of the Chosŏn Catholic Church's history has been confined to diocesan-level historiography and the veneration of martyrs. Nevertheless, considering that the Korean Catholic Church was born as a community through communication with Beijing and, further, with the world, the significance of the establishment of the Chosŏn Catholic Church cannot be limited merely within the Church itself. Just as the Chosŏn Catholic Church, as a local church, is connected to the universal Church, the history of the Chosŏn Catholic Church also unfolded in conjunction with Chosŏn history and East Asian history within a broader framework. This study aims to provide a macroscopic perspective on the history of the Chosŏn Catholic Church by examining the major trends in the research conducted on the Chosŏn Catholic Church's history both domestically and in Western academia, demonstrating that these perspectives are meaningful for studying not only the Chosŏn period but also traditional East Asian history. Furthermore, by presenting the major issues that both academic fields have focused on regarding certain aspects of Chosŏn Catholic history, it will explore the points of intersection and directionality in the understanding of Church history by both academic communities.

2. Debates on the Origins of the Korean Catholic Church

The Korean Catholic Church designates 1784 as the beginning of the Church. Yi Sŭnghun, who visited Beijing in 1783 as a member of the regular diplomatic mission of the Chosŏn Dynasty, received baptism there in secret, and upon returning home the following year, administered baptism to his fellow believers.[3] What is noteworthy is that the focus is not on the individual baptism of Yi Sŭnghun, but rather on the establishment of the community that mediated this event, which is regarded as the birth of the Church.[4] This point is significant, as the Church is regarded not merely as an individual's observance of faith or a general faith community, but as a community formed through the mediation of baptism. Catholicism emphasizes baptism and the sacraments as fundamental elements of the "*Ecclesia*," and in the Chosŏn, these requirements were first fulfilled in September 1784 when Yi Sŭnghun conducted the baptismal ceremony at the home of Yi Pyŏk 李蘗. As a result, the chronology of the Korean Catholic Church, which began in 1784, extends to the present.

However, a debate arose concerning the origin of the Korean Catholic Church, with some asserting different periods and events as its foundation. This debate is relevant to the topic of this study not only because it goes beyond the simple "search for origins" of the Chosŏn Catholic Church, but also because it is related to the particularity of the Chosŏn Catholic Church and developed into an international dimension.

1) Origin Hypothesis for the Korean Catholic Church During the Imjin War (1592-1598)

The comprehensive questioning of the origin of the Korean Catholic Church began with Medina, a Spanish priest and church historian. Medina focused on the beginning of the Korean Catholic Church in relation to the Imjin War (1592–1598), an international conflict in which Chosŏn, Toyotomi Hideyoshi's Japan, and the Ming China participated. In his work *The Catholic Church in Korea, Its Origins 1566–1784*, he dealt with the historical relationship between the Chosŏn Dynasty and the Catholic Church prior to 1784. This book has been translated into Korean, Japanese, and English, with the English version having a significant influence as an early work that introduced the history of the Korean Catholic Church to English-speaking readers. Medina viewed the transmission of the Gospel to the unknown land of Chosŏn as the origin of the Church.

Medina's discussion begins with the collection of information on Chosŏn from the Jesuit mission in East Asia, specifically from Japan, which was the first mission field. In 1549, Jesuit priests Francisco de Xavier, Cosme de Torres, and Juan Fernández, who arrived in Japan, obtained information about Chosŏn from Japanese and Chinese people they encountered during their voyage. From 1550 to 1556, they stayed in Yamaguchi [山口], a place frequented by Chosŏn envoys, where they had the opportunity to observe Chosŏn people. The Jesuits planned to dispatch missionaries to Chosŏn, and although this plan was not realized, the Chosŏn Catholic Church began to "take root" through their efforts.[5] During the war, Jesuit missionaries also traveled to Chosŏn. In December 1593, Father Gregorio de Cespedes and Brother Hankan Leon, at the invitation of Konishi Yukinaga [小西行長], who was a Catholic believer, officiated sacraments at the military camp located in Ungchŏn 熊川, Chosŏn, for over a year until approximately May 1595.

Medina identified the year 1592 as the foundation of the Chosŏn Catholic Church. This claim is based on the records of Jesuit priest Luis Froïs, which indicate that a Catholic samurai from Bungo [豊後], who had joined the war, baptized around 200 children near Seoul, who were dying after losing their parents in the war. Medina emphasizes, "From a theological perspective, it is certain that the Chosŏn Catholic Church was established in 1592" (pp. 37–38). In doing so, he characterizes this event as the "birth" rather than the "foundation" of the Church, explaining that this distinction was made to counter the notion that the Church emerged from the sacramental and charismatic mission of the universal Catholic Church, rather than being born out of local social structures (pp. 127–128).

Thus, Medina interprets the origin of the Korean Catholic Church as the baptism of "locals (around 200 dying children)" by a "legitimate Church representative (the samurai from Bungo)."

From this perspective, the history of the Chosŏn Catholic Church, which "was born" in 1592, continued in Japan, as the Chosŏn people who had been taken as captives and baptized in the Japanese military camp were transferred to Japan. As a result, in 1613, Hachikan Joaquin, the "first Chosŏn martyr," was beheaded near Asakusa [淺草] (p. 52). After the captive Chosŏn believers were repatriated, Chosŏn had numerous Catholic believers (pp. 75–77), and by sometime before 1784, a "beautiful cathedral" constructed in a modern style had already been established (pp. 88–92). According to Medina's account, the timeline of the Korean Catholic Church could be moved forward by almost 200 years compared to the existing view.

Such a claim faced widespread criticism from Korean academia. Medina's argument not only denies the traditional chronology of the Korean Catholic Church, but also dismisses the 1784 founding year of the Korean Catholic Church as a "pseudo-historical assertion provided for free" and as a "claim fabricated by a small group within the Church to foster irrational and romantic nationalism" (p. v). However, Medina's argument has been pointed out to have factual inaccuracies, as well as theological inconsistencies that make the establishment of his theory impossible.

First of all, Medina identifies the event of 200 dying children baptism by samurai during the Imjin War as the starting point of the "birth" of the

Korean Catholic Church, but this event cannot be given much significance either historically or theologically. Medina emphasizes the baptism of "locals" by a "legitimate Church representative," but this does not always lead to the establishment of a Church. The actions of the samurai during the Imjin War, which involved baptizing 200 dying children (an event mentioned only in the missionary's letter, thus its authenticity itself is uncertain), were indeed baptisms, but there are no records indicating that the baptized 200 dying children grew up to form a community or lead a life of faith. Moreover, the baptism performed by the samurai from Bungo, as described by Medina, was administered to 200 dying children who were dying after losing their parents in the war, making their survival prospects extremely unlikely. Therefore, even if the Church was said to have been born through the baptism by the samurai from Bungo, it would be a Church of deceased children, unrelated to the Church as discussed in the real world.[6] The fundamental difference between the baptism by the Bungo samurai in 1592 and that of Yi Sŭnghun in 1784 lies in whether the act of "baptism" led to the emergence of a community that mediated baptism within Chosŏn society and performed a series of religious practices, including sacraments.

Even from the perspective of the distinction between the universal Church and the local Church, the activities of Chosŏn martyrs in Japan after the Imjin War, as mentioned by Medina, are part of the history of the local Church known as the "Japanese Church," also referred to as "Kirishitan [吉利支丹]," rather than evidence for the establishment of a local "Chosŏn Church."[7] Just as the Chinese Father Zhou Wenmo 周文謨, who worked for the Chosŏn Church and was martyred, was included among the blessed of the Korean Catholic Church, the Chosŏn martyrs who were martyred while working in the Japanese Church are also members of the local Japanese Church. In this respect, Medina's argument is difficult to avoid criticism for hastily discussing the "birth" of the Korean Catholic Church without distinguishing between the universal Church and the local Church.

Yun Min-gu comprehensively criticized Medina's argument, listing each point in detail.[8] He synthesized existing critiques of Medina's claims and additionally pointed out the bias in the sources and translation issues. Specifically, the "Chosŏn Church" prior to 1784, found only in the records of Jesuit priests active in Japan, appears only in fragmentary hearsay, and Father Medina, a Jesuit himself, accepted this without any critical assessment of the sources, which Yun argues reflects Medina's excessive affection for the Jesuits.[9] Through this review, Medina's argument lost its standing, and with Medina's passing, further debates did not continue. However, the recent translation and introduction of letters by Father Cespedes and the continued discussion on Chosŏn Kirishitan martyrs who were martyred in Japan indicate sustained interest in Chosŏn believers active in Japan.

In short, the "Imjin War origin theory of the Korean Catholic Church" suggests that due to the unique circumstances of the late 16th and early 17th centuries surrounding the Imjin War, some Chosŏn individuals were involved in the local "Japanese Church," i.e., the Kirishitan. However, this involvement has no relation to the establishment of a local "Chosŏn Church," and therefore cannot be considered the origin of the Chosŏn Church. While the "Imjin War origin theory of the Chosŏn Catholic Church," as represented by Medina, is no longer a topic of scholarly debate today, it holds historiographical significance in that it invites contemplation on the relationship between the universal Church and the local Church concerning the origins of the Chosŏn Catholic Church.

2) Origin Hypothesis for the Korean Catholic Church through the Academic Gatherings at Chuŏ-sa (Chŏnjinam) Temple

The "Academic Gatherings at *Chuŏ-sa* 走魚寺 (also known as *Chŏnjinam* 天眞菴) temple Origin Hypothesis for the Korean Catholic Church" further emphasizes the "uniqueness" of Chosŏn in the question of the origins of the Chosŏn Catholic Church, thereby opening a new chapter in the debate on the origins of the Korean Catholic Church. This issue is also relevant in the contemporary context, as it is connected to the current efforts within the Korean Catholic Church, as of 2024, to beatify and canonize "Servant of God Yi Pyŏk John the Baptist and his 133 Companions."[10] The "*Chuŏ-sa* temple Academic Gatherings Origin Hypothesis" argues that during the winter of 1779 (or possibly 1777), scholars, including Yi Pyŏk, held academic gatherings at *Chuŏ-sa* temple, where they discussed Western learning. It was during this time that a Catholic community was established around several key figures, suggesting that the origin of the Korean Catholic Church should be considered as 1779, when these gatherings took place, rather than 1784, when Yi Sŭnghun returned after receiving baptism.[11] According to this hypothesis, the group of scholars at *Chuŏ-sa* temple, after discussing Western texts, accepted Catholicism as their faith. These scholars, acting independently before Yi Sŭnghun's return from China, established a church community, giving the Korean Catholic Church a unique status that stands apart from any other local church in the world.

In this process, the status of the gathering place and the leaders who led the academic discussions also changed. The significance of *Chuŏ-sa* temple as the location of the gatherings expanded from being the cradle of faith to the birthplace of the Korean Catholic Church and, eventually, to a founding "sacred site." Those who participated in the gatherings came to be revered as founding "saints." This has led to questions regarding why figures such as Yi Pyŏk, Yi Sŭnghun, Kwon Ch'ŏlsin 權哲身, and Kwon Ilsin 權日身, who are considered "founding leaders" of the Korean Catholic Church, have not been recognized as martyrs, prompting the push for their beatification and canonization. This is because historical evaluation of the so-called "founding saints" and whether the event at *Chuŏ-sa* temple can be considered the origin of the Korean Catholic Church must be conducted.

First of all, questions were raised regarding the nature of the academic gatherings. The *Chuŏ-sa* temple gatherings were led by Kwon Ch'ŏlsin, a disciple of Yi Ik 李瀷. The term "academic gatherings" traditionally refers to meetings where Confucian scholars discuss Confucian classics and practice self-cultivation. The gatherings at *Chuŏ-sa* temple were no different from these traditional academic gatherings, and the question arises whether the discussion of some Western texts during these gatherings could be seen as the origin of the Korean Catholic Church. The leaders of the gatherings examined Neo-Confucianism, and while some Western texts were reviewed, the main purpose of the gatherings was clearly the pursuit of Confucian scholarship.[12] Thus, it is difficult to consider the discussion of some Western texts at *Chuŏ-sa* temple, and the budding faith of a few participants, as the origin of the Korean Catholic Church. Not only was the nature of the academic gatherings not aimed at establishing a Church, but even if some participants formed a community and practiced their faith, it cannot be seen as a "Church" formed through the mediation of baptism. Therefore, it would be more appropriate to regard the 1779 *Chuŏ-sa* temple gatherings as a kind of prehistory rather than the true origin of the Church.

Meanwhile, apart from the question of whether *Chuŏ-sa* temple is indeed the birthplace of the Korean Catholic Church, the issue of honoring the so-called "founding saints" was also discussed. The 1779 *Chuŏ-sa* temple origin hypothesis for the Korean Catholic Church venerates figures such as Yi Pyŏk, Yi Sŭnghun, Kwon Ch'ŏlsin, and Kwon Ilsin as the "founding leaders" and "founding saints" of the Korean Catholic Church, but they have not been recognized as martyrs. Although they played significant roles in the early establishment of the Korean Catholic Church, they were not included in the list of martyrs due to the ambiguity of their martyrdom and the record of apostasy. For example, Yi Pyŏk was a leading figure in the early Chosŏn Catholic Church, introducing Western texts at the *Chuŏ-sa* temple gatherings and influencing Yi Sŭnghun's baptism. However, after 1795, when Catholicism began to be persecuted by the Chosŏn dynasty, Yi was dissuaded by his family from practicing his faith and later died of the plague, as recorded. Similarly, Yi Sŭnghun, Kwon Ch'ŏlsin, and Kwon Ilsin were all interrogated by the authorities for being Catholics, and records show that they renounced their faith. Consequently,

Yi Pyŏk, who died of illness, and Yi Sŭnghun, Kwon Ch'ŏlsin, and Kwon Ilsin, who have records of apostasy, have not been recognized as martyrs.

In an effort to resolve these issues, *Cheonjinam* Shrine and the Diocese of Suwon convened Church historians and relevant scholars in 2002, 2005, 2009, and 2011 to examine the martyrdom of the "founding leaders" of the Korean Catholic Church. The results of these examinations were published in the series "The Catholic Faith of the Founding Leaders of the Korean Catholic Church" (hereinafter referred to as the "Series").[13] Parts of the "Series" have also been translated into English, where a new understanding of martyrdom from a 'theological' perspective was sought, focusing on the martyrdom of Yi Pyŏk, Yi Sŭnghun, Kwon Ilsin, and Kwon Ch'ŏlsin.[14] The "Series" emphasizes, in its introduction, the 'uniqueness' of the Korean Catholic Church, which has hundreds of martyrs, while also pointing out the fact that the founding leaders have not been beatified or canonized. "From a human perspective, (those canonized ahead of the founding leaders: author's note) saint Kim Taegŏn and the martyrs who followed him would be praying in heaven for the beatification and canonization of the founding leaders. Logically speaking, the founding leaders, who are the most venerable and respected in our faith, should have been canonized before others, but their successors have been canonized first and are now venerated by the universal Church. This is not the proper order."[15] Thus, it emphasizes the 'human and logical' necessity of the beatification and canonization of the so-called founding leaders.

Amidst the emphasis on the necessity of the beatification and canonization of these 'founding leaders,' the "Series" particularly reinterprets the martyrdom status of Yi Pyŏk, who died of illness and thus was not a martyr, and Yi Sŭnghun, who faced controversy over apostasy. According to Church historical records, Yi Pyŏk clearly died of an illness. However, the "Series" raised the so-called 'Yi Pyŏk poisoning allegation based solely on the testimony of an anatomy professor who observed the state of Yi Pyŏk's remains during their relocation in June 1979.[16] Furthermore, the "Series" examined the authority and responsibilities of the head of a household 家長 during the Chosŏn dynasty, suggesting that

Yi Pyŏk's father, in his role as the head of the family, might have 'poisoned' Yi Pyŏk in an effort to protect the household.[17] No forensic examination has been conducted on his remains, which have been buried for nearly 200 years, and there is no evidence that his father killed him. Nevertheless, the "Series" strongly suggests the possibility that Yi Pyŏk was 'poisoned,' based on anecdotal accounts regarding his remains and extreme examples from late Chosŏn.

Meanwhile, Yi Sŭnghun faced severe hardship as he was accused of bringing Western texts on Catholicism from Beijing and introducing Catholicism to Chosŏn, He actively communicated with the Catholic Church in the process of inviting and participated in bringing Father Zhou Wenmo to Chosŏn, but in 1801, he was eventually executed after continuously denying his association with Catholicism. Charles Dallet criticized Yi Sŭnghun's actions in his final moments, stating, "He, who was baptized first, who brought the sacrament and the Gospel to his compatriots, went towards death alongside the martyrs, but he was not a martyr. He was beheaded as a Catholic, but he died as an apostate."[18] Although acknowledging Yi Sŭnghun's significant contribution to the establishment of the Chosŏn Catholic Church, it also pointed out that, unlike other martyrs, he did not make a confession of faith in his final moments. However, the "Series" interpreted the meaning of 'martyrdom' overly broadly, suggesting that one could still be considered a martyr even without being killed, or that even if one had renounced their faith, if it was due to persecution by state power, it could still be viewed as martyrdom. Such interpretations deviated from not only historical facts but also the commonly accepted meaning of 'martyrdom' within the Catholic Church.[19] This was because, rather than first considering the historical facts or the theological implications of the actions of historical figures of the time, the individuals who participated in the *Chuŏ-sa* temple academic gatherings were too quickly identified as 'founding saints.'

The somewhat excessive veneration of those who participated in the *Chuŏ-sa* temple academic gatherings can be traced to the influence of Yi Sŭnghun's posthumous collection, *Manchŏn Yugo* 蔓川遺稿, which includes writings attributed to Yi Pyŏk. *Manchŏn Yugo* contains works such as *Sŏngkyo Yoji* 聖教要旨 and *Chŏnjukongkyŏngga* 天主恭敬歌, both of which were revealed to the world by the late Kim Yang-sŏn in the 1960s. Since their release, these writings, including *Manchŏn Yugo*, have been regarded as the essence of early Korean Catholic thought. Numerous studies interpreting Korean Catholic ideology based on Yi Pyŏk's writings emerged, and a translated edition introduced *Sŏngkyo Yoji* as a great 'epic poem' comparable to Milton's "Paradise Lost" and Dante's "Divine Comedy."[20] In this context, the status of Yi Sŭnghun and Yi Pyŏk, major figures in the history of the Chosŏn Catholic Church, was elevated, leading to a re-evaluation of their recognition as martyrs.

The problem lies in the fact that *Sŏngkyo Yoji* and *Manchŏn Yugo*, along with the materials donated by Pastor Kim Yang-sŏn, were all forgeries. This issue was comprehensively raised by Yun Min-gu, who revealed that *Sŏngkyo Yoji*, *Manchŏn Yugo*, as well as *Yi Pyŏk jŏn* 李蘗傳 and *Yuhandang Ŏnhaeng Sillok* 柳閑堂言行實錄, housed in the Korean Christian Museum at Soongsil University, were all counterfeit.[21] Yun's awareness of the issue arose incidentally when, as someone familiar with Catholic culture, he noticed that "*Seonggyo Yoji*" contained an excessive number of Protestant terms such as '*Kamram* 橄欖 (The Catholic Church, on the other hand, translated this word as '*Oriwa*' or '*Olive*'.) Protestant terminology that entered Korea long after Yi Pyŏk's death could not have been present in his writings. Yun conducted a thorough investigation of the Protestant terms found in *Sŏngkyo Yoji* and revealed that its content was filled with non-Christian ideas, such as Noah causing the flood or the existence of multiple creators. He pointed to the sociocultural context of the 1930s as the background for these forgeries. On July 5, 1925, seventy-nine martyrs of the Korean Catholic Church were beatified in Rome, which sparked increased interest in Catholicism, and opportunists took advantage of this atmosphere to produce and sell forgeries.

However, the response to this revelation was passive. Despite *Manchŏn Yugo* and *Sŏngkyo Yoji* being revealed as forgeries, the atmosphere of emphasizing Yi Pyŏk and Yi Sŭnghun as the founding saints of the Chosŏn

Catholic Church continued, dismissing the issue as merely a problem of textual versions. A review published the year following Yun Min-gu's book still stated that the Classical Chinese version of *Sŏngkyo Yoji* was extremely difficult, containing many elements from the Bible and doctrine, and emphasized that accurately translating and annotating it was an urgent task. This repeated assertion clearly illustrates the prevailing atmosphere at that time.[22] Eventually, the controversy surrounding *Sŏngkyo Yoji* was resolved when Protestant scholars identified its original source. It was revealed that the original text of *Sŏngkyo Yoji* was "*The Analytical Reader: A Short Method For Learning To Read And Write Chinese* 雙千字文," published by missionary William A. P. Martin in 1863 (revised edition in 1897) in China.[23] Subsequent research revealed that the purpose of "*The Analytical Reader*" was to serve as an educational textbook to help Westerners and students at mission schools in China learn Chinese. It was not intended to explain Christian doctrines or biblical content.[24] Earlier in Yun Min-gu's book, it was pointed out that *Manchŏn Yugo* and *Sŏngkyo Yoji* not only contained Protestant terms but also diverged from Christian doctrines. The reason for this was clarified through an analysis of *The Analytical Reader*.

Ultimately, the historical reassessment of Yi Pyŏk and Yi Sŭnghun, which was based on *Sŏngkyo Yoji* and *Manchŏn Yugo*, had to return to its starting point. However, what we highlights even more is the excessive veneration of the so-called 'founding saints' of the Korean Catholic Church, which was carried out while emphasizing the uniqueness of the Korean Catholic Church. The history of the Korean Catholic Church undoubtedly began on a 'unique' path, distinct from other regional churches worldwide. How, then, is this 'uniqueness' reflected in the progression of Korean Catholic history? Furthermore, what implications does it have in the context of Korean history? These questions will be explored in a separate section, focusing on recent research achievements in the history of the Korean Catholic Church.

3. Issues and Discussions

Should we view the birth of the Chosŏn Catholic Church as solely resulting from contact with the universal Church (as in the Imjin War origin theory), or should we see the formation of an indigenous community within Chosŏn as the emergence of the Church without external influence (as in the *Chuŏ-sa* temple academic gathering origin theory)? This question is closely related to the emphasis we place on either the universal or the particular aspects when understanding the history of the Chosŏn Catholic Church. The former defines the establishment of the Chosŏn Catholic Church as part of the Jesuit 'propagation of the Gospel,' while the latter minimizes external influences like the Beijing Catholic Church in the establishment of the Chosŏn Catholic Church, emphasizing the significance of a community that emerged 'indigenously' in Chosŏn. However, the historical reality of the emergence of the Chosŏn Catholic Church was neither simply the result of the propagation of a universal religion into Chosŏn nor an event that emerged in isolation from the outside world. Rather, it was the result of Chosŏn individuals wrestling with the acceptance of Catholicism on the broader stage of East Asia.

Therefore, understanding the history of the Chosŏn Catholic Church solely as the history of a small church community or limiting it to the veneration of martyrs does not allow for a full comprehension of the Chosŏn Catholic Church as a historical entity.[25] The trend in Western scholarship has also focused not on the history of the church itself but on the significance of the transmission of Catholicism to Chosŏn and the response of the state to its acceptance.[26] Thus, this section will examine the intersection and orientation of research trends regarding the history of the Chosŏn Catholic Church as undertaken in both Korean and Western academic circles.

1) The Divergence of *Sŏhak* (Western Learning, 西學): *Sŏkyo* (Western Religion, 西教) and *Chŏksa* (Rejection of Heterodoxy, 斥邪)

The foremost issue in understanding the emergence of the Chosŏn Catholic Church is the question of the nature of *Sŏhak* (Western Learning 西學). Western knowledge and culture, introduced to Chosŏn through diplomatic missions, stimulated Chosŏn intellectuals, with the influx of Chinese-translated Western texts serving as a critical impetus for the establishment of the Chosŏn Catholic Church. Therefore, examining the characteristics of *Sŏhak* and the various aspects of change it brought upon its introduction to Chosŏn represents a significant concern in intellectual history. Particularly, the context in which certain Chosŏn individuals accepted *Sŏhak* as a religion, specifically Catholicism, must be addressed to make clear the historical phenomenon of the Chosŏn Catholic Church in Korea—a society devoid of the modern concept of religion.

The general explanation offered by Korean academia regarding this issue is that when Chosŏn people accepted *Sŏhak*, they predominantly embraced its technological aspect (*ki*, 器) while excluding its religious and ethical dimension (*li*, 理).[27] Contrary to the expectations of Jesuit missionaries who authored texts on *Sŏhak* as part of their East Asian missionary efforts, Chosŏn intellectuals showed interest only in subjects such as mathematics, astronomy, and calendrical science, while displaying little to no interest in the "religious" aspects of *Sŏhak*. Moreover, even when they accepted the "technological" aspects (*ki*, 器) of *Sŏhak*, they justified this acceptance by framing it as knowledge originating from China, thereby legitimizing the adoption of Western science and technology as *Sŏhak* rather than as *Sŏkyo* (Western religion 西教).[28] This discussion highlights the context in which *Sŏhak* was accepted as a form of scholarship in the Chosŏn dynasty, which lacked the modern concept of religion. It also explains the background that allowed *Sŏhak* to be discussed in public spaces in Chosŏn before the state-level suppression of Catholicism took place.

Those who accepted *Sŏhak* as a religion were predominantly young scholars from the *Namin* (Southern faction 南人) faction. As a result, this group is sometimes understood as a collective that reflects the reformist discourse among *Namin* intellectuals, culminating in the establishment of the Chosŏn Catholic Church. Within the *Namin* faction, the acceptance of *Sŏhak* led to a division between the "*Sin Sŏ*" (Pro-*Sŏhak*, 信西) group, who embraced *Sŏhak* as a religion, and the "*Kong Sŏ*" (Anti-*Sŏhak*, 攻西) group, who criticized it. Furthermore, it has been explained that as political conflicts within the *Namin* faction intensified in the late 18th century, this division sparked the emergence of widespread *chŏksa* (rejection of heterodoxy, 斥邪) sentiments across Chosŏn society, beginning with the *Kong Sŏ* faction.[29] In the discourse of *chŏksa*, *Sŏhak* was defined as *sahak* (heretical or evil learning, 邪學). Once *Sŏhak* was categorized as *sahak*, Catholicism could no longer be tolerated within the public sphere of the Chosŏn dynasty. Consequently, scholarly discussions within Korea regarding the acceptance of *Sŏhak* have primarily understood it as encompassing both Western science and technology as well as religion, and have focused on attitudes toward this comprehensive body of knowledge.

This interpretation appears to be largely agreed uponby Western scholars as well. Donald Baker notes that King Chŏngjo (r. 1776-1800) also distinguished between science and religion within *Sŏhak*. Like other Confucian scholars, he is understood to have protected Jesuit science while rejecting Catholic faith. While theology and science were inseparable for Jesuit missionaries, Chosŏn intellectuals made a clear distinction between the two, which ultimately led to the failure of Jesuit missionary efforts in Chosŏn Korea.[30] Baker maintains the perspective that *Sŏhak* fundamentally represented Catholicism as a religion. According to him, the fierce opposition that Catholicism faced in Chosŏn stemmed from the fundamental differences between Confucianism and Catholicism. Unlike Confucianism, which emphasized "morality" as a means to maintain social order among members of society, Catholicism posited the existence of God as an absolute object of obedience and placed "truth" above morality, making the two systems fundamentally incompatible.[31] While Korean academic discussions have primarily interpreted the acceptance and differentiation of *Sŏhak* in relation to factional disputes and political contexts, Baker's argument distinguishes itself by emphasizing the fundamental differences between Confucianism and Catholicism. Rather than focusing on the process of *Sŏhak*'s acceptance, Baker highlights the irreconcilable disparity between the two ideologies, bringing a unique perspective to the discourse.

Recently, fundamental questions have been raised regarding whether *Sŏhak* adopted by Chosŏn intellectuals can indeed be understood by dividing it into two distinct categories of "science and technology" and "religion." Since the consciousness of Jesuit missionaries, including Matteo Ricci, did not entail a clear distinction between religious knowledge and scientific knowledge, it has become necessary to reexamine the assumption that Chosŏn intellectuals also separated the scientific aspects of *Sŏhak* from its religious dimensions when they accepted it.[32] Furthermore, questions have been raised regarding the previously uncritical assumption about the "scientific and technological" aspects of *Sŏhak*. Specifically, it has been pointed out that the science and technology transmitted by Jesuit missionaries carried the medieval worldview of the Catholic Church and therefore could not represent the contemporary scientific advancements of Europe. Instead, it reflected somewhat anachronistic knowledge tied to outdated frameworks.[33] It can now be said that the history of Chosŏn intellectuals' acceptance of *Sŏhak* is being called into question, requiring a comprehensive reexamination from its very premises.

In this context, while ongoing questions regarding the nature and acceptance of *Sŏhak* continue to arise, it seems that no consensus has yet been reached within Korean academia. Nevertheless, there is growing attention to the need for reflection on the long-standing focus on the relationship between *Sŏhak* and *Silhak* (Practical Learning 實學) or modernity, along with the importance of examining the context in which Chosŏn intellectuals conditionally accepted *Sŏhak*.[34] This perspective shifts the focus away from associating the speed of Chosŏn people's acceptance of *Sŏhak* with modernity, instead emphasizing the changes that *Sŏhak* itself brought about in the Chosŏn dynasty—a point worth noting. Additionally, the view that Chosŏn people in the late 18th century accepted and circulated *Sŏhak* strictly as "authorized" knowledge is also significant. In both the Chosŏn and Qing, *Sŏhak* was positioned as a field of study carried out by a limited group of state-sanctioned officials for the purpose of governance. At an academic level, *Sŏhak* functioned only as an auxiliary to the highest form of learning, *Kyŏnghak* (the study of Confucian classics, 經學), which aimed at cultivating sagehood.[35] Taking these points into consideration, we can gain a multifaceted understanding of how *Sŏhak* was openly discussed in late Chosŏn society, while, paradoxically, the Chosŏn Catholic Church faced fierce opposition from both the state and society immediately after its establishment.

An additional point that must be noted is the need for continued exploration of the actual texts of *Sŏhak* and the reconstruction of the various contexts in which they were received. Korean academia has yet to compile a comprehensive catalog of the *Sŏhak* texts introduced during the late Chosŏn period. Given the historical reality that the majority of these texts were destroyed in large-scale book burnings during periods of intense persecution, this task remains exceedingly difficult. However, some lists of *Sŏhak* texts have been revealed in official records, including interrogation reports of Catholic believers.[36] More recently, there have been attempts to analyze physical copies of Catholic books written in Korean from the late 19th century.[37] While earlier research focused primarily on the circulation of translated *Sŏhak* texts, these recent efforts stand out for paying attention to the physical books that were actually distributed, marking a notable distinction in approach.

Meanwhile, just as the *chŏksa* discourse varied depending on the individuals and periods involved, it is important to note that differences also existed among those who accepted *Sŏhak* as *Sŏkyo*. This aspect has often been overlooked, as those who accepted *Sŏhak* were commonly understood within the singular framework of the "Chosŏn Catholic Church." However, not all individuals who accepted or rejected *Sŏhak* in the late Chosŏn period did so under the same terms or necessarily embraced Catholicism. Even within the Chosŏn Catholic Church, there were internal conflicts regarding the direction of the Church. Moreover, among the government officials labeled as "persecutors" by the Church, some opposed anti-Catholic measures or sought to "protect" the Chosŏn Catholic Church. For instance, Kim Yu-gŭn 金逌根, a key figure in the Andong Kim clan's regency, showed a favorable attitude toward Catholicism as a new folk religious practice, while Kim Chŏng-hŭi 金正喜 and Cho Pyŏng-hyŏn 趙秉鉉 adopted a more lenient stance toward the persecution of Catholic believers.[38] This fact demonstrates that even during the so-called *Kihae* persecution of 1839 in the mid-19th century, the stance of the Chosŏn court toward Catholicism was not entirely consistent. Additionally, research comparing the understanding of *Sŏhak* by Yi Pyŏk, Hwang Sayŏng 黃嗣永, and *Chŏng Hasang* 丁夏祥—key figures within the Chosŏn Catholic Church—is also noteworthy.[39] The discussion surrounding the acceptance of *Sŏhak* has begun to move beyond the binary analysis of *Sŏkyo* versus *chŏksa*, to explore the commonalities and differences among those who accepted *Sŏhak* as a religion. More recently, the patterns of *Sŏhak* acceptance by three students—Kim Taegŏn, Ch'oe Yangŏp 崔良業, and Ch'oe Pangje 崔方濟—who were selected by the Chosŏn Catholic Church and studied abroad at the seminary in Macau, have also been examined.[40] The context in which Chosŏn people accepted Catholicism is expected to remain a subject of diverse discussions in the future. Efforts to reconstruct the various contexts that existed between the polar extremes of *Sŏkyo* and *chŏksa* must continue moving forward.

2) The History of Catholicism as a Lens into Late Chosŏn Society

While studies exploring the acceptance of *Sŏhak* have predominantly focused on the understanding of Catholicism among the *yangban* intellectual elite, other research has examined the role of laypeople, including commoners and women, who constituted the majority of the Chosŏn Catholic Church. Although the growth of the Church experienced fluctuations over time, its membership expanded significantly—from over 10,000 following the first nationwide persecution during the 1801 to approximately 23,000 by the 1866.[41] These figures were sufficient to form a distinct "society," leading to studies that examined aspects of late Chosŏn society through an analysis of the Chosŏn Catholic Church. Such studies often attempted quantitative analyses of the Church. The focus of these studies on the so-called "Great Persecutions" during the *Shinyu* 辛酉 year (1801), *Kihae* 己亥 year (1839), and *Byŏngin* 丙寅 year (1866) is largely due to the extensive documentation left behind from the large-scale arrests of Catholic believers during these periods.

Among these, the *Shinyu* year (1801) stands out due to the abundance of church-related materials and interrogation records from the government, which provide diverse insights. These records have enabled in-depth analyses not only of the early composition of the Chosŏn Catholic Church but also of the broader societal context of the Chosŏn dynasty during this period. Particularly intriguing are the contrasting conclusions reached by Cho Kwang and Kim Han-kyu, who both analyzed the composition of the Chosŏn Catholic Church during the Shinyu persecution. Both studies aimed to uncover aspects of society through quantitative analyses of the Church's membership during that year. However, while Cho Kwang emphasized the rise of disenfranchised *yangban* and the *chungin* 中人 class within the Church, arguing that the Church contributed to the dismantling of feudal society, Kim Han-kyu concluded that the core of the Church's organization at the time consisted of male *yangban*, making it difficult to identify any so-called "popular" elements during the Church's formative years.[42] The differences in interpretation extend beyond the variations in the sources referenced by the two studies, demonstrating that the character of the Church can also be understood differently depending on the researcher's perspective on the sociopolitical context of late Chosŏn society.

Recent studies related to late Chosŏn society have focused on a more detailed reading of historical sources to uncover the lived experiences and faith practices of Chosŏn Catholic believers. Since research in the 1970s revealed the overall structure of the Chosŏn Catholic Church, attention has shifted toward examining the lives of individual Catholic believers through newly uncovered sources. In particular, research on women has gained prominence. Unlike most women of the Chosŏn period, who left behind few records, female Catholic believers can be heard through direct sources such as interrogation records and letters. As a result, academic interest in female Catholic believers began relatively early,[43] with notable figures like Kang Wan-suk 姜完淑, Chŏng Nanjoo 丁蘭珠, and Yi Suni 李順伊 being analyzed not only for their historical roles but also for how their lives have been represented in literary narratives and oral traditions.

One of the most notable differences between ordinary women in the Chosŏn period and female Catholic believers was their practice of celibacy (*tongjŏng* 童貞). Recent studies have emphasized that these women not only rejected the patriarchal structure of Chosŏn society but also resisted the Western-style patriarchy embedded in Catholicism, actively navigating the spaces between the two systems to assert themselves as agents of their own lives. Some of these women are known to have disguised themselves as widows, leveraging the social mobility and autonomy traditionally associated with widowhood in Chosŏn society to actively participate in church activities.[44] In summary, studies on female Catholic believers during the Chosŏn period have highlighted their "agency" as a key focus. Such efforts are significant not only for understanding Catholic women but also for providing a lens through which the question of agency in the broader history of women in Chosŏn society can be examined.

While Korean research has primarily used quantitative methodologies to analyze various aspects of the Chosŏn Catholic Church by class and gender, Western scholarship has shown interest in the societal changes brought about by the introduction of Catholicism as a foreign religion into Chosŏn or the reasons why Chosŏn society was able to accept Catholicism. Donald Baker argues that the late 18th-century Chosŏn Catholic Church introduced a new concept of "religion" previously absent from the Chosŏn dynasty and attempted to establish a new relationship between the state and religion. He describes this phenomenon as a form of "religious revolution," asserting that this "religious revolution" marked the emergence of an independent religious community with its own ecclesiastical structure and ritual practices, distinct from the state. Ultimately, this movement sought individual salvation and freedom of faith, bringing about a paradigm shift in Korean history.[45] In other words, Catholicism was the first to establish a community of believers, or a "church," in the Chosŏn dynasty that was independent from the state and mediated by faith. The emergence of these "alternative centers of power" played a crucial role in the later development of democracy in Korea.[46] The significance of the Korean Catholic Church has been actively interpreted not merely as the propagation of a foreign religion but as a driving force in historical developments such as Korea's modernization and democratization.

However, given the recent historiographical reflections within Korean historical studies on previously established discourses such as *Silhak* or *Pukhak* (Northern Learning 北學) in relation to modernity, it is necessary to exercise caution in directly linking the emergence of the Chosŏn Catholic Church and the new spaces it created to modern concepts such as modernization or democratization.[47] Instead, some emphasize the distinct characteristics of Chosŏn society that enabled Catholicism to take root, while others highlight the ways in which Catholicism adapted to Chosŏn culture upon its introduction.

Andrew Finch has argued that one of the key characteristics of the Chosŏn Catholic Church—its pursuit of "martyrdom"—was underpinned by Confucian values that existed even before the introduction of Catholicism.[48] Specifically, the Confucian ideal of sacrificing one's life for the sake of moral virtue, combined with the prolonged era of "persecution," contributed to the emergence of the "Korean martyrs" as a respected figure within Chosŏn society. This perspective is particularly noteworthy as it is based on an analysis of 117 devout lay believers arrested between 1839 and 1840, the majority of whom were commoners and women. In a Chosŏn Catholic Church context where access to Classical Chinese theological texts, complex doctrinal teachings, or even missionaries was limited, the large-scale martyrdom of these faithful lay believers highlights the unique characteristics of the Church, shaped by Chosŏn's cultural values and the emergence of Korean martyrs.

This perspective has been further reinforced by the works of Deberniere J. Torrey and So Jung Kim. Deberniere J. Torrey conducted a micro-level analysis of the Virgin Barbara as depicted in the letters of Father Ch'oe Yangŏp, offering deeper insights into the agency of female believers in their practice of celibacy.[49] Meanwhile, So Jung Kim analyzed the rhetorical strategies employed in the Korean-language letters of Yi Suni Lucarda, a female martyr from 1801, to demonstrate that the spirituality of early Chosŏn Catholic believers could develop independently of direct influence from Western missionaries.[50] Such efforts are significant in that they explore the "foundations" upon which Catholicism was accepted into Chosŏn society, prior to examining the "changes" brought about by Catholicism in that context. Understanding the foundational conditions that allowed Catholicism to take root in the Chosŏn dynasty is essential for fully grasping both the transformations in late Chosŏn society and their broader implications.

3) East Asian or a Global Historical Perspective

The issues of regional dissemination of Catholicism, along with the resulting conflicts and adaptations, are not confined to Chosŏn alone. This is because the East Asian missionary activities of this universal religion were not limited to Chosŏn. Accordingly, the various issues that emerged in Korea with the introduction of Catholicism can naturally be found in other regional contexts as well. For instance, in the *Jiangnan* 江南 region of China during the Ming and Qing dynasties, social conflicts arose over issues such as ancestor worship, gender roles, and interactions with missionaries. In this process, discussions about Catholicism as a "regional religion" in the Chinese context also emerged.[51] Therefore, a comparative historical perspective is essential for understanding the unique characteristics of the Chosŏn Catholic Church. Recently, research on the history of Catholicism in China has been published within Korean academia,[52] and attempts to understand the history of the Chosŏn Catholic Church within the contexts of East-West relations or the East Asian region have continued to develop. This section aims to highlight such research trends, emphasizing the necessity of a comparative perspective in the study of Catholic Church history.

From its establishment, the Chosŏn Catholic Church obtained information about Catholicism through Western texts on *Sŏhak* and continued to develop its institutions through exchanges with Western missionaries based in Beijing. In this regard, the space of diplomatic missions and Beijing, as the only route through which Chosŏn individuals could collect *Sŏhak* texts and engage with Western missionaries, held a particularly unique significance in the foundation of the Chosŏn Catholic Church. Especially in the 18th century, when interactions between Chosŏn delegations and Western missionaries in Beijing were most active, a conducive environment was created for mutual exchanges, as Western missionaries became increasingly interested in Chosŏn and Chosŏn intellectuals similarly sought engagement. According to Pierre-Emmanuel Roux, Jesuit missionaries viewed Chosŏn as a "bridge" in the 16th century as a stepping stone for advancing into China from Japan, and in the 17th and 18th centuries as a base for reinitiating missions to Japan from China.[53] In the context of Jesuit missionary activities in East Asia, Chosŏn's strategic importance was thus prominently emphasized.

The interest of Western missionaries in Chosŏn naturally led to exchanges at the Beijing Catholic Church. In Korea, studies have particularly focused on the interactions between Chosŏn diplomatic missions and Western missionaries as a subfield of research on *sahaeng* (official diplomatic missions 事行), yielding significant scholarly achievements. However, most of these studies have primarily addressed the fragmented encounters between Chosŏn delegations and Beijing-based missionaries, leaving unexplored the broader question of how these exchanges influenced the establishment of the Chosŏn Catholic Church or shaped Chosŏn intellectuals' perceptions of Catholicism. Focusing exclusively on the personal interactions between Chosŏn envoys and missionaries risks reducing the analysis to isolated episodes, as the extent and nature of these interactions were heavily influenced by individual circumstances and personal inclinations. To better understand the exchanges between Chosŏn envoys and Western missionaries, it is essential to adopt a more comprehensive framework that considers these interactions within the broader context of East Asian history.

In this regard, Pierre-Emmanuel Roux's research, which focuses on the spatial significance of Beijing rather than individual cases of interactions between Chosŏn envoys and missionaries, is particularly noteworthy.[54] According to his findings, Chosŏn intellectuals visiting Beijing not only frequented the Beijing Catholic Church but also engaged with Chinese Catholic literati and lay believers residing in the city. Therefore, the historical event of the Chosŏn Catholic Church's emergence cannot simply be reduced to isolated encounters between a few Chosŏn intellectuals and Jesuit missionaries stationed in Beijing. Rather, it was deeply intertwined with the complexities of Sino-Korean relations and the Jesuit missionary strategy of top-down conversion. This perspective is significant, especially given that classical Chinese based *Sŏhak* texts were not merely the works of Western Jesuit missionaries but collaborative efforts between Jesuits and Chinese Catholic literati. Recent studies have also explored the modes of communication between missionaries in Beijing and the Chosŏn Catholic Church.[55] It is anticipated that future research will further investigate the exchanges between the Chosŏn Catholic Church and the universal Church through the lens of Beijing as a medium, considering its broader East Asian dimensions.

Joo Hyun Sheen analyzed the historical and intellectual significance of Catholic acceptance in East Asia by conducting a comparative study of cases in China and Korea, as outcomes of the Jesuit strategy of accommodation.[56] In contrast to previous studies on the acceptance of

Sŏhak in Chosŏn, which largely assumed that Western missionaries' writings directly influenced Chosŏn intellectuals, Sheen's work stands out for its comparison with figures such as Xu Guangqi 徐光啟, a Chinese Catholic (or a Chinese literatus sympathetic to Catholicism), who mediated between Western missionaries and Chosŏn scholars. Intellectuals in both late Ming China and Chosŏn who accepted Catholicism shared the legacy of Jesuit accommodationism, particularly embodied in classical Chinese *Sŏhak* texts, and this commonality enabled the coexistence of East Asian and Catholic modes of thought among Catholic adherents in the region. Similarly, studies that examine Chosŏn attitudes of suspicion toward *Sŏhak* from an East Asian perspective are also of significant utility. Gregory N. Evon noted parallels between King Chŏngjo of Chosŏn's perception of Catholicism as heretical and similar stances taken by the Qianlong Emperor (r. 1735-1796) of the Qing and Matsudaira sadanobu [松平定信] of Edo-period Japan.[57] The works of Sheen and Evon are noteworthy in that they demonstrate how debates over the acceptance or rejection of *Sŏhak* in late Chosŏn history can be interpreted within a broader East Asian framework.

Within Korean academia, a trend emphasizing East Asian or global historical contexts in understanding the history of the Chosŏn Catholic Church has emerged. In particular, empirical research on missionaries has been prioritized within the field of church history. Cho Hyŏnbŏm analyzed the social backgrounds of missionaries dispatched to Chosŏn from France, alongside their missionary strategies and their perspectives on Chosŏn society. Meanwhile, Yi Sŏkwŏn explored the efforts of Vicars Apostolic in Chosŏn to gain official recognition of the Church and the Chosŏn government's responses to these attempts.[58] Furthermore, studies conducted in Western academia have examined the significance of missionary activity in Chosŏn from the perspective of the missionaries themselves.[59] These scholarly endeavors have facilitated a deeper understanding of the role Western missionaries played as counterparts to Chosŏn Catholic believers in the Church's practical operations. Such efforts have thus laid the groundwork for future comparative studies of the

Choson Catholic Church

Meanwhile, Kim Taegŏn, the first priest of Chosŏn Catholic Church, was selected as a seminarian along with Ch'oe Yangŏp and Ch'oe Pangje and studied at seminaries in Macau and Lumban, Philippines. Later, during the height of the First Opium War in 1842, he boarded a French naval vessel and attended the signing ceremony of the Treaty of Nanking. Subsequently, Kim Taegŏn traveled between Manchuria and the western coastal regions of Chosŏn in search of routes for missionaries to enter Chosŏn. Captured and martyred during these activities, his endeavors encompassed the entire East Asian region, demanding an analysis of Kim Taegŏn from an East Asian perspective rather than solely as a priest or martyr. In this regard, the series of studies by Doh Jin-soon deserve attention. He meticulously examined various sources to reconstruct Kim Taegŏn's journey and his attendance at the Nanking Treaty signing.[60] He also analyzed how the plans of French Admiral Jean-Baptiste Cécille, special envoy Dubois de Jancigny, and Napoleon Libois, a priest of the Paris Foreign Missions Society's Macau East Asia Delegation, influenced the entry and martyrdom of Fathers Kim Taegŏn and Ch'oe Yangŏp.[61] According to his findings, a secret plan devised in February 1842 by Cécille, Jancigny, and Libois to have Fathers Joseph A. Maistre, Kim Taegŏn, and Ch'oe Yangŏp enter Chosŏn aboard a French warship was delayed and altered in the wake of the signing of the Nanking Treaty in August 1842 and shifts in French foreign policy. Ultimately, no missionaries entered Chosŏn via the planned naval route, and premature French involvement hastened Kim Taegŏn's martyrdom. This perspective evaluates Kim Taegŏn's activities not only within the realm of martyrdom but also within the broader East Asian context, highlighting its significance.

4) Chosŏn Catholic Church and the State

The final topic that must be addressed in discussions about recent research on the history of the Catholic Church in Chosŏn, conducted in both Korea and the Western academic sphere, concerns the relationship between the Catholic Church and the state. This is because the history of the Chosŏn Catholic Church, often described as a history of "persecution," highlights the state as the primary agent of persecution. The Chosŏn dynasty strictly prohibited its people from practicing Catholicism, detaining and executing those who violated this prohibition under the name of the law.

Thus, exploring the legal treatment of Catholic believers under the Chosŏn dynasty offers valuable insights into the relationship between the Church and the state. However, until relatively recently, research in this field had not delved deeply into this issue. This is primarily due to the characterization of the execution of Catholic believers as "martyrdom" and the legal actions of the Chosŏn dynasty as "persecution," which made it challenging to attribute a particular significance to the state's enforcement of the law. For instance, Dallet described the legal processes of the Chosŏn dynasty as barbaric practices filled with torture, coerced confessions, and fabrications. Likewise, Hwang sayŏng referred to the officials who suppressed Catholicism as a "wicked" faction.[62] In such circumstances, it has been difficult to engage in scholarly discourse about the legal basis underpinning the Chosŏn dynasty's suppression of Catholic believers.

The fact that the Chosŏn dynasty specifically utilized "law" as one of its tools to suppress the Catholic Church in Chosŏn reveals the distinctive nature of the relationship between the Chosŏn state and the Catholic Church. The Chosŏn ruling class perceived Catholicism as a threat to the Confucian-centered national identity and cultural integrity of Chosŏn. As a result, the state classified Catholic believers as "criminals" and sought to establish legal measures to address the newly emerging Catholic community.

A pioneering example of research in this area is Wŏn Jae-yŏn's study, which examined the legal procedures surrounding the first execution of Catholic believers in the *Chin-san* Incident (1791), as well as the forms of property confiscation imposed on Catholic believers, and the indiscriminate punishments enacted around the *Pyŏng-in* Persecution (1866~).[63] However, instead of approaching the state's treatment of Catholic believers within a diachronic context, these studies have tended to focus on specific cases, emphasizing the "lawless" aspects of the Chosŏn dynasty's suppression of Catholicism. In terms of critical perspectives guiding these discussions, many studies have largely adhered to conventional approaches.

Recent studies have examined the diachronic application of laws by the Chosŏn dynasty toward Catholic believers, aiming to uncover the historical implications embedded in the legal measures taken against them. Of particular note is Pierre-Emmanuel Roux's research, which focuses on the fact that legal measures against Catholic believers in Chosŏn were grounded in the Great Ming Code 大明律. Roux highlights the East Asian context of Chosŏn's use of the Great Ming Code to execute Catholic believers, emphasizing that the use of law was seen as the most ideal means to suppress Catholicism.[64] By analyzing specific legal provisions, Roux demonstrates how the Chosŏn state applied—or in some cases, misapplied—the Great Ming Code to Catholic believers, shedding light on the detailed circumstances surrounding such legal practices.

This perspective effectively illustrates the contexts in which Catholic believers in Chosŏn were legally executed and highlights the importance of the Great Ming Code in East Asian legal culture, particularly in its application to the persecution of Catholics in Chosŏn. However, Roux conceptualizes all instances of legal application outside the Great Ming Code's framework as "abuse," a term that warrants reconsideration. While the Great Ming Code served as Chosŏn's foundational legal framework from its early establishment, the Chosŏn state also displayed significant ingenuity in adapting and operationalizing its legal system. By basing its legal practices on Chinese law but simultaneously developing a distinctive legal identity unique to Chosŏn, the state demonstrated legal flexibility. Therefore, the "abuse" Roux identifies in cases of legal measures against Catholic believers requires further contextualization and diachronic analysis. Such an approach could clarify the historical significance of these instances and offer a more nuanced understanding of Chosŏn's legal practices regarding Catholicism.

Research examining the relationship between the Chosŏn state and the Catholic Church in Chosŏn through the lens of legal mediation has primarily focused on the period around 1801 when legal restrictions against Catholic believers were formalized, as well as on the analysis of legal statutes.[65] These studies have explored the specific criminal laws applied to Catholic believers during the late Chosŏn dynasty and analyzed their implications, particularly in the context of the political circumstances of the time. In 1801, the Chosŏn dynasty officially categorized the persecution of Catholics under the term *sa'ok* (heresy cases 邪獄), signifying a new legal category distinct from *sal'ok* (murder cases 殺獄) or *yŏk'ok* (treason or rebellion cases 逆獄). This shift indicated that the Chosŏn state had established Catholicism as a distinct category of legal offense. Under King Chŏngjo's reign, Catholic issues were treated as matters of "individual deviance," but by 1801, the state had transitioned to a mode of handling Catholic believers that involved "significant administrative mobilization."[66] This substantial shift in approach is understood to have been influenced by growing concerns over the West, as well as political motives to eliminate the *Namin* literati, particularly the *Shinsŏ* School, who had played a key role in establishing the Catholic community in Chosŏn. These studies go beyond merely listing the chronological application of criminal codes to Catholic believers; instead, they examine how specific laws were tailored to address Catholic cases during certain periods, providing insights into the contemporary perceptions embedded in the legal treatment of Catholic believers.

The study of the relationship between the late Chosŏn state and the Catholic Church, mediated through law, has recently gained momentum, but many unresolved issues remain. Notably, earlier research has identified the year 1801 (*Sinyu*) as a turning point in the state's legal treatment of Catholic believers. However, legal regulations against Catholics persisted beyond 1801, and their characteristics evolved according to the broader trends of the 19th century. This evolution demands further attention.

In this regard, the work of Nam Hohyun is particularly noteworthy for establishing a diachronic understanding of the legal treatment of Catholics in late Chosŏn.[67] He categorizes the legal actions against Catholics from the establishment of the Catholic Church in Chosŏn and traces the gradual "hollowing out" of the Chosŏn state's judicial measures against Catholics until 1871. His study sheds light on the historical shifts in legal policies and explores how these shifts reflected contemporary perceptions embedded in the application of law against Catholic believers.

These attempts hold significance as they address the state-level implications of Chosŏn's judicial treatment of Catholics, previously dismissed in historical narratives of Chosŏn Catholicism as merely violent or inconsequential. This research trend is expanding beyond the central court to include discussions of local officials who implemented national policies, suggesting a deeper and more nuanced approach.[68] In essence, studies on the relationship between the state and the Catholic Church, as defined by law in late Chosŏn, have moved away from a one-sided narrative of persecution and suppression. Instead, they delve into the motivations behind such actions, which persisted for over a century, and the broader context of how these actions reflected late Chosŏn's understanding of its realities and responses. With ongoing discussions on the interplay between the state and legal frameworks in late Chosŏn, it is anticipated that this research trajectory will continue to develop in the near future.

4. Conclusion

The process by which Catholicism, a universal religion, was introduced and the Chosŏn Catholic Church was established was anything but universal. The Chosŏn Catholic Church emerged at the confluence of East Asian Catholic missions, the Chosŏn intellectuals' acceptance of Western knowledge, and the unique characteristics of Chosŏn society, which at times fused with and at other times clashed with external influences. Consequently, the Chosŏn Catholic Church embodies the complexity of its formation process, possessing unique characteristics that have garnered extensive scholarly attention. This chapter sought to examine the differing perspectives of Korean and Western academia on the Chosŏn Catholic Church, arguing that Catholic history can serve as a meaningful lens not only for understanding Chosŏn society but also for interpreting early modern East Asia.

The debates surrounding the origins of the Chosŏn Catholic Church, paradoxically, have stimulated scholarly reevaluation of what was previously considered self-evident about the Church's early circumstances. The theory of an Imjin War origin, based on the Jesuit missionaries' letters, reveals the strategic perception of Chosŏn as a "bridgehead" for East Asian missions. Similarly, the claim that the Chosŏn Catholic Church originated in the scholarly gatherings at *Chuŏ-sa* temple has facilitated rigorous source criticism of early Catholic materials. Although both theories ultimately failed to redefine the Church's origins due to inherent flaws and inconsistencies, they drew scholarly attention to the nuanced details of Catholicism's initial reception in Chosŏn. This, in turn, has enhanced our ability to scrutinize the early phases of Catholicism in Chosŏn society. With new sources being unearthed and innovative readings of Jesuit letters emerging, it is now imperative to move beyond origin debates and recover the multifaceted realities of early Catholicism in Chosŏn.

While Korean scholarship has concentrated on ecclesiastical, diocesan, and martyrological perspectives, analyzing numerous events and deepening our understanding of countless martyrs, Western scholarship on Chosŏn Catholicism engages with Korean research while proposing new discourses. Noteworthy among these is the examination of the societal characteristics of Chosŏn revealed through the acceptance and rejection of Catholicism, as well as studies that contextualize Chosŏn Catholic history within an East Asian perspective. Such approaches, as discussed in this paper, offer a broader framework for interpreting Chosŏn Catholicism, expanding the scope of Korean ecclesiastical research. Above all, comparative studies on how Catholicism was accepted as a "religion" in

East Asia are urgently needed.

Furthermore, as recent studies have pointed out, the contexts of *Sŏhak* reception and the Chosŏn Catholic Church's relationship with the state demand more nuanced analysis than the linear narratives presented so far. The interactions between foreign ideologies and religions like *Sŏhak* and Catholicism with the Chosŏn monarchy cannot be reduced to mere "transmission and acceptance (or rejection)." Similarly, the Chosŏn court's century-long responses to Catholicism cannot be simply labeled as "persecution." Future research on Korean Catholic history must elucidate the diverse aspects of the Chosŏn Catholic Church and demonstrate how its historical trajectory was deeply intertwined with the socio-political dynamics of its time.

In essence, the integration of Catholicism, a universal religion, into Korean society was marked by particularity, allowing the Chosŏn Catholic Church to become both part of the universal Catholic tradition and a unique regional church reflecting Korean heritage. The Chosŏn Catholic Church did not operate solely according to missionary intentions, nor did Catholicism, as envisioned by its Korean adherents, materialize to resolve the various contradictions of the Chosŏn state. Yet, through these tensions and intersections, the Chosŏn Catholic Church increasingly became part of Chosŏn society, whether or not this was desired by the Chosŏn government. In the 19th century, during the era of Western imperial encroachment, the Chosŏn Catholic Church, willingly or unwillingly, also became intricately tied to global political dynamics. This underscores the broader truth that the history of the Chosŏn Catholic Church cannot be understood in isolation. The significance of Korean Catholic history lies precisely in its refusal to remain merely the history of a church or a purely ecclesiastical narrative.

Note

1 "The Statue of St. Andrew Kim Soars High in the Vatican: Hoping the Martyrdom Spirituality of the Korean Church Spreads Widely," *Korean Catholic Newspaper*, September 24, 2023.

2 Don Baker and Franklin Rausch, *Catholics and Anti-Catholicism in Chosŏn Korea*, University of Hawai'i Press and Center for Korean Studies, 2017, p. 7.

3 The baptism of Yi Sŭnghun and the process of mass baptism upon his return to Chosŏn are detailed in Charles Dallet, trans. Ch'oe Sŏk-u and An Ŭng-ryŏl, *A History of the Korean Catholic Church* (Volume 1), Han'guk Kyohŏsa Yŏn'guso, 1996, pp. 305-308.

4 Ch'oe Sŏk-u, "Han'guk Ch'ŏnju-gyohoeŭi Kiwŏn Munje (The Issue of the Origins of the Korean Catholic Church)," *Han'guk Kidokkyo wa Yŏksa* 1, 1991, pp. 19-20.

5 Medina J. G. R., "*The Catholic Church in Korea, Its Origins 1566-1784*", Royal Asiatic Society, 1994, p. 19. When citing this book below, include the page number in parentheses within the main text.

6 Cho Kwang, "*Chosŏn hugi Sahoe wa Ch'ŏnju-gyo* (Korean Society and Catholicism in the Late Chosŏn Period)," Kyŏngin Munhwasa, 2010, p. 83.

7 Ch'oe Sŏk-u, *op. cit*., pp. 12-16.

8 Yun Min-gu, "*Han'guk Ch'ŏnju-gyohoeŭi Kiwon* (the Origins of the Korean Catholic Church)", Kukhak Charyowŏn, 2002, pp. 339-487. Father Yun Min-gu was directly involved as the postulatorin Rome during the canonization process of the "103 Blessed Martyrs" in 1983. Consequently, he is also considered a prominent figure representing the "excessive nationalism" criticized by Medina.

9 For example, Medina emphasized the existence of a "beautiful cathedral" in Chosŏn around 1666 based on letters written by Jesuit missionaries. However, this claim relies on the testimony of a Chinese captain who was active in Japan, rendering its credibility highly questionable. Most importantly, no records from the period around 1666 mention the existence of such a "beautiful cathedral" in Chosŏn. (Yun Min-gu, *ibid*., pp. 438-441.)

10 In the Catholic Church, the canonization process is divided into the stages of "Servant of God," "Venerable," "Blessed," and "Saint." The title of "Servant

of God" refers to an individual whose canonization cause has been officially submitted to the Congregation for the Causes of Saints in the Vatican by a diocese, religious order, or faith organization. Once the Congregation examines and accepts the petition and documents, the individual is officially declared "Venerable." Subsequently, through the beatification and canonization procedures, the individual is elevated to the statuses of "Blessed" and finally "Saint." The beatification process for the "133 Servants of God," including Yi Pyŏk, began in 2009. In March 2021, the preparatory investigation by the Special Episcopal Commission for the Beatification and Canonization of the Catholic Bishops' Conference of Korea was completed, and the beatification dossier was submitted to the Congregation for the Causes of Saints.

11 The years 1777 and 1779, along with the locations *Ch'ŏnjinam* and *Chuŏ-sa* temple, have been suggested as the time and place of the academic discussions in question. This is because different sources, such as Dallet's and Chŏng Yak-yong's notes, refer to the event in varying ways. They describe the years of the discussions as the *Chŏngyu* 丁酉 Year (1777) and *Kihae* 己亥 Year (1779) and the location as "a certain temple," "*Ch'ŏnjinam*," or "*Ch'ŏnjinam Chuŏ-sa*." Since *Ch'ŏnjinam* and *Chuŏ-sa* temple are geographically close, they are sometimes considered as one location. Currently, no definitive historical sources pinpoint the exact time and place of these discussions. For convenience, this article will refer to the event as the "Academic gatherings at 1779 *Chuŏ-sa* temple."

12 Ch'oe Sŏk-u, *op. cit.*, pp. 16–19; Cho Kwang, *op. cit.*, pp. 96–106.

13 The Catholic Diocese of Suwŏn's Committee for the Promotion of Beatification and Canonization published the following works, "*Han'guk Ch'ŏnju-gyohoe Ch'angsŏl Chuyŏg ŭi Ch'ŏnju Sinang 1: Ch'angsŏl Chuyŏg kwa Yi Pyŏk* (The Catholic Faith of the Founding Figures of the Korean Catholic Church 1: Founding Figures and Yi Pyŏk), Hasang Publications, 2011a; "*Han'guk Ch'ŏnju-gyohoe Ch'angsŏl Chuyŏg ŭi Ch'ŏnju Sinang 2: Ch'angsŏl Chuyŏg ŭi Sungyo wa Kŭ Pyŏngp'an* (The Catholic Faith of the Founding Figures of the Korean Catholic Church 2: The Martyrdom of the Founding Figures and Their Reputation)," Hasang Publications, 2011b; "*Han'guk Ch'ŏnju-gyohoe Ch'angsŏl Chuyŏg ŭi Ch'ŏnju Sinang 3: Han'guk Ch'ŏnju-gyohoe Ch'angnip Sŏnjo Husondŭl ŭi Ch'ŏnju Sinang* (The Catholic Faith of the Founding Figures of the Korean Catholic Church 3: The Catholic Faith of the Descendants of the Founding Ancestors of the Korean Catholic

Church)," Hasang Publications, 2013. Volume 1 of this series includes presentations from the academic conferences held in 2002 and 2005, Volume 2 contains materials from the 2009 conference, and Volume 3 compiles presentations from the 2011 conference. In response to controversies surrounding the authenticity of works such as Sŏnggyo Yoji and the martyrdom status of the so-called "founding saints," the Catholic Diocese of Suwŏn organized the fifth symposium on the theme "A Comprehensive Review of *Manchŏn Yugo and* Sŏngkyo *Yoji*." However, unlike the previous four symposia, the proceedings of the fifth symposium were not published.

14 Msgr. Shim sang-Tai and Others, *The Founding Ancestors of the Catholic Church in Korea*, Hasang Publishing, 2014.

15 *ibid*, p. 10.

16 The Catholic Diocese of Suwŏn's Committee for the Promotion of Beatification and Canonization, *op. cit.*, 2011a, pp. 51-52.

17 The Catholic Diocese of Suwŏn's Committee for the Promotion of Beatification and Canonization, *op. cit.*, 2011a, p. 225.

18 Charles Dallet, trans. Ch'oe Sŏk-u and An Ŭng-ryŏl, *op. cit.*, 1996, pp. 448-449.

19 Msgr. Shim sang-Tai and Others, *op. cit.*, 2014, pp.154-157; pp.200-203.

20 Yi Pyŏk. *Sŏngkyo Yoji*. Edited and translated by Ha, Sŏng-rae. Sŏng hwang Sŏkdu Ruga Sŏwŏn, 2007.

21 Yun Min-gu. "*Ch'ogi Han'guk Ch'ŏnju Kyohoesaui Chaengchŏm Yŏn'gu: Sŏngkyo Yoji, Sipkemyŏngga, Manch'ŏnyugo, Ibyŏkchŏn, Yuhandang Ŏnhaengsilnogŭn Sagida* (A Study on the Issues in the Early History of the Korean Catholic Church: Sŏnggyo Yoji, Ten Commandments Song, Manchŏn Yugo, The Biography of Yi Pyŏk, and Yuhandang's Records Are Fabrications)." Gukhakjaryowon, 2014.

22 Seo Jong-tae. "(Book Review) A Study on the Issues in the Early History of the Korean Catholic Church." *Kyohŏsa Yŏn'gu* 46, 2015, p.188.

23 Kim Hyŏn-u and Kim Sŏk-ju, "Yi Pyŏk ŭi *Sŏngkyo Yoji* nŭn Wijo Munhŏn in'ga? (Is Yi Pyŏk's *Sŏngkyo Yoji* Forged Document?)" *Kidokkyŏ Sasang* 729, 2019.

24 Hwang Chae-bŏm. "*Sŏngkyo Yoji* ŭi Wŏnbon Mat'in Sŏn'gyosa ŭi *Ssangch'ŏnjamun* Yŏn'gu (A Study on the Original Text of *Sŏngkyo Yoji*: Missionary Martin's *Ssangch'ŏnjamun*)." *Sinhak Sasang* 190, 2020, p. 50.

25 That being said, the significance of the "Church History" or "Martyrdom History," which represents a major thread in the historiography of the Korean

Catholic Church, must not be undervalued. The discovery and translation of historical materials related to the Korean Catholic Church, carried out within the framework of diocesan histories or the commemoration of martyrs, as well as the heightened interest in the Korean Catholic Church during the beatification and canonization processes of martyrs, undeniably form the foundation of Church History research. However, due to the limitations of space, the author's capacity, and the objective of selecting studies aligned with the overarching theme of the "intersections and directions" of Korean and Western academia, this article does not attempt to comprehensively present the extensive body of research on martyrs and martyr-related historical materials, which constitute the mainstream of Church History studies.

26 Anders Karlsson, "Beyond the Great Tradition: Recent European Scholarship on the History of Chosŏn Korea", *Yŏksa wa Hyŏnsil* 90, 2013, p. 406.

27 Yi, Wŏn-sun. "Ch'ŏnju-gyo ŭi Suyong kwa Chŏn'p'a (Acceptance and Propagation of Catholicism)." Edited by the Kuksa Pyŏnch'an Wiwŏnhoe, *Sinp'yŏn Han'guksa* 35, 2002, pp. 87-91.

28 No Tae-hwan. *Tongdo Sŏgi-ron Hyŏngsŏng Kwajŏng Yŏn'gu* (A Study on the Formation Process of Tongdo Sŏgi Theory)," Iljisa, 2005, pp. 57-83.

29 Cha Ki-jin, "*Chosŏn Huggi ŭi Sŏhak kwa Ch'ŏksaron Yŏn'gu* (A Study on Western Learning and the Theory of Rejecting Heterodoxy in Late Chosŏn). Han'guk Kyohŏsa Yŏn'guso, 2002. For a discussion on the internal division of the Namin faction based on political conflicts and attitudes toward Catholicism, see pp. 305-310.

30 Donald Baker, "Jesuit Science through Korean Eyes," *Journal of Korean Studies* 4, 1982~1983.

31 Donald Baker, "A Different Thread: Orthodoxy, Heterodoxy, and Catholicism in a Confucian World," Confucian and Late Chosŏn Korea. (unpublished)

32 Cho Hyŏn-bŏm. "Chosŏn Huggi Yuhakjadŭl ŭi Sŏhak Insik: Chonggyo/Kwahak Kubunron e Taehan Chaegŏmto (Late Chosŏn Confucian Scholars' Perceptions of Western Learning: A Reexamination of the Religion/Science Dichotomy)." *Han'guk Sasangsahak* 50, 2015, pp.134-138.

33 Chŏn, Yong-hun, "19-segi Chosŏn esŏ Sŏyang Kwahak kwa Ch'ŏnmunhak ŭi Sŏnggyŏk (The Nature of Western Science and Astronomy in 19th Century Chosŏn)." *Han'guk Kwahaksahakhoeji* 35(3), 2013

34 So, Chin-hyŏng. "Chosŏn Huggi Sŏhak Yŏn'gu ŭi Chuje Hwaktang e Taehan Cheŏn: Ponyŏk, Ch'ŏksap'a Yŏn'gu wa Sŏhak ŭi Kwangye rŭl Chungsim ŭro

(A Proposal for Expanding the Themes of Western Learning Studies in Late Chosŏn: Focusing on Translation, the Ch'ŏksap'a, and Their Relationship with Western Learning)." *Chosŏn Sidae Sahakbo* 107, 2023, pp. 154–160.

35 Chŏn, Yong-hun. "Chŏngjo Sidae Tasi Pogi: Ch'ŏnmunhaksa ŭi Kwanchŏm esŏ (Revisiting the Reign of King Chŏngjo: From the Perspective of the History of Astronomy)." *Yŏksa Pip'yŏng* 115, 2016 ; Kim, Sŏn-hŭi. *Sŏhak, Chosŏn Yuhak i Mannan Natsŏn Kŏul* (Western Learning, A Strange Mirror Encountered by Chosŏn Confucianism). Mosinŭn Saramdŭl, 2018, pp. 13–19.

36 During the reign of King Chŏngjo, Pak Chong-ak, who confiscated Catholic believers' books in the *Naepo* 內浦 region, reported a list of books possessed by Catholics in his *Sug'i* 手記. For further details, see Chang Yu-sŭng, "1791-nyŏn Naepo: Pak Chong-ak kwa Ch'ŏnju-gyo Pakhae (Naepo in 1791: Pak Chong-ak and the Persecution of Catholics)," *Kyohŏsa Yŏn'gu* 44, 2014.

37 No, Kyŏng-hŭi. "19-segi Huban Sŏyang Hwalpan Kisul ŭi Toip kwa Han'gŭl Ch'ŏnju-gyo Sŏjŏk ŭi Ch'ulp'an (The Introduction of Western Printing Technology and the Publication of Korean Catholic Books in the Late 19th Century)." *Han'guk Silhak Yŏn'gu* 47, 2024.

38 Doh, Jin-soon. "1839-nyŏn Kihae Pakhae wa Kŭ Pandaejadŭl: 'Cheil Sŏpjŏng' Kim Yu-gŭn, 'Yebi Sinja' Kim Chŏng-hŭi, Hyŏngjo P'ansŏ Cho Pyŏng-hyŏn (The 1839 *Gihae* Persecution and Its Opponents: 'First Regent' Kim Yu-gŭn, 'Catechumen' Kim Chŏng-hŭi, and Minister of Justice Cho Pyŏng-hyŏn)." *Kyohŏ Sahak* 25, 2024.

39 Yi, Kyŏng-gu. "Yi Pyŏk, Hwang Sayŏng, Chŏng Hasang ŭi Ch'ŏnju-gyo, Yugyo Insik ŭi Tongilsŏng kwa Ch'ai-jŏm (The Similarities and Differences in the Perception of Catholicism and Confucianism by Yi Pyŏk, Hwang Sayoung, and Chŏng Hasang)." *Kyohŏsa Yŏn'gu* 52, 2018.

40 Wŏn, Chae-yŏn. "19-segi Chŏnban Kyŏnggi-do Kŏju Se Sonyŏn ŭi Haewoe Yuhaksaeng Kongdongch'e wa Sŏhak Suyong (The Overseas Student Community and the Reception of Western Learning by Three Boys Residing in Gyeonggi-do in the Early 19th Century)," *Kijŏn Munhwa Yŏn'gu* 45(1), 2024.

41 For details on the status of the Catholic Church in Joseon, see Pang, Sang-gŭn. *19-segi Chungban Han'guk Ch'ŏnju-gyo-sa Yŏn'gu* (A Study on the History of Korean Catholicism in the Mid-19th Century)." Han'guk Kyohŏsa Yŏn'guso, 2006.

42 Cho Kwang. "Sin'yu Pakhae ŭi Punsŏkchŏk Kosal (An Analytical Study of

the Sin'yu Persecution)." *Kyohŏsa Yŏn'gu* 1, 1977 ; Kim Han-kyu. "Sahak Chingŭi rŭl T'onghaesŏ Pon Ch'ogi Han'guk Ch'ŏnju-gyohoe ŭi Myŏt Kaji Munje (Several Issues in the Early Korean Catholic Church as Seen Through Sahak Chingŭi)." *Kyohŏsa Yŏn'gu* 2, 1979.

43 Kim Ok-hy, "Women in the History of Catholicism in Korea," *Korea Journal* 24(8), 1984.

44 Song Chi-yŏn. "Chosŏn Sidae Ch'ŏnju-gyo Yŏsŏng ŭi Yŏksa Tasi Ilgi: Tongjŏngnyŏ e Taehan Nonŭi rŭl Chungsim ŭro (Reinterpreting the History of Catholic Women in Chosŏn: Focusing on Discussions of Virgins)." *Tongbang Hakchi* 169, 2015 ; Pak Min-ye. "Sin'yu Pakhae rŭl T'onghae Pon Ch'ŏnju-gyohoe Nae Kwabu Sinja wa Wisang Kwabu (Widow Believers and Pseudo-Widows in the Catholic Church Through the Lens of the Sin'yu Persecution)." *Sŏgang Inmun Nonch'ong* 54, 2019.

45 Don Baker, "The Religious Revolution in Modern Korean History: From ethics to theology and from ritual hegemony to religious freedom," T*he review of Korean Studies* 9(3), 2006.

46 Don Baker, "The Impact of Christianity on Modern Korea: An overview," *Acta Koreana* 19(1), 2016, pp. 57-60.

47 For a historiographical reflection on the trend of associating *Silhak* and *Bukhak* with modernity, see Hŏ T'ae-yong, "'Silhak' Iraneŭn T'ŭl ŭi Yŏksa-jŏk Chokan (A Historical Bird's-Eye View of the Framework of 'Practical Learning',) *Chosŏn Sidae Sahakbo* 102, 2022. Meanwhile, in studies on *Sŏhak* and the history of Catholic women, critical perspectives have also been presented on the tendency to relate the historical significance of the Chosŏn Catholic Church to modernity (Song Chi-yŏn, *op. cit*., 2015, pp. 34-35 ; So Chin-hyŏng, *op. cit*., 2023, pp.138-143).

48 Andrew Finch, "The Pursuit of Martyrdom in the Catholic Church in Korea before 1866," *Journal of Ecclesiastical History* 60(1), 2009.

49 Deberniere J. Torrey, "Young Barbara's Devotion and Death: Reading Father Ch'oe's Field Report of 1850," *Korean Studies* 42, 2018.

50 So Jung Kim, "Speaking In-Between: Vernacular Spirituality of a Woman in Late Chosŏn Korea," *Journal of Ecumenical Studies* 58(4), 2023.

51 Eugenio Menegon, "*Ancestors, Virgins, and Friars: Christianity as a Local Religion in Late Imperial China*," Harvard University Asia Center, 2010.

52 Ch'oe Pyŏng-uk. *Chungguk Kŭnhyŏndae Ch'ŏnju-gyo-sa Yŏn'gu* (A Study on the History of Modern and Contemporary Chinese Catholicism). Kyŏngin

Munhwasa, 2020 ; Yi Chun-gap. *Kŏnrŭngje wa Ch'ŏnju-gyo* (The Qianlong Emperor and Catholicism). Hyean, 2022.

53 Pierre-Emmanuel Roux. "Chosŏn Kakyŏ ŭi Chaebalgyŏn: 16-19-segi Ch'ŏnju-gyo Sŏn'gyosa ŭi Chosŏn Chin'ch'ul Chŏllyak e Taehan Kich'o Yŏn'gu (Rediscovery of the Bridge-Building Role of Chosŏn: A Preliminary Study on the Missionary Strategies of Catholic Missionaries in Joseon from the 16th to 19th Centuries)." *Yŏnmin Hakchi* 16, 2011.

54 Pierre-Emmanuel Roux, "The Catholic Experience of Chosŏn Envoys in Beijing: A Contact Zone and the Circulation of Religious knowledge in the Eighteenth century", *Acta Koreana* 19(1), 2016.

55 Kim, Chang-hwan. "Yŏnhaeng Milsa Sot'ong Bangsik kwa Pyŏnhwa: Ch'ŏnju-gyo Milsa Kirok ŭl Chungsim ŭro (Communication Methods and Changes of Envoys to Beijing: Focusing on Records of Catholic Envoys)." *Kyohŏsa Yŏn'gu* 64, 2024.

56 Joo Hyun Sheen, "Religious Hybridization and the Legacy of Jesuit Accommodationism in the Early Modern East Asia: A Comparative Analysis of Apologetics by Early Catholics in China and Korea," unpublished Ph.D. dissertation, Pennsylvania State University, 2018

57 Gregory N. Evon, "Tobacco, God, and Books: The Perils of Barbarism in Eighteenth-Century Korea," *The Journal of Asian Studies* 73(3), 2014.

58 Cho, Hyŏn-bŏm. *Chosŏn ŭi Sŏn'gyosa, Sŏn'gyosa ŭi Chosŏn* (Missionaries in Chosŏn, Chosŏn Through Missionaries). Han'guk Kyohŏsa Yŏn'guso, 2015 ; Yi, Sŏk-wŏn. *19-segi Tong-Sŏyang Ch'ungdol kwa Chosŏn Ch'ŏnju-gyo* (The Clash of East and West in the 19th Century and Chosŏn Catholicism). Suwŏn Kyohŏsa Yŏn'guso, 2018.

59 Daniel Kane, "The Beautiful Mission: The Catholic Missionary Experience in Korea, 1853-1866," *Acta Koreana* 4, 2001.

60 Doh Jin-soon, and Nam Ji-woo. "1842-nyŏn Kim Taegŏn ŭi Erigon-ho Hanghae wa Ap'yŏn Chŏnjaeng: Hanghae Ilji wa Yŏjŏng (Kim Dae-gŏn's Voyage on the Erigon in 1842 and the Opium War: Logbooks and Journey)." *Kyohŏsa Yŏn'gu* 59, 2021 ; Doh Jin-soon. "1842-nyŏn Kim Dae-gŏn ŭi Namgyŏng Joyak Join-sik Ch'amgwan kwa Pogo (Kim Taegŏn's Observation and Report on the Nanjing Treaty Signing in 1842)." *Han'guk Kŭnhyŏndaesa Yŏn'gu* 98, 2021a.

61 Doh Jin-soon. "Kunham kwa Sŏn'gyo: 1842-nyŏn Sesil·Changshini·Ribŭ wa ŭi <Chosŏn Kusang> kwa Chŏndoedoen Silhaeng, Kim Taegŏn·Ch'oe

Yangŏp ŭi Ip'guk kwa Sunkyo (Warships and Missionary Work: The 1842 Plans for Joseon by Cecille, Jangsin, and Rive, the Misguided Execution, and the Entry and Martyrdom of Kim Taegŏn and Ch'oe Yangŏp)." *Yŏksa Hakbo* 252, 2021b.

62 Franklin Rausch, "Wicked Officials and Virtuous Martyrs: an analysis of the martyr biographies in Alexius Hwang sayŏng's Silk Letter", *kyohŏsa Yŏn'gu* 32, 2009.

63 Wŏn, Chae-yŏn. *Chosŏn Wangjo ŭi Pŏp kwa Kŭrisŭdo-gyo* (The Law of the Chosŏn Dynasty and Christianity). Handŭl Ch'ulp'ansa, 2003.

64 Pierre-Emmanuel Roux, "The Great Ming Code and the Repression of Catholics in Chosŏn Korea," Acta Koreana 15(1), 2012.

65 Byungsul Jung, "The Joseon Government's Changing Perception of Early Catholicism Examined through Law Application", *Seoul Journal of Korean Studies* 33(2), 2020 ; Pang, Sang-gŭn. "Chosŏn Huggi Ch'ŏnju-gyo-do ŭi Sun'gyo Kwajŏng (Ch'epo~Ch'ŏhyŏng) Yŏn'gu (A Study on the Martyrdom Process of Catholics in Late Chosŏn (Arrest to Execution))." *Kyohŏsa Yŏn'gu* 61, 2022.

66 So Chin-hyŏng. "Sinyu Saok Ijŏn Ch'ŏnju-gyo e Taehan Kuk'kajŏk Taeŭng kwa Kŭ Chŏngch'ijŏk Ŭimi: Ch'ŏnju-gyo e Taehan Yŏron Hyŏngsŏng kwa Sahoe ŭi Posu-hwajŏk Kwanchŏm esŏ (The State's Response to Catholicism Before the Sinyu Persecution and Its Political Implications: From the Perspective of Public Opinion Formation and Social Conservatization)." *Chŏngch'i Sasang Yŏn'gu* 28(1), 2022.

67 Nam, Ho-hyun. "*Chosŏn Huggi Kukka ŭi Ch'ŏnju-gyo Taeŭng kwa Hyŏngjŏng* (The State's Response to Catholicism and Penal Administration in Late Chosŏn Dynasty). PhD diss., Department of History, Sogang University, 2024.

68 Yun Yŏng-hyŏn. "Chosŏn Huggi Sahak Ihae wa Chibang ŭi Saok Hyŏngjŏng (Understanding Western Learning and Penal Administration of Local Persecutions in Late Chosŏn)." *Kyohŏ Sahak* 24, 2024a ; ———. "Chŏllado Kwanch'alsa ŭi Sahak Choenin Taeŭng: Chŏnghae Saok (1827) ~ Kiyŏ Saok (1839) e Hanjŏnghayŏ (The Response of Jeolla Province Governor to Western Learning Criminals: Focusing on the Persecutions of 1827 and 1839)." *Chŏnbuk Sahak* 70, 2024b.

Bibliography

Baker, Donald. "Jesuit Science through Korean Eyes," *Journal of Korean Studies* 4, 1982~1983.

_________. "The Religious Revolution in Modern Korean History: From ethics to theology and from ritual hegemony to religious freedom," T*he review of Korean Studies* 9(3), 2006.

_________. "The Impact of Christianity on Modern Korea: An overview," *Acta Koreana* 19(1), 2016.

_________. "A Different Thread: Orthodoxy, Heterodoxy, and Catholicism in a Confucian World," Confucian and Late Chosŏn Korea. (unpublished)

Baker, Don and Rausch, Franklin. *Catholics and Anti-Catholicism in Chosŏn Korea*, University of Hawai'i Press and Center for Korean Studies, 2017.

Catholic Diocese of Suwŏn's Committee for the Promotion of Beatification and Canonization. "*Han'guk Ch'ŏnju-gyohoe Ch'angsŏl Chuyŏg ŭi Ch'ŏnju Sinang 1: Ch'angsŏl Chuyŏg kwa Yi Pyŏk* (The Catholic Faith of the Founding Figures of the Korean Catholic Church 1: Founding Figures and Yi Pyŏk), Hasang Publications, 2011a.

_________. "*Han'guk Ch'ŏnju-gyohoe Ch'angsŏl Chuyŏg ŭi Ch'ŏnju Sinang 2: Ch'angsŏl Chuyŏg ŭi Sungyo wa Kŭ Pyŏngp'an* (The Catholic Faith of the Founding Figures of the Korean Catholic Church 2: The Martyrdom of the Founding Figures and Their Reputation)," Hasang Publications, 2011b.

_________. "*Han'guk Ch'ŏnju-gyohoe Ch'angsŏl Chuyŏg ŭi Ch'ŏnju Sinang 3: Han'guk Ch'ŏnju-gyohoe Ch'angnip Sŏnjo Husondŭl ŭi Ch'ŏnju Sinang* (The Catholic Faith of the Founding Figures of the Korean Catholic Church 3: The Catholic Faith of the Descendants of the Founding Ancestors of the Korean Catholic Church)," Hasang Publications, 2013.

Cha, Ki-jin. "*Chosŏn Huggi ŭi Sŏhak kwa Ch'ŏksaron Yŏn'gu* (A Study on Western Learning and the Theory of Rejecting Heterodoxy in Late Chosŏn). Han'guk Kyohŏsa Yŏn'guso, 2002.

Chang, Yu-sŭng. "1791-nyŏn Naepo: Pak Chong-ak kwa Ch'ŏnju-gyo Pakhae (Naepo in 1791: Pak Chong-ak and the Persecution of Catholics)," *Kyohŏsa Yŏn'gu* 44, 2014.

Ch'oe, Pyŏng-uk. *Chungguk Kŭnhyŏndae Ch'ŏnju-gyo-sa Yŏn'gu* (A Study on the History of Modern and Contemporary Chinese Catholicism). Kyŏngin Munhwasa, 2020.

Ch'oe, Sŏk-u. "Han'guk Ch'ŏnju-gyohoeŭi Kiwŏn Munje (The Issue of the Origins of the Korean Catholic Church)," *Han'guk Kidokkyo wa Yŏksa* 1, 1991.

Cho, Hyŏn-bŏm. "Chosŏn Huggi Yuhakjadŭl ŭi Sŏhak Insik: Chonggyo/Kwahak Kubunron e Taehan Chaegŏmto (Late Chosŏn Confucian Scholars' Perceptions of Western Learning: A Reexamination of the Religion/Science Dichotomy)." *Han'guk Sasangsahak* 50, 2015.

_________. *Chosŏn ŭi Sŏn'gyosa, Sŏn'gyosa ŭi Chosŏn* (Missionaries in Chosŏn, Chosŏn Through Missionaries). Han'guk Kyohŏsa Yŏn'guso, 2015.

Cho, Kwang. "Sin'yu Pakhae ŭi Punsŏkchŏk Kosal (An Analytical Study of the Sin'yu Persecution)." *Kyohŏsa Yŏn'gu* 1, 1977.

_________. "*Chosŏn hugi Sahoe wa Ch'ŏnju-gyo* (Korean Society and Catholicism in the Late Chosŏn Period)," Kyŏngin Munhwasa, 2010.

Chŏn, Yong-hun. "19-segi Chosŏn esŏ Sŏyang Kwahak kwa Ch'ŏnmunhak ŭi Sŏnggyŏk (The Nature of Western Science and Astronomy in 19th Century Chosŏn). *Han'guk Kwahaksahakhoeji* 35(3), 2013.

_________. "Chŏngjo Sidae Tasi Pogi: Ch'ŏnmunhaksa ŭi Kwanchŏm esŏ (Revisiting the Reign of King Chŏngjo: From the Perspective of the History of Astronomy)." *Yŏksa Pip'yŏng* 115, 2016 ; Kim, Sŏn-hŭi. *Sŏhak, Chosŏn Yuhak i Mannan Natsŏn Kŏul* (Western Learning, A Strange Mirror Encountered by Chosŏn Confucianism). Mosinŭn Saramdŭl, 2018.

Dallet, Charles. trans. Ch'oe, Sŏk-u and An, Ŭng-ryŏl, *A History of the Korean Catholic Church* (Volume 1), Han'guk Kyohŏsa Yŏn'guso, 1996.

Doh, Jin-soon. "Kunham kwa Sŏn'gyo: 1842-nyŏn Sesil·Changshini·Ribŭ wa ŭi <Chosŏn Kusang> kwa Chŏndoedoen Silhaeng, Kim Dae-gŏn·Ch'oe Yangŏp ŭi Ip'guk kwa Sunkyo (Warships and Missionary Work: The 1842 Plans for Joseon by Cecille, Jangsin, and Rive, the Misguided Execution, and the Entry and Martyrdom of Kim Taegŏn and Ch'oe Yangŏp)." *Yŏksa Hakbo* 252, 2021b.

_________. "1839-nyŏn Kihae Pakhae wa Kŭ Pandaejadŭl: 'Cheil Sŏpjŏng'

Kim Yu-gŭn, 'Yebi Sinja' Kim Chŏng-hŭi, Hyŏngjo P'ansŏ Cho Pyŏng-hyŏn (The 1839 *Gihae* Persecution and Its Opponents: 'First Regent' Kim Yu-gŭn, 'Catechumen' Kim Chŏng-hŭi, and Minister of Justice Cho Pyŏng-hyŏn)." *Kyohŏ Sahak* 25, 2024.

Doh, Jin-soon, and Nam, Ji-woo. "1842-nyŏn Kim Taegŏn ŭi Erigon-ho Hanghae wa Ap'yŏn Chŏnjaeng: Hanghae Ilji wa Yŏjŏng (Kim Taegŏn's Voyage on the Erigon in 1842 and the Opium War: Logbooks and Journey)." *Kyohŏsa Yŏn'gu* 59, 2021.

Evon, Gregory N. "Tobacco, God, and Books: The Perils of Barbarism in Eighteenth-Century Korea," *The Journal of Asian Studies* 73(3), 2014.

Finch, Andrew. "The Pursuit of Martyrdom in the Catholic Church in Korea before 1866," *Journal of Ecclesiastical History* 60(1), 2009.

Hŏ, T'ae-yong. "'Silhak' Iraneŭn T'ŭl ŭi Yŏksa-jŏk Chokan (A Historical Bird's-Eye View of the Framework of 'Practical Learning',) *Chosŏn Sidae Sahakbo* 102, 2022.

Hwang, Chae-bŏm. "*Sŏngkyo Yoji* ŭi Wŏnbon Mat'in Sŏn'gyosa ŭi *Ssangch'ŏnjamun* Yŏn'gu (A Study on the Original Text of *Sŏngkyo Yoji*: Missionary Martin's *Ssangch'ŏnjamun*)." *Sinhak Sasang* 190, 2020.

Kane, Daniel. "The Beautiful Mission: The Catholic Missionary Experience in Korea, 1853-1866," *Acta Koreana* 4, 2001.

Jung, Byungsul. "The Joseon Government's Changing Perception of Early Catholicism Examined through Law Application", *Seoul Journal of Korean Studies* 33(2), 2020.

Karlsson, Anders. "Beyond the Great Tradition: Recent European Scholarship on the History of Chosŏn Korea", *Yŏksa wa Hyŏnsil* 90, 2013.

Kim, Chang-hwan. "Yŏnhaeng Milsa Sot'ong Bangsik kwa Pyŏnhwa: Ch'ŏnju-gyo Milsa Kirok ŭl Chungsim ŭro (Communication Methods and Changes of Envoys to Beijing: Focusing on Records of Catholic Envoys)." *Kyohŏsa Yŏn'gu* 64, 2024.

Kim, Han-kyu. "Sahak Chingŭi rŭl T'onghaesŏ Pon Ch'ogi Han'guk Ch'ŏnju-gyohoe ŭi Myŏt Kaji Munje (Several Issues in the Early Korean Catholic Church as Seen Through Sahak Chingŭi)." *Kyohŏsa Yŏn'gu* 2, 1979.

Kim, Hyŏn-u and Kim, Sŏk-ju. "Yi Pyŏk ŭi *Sŏngkyo Yoji* nŭn Wijo Munhŏn in'ga? (Is Yi Pyŏk's *Sŏngkyo Yoji* Forged Document?)" *Kidokkyŏ Sasang*

729, 2019.
Kim, Ok-hy. "Women in the History of Catholicism in Korea," *Korea Journal* 24(8), 1984.
Kim, So Jung. "Speaking In-Between: Vernacular Spirituality of a Woman in Late Chosŏn Korea," *Journal of Ecumenical Studies* 58(4), 2023.
Medina, J. G. R. "*The Catholic Church in Korea, Its Origins 1566-1784*", Royal Asiatic Society, 1994.
Menegon, Eugenio. "*Ancestors, Virgins, and Friars: Christianity as a Local Religion in Late Imperial China*," Harvard University Asia Center, 2010.
Msgr. Shim sang-Tai and Others. *The Founding Ancestors of the Catholic Church in Korea*, Hasang Publishing, 2014.
Nam, Ho-hyun. *Gonjang kwa Sipchaga: Chosŏn Hugi Ch'ŏnjugyo Sinja ŭi Hyŏngjŏng kwa Kukka* (Cudgel and Cross: Legal Application and the State's Response to Catholicism in Late Chosŏn Korea). Gyeongin Munhwasa, 2025.
No, Kyŏng-hŭi. "19-segi Huban Sŏyang Hwalpan Kisul ŭi Toip kwa Han'gŭl Ch'ŏnju-gyo Sŏjŏk ŭi Ch'ulp'an (The Introduction of Western Printing Technology and the Publication of Korean Catholic Books in the Late 19th Century)." *Han'guk Silhak Yŏn'gu* 47, 2024.
No, Tae-hwan. *Tongdo Sŏgi-ron Hyŏngsŏng Kwajŏng Yŏn'gu* (A Study on the Formation Process of *Tongdo Sŏgi* 東道西器 Theory)," Iljisa, 2005.
Pak, Min-ye. "Sin'yu Pakhae rŭl T'onghae Pon Ch'ŏnju-gyohoe Nae Kwabu Sinja wa Wisang Kwabu (Widow Believers and Pseudo-Widows in the Catholic Church Through the Lens of the Sin'yu Persecution)." *Sŏgang Inmun Nonch'ong* 54, 2019.
Pang, Sang-gŭn. "*19-segi Chungban Han'guk Ch'ŏnju-gyo-sa Yŏn'gu* (A Study on the History of Korean Catholicism in the Mid-19th Century)." Han'guk Kyohŏsa Yŏn'guso, 2006.
________. "Chosŏn Huggi Ch'ŏnju-gyo-do ŭi Sun'gyo Kwajŏng (Ch'epo~Ch'ŏhyŏng) Yŏn'gu (A Study on the Martyrdom Process of Catholics in Late Chosŏn (Arrest to Execution))." *Kyohŏsa Yŏn'gu* 61, 2022.
Rausch, Franklin. "Wicked Officials and Virtuous Martyrs: an analysis of the martyr biographies in Alexius Hwang sayŏng's Silk Letter", *kyohŏsa Yŏn'gu* 32, 2009.

Roux, Pierre-Emmanuel. "Chosŏn Kakyŏ ŭi Chaebalgyŏn: 16-19-segi Ch'ŏnju-gyo Sŏn'gyosa ŭi Chosŏn Chin'ch'ul Chŏllyak e Taehan Kich'o Yŏn'gu (Rediscovery of the Bridge-Building Role of Chosŏn: A Preliminary Study on the Missionary Strategies of Catholic Missionaries in Joseon from the 16th to 19th Centuries)." *Yŏnmin Hakchi* 16, 2011.

_________. "The Great Ming Code and the Repression of Catholics in Chosŏn Korea," Acta Koreana 15(1), 2012.

_________. "The Catholic Experience of Chosŏn Envoys in Beijing: A Contact Zone and the Circulation of Religious knowledge in the Eighteenth century", *Acta Koreana* 19(1), 2016.

Seo, Jong-tae. "(Book Review) A Study on the Issues in the Early History of the Korean Catholic Church." *Kyohŏsa Yŏn'gu* 46, 2015.

Sheen, Joo Hyun. "*Religious Hybridization and the Legacy of Jesuit Accommodationism in the Early Modern East Asia: A Comparative Analysis of Apologetics by Early Catholics in China and Korea*," unpublished Ph.D. dissertation, Pennsylvania State University, 2018.

So, Chin-hyŏng. "Sinyu Saok Ijŏn Ch'ŏnju-gyo e Taehan Kuk'kajŏk Taeŭng kwa Kŭ Chŏngch'ijŏk Ŭimi: Ch'ŏnju-gyo e Taehan Yŏron Hyŏngsŏng kwa Sahoe ŭi Posu-hwajŏk Kwanchŏm esŏ (The State's Response to Catholicism Before the Sinyu Persecution and Its Political Implications: From the Perspective of Public Opinion Formation and Social Conservatization)." *Chŏngch'i Sasang Yŏn'gu* 28(1), 2022.

_________. "Chosŏn Huggi Sŏhak Yŏn'gu ŭi Chuje Hwaktang e Taehan Cheŏn: Ponyŏk, Ch'ŏksap'a Yŏn'gu wa Sŏhak ŭi Kwangye rŭl Chungsim ŭro (A Proposal for Expanding the Themes of Western Learning Studies in Late Chosŏn: Focusing on Translation, the Ch'ŏksap'a, and Their Relationship with Western Learning)." *Chosŏn Sidae Sahakbo* 107, 2023

Song, Chi-yŏn. "Chosŏn Sidae Ch'ŏnju-gyo Yŏsŏng ŭi Yŏksa Tasi Ilgi: Tongjŏngnyŏ e Taehan Nonŭi rŭl Chungsim ŭro (Reinterpreting the History of Catholic Women in Chosŏn: Focusing on Discussions of Virgins)." *Tongbang Hakchi* 169, 2015.

Torrey, Deberniere J. "Young Barbara's Devotion and Death: Reading Father Ch'oe's Field Report of 1850," *Korean Studies* 42, 2018.

Wŏn, Chae-yŏn. *Chosŏn Wangjo ŭi Pŏp kwa Kŭrisŭdo-gyo* (The Law of the Chosŏn Dynasty and Christianity). Handŭl Ch'ulp'ansa, 2003.

________. "19-segi Chŏnban Kyŏnggi-do Kŏju Se Sonyŏn ŭi Haewoe Yuhaksaeng Kongdongch'e wa Sŏhak Suyong (The Overseas Student Community and the Reception of Western Learning by Three Boys Residing in Gyeonggi-do in the Early 19th Century)," *Kijŏn Munhwa Yŏn'gu* 45(1), 2024.

Yi, Chun-gap. *Kŏnrŭngje wa Ch'ŏnju-gyo* (The Qianlong Emperor and Catholicism). Hyean, 2022.

Yi, Sŏk-wŏn. *19-segi Tong-Sŏyang Ch'ungdol kwa Chosŏn Ch'ŏnju-gyo* (The Clash of East and West in the 19th Century and Chosŏn Catholicism). Suwŏn Kyohŏsa Yŏn'guso, 2018.

Yi, Kyŏng-gu. "Yi Pyŏk, Hwang Sayŏng, Chŏng Hasang ŭi Ch'ŏnju-gyo, Yugyo Insik ŭi Tongilsŏng kwa Ch'ai-jŏm (The Similarities and Differences in the Perception of Catholicism and Confucianism by Yi Pyŏk, Hwang Sayoung, and Chŏng Hasang)." *Kyohŏsa Yŏn'gu* 52, 2018.

Yi, Wŏn-sun. "Ch'ŏnju-gyo ŭi Suyong kwa Chŏn'p'a (Acceptance and Propagation of Catholicism)." Edited by the Kuksa Pyŏnch'an Wiwŏnhoe, *Sinp'yŏn Han'guksa* 35, 2002.

Yun, Min-gu. "*Han'guk Ch'ŏnju-gyohoeŭi Kiwon* (the Origins of the Korean Catholic Church)", Kukhak Charyowŏn, 2002.

________. "*Ch'ogi Han'guk Ch'ŏnju Kyohoesaui Chaengchŏm Yŏn'gu: Sŏngkyo Yoji, Sipkemyŏngga, Manch'ŏnyugo, Ibyŏkchŏn, Yuhandang Ŏnhaengsilnogŭn Sagida* (A Study on the Issues in the Early History of the Korean Catholic Church: Sŏnggyo Yoji, Ten Commandments Song, Manchŏn Yugo, The Biography of Yi Pyŏk, and Yuhandang's Records Are Fabrications)." Gukhakjaryowon, 2014.

Yun, Yŏng-hyŏn. "Chosŏn Huggi Sahak Ihae wa Chibang ŭi Saok Hyŏngjŏng (Understanding Western Learning and Penal Administration of Local Persecutions in Late Chosŏn)." *Kyohŏ Sahak* 24, 2024a.

________. "Chŏllado Kwanch'alsa ŭi Sahak Choenin Taeŭng: Chŏnghae Saok (1827) ~ Kihae Saok (1839) e Hanjŏnghayŏ (The Response of Jeolla Province Governor to Western Learning Criminals: Focusing on the Persecutions of 1827 and 1839)." *Chŏnbuk Sahak* 70, 2024b.

8

Conflicts and Divergences: Review of Research Trends on Chin'gyŏng Landscape Painting in Late Chosŏn Period

Dawoon Jeong

Sogang University

8 Conflicts and Divergences: Review of Research Trends on Chin'gyŏng Landscape Painting in Late Chosŏn Period

Dawoon Jeong (Sogang University)

1. Introduction

The keyword representing the culture and arts of late Chosŏn Korea would be landscape paintings, and among them, the Chin'gyŏng (True-View, 眞景) landscape painting. Though there are various interpretations of its definition, it generally refers to landscape paintings during the eighteenth century, depicting actually existing landscapes of Chosŏn Korea.[1] The painter who is regarded as having prioneered and completed this new genre is Chŏng Sŏn (1676~1759), evaluated as having created original landscape paintings by fusing a new technique from the genre of painting originating in China, Namjong-hwa (The Southern School painting, 南宗畵), with conventional landscape painting traditions. His works depicting natural scenery, such as Mt. Inwang, Mt. Kŭmgang, and the Han River, have become representative images of late Chosŏn culture, showcased through various media, exhibitions, and even textbooks.

However, it's interesting to note that despite its undisputed popularity as a beautiful and proud national cultural heritage, the Chin'gyŏng landscape painting has been at the center of academic debate. The Chin'gyŏngshidae (Chin'gyŏng era, 眞景時代) theory is a prime example.

The Chin'gyŏngshidae theory emerged with growing interest and research on Chin'gyŏng landscapes and moreover Korean art history itself since Korea's 1945 liberation from Japan. It has been advocated by Ch'oe Wansu, a curator of Kansong art museum who has deeply studied Chŏng Sŏn, and some historians such as Chŏng Okcha and Yu Ponghak. They defined late Chosŏn as the pinnacle of culture that revealed Korea's unique characteristics, as exemplified by Chin'gyŏng landscapes, and explained its foundation through Chosŏn Neo-Confucianism (朝鮮性理學), the ideology of Chosŏn Zhonghua (朝鮮中華), and the resulting consciousness of autonomy. What can be discerned from this is that the theory is intrinsically linked to a historiographical perspective emphasizing the cultural independence and autonomy of the late Chosŏn period.

The Chin'gyŏngshidae theory attracted both approval and criticism from scholars right after its emergence. Scholars raised sharp criticisms, especially of its excessive schematic view and nationalistic purpose. In 2006, for example, the conference was held with the title "Chin'gyŏngmunhwa, kŭ shilsanggwa hŏsang (The reality and illusions of Chin'gyŏng culture)", and a critical review paper on the theory was published as a result.[2] Despite such criticisms, the Chin'gyŏngshidae theory continues to maintain its presence as an active scholarly discourse, with a new advocating research emerging again in 2014.[3] Furthermore, studies that have inherited and developed this argument continue to appear in the domains of intellectual history and cultural theory of late Chosŏn.

These research trends are evident in both Korean and international academia. Compared to Chinese or Japanese art history, Korean art history has received markedly less attention from scholars outside Korea. However, since the beginning of the twenty first century, Korean research achievements have gradually been introduced to and incorporated into international scholarship. Consequently, both responsive and critical studies on the Chin'gyŏngshidae theory began to emerge. While there was not much controversy as in Korea, the novel perspectives and approaches to late Chosŏn cultural arts in some studies merit attention, particularly when compared with Korean scholarship.

Therefore, this chapter examines the developments, conflicts, and divergences of theories related to Chin'gyŏng landscape painting, with particular focus on the Chin'gyŏngshidae theory. This analytical approach has significant historiographical implications, as the Chin'gyŏngshidae theory reflects the historical experiences and memories of modernity in Korean art history. Given that these historical experiences and traumas of modern Korea have influenced not only art history but Korean studies broadly, this investigation is also about the historical perspective on late Chosŏn and the process of its formation. Furthermore, the comparative analysis of scholarship both within and beyond Korea constitutes another distinctive contribution of this study.

This chapter is structured in two parts. First, it examines chronological development of research on Chin'gyŏng landscape painting, taking the early 2000s as a pivotal point in scholarly trends. This section presents the theoretical conflicts and the subsequent diversification of the research approach. Second, based on this historiographical review, it analyzes the characteristics of research trends, offering some commentaries and suggestions on research perspectives. The broader aim of this work is to expand the discourse on the culture and history of Chosŏn Korea, thereby contributing to the growing scholarly interest in this field.

2. Research Trends on Chin'gyŏng Landscape Painting

1) 1970s~Early 2000s: The Emergence and Conflicts over the Chin'gyŏngshidae Theory

Although the Chin'gyŏngshidae theory emerged in detail during the 1990s, its arguments were, in fact, the result of discourses that had accumulated in earlier periods. The study of Korean art history as a modern discipline emerged during Japanese colonial rule, making it inevitable that post-liberation scholarship would emphasize national autonomy.[4]

Chosŏnmisulsayŏn'gu (A Study of Chosŏn Art History, 1946) by Yun Hŭisun, for example, constructed a dichotomous framework of art history that contrasted autonomous versus toadying, national versus sinocentric, and original versus imitative characteristics, focusing particularly on the relationship between Chinese and Korean art.[5] Within this context, Chin'gyŏng landscapes came to be regarded as a representative example of independent and developmental national art.

However, the development of Korean art history was significantly delayed. Substantive research on Chin'gyŏng landscapes did not begin until the 1970s, following several impediments such as the Korean War and a dearth of specialists in the field of study. One of the pioneering scholars in this field was Yi Dong-ju. He published an introductory book, *Urinaraŭi yetkŭrim* (Old paintings of our country, 1975), that compiled his papers from the 1960s, focusing on Chŏng Sŏn's Chin'gyŏng landscapes. Through chronological organization and analysis of Chŏng's paintings, Yi argued that his works were original and unique in depicting Korean scenes, transcending Chinese influences and techniques. Moreover, Yi criticized the Japanese colonial historiography of Korean art by characterizing the eighteenth century, particularly the reigns of Kings Yŏngjo (r. 1724~1776) and Chŏngjo (r. 1776~1800), as a period of cultural renaissance.[6] These arguments reflected the academic zeitgeist of the time, a shared imperative consciousness to overcome Japan's colonial legacies.

In the 1980s, scholarship on Chin'gyŏng landscapes further advanced both quantitatively and qualitatively, especially by Ch'oe Wansu and Yi Tae-ho. They shared a common methodological approach of conducting research in conjunction with organizing exhibitions of Chin'gyŏng landscapes at museums and galleries.[7] In the case of Ch'oe, he initiated investigations on Chŏng Sŏn while curating exhibitions at the Kansong art museum. In 1981, he published articles on Chŏng's landscapes in conjunction with the exhibition[8], releasing an art book on Chŏng Sŏn and its commentary book. That same year, Yi Tae-ho organized exhibitions at the Gwangju National Museum, subsequently producing several studies on Chin'gyŏng landscapes.[9]

Their research achievements were published as comprehensive results in the 1990s. The rapid proliferation of Chin'gyŏng landscapes studies during this period was closely linked to the context of that time. For example, the 1997 financial crisis in Korea also served as a catalyst that intensified Korean scholars' engagement with traditional culture and attempts to find its values, along with the imperative of the post-liberation era. As the limitations of Western culture and values became apparent, scholars' attention shifted toward the rediscovery and preservation of traditional cultural heritage.[10] Within these historical context and influences, Yi Tae-ho wove together the trends of late Chosŏn painting, including Chin'gyŏng landscape painting, genre painting, and portrait, under the unifying core theme of "realistic mindset." He argued that economic growth and transformation in feudal social structures fostered both a heightened interest in reality and an autonomous artistic consciousness. Ultimately, he interpreted this realistic spirit as background for the distinctive late Chosŏn style in art history.[11] His research thus aligned with contemporary scholarship on Chin'gyŏng landscapes, and furthermore with studies on the art history of the late Chosŏn dynasty that emphasize the artistic excellence and cultural autonomy.

Ch'oe Wansu's works further advanced these theoretical perspectives. He wrote *Kyŏmjae chŏngsŏn chin'gyŏngsansuhwa* (Chin'gyŏng Landscape Paintings of Kyŏmjae Chŏng Sŏn, 1993), a compilation of his published papers and commentaries on the works of Chŏng Sŏn, through which he sought to establish the significance of Chin'gyŏng landscapes within the ideological and cultural currents of late Chosŏn Korea. According to Ch'oe, after Yi Hwang (1501~1570) digested Neo-Confucian philosophy and Yi I (1536~1584) completed Chosŏn Neo-Confucianism, the Sŏin (The Western faction, 西人), who succeeded the school of Yi I, initiated a cultural movement to manifest Chosŏn's distinctive characteristics. Ch'oe also argued that after the Ming-Qing transition in China, a discourse centered on Song Siyŏl (1607~1689) emerged that positioned Chosŏn as the actual heir of Zhonghua culture, fostering pride in Chosŏn's own cultural identity and advancing its characteristics. He evaluated the Noron

(The Old Doctrine faction, 老論), represented by Kim Ch'anghyŏp (1651~1708), as the leading force of this cultural trend, and Chŏng Sŏn, its proponent, as a great master who demonstrated the excellence and pride of national culture through his paintings.[12]

Furthermore, Ch'oe gathered scholars who agreed with this view, centered on the Institute of Korean National Art and the Kansong art museum, and published *Urimunhwaŭi hwanggŭmgi, chin'gyŏngshidae* (The Golden Age of Our Culture: The Chin'gyŏng era, 1998). Throughout the book, he extended the cultural movement, led by the Sŏin and the Noron and based on the ideology of Chosŏn Zhonghua, to encompass the entirety of late Chosŏn culture, defining the seventeenth and eighteenth centuries as the Chin'gyŏngshidae. The co-authors of each chapter described various cultural and artistic forms, including calligraphy, genre painting, portraits, and ceramics, as products of the Chin'gyŏng era. Historians such as Chŏng Okcha and Yu Ponghak also examined the intellectual, literary, religious, and socioeconomic transformations in the late Chosŏn period, trying to substantiate this theory.[13]

The Chin'gyŏngshidae theory, which asserted the cultural uniqueness of late Chosŏn and cultural pride of both ruling elites at that time and scholars today, seems to be a natural conclusion of the trajectory of Korean art history scholarship after liberation from Japanese colonial rule. The theory's significance lies in its attempt to illuminate and integrate sociocultural aspects of the late Chosŏn society within a macro-level context. As a scholarly theory, however, it has a fundamental limitation: the lack of conceptual precision, most notably in the absence of a consistent definition of key theoretical terms such as "Chin'gyŏng" and "Chin'gyŏng era." There were divergent definitions regarding temporal boundaries and characteristics of Chin'gyŏng, with a lack of scholarly consensus, even among the co-authors. Moreover, extending the limited concepts and discussion on the Sŏin, the Noron, and Chŏng Sŏn's landscape paintings to represent the entirety of late Chosŏn culture is nearly an unsubstantiated logical leap.

Therefore, the Chin'gyŏngshidae theory encountered significant critiques since its inception. In response to Ch'oe Wansu's earlier articles, scholars already questioned and pointed out the weak connection between Chin'gyŏng landscapes and Chosŏn Zhonghua ideology, calling for research grounded in broader perspectives, including the art history of East Asia. Hong Sŏnp'yo was the leading figure in the critique of the Chin'gyŏngshidae theory. He criticized the theory for overemphasizing the opposition between Chin'gyŏng landscapes and traditional ideal landscape paintings that depict imaginary scenery, and for interpreting the former as a product of nationalistic, original, modern-oriented, and uniquely Korean characteristics. Hong argued that this interpretation contradicted the historical evidence: late Chosŏn painters engaged with both genres simultaneously. According to him, it was a practice paralleled in contemporary Chinese and Japanese painting traditions under the influence of Ming's literary figure Dong Qichang (1555~1636).[14]

Han Chŏnghŭi also challenged the presumed correlation between Chin'gyŏng landscapes in the eighteenth century and the autonomous consciousness of Chosŏn Zhonghua. He argued that cultural sinocentrism never disappeared and persisted even during periods of widespread anti-Qing sentiment. Instead of accepting the Chin'gyŏngshidae theory, Han proposed that the Chinese ideas of Silhak (Practical Learning, 實學) and Daoism formed the ideological foundation of Chŏng Sŏn's Chin'gyŏng landscape paintings.[15] This perspective led to a subsequent investigation that compared artworks depicting Mt. Huang in China, Mt. Kŭmgang in Korea, and Mt. Huji in Japan, highlighting the phenomenon of the East Asian trend toward realistic paintings.[16]

Critical book reviews of the Chin'gyŏngshidae theory also emerged. Ch'oe Yŏngchin acknowledged the merit of the discourse, as it offered an opportunity to reexamine Neo-Confucianism and the late Chosŏn period, which had been negatively maligned under the influence of Japanese colonial historiography, and redefine it as a cultural golden age. However, Ch'oe also identified descriptive inaccuracies in the explanation of Neo-Confucianism and questioned the discourse's claim of evaluating Chosŏn Neo-Confucianism as a "more developmental" approach distinct from Zhu

Xi (1130~1200)'s philosophy. Furthermore, the critic raised concerns about the narrow perspective that defined only the Sŏin and the Noron, centered on Yulgok, as the Chosŏn Neo-Confucian scholars and categorized the rest as conservative.[17]

Yi Sŏng-Mi, meanwhile, proposed a strong critique of the validity of the term "Chin'gyŏng" as a representative criterion for categorizing the late Chosŏn period. She argued that this contradictory argument originated from Ch'oe Wansu's research, which focused predominantly on a single historical figure, Chŏng Sŏn. Moreover, Yi identified several critical flaws in the Chin'gyŏngshidae theory, such as its excessive emphasis on domestic Korean history, its problematic justification of the manifestation of unique characteristics, and its overly faction- and school-centric approach to cultural history.[18]

Another scholar who deepened the critique of the Chin'gyŏngshidae theory was Ko Yŏnhŭi, proposing the concept of "Sansugihaengyesul (Travelogue and Real-Scenery painting)" of the eighteenth century instead of Chin'gyŏng landscape painting. Through her alternative approaches, which concurrently examined painting and literature of late Chosŏn, she identified Chŏng Sŏn and the brothers Kim Ch'anghyŏp and Kim Ch'anghŭp (1653~1722) as the founders of this new cultural genre. Examining their views of nature and theories of creative writing, Ko demonstrated how the intellectual climate of late Chosŏn was significantly influenced by the flourishing literature of the Ming and Qing dynasties, the popularity of print collections of natural landscape, and the aesthetics and creative theories embedded within them.[19] It was a notable achievement in that she approached cultural phenomena from an international perspective and further sought to establish a new academic terminology.

The academic controversy over the Chin'gyŏngshidae theory culminated in Pak Ŭnsun's critical article. Following her participation in the 2006 conference, Pak published a paper summarizing the historiography of Chin'gyŏng landscape painting research and criticizing the Chin'gyŏngshidae theory. In her analysis, she identified three theoretical frameworks explaining the emergence of Chin'gyŏng landscapes: the internal development of Korean culture, external influences from Chinese and Japanese cultures, and the ideology of Chosŏn Zhonghua. Pak strongly criticized the Chin'gyŏngshidae theory, of these frameworks, that positioned Chosŏn Zhonghua ideology as the background for the emergence of Chin'gyŏng landscape paintings.

For example, Pak contended that the theory misrepresented historical complexity by explaining the late Chosŏn solely through concepts such as Chŏng Sŏn, Chin'gyŏng landscapes, the Sŏin, and Chosŏn Zhonghua ideology. She also criticized that it interpreted Chin'gyŏng landscapes paintings as overly nationalistic and subjective products, reflecting a narrow understanding of Chŏng Sŏn. Moreover, she noted that the theory failed to encompass the diverse aspects of Chin'gyŏng landscapes and their painters, while disregarding the cultural achievements during King Chŏngjo's reign by establishing periodization based on Chŏng Sŏn, who was active during the reign of King Yŏngjo. Pak emphatically argued that Chin'gyŏng landscapes were not the result of ideological and speculative thinking, but rather the manifestation of the realistic tendencies of the Silhak, practical learning that had developed within the context of the Qing's prosperity and socioeconomic transformation in the eighteenth century of Chosŏn.[20]

As demonstrated above, the Chin'gyŏngshidae theory advocated by Ch'oe Wansu is closely aligned with the contemporary imperative to establish an autonomous and developmental national art. This temporal context constituted both the theory's significance and its limitations, leading to scholarly conflicts within Korean academia from the time of its emergence. Critics commonly questioned the strong intrinsic motivation underlying the theory, an ideological justification that emphasized the uniqueness and autonomy of Chosŏn Korea in response to Japanese colonial historiography. In addition, they argued that the theory's concept of Chin'gyŏng failed to encompass the diverse cultural images of late Chosŏn society. These critiques were primarily raised by art historians, highlighting the methodological differences and boundaries between the disciplines of history and art history. This is why Pak strongly argued for the application of art historical methodology, which basically focused on individual works, rather than broader cultural and historical approaches.[21]

2) After the 2000s: The Diversification of the Chin'gyŏng Landscape Painting Studies

After intense scholarly conflicts, the controversy surrounding the Chin'gyŏngshidae theory subsided, accompanied by a conceptual refinement of academic terminology. Art historians have since concretized its scope and significance, being wary of the overuse of the term Chin'gyŏng landscapes. The attempts to redefine the terminology by distinguishing between "Chin'gyŏng (眞境)" and "Chin'gyŏng (眞景)" reflected this movement toward conceptual clarity.[22] As a result, the two terms were distinguished and categorized. "Silgyŏng (Real-Scenery, 實景) landscape painting," referring to depictions of real scenery, came to be used in a broader and more general sense. Today, Silgyŏng landscape painting is more commonly used as a value-neutral and encompassing term in research papers and art brochures of museums and art galleries.[23] "Chin'gyŏng landscapes," meanwhile, has evolved into a more specific concept for painting that flourished in the eighteenth century, influenced by Chŏng Sŏn and the genre of Namjong-hwa, the Southern School of Chinese painting.[24]

However, on the other hand, some scholars actively embrace and expand the terminology of the Chin'gyŏngshidae theory. For example, there is a study that has fully embraced the Chin'gyŏngshidae theory, understanding the late Chosŏn culture as an exemplary model that simultaneously achieved both national distinctiveness and universal Zhonghua civilization. From this perspective, the culture of late Chosŏn serves as an ideal precedent, demonstrating the necessity and possibility of a medieval East Asian community, relevant to contemporary nations in conflict within the modern nationalist order.[25] Furthermore, scholars have undertaken efforts to analyze the Chin'gyŏng culture in the eighteenth century through the lens of specific aesthetic, literary, and moral theoretical frameworks.[26]

These studies reveal that, despite substantial criticisms, the Chin'gyŏngshidae theory remained appealing and influential, particularly in historical and philosophical domains. Interestingly, even within art history, where the theory encountered strong opposition, parallel arguments emerged. Scholars continued to emphasize the significance of Chin'gyŏng landscapes as manifestations of an original and autonomous culture of late Chosŏn, even without explicitly employing the theory's concepts or acknowledging the discourse of Chosŏn Zhonghua as its ideological foundation. This tendency is evident in studies that, while criticizing the theory's arbitrary and overly nationalistic objectives, simultaneously analyzed Chŏng Sŏn's paintings as independent, original, and even "the most Korean" artworks.[27] Such scholarly positions, though seemingly contradictory, were fundamentally aligned with the Chin'gyŏngshidae theory. This alignment becomes more comprehensible when considered within the broader historiographical context of Korean art history.

Under these circumstances, proponents of the Chin'gyŏngshidae theory reasserted their scholarly position. Ch'oe Wansu maintained his theoretical framework and published *Kyŏmjae Chŏng Sŏn* (2009), synthesizing his research on Chŏng Sŏn and his paintings.[28] Yu Ponghak, who co-developed the Chin'gyŏngshidae theory, continued to advance the argument that the Gyeonghwasajok (京華士族), the ruling elite centered around the capital region in late Chosŏn, led developments in both Silhak and Chin'gyŏng culture.[29] In 2014, a follow-up study was published by the Institute of Korean National Art, commemorating Ch'oe Wansu's seventieth year, which upheld the same thesis of the theory.[30] Another proponent of the theory, Kang Kwansik, rejoined the discourse by emphasizing that "Chin'gyŏng" exemplified the realistic and practical tendencies of the late Chosŏn culture, and advocating for its validity as a periodizing concept, comparable to Western terms like "Baroque" or "Rococo". Meanwhile, he appeared to be aware of the criticisms directed at the theory in that he acknowledged that this realistic mindset was widely shared, even among intellectuals outside the Noron, and emphasized the influence of Chinese paintings in Chŏng Sŏn's works.[31]

A parallel trajectory can be observed in Western scholarship. However, comparing Western and Korean academic achievements in this field presents significant challenges. This disparity stems not only from the relative paucity of research on Korean landscapes but also from the marginalization of Korean art itself within Western art history, which has traditionally focused more on Chinese and Japanese art. Despite initiatives such as the touring exhibition "Five Thousand Years of Korean Art (1979–1981)" in the United States, Korean art struggled to transcend its perceived status as derivative of Chinese art.[32] Consequently, substantial Western scholarship on Korean art did not emerge until the 2000s[33]; even then it was primarily composed of introductory texts that either introduced or reflected the work of Korean scholars. The English translation and publication of Ch'oe Wansu's *Kyŏmjae chŏngsŏn chin'gyŏngsansuhwa* (1993) during this period exemplifies this pattern.[34]

The first comprehensive Western study of Chin'gyŏng landscapes was undertaken by Yi Sŏng-Mi, who published a book on Korean landscape paintings as the fourth volume in the Korea Foundation's the *Korean Culture Series*, an initiative to introduce Korean art and culture to Western audiences. She provided an overview of landscape painting of Korea from the early centuries of the Three Kingdoms period to the early twentieth century, examining the representative works and characteristics of each period. However, with half of the book's six chapters devoted to Chin'gyŏng landscapes, this work, while covering Korean landscapes broadly, demonstrated a clear emphasis on Chin'gyŏng landscape paintings.

The book analyzed Korean landscape paintings through the lens of the relationship between "continuity" and "innovation". The author argued that, despite the influence of Chinese art, late Chosŏn developed distinctive aesthetic characteristics, achieving a process of "Koreanization" in landscape painting through the Chin'gyŏng landscapes of the eighteenth century. She also noted that Chŏng Sŏn was able to pioneer Chin'gyŏng landscape painting because of the zeitgeist that positioned Chosŏn as the cultural heir to the Zhonghua and the resultant cultivation of cultural pride, along with the influences of Silhak and Western styles of painting.[35]

The narrative above mirrors the arguments found in early Korean scholarly research, especially the Chin'gyŏngshidae theory, which interpreted Chin'gyŏng landscapes through a dichotomous framework and Chosŏn Zhonghua ideology. Although the detailed presentation of Ming art history and the broader perspective on Chosŏn's international relations distinguished the work from the Chin'gyŏngshidae theory, which is centered on a single-country perspective, Chin'gyŏng landscape paintings were emphasized throughout the book as undeniably the most creative achievement in Korean art history.[36] A similar argument was reiterated in her second study, *Searching for Modernity* (2015). While cultural exchanges between Chosŏn and the outside world were acknowledged, including the visits to China by Chosŏn emissaries and the adoption of Western painting techniques, Chin'gyŏng landscapes were still described as the embodiment of Korean national culture, grounded in the ideological background of Chosŏn Zhonghua and Silhak.[37]

Interpretations parallel to the Chin'gyŏngshidae theory continued to emerge in scholarly discourse. Joan Kee analyzed Kang Sehwang's (1713~1791) works in *Songdogihaengch'ŏp* (*Journey to Kaesŏng,* 松都紀行帖) connecting the dissolution of hierarchical order in his paintings to the perception of the time, regarding Chosŏn as the new "Middle Kingdom" (Zhonghua, 中華).[38] Through this analysis, she applied the Chosŏn Zhonghua-based interpretation of Chin'gyŏng landscapes to Kang Sehwang's artworks.

An alternative approach to understanding Chin'gyŏng landscapes emerged beyond the influence of Chin'gyŏngshidae theory. Burglind Jungmann, in her research on Korean art, examined Chosŏn paintings through the lens of East Asian international exchange. In analyzing the artistic perspective of the Noron intellectuals who engaged with Chŏng Sŏn, she emphasized anti-Qing sentiment and disregard for realpolitik as key characteristics, rather than Chosŏn Zhonghua ideology.[39] Though, this alternative interpretation seems to have received limited attention.

As in Korea, scholars across various disciplines continued to employ Chin'gyŏngshidae theory to explain the eighteenth-century Koreanization of culture, weaving it with the transcendence of traditional Sino-centric attitudes and the formation of a distinctive Chosŏn identity.[40]

The Chin'gyŏngshidae theory thus established itself as a framework for interpreting Chin'gyŏng landscape painting both in Korea and abroad, maintaining its influence despite various controversies and debates. However, this sustained influence does not necessarily validate its theoretical status or legitimacy. Indeed, recent studies have emerged that criticize the existing research on Chin'gyŏng landscape paintings and the Chin'gyŏngshidae theory, while pursuing alternative approaches. The following studies illustrate these new trends.

First, there are studies questioning Kyŏmjae Chŏng Sŏn's established position as the definitive master of Chin'gyŏng landscape painting. This marked a shift from previous tendencies where both proponents and critics of the Chin'gyŏngshidae theory had vied to emphasize Chŏng Sŏn's influence and significance.[41] Chang Chinsŏng's research pioneered this shift by deconstructing the "Hwasŏng (Sage of Painting, 畵聖)" image of Chŏng Sŏn, primarily advanced by Ch'oe Wansu. With a critical analysis of historical records of the time, he highlighted several overlooked factors: the absence of Chŏng Sŏn's own writings, his status as a professional painter who earned his living by selling paintings, and the mixed reception of his work during his lifetime, including significant criticism. Through this investigation, Chang cautioned against allowing affection to compromise academic objectivity.[42]

In response to this criticism, some studies have reexamined the Chin'gyŏngshidae theory within the context of the colonial period. Ko Yŏnhŭi argued that today's high regard for Chŏng Sŏn and Chin'gyŏng landscapes was a product of nationalist needs during the Japanese occupation. In her view, their prominence was constructed within the context of modern nationalist intentions. Furthermore, she refuted the Chin'gyŏngshidae theory's claim that Chin'gyŏng landscape paintings originated from Chosŏn Zhonghua ideology, highlighting that Ch'oe

Wansu's admiration for Chŏng was rooted in a misinterpretation of historical sources.[43]

Yi Gyeong-hwa also revealed that the discourse associating Chŏng Sŏn's paintings with national identity or cultural competence emerged during the colonial period. According to her, under the influence of Chŏn Hyŏngp'il (1906~1962), a collector who laid the foundation for Kansong art museum, and his mentor O Sech'ang (1864~1953), Chŏng Sŏn was revived as a symbol of national culture and became a favorite object of art collectors.[44] These studies have broadened the scope of research on Chin'gyŏng landscapes, arguing from various sources that the discourse surrounding Chŏng Sŏn and his works was a modern invention.

Secondly, some scholars have examined Chin'gyŏng landscape paintings as media for reflecting political, socioeconomic, and cultural circumstances, moving beyond their conventional interpretation as mere depictions of natural scenery. A representative scholar of this research is Cho Kyuhŭi. Her study revealed that the landscape paintings of Chosŏn were not merely works for aesthetic appreciation but were practical media for recording, commemorating, and transmitting landownership within a socioeconomic context. Such paintings, which functioned as a kind of record, can also be observed in some of Chŏng Sŏn's Chin'gyŏng landscapes.[45]

Through her recent publication, she reaffirmed that landscape paintings in East Asia were not merely representations of nature, but also political and sociocultural symbols embedded with cultural codes. In other words, landscape paintings served as hieroglyphics, reflecting sociocultural changes, and acted as powerful mediators capable of altering perceptions of the real world. Therefore, from this perspective, Chŏng's paintings were not only poetic works that reflected Kim Ch'anghŭp's literary view, but also exerted realistic and cultural power, such as symbolizing the wish for the rebirth of Kim's family and reconstructing the P'algyŏng (Eight Scenic Views, 八景) of the capital.[46] In short, her research clarified that Chin'gyŏng landscape paintings reveal the existence of a privileged group of people and their cultural competence in understanding and shaping the power and impact of landscape paintings.

A similar argument can also be found in Yi Seong-hyeon's research. He criticized previous studies on Chin'gyŏng landscapes for overlooking the traditional meanings of landscape painting, instead interpreting them primarily as expressions of national pride. Yi argued that "Chin'gyŏng" refers to an idealized politics grounded in the Dao (道), and that landscape paintings served as vehicles for political messages. Therefore, Chin'gyŏng landscapes were media for conveying perspectives on the political reality of late Chosŏn. Chŏng Sŏn's paintings, in this view, were not merely realistic representations of his travels and impressions of natural scenery, but rather tools for expressing his political stance in relation to the Noron.[47] Although lacking concrete evidence, his research is significant for introducing a new interpretation by viewing Chin'gyŏng landscapes as a means of conveying political messages.

Third, it is worth noting that a significant shift is occurring within Western scholarship, moving away from conventional interpretations of Chin'gyŏng landscapes toward new interpretations. The work of J. P. Park exemplified this transformation, offering a critical assessment of modern scholars' nationalistic tendencies to hastily correlate the late Chosŏn period with national autonomy and modernity. Instead, he advocated for contextualizing these artworks within the historical context of the time. According to his perspective, rather than conveying an aesthetic view of nature and its beauty, landscape paintings served as "real-life" documents reflecting the voice of a social group regarding a particular place. The author thus argued that Chin'gyŏng landscapes were a medium through which the ruling elites of late Chosŏn projected their aspirations for status legitimization and social positioning.[48] J. P. Park further critiqued the scholarly tendency to emphasize the unilateral influence of Chosŏn Korea's culture in asserting its cultural distinctiveness and supremacy. Instead, he highlighted the reciprocal artistic exchanges with Chinese, Japanese, and European paintings.[49]

What these recent studies have in common is that they have broadened the scope of Chin'gyŏng landscapes research by posing critical and reflective questions to scholars of Korean art history, both in Korea and internationally. The driving force behind these new interpretations and approaches to Chin'gyŏng landscapes is a critical attitude toward the prevailing research climate, which, as the scholars themselves point out, has prioritized Korean characteristics and national identity. Given this context, one of the historiographical significances of the Chin'gyŏngshidae theory is that it triggered a reflective reassessment and diversification of research on landscape painting in late Chosŏn Korea.

3. Critical Analysis and Recommendations

This part aims to reexamine several characteristics of research on Chin'gyŏng landscape painting, based on the preceding discussion, and to offer brief commentaries.

First, the research on Chin'gyŏng landscape painting is a historically significant subject that exemplifies the trajectory of academic development in Korea, where ideological self-justification often preceded rigorous empirical inquiry. The experience of Japanese colonization led to a post-liberation academic response that, across disciplines, prioritized overcoming colonial historiography. The field of art history followed this pattern, with Chin'gyŏng landscape painting being one of the most prominent domains where the theory of internal development was applied.

This normative orientation embedded within earlier research has been frequently highlighted by critical reassessments of the Chin'gyŏngshidae theory. What is particularly noteworthy, however, is that some recent scholarship has gone beyond simple critiques of nationalist perspectives to conduct historiographical reflections on the discourse itself. Hong Sŏnp'yo, for instance, acknowledged Ch'oe Wansu's work, driven by a strong intention to overcome colonialist historiography, despite its scholarly limitations, as a contribution to fulfilling historical responsibility for the nation.[50] The research of Ko and Yi, as noted above, also traced the origins and development of contemporary discourse on Chŏng Sŏn and Chin'gyŏng landscape painting to modern historical experiences.[51] Additionally, a recent study examined how Japanese colonial discourse on "tradition" influenced Chosŏn Korea under the Japanese rule, investigating the context in which Chosŏn intellectuals' "tradition" discourse came to include Chin'gyŏng landscapes.[52] Another recent study also analyzed the reinterpretation of Chŏng Sŏn's paintings during the Japanese colonial period, noting their connection to modern-oriented terms such as "sketching" and "landscape painting."[53]

Considering these developments, research on Chin'gyŏng landscape paintings of late Chosŏn has expanded its scope and subject matter to encompass modern and contemporary Korean academic discourse on Chin'gyŏng landscape painting. This research has been strengthened their historiographical significance by examining how the constraints and trauma of modernity influenced the formation and development of Korean art history.

Furthermore, the potential for further expansion in Chin'gyŏng landscape painting research appears considerable. Particularly, broadening the scope of inquiry to encompass discourses on "national art" and "national culture" could stimulate more comparative historical studies within the East Asian context. East Asian intellectuals grappled intensely with their cultural identity as new political and sociocultural values were introduced from the West. For instance, in Japanese art history as well, understanding and establishing the position of national culture in relation to Chinese art was also a major concern.[54] This opens the possibility of comparative studies on the discourse of Chin'gyŏng landscape painting and the discourses of national art in modern China and Japan.

This subject also holds potential for collaboration, as exemplified by *Tongashia misurŭi kŭndaewa kŭndaesŏng* (Modernity and Modernism in East Asian Art, 2009), in which scholars from Korea, China, and Japan each discussed the development of national art and modernities in their respective contexts. Although the work may lack overall cohesion, it is significant for applying a transnational East Asian perspective. Continued engagement with such collaborative efforts could contribute to a deeper understanding of national art discourses within the context of modern and contemporary East Asia.

Secondly, it is worth noting that one of the most prominent features of Chin'gyŏng landscape painting research is the problem of terminology. That is, the major limitation of the Chin'gyŏngshidae theory as an academic framework is the absence of precise discussions of its core concept. This is evidenced by the fact that there were inconsistencies, even among scholars aligned with the theory, regarding the temporal scope of the Chin'gyŏngshidae. In addition, within contemporary scholarship, there seems to be potential for developing a more precise consensus on the concept of Chin'gyŏng landscape painting. As previously mentioned, following the emergence of the Chin'gyŏngshidae theory, the scholars have clarified the definitions and relationships between Chin'gyŏng and Silgyŏng landscape paintings. Chin'gyŏng landscape painting is generally understood as Silgyŏng landscape paintings created by Chŏng Sŏn and his followers, under the influence of the eighteenth-century Namjong-hwa, the Southern School painting. However, close analysis of the existing research reveals that this definition alone is insufficient to account for the diversity of the works.

For example, Chŏng Sŏn's Chin'gyŏng landscapes were map-like paintings that emerged in response to the growing demand for accurate geographical information and the rising popularity of travel to Mt. Kŭmgang.[55] At the same time, they reflected the transition in traditional Sillgyŏng landscape painting, from a documentary mode with practical functions to one oriented toward aesthetic appreciation.[56] Even these basic observations reveal that there are multiple layers of interpretation regarding Chin'gyŏng landscape painting among scholars. Rather than suggesting that any one interpretation is definitively incorrect, it may be more accurate to recognize that Chin'gyŏng landscape painting did not follow a singular, fixed trajectory but developed through multiple and diverse forms.

However, this situation raises critical questions about the appropriateness of grouping paintings with such multifaceted characteristics and developmental trajectories under the singular category of Chin'gyŏng landscape painting, and whether such a classification is truly suitable. This concern arises from the potential risk of arbitrarily applying the concept of Chin'gyŏng landscape painting. Indeed, Cho Kyuhŭi has already pointed out that the current use of the term in Korean academia is arbitrary, arguing that it is essentially equivalent to Cahill's concept of "Topographical painting," which refers to paintings that depict real places or journeys to specific locations. She also noted that this conceptual ambiguity originated from a research tendency to prioritize the context surrounding the emergence of Chin'gyŏng landscape painting. Thus, she called for a shift in the focus of discussion toward the perception and reception of Chŏng's paintings at that time.[57]

The existence of diverse interpretations regarding the concept of Chin'gyŏng landscape painting, despite its prominent position in Korean art history, suggests that the current research approaches and terminology may have been inherited without sufficient critical examination. This is perhaps unsurprising, given the historical context in which early research was shaped by the urgent imperatives of overcoming colonial historiography and constructing a national culture. The existing concept of Chin'gyŏng landscape painting, still overshadowed by nationalism and labeled as "uniquely Korean" or "original," fails to adequately capture the specific and diverse cultural dynamics of the real history. Only by moving beyond the conventional understanding of Chin'gyŏng landscapes can multiple analytical interpretations emerge, thereby enriching our understanding of late Chosŏn art and culture. Representative examples include studies that reclassify paintings, which were previously interpreted solely as Chin'gyŏng landscapes or Silgyŏng landscapes, into a new category of landscape paintings for the estate,[58] or that capture political messages within paintings viewed merely as precedents for Chin'gyŏng landscapes.[59]

Meanwhile, it is also noteworthy that Western research on Chin'gyŏng landscapes has not been free from this terminological limitation. Western studies generally translate Chin'gyŏng landscapes into "True-View landscape painting" and Silgyŏng landscapes into "Real-Scenery landscape painting," similar to Korean studies, with the latter term frequently applied in a broader sense. While the term "Topographical landscape painting" is also often mentioned, few studies have examined the relationships among these terms or provided in-depth discussions of their definitions. A recent study adopted the term "True-Scenery" instead of "True-View,"[60] but this alternative has not gained significant traction. This situation is somewhat discouraging, especially considering the substantial achievements of art history in Western academia. Therefore, there is a need to expand the discussion on Chin'gyŏng landscapes by actively engaging with the rich achievements of existing scholarship.

Third, research on Chin'gyŏng landscape painting presents the continuing challenge of fostering closer cooperation between historical and art historical scholarship, while maintaining distinct disciplinary identities. One reason why the Chin'gyŏngshidae theory has retained influence despite evident limitations may lie in its attempt to read the zeitgeist beyond the artworks themselves. In essence, this approach represented an effort to comprehend culture holistically by connecting the artworks to the thought and consciousness of the period. The fundamental issue, however, lies in the structure of its logic—presupposing macro-level, normative assertions and subsequently wresting specific cultural phenomena to conform to these premises. A similar pattern emerged in early research on Chosŏn's Zhonghua ideology, which maintained a mutually reinforcing relationship with the Chin'gyŏngshidae theory. The normative objectives of reinterpreting and rediscovering the late Chosŏn period guided the entire process of interpreting and synthesizing historical materials, thereby directly informing the theory's development.

At this point, the art historians' argument that Chin'gyŏng landscape paintings should be approached with an art historical methodology centered on individual works merits reconsideration.[61] Given early studies where macro-level theories and normative assertions preceded but failed to align with concrete realities and actual artworks, such methodological considerations and observations hold significant value. However, if research that begins with specific case studies merely concludes with those individual cases, its significance remains confined to the micro-level. The meaning and importance of research can be fully realized only when investigations of individual works or artists are connected to broader historical contexts and realities at the macro-level.

This underscores the necessity for scholars to adopt a more interdisciplinary and collaborative research approach. Art historians should engage with recent historical research to gain a more comprehensive understanding of the historical context of late Chosŏn. The recent groundbreaking studies mentioned above shared a common perspective regarding paintings as historical documents reflecting their temporal context. This methodological approach has allowed scholars to transcend discussions of individual works, thereby enabling them to capture social conditions and expand the scope of research to include aspects such as patrons and cultural power dynamics. Nevertheless, even these studies seem to insufficiently incorporate the accumulated research achievements in the field of history. There remained traces of historical theories developed based on the internal development framework, as the Chin'gyŏngshidae theory, including concepts such as the socioeconomic development, the rise of folk culture, and the destabilization of the social status system in late Chosŏn. Given that historians themselves have engaged in critical reflection on conventional theories that relied on normative assumptions rather than maintaining scholarly objectivity, there is a necessity to broaden and deepen the historical understanding of late Chosŏn.

Within historical scholarship, there is a need to expand research domains beyond traditional disciplinary boundaries. While historians have actively engaged in debates concerning Chosŏn Zhonghua ideology, they have shown limited interest in the Chin'gyŏngshidae theory, despite its foundational relationship with Zhonghua ideology discourse. The discussions have primarily focused on the meaning of Zhonghua, the discrepancy between the values of Chosŏn intellectuals and political realities, and the resulting existential concerns.[62] Bae

Usŏng's research is therefore notable in that it extends discussions on Chosŏn Zhonghua ideology into the realm of cultural art, tracing the worldview of intellectuals of the time through maps.[63] His perspective on maps as products of the worldviews and beliefs of their creators and contemporaries has enriched the discussion. Similarly, historical research would be further expanded by applying the perspectives of recent art history studies, treating paintings as sources "to be read."

Meanwhile, focusing on shared research interests may present a valuable opportunity for interdisciplinary studies. A comprehensive understanding of the eighteenth and nineteenth centuries, for instance, necessitates close collaboration across disciplines. Both historical and art historical scholarship firmly establish the eighteenth century as a period of cultural renaissance under the reigns of two exceptional monarchs, Yŏngjo and Chŏngjo. This period's significance is so evident that even criticisms of the Chin'gyŏngshidae theory highlight its focus solely on Chŏng Sŏn, who was active during Yŏngjo's reign, thereby overlooking the cultural achievements of the Chŏngjo era.

However, the higher the regard for the eighteenth century, the greater the risk of overshadowing the significance of the nineteenth century by comparison. Under the conventional perspective in Korean art history, which emphasizes the originality and excellence of eighteenth-century Chosŏn culture, the nineteenth century, marked by the increasing influence of Namjong-hwa has often been viewed as a period of relative decline. Similar concerns over a fragmented understanding of historical periods have also been noted in historical scholarship.[64] The emphasis on the eighteenth century, particularly the reigns of Yŏngjo and Chŏngjo, especially the latter, has raised concerns about its potentially constraining effect on interpretations of the nineteenth century. Such considerations highlight the necessity of an interdisciplinary research approach. While the discourses on the Chin'gyŏngshidae theory have revealed significant differences and tensions between academic disciplines, they ultimately have demonstrated an even greater need for close communication and collaboration among scholars.

Lastly, it is crucial to recognize that research trends on Chin'gyŏng landscape paintings exhibit minimal substantial difference between Korean and international scholarship. It would not be an exaggeration to assert that Western scholarship on Chin'gyŏng landscape paintings largely aligns with the framework of Korean academic discourse. This alignment reflects a general lack of interest in Korean art among international scholars and indicates that Chin'gyŏng landscape painting is not regarded as a significant topic in international academia. In other words, existing research on Chin'gyŏng landscape paintings has not effectively engaged with international academic discourse, resulting in its isolation, predominantly produced and consumed within domestic circles.

This situation reaffirms that research on Chin'gyŏng landscape painting is itself a historical product of Korea's complex modern experience. Following the developmental trajectory of Korean art history, which began under the influence of colonial historiography, research on Chin'gyŏng landscape painting has been tasked from its inception with demonstrating that Korean art had achieved an independent and original stage of development beyond Chinese influence. The majority of studies on Chin'gyŏng landscapes, as previously discussed, exhibit this tendency regardless of their stance on the Chin'gyŏngshidae theory.

However, just as uniqueness becomes evident within the context of universality, the characteristics and significance of Korean art can be fully appreciated within the broader East Asian context, including China and Japan. Given that paintings of actual scenery were not a genre exclusive to Korea, such comparative analysis becomes even more essential. While previous research has largely focused on identifying the distinctions of Korean art from Chinese art, what is now required is a more expansive perspective that considers not only the East Asian context but Western art history, adopting a more objective approach to make Korean art history accessible and relatable to international scholarship.

In summary, the emergence of Chin'gyŏngshidae theory marked a pivotal moment that highlighted the necessity for a paradigm shift in the study of Chosŏn paintings. The limitations of nation-centric perspectives and the excessive emphasis on cultural uniqueness have prompted art historians to critically reassess existing research. As a result, recent studies have sought to situate Korean art within the context of international exchange and networks of influence in East Asia.[65] Similar perspectives have also emerged in international academic circles. However, considering that many studies are still influenced by the nationalist agenda of overcoming colonial historiography, there is an increasing need to examine Chin'gyŏng landscape painting from more diverse viewpoints. It will be important to trace how future research on Chin'gyŏng landscape painting, and Korean art history more broadly, evolves to transcend its isolation and conventional frameworks.

4. Conclusion

This study provides an overview of Chin'gyŏng landscape painting research, with a particular focus on the Chin'gyŏngshidae theory. Following liberation from Japanese occupation, Korean academia was committed to the common objective of overcoming colonial historiography. Under this same banner, Korean art historians strived to demonstrate the development of an autonomous and original national art that transcended Chinese influence. The Chin'gyŏngshidae theory represented the culmination of these efforts. Ch'oe Wansu, drawing upon Korean historical scholarship's research on Chosŏn Neo-Confucianism and Chosŏn's Zhonghua ideology as a mutual foundation, highly valued Chin'gyŏng landscape painting as both a product of autonomous cultural consciousness and evidence of a cultural zenith.

The Chin'gyŏngshidae theory, emerging from such strong ideological imperatives, faced considerable criticism and controversy immediately after its inception. Particularly within art historical circles, critiques centered on the prioritization of ideological imperatives over scholarly objectivity and the theory's inadequacy in explaining the cultural realities of late Chosŏn. Following the conflicts between the Chin'gyŏngshidae theory and its critics, research on Chin'gyŏng landscape painting diverged into two distinct paths. On one side, studies either actively embraced the Chin'gyŏngshidae theory or maintained similar nationalist perspectives; on the other, scholars attempted to reassess Chin'gyŏng landscape painting, examining it from an East Asian perspective and historical context. This bifurcation was also reflected in international scholarship on Chin'gyŏng landscape painting, which largely operated under the influence of Korean academic discourse.

Considering these research trajectories, the Chin'gyŏngshidae theory holds historiographical significance as it reflects a self-portrait of modern Korean academia shaped by the scars of colonial rule. Its importance also lies in its role as a catalyst for scholarly debate, fostering the diversification of research on Chin'gyŏng landscape painting. These very facts, however, also clearly demonstrate the theoretical limitations of the Chin'gyŏngshidae theory. Ultimately, research grounded primarily in conviction without sufficient empirical investigation has inevitably proven its limitations in comprehending Chin'gyŏng landscape painting and, by extension, the culture and history of late Chosŏn.

Recent research on Chin'gyŏng landscape painting, therefore, while critically reflecting on previous academic approaches, has sought to broaden its investigative scope. These studies presented both positive prospects and several challenges for contemporary researchers, which can be summarized as follows: expanding research into modern discourses on national cultures; conducting deeper examination of academic terminology, such as Chin'gyŏng landscape painting and Silgyŏng landscape painting; promoting interdisciplinary research between art history and history; and situating research within a broader East Asian context. These directions are essential for the development of late Chosŏn painting studies to move beyond national trauma and the uncritical replication of existing studies, to enhance research significance through both specific analysis and macro-level understanding, and, most importantly, to overcome scholarly isolation by developing internationally communicable research, rather than remaining confined as domestic discourse. Through such endeavors, it is anticipated that future research on Chin'gyŏng landscape painting will continue to broaden our understanding of late Chosŏn culture, expanding the prospects of Korean art historical studies.

Note

1 Refer to the contents of "Chin'gyŏngsansuhwa" from the *Encyclopedia of Korean Culture* (https://encykorea.aks.ac.kr/Article/E0054575).

2 See Pak Ŭnsun, "Chin'gyŏngsansuhwa yŏn'gue taehan pip'anjŏng kŏmt'o: Chin'gyŏngmunhwa, chin'gyŏngshidaeronŭl chungshimŭro" (A critical review of studies on Chin'gyŏng landscape paintings: focusing on Chin'gyŏng Culture and the Chin'gyŏng Era theory), *Han'guksasangsahak* Vol. 28, 2007. This article was republished in Pak Ŭnsun, *Chosŏnhugi chin'gyŏngsansuhwa* (Chin'gyŏng landscape paintings of Late Chosŏn), Tolbegae, 2024, pp. 65–93.

3 Han'gungminjongmisuryŏn'guso, *Chin'gyŏngmunhwa: Ch'allanhan uri munhwaŭi kkot* (Chin'gyŏng Culture: The gloriousness of our cultural heritage), Hyŏnamsa, 2014.

4 For an overview of research trends in Korean painting history before and after the Korea's liberation, see Hongsŏnp'yo, *Chosŏnshidaehoehwasaron* (Theories of Chosŏn painting history), Munye, 1999, pp. 16–108.

5 *Ibid.*, pp. 80–81.

6 Yi Dong-ju, "Kyŏmjaeilp'aŭi chin'gyŏngsansu" (Chin'gyŏng landscape paintings by Kyŏmjae school) in *Urinaraŭi yetkŭrim* (Old paintings of our country), Pakyŏngsa, 1975, pp.151-192. The same article was also included in *Kyŏmjae Chŏng Sŏn* (Kyŏmjae Chŏng Sŏn), Chungangilbo·tongyangbangsong, 1977, pp.141-158. For another first- generation scholars, such as Kim Rina and Yu Chunyŏng, see Pak Ŭnsun, *op.cit.*, 2007, pp. 78–79.

7 For more details, see Pak Ŭnsun, *op. cit.*, 2007, p. 79.

8 For example, Ch'oe Wansu, "Kyŏmjae chin'gyŏngsansuhwago" (A study on Chin'gyŏng landscape paintings by Kyŏmjae), *Kansongmunhwa* Vol. 21·29·35, 1981·1985·1988.

9 For example, Yi Tae-ho, "Chŏng Sŏn chin'gyŏngsansuhwap'ungŭi kyesŭnggwa pyŏnmo" (Succession and transformation of art styles of Chŏng Sŏn's Chin'gyŏng landscapes) in *Han'gungmisulsanonmunjip* (Journal of Korean Art History), Han'gukchŏngshinmunhwayŏn'guwŏn, 1984; "18~19segi hoehwaŭi chosŏnp'ung, tokch'angsŏng, sashilchŏngshin" (Chosŏn style, originality, and realistic mindset in 18-19th century painting) *Yŏksabip'yŏng* Vol. 23, 1993.

10 For example, see Chŏng Okcha, *Chosŏnhugi chosŏnjunghwasasang yŏn'gu* (A study on Chosŏn zhonghua in Late Chosŏn period), Ilchisa, 1998, pp. 286–287.

11 Yi Tae-ho, *Chosŏnhugi hoehwaŭi sashilchŏngshin* (The realistic mindset in Late Chosŏn period painting), Hakkojae, 1996.

12 Ch'oe Wansu, *Kyŏmjae chŏngsŏn chin'gyŏngsansuhwa* (Chin'gyŏng landscape paintings of Kyŏmjae Chŏng Sŏn), Beomwoosa, 1993, pp. 266–337.

13 Ch'oe Wansu et al., *Urimunhwaŭi hwanggŭmgi, chin'gyŏngshidae* (The golden age of our culture: The Chin'gyŏng era) Vol 1·2, Tolbegae, 1998.

14 Hong Sŏnp'yo, "Chin'gyŏngsansuhwa yŏn'guŭi pip'anjŏng kŏmt'o" (A critical review of research on Chin'gyŏng landscape paintings), *Kanaart* July·August, 1994; *op. cit.*, 1999, p. 64.

15 Han Chŏnghŭi, "Chosŏnhugi hoehwae mich'in chunggugŭi yŏnghyang" (Chinese influence on late Chosŏn paintings), *Misulsahakyŏn'gu* Vol. 206, 1995. This article was republished in *Han'gukkwa chunggugŭi hoehwar: kwan'gyesŏnggwa pigyoron* (Korean and Chinese paintings: relationships and comparative theories), Hakkojae, 1999, pp. 216–255.

16 Han Chŏnghŭi, "17–18segi tongashiaesŏ shilgyŏngsansuhwaŭi sŏnghaenggwa kŭ ŭimi" (The rise of Silgyŏng landscapes in the seventeenth and eighteenth centuries in East Asia and its implications), *Misulsahakyŏn'gu* Vol. 237, 2003.

17 Ch'oe Yŏngchin, "Uri munhwaŭi hwanggŭmgi chin'gyŏngshidae, kŭrigo kŭ ppurirosŏŭi chosŏnsŏngnihak: Ch'oe Wansu oe, *chin'gyŏngshidae*" (The golden age of our culture: The Chin'gyŏng era, and Chosŏn Neo-Confucianism as its roots: Ch'oe Wansu et al., *chin'gyŏngshidae*), *Tongashia munhwawa sasang* Vol. 1, 1998.

18 Yi Sŏng-Mi, "Uri munhwaŭi hwanggŭmgi chin'gyŏngshidae" (The golden age of our culture: The Chin'gyŏng era), *Misulsahakyŏn'gu* Vol. 227, 2000.

19 Ko Yŏnhŭi, *Chosŏnhugi sansugihaengyesul yŏn'gu: chŏngsŏn'gwa nongyŏn'gŭrubŭl chungshimŭro* (Research on Travelogue and Real Scenery Painting of late Chosŏn centered on Chŏng Sŏn and Nongyŏn group), Ilchisa, 2001.

20 Pak Ŭnsun, *op. cit.*, 2007; *op.cit.*, 2024, pp. 65–93.

21 Pak Ŭnsun, *op. cit.*, 2007, p. 99.

22 According to Pak Ŭnsun's analysis, the term "Chin'gyŏng" (眞境) was primarily used in the early eighteenth century to refer to landscapes that were beautiful and extraordinary, conveying the principles of nature and inspiration to viewers. This concept was grounded in the Ch'ŏn'gi theory, a literary

theory that sought to uncover the principles of the universe within landscape and express them in unadorned form. From the mid-eighteenth century, the term "Chin'gyŏng" (眞景), which emphasized the observation and realistic depiction of nature, began to be used interchangeably with "Chin'gyŏng" (眞境). See Pak Ŭnsun, *op. cit.*, 2024, pp.23-28. Hong Sŏnp'yo also pointed out that Chin'gyŏng landscape paintings in eighteenth century depicted actual landscapes, "Chin'gyŏng" (眞景), in order to embody the ideal landscape, "Chin'gyŏng" (眞境), where universal order was revealed. See Hong Sŏnp'yo, *op. cit.*, 1999, p.301.

23 For example, see Kim Ulrim, O Tayŏn, Yi Jae-ho, *Chosŏnshidae shilgyŏngsansuhwa* (Silgyŏng landscape paintings of Chosŏn period), Kungnipchungangbangmulgwan, 2018.

24 An Hwi-jun contended that only those paintings painted by Chŏng Sŏn and his influences that incorporated the Namjong-hwa method should be called Chin'gyŏng landscape paintings. See An Hwi-jun, *Han'guk'oehwasa* (History of Korean paintings), Ilchisa, 1980, pp. 255-258; "Kyŏmjae Chŏngsŏn(1676~1759)kwa kŭŭi chin'gyŏngsansuhwa, ŏttŏk'e pol kŏshin'ga" (Kyŏmjae chŏngsŏn and his Chin'gyŏng landscape paintings: how should we view them?), *Yŏksahakpo* Vol. 214, 2012, p. 14.

25 Chŏn Hongsŏk, "Tongashia moderŭi chŏnhwan: chungsehwaron'gwa chin'gyŏngmunhwa-tongashia kukchegonggongsŏng mosaekŭl chungshimŭro" (Transition of the East Asian model: medieval theory and Chin'gyŏng culture-focusing on the search for international publicness for East Asian), *Tongyangch'ŏrhakyŏn'gu* Vol. 76, 2013.

26 Kim Chiyŏng, "18segi chin'gyŏngŭi yŏksajŏng ihae" (Historical understanding of Chin'gyŏng in the eighteenth century), *Han'guksasangsahak* Vol. 28, 2007.

27 For example, see Kim Chinkyŏng, "Kyŏmjae chin'gyŏngsansuhwae nat'anan nambukchong hwabŏbyunghabŭi tokch'angsŏng yŏn'gu" (A study on the originality of the fusion of Southern and Northern Schools' painting techniques in Kŏmjae's Chin'gyŏng landscapes), *Yangmyŏnghak* Vol. 34, 2013.

28 Ch'oe Wansu, *Kyŏmjae Chŏng Sŏn 1·2·3* (Kyŏmjae Chŏng Sŏn), Hyŏnamsa, 2009.

29 Yu Ponghak, *Shirhakkwa chin'gyŏngmunhwa* (Silhak and Chin'gyŏng culture), Shin'gumunhwasa, 2013.

30 Han'gungminjongmisuryŏn'guso, *op. cit.*

31 Kang Kwansik, "Chin'gyŏngshidae hoehwaŭi chasaengjŏng chip'yŏnggwa chosŏnjŏng p'unggyŏk," (The autonomous prospect and Chosŏn style of paintings in Chin'gyŏng Era) in *Ibid.,* pp. 143-178.

32 For more detail, see Kwŏn Kichun, "Chŏpch'okchidaerosŏ han'gung munhwajae kugoe chŏnshi: Han'gukkukpojŏn'(1957~1959) gwa han'gungmisul och'ŏnnyŏnjŏn(1979~1981)" (Overseas exhibitions of Korean cultural assets as a contact zone - The Korean National Treasures Exhibition (1957-1959) and Five Thousand Years of Korean Art (1979-1981)), *Han'guk'akyŏn'gu* Vol. 72, 2024.

33 J. P. Park, Burglind Jungmann, Juhyung Rhi. ed., *A companion to Korean art*, Hoboken: Wiley Blackwell, 2020, pp. xiii -xiv.

34 Wan-Su Choe, edited translation by Pak Youngsook and Roderick Whitfield, *Korean true-view landscape : paintings by Chŏng Sŏn (1676-1759)*, London, England : Saffron, 2005.

35 Sŏng-mi Yi, *Korean landscape painting: Continuity and Innovation through the Ages,* Elizabeth: Hollym, 2006.

36 *Ibid.*, p.129; Marsha Weidner, "Korean Landscape Painting: Continuity and Innovation through thte Ages by Yi Song-mi," *The Journal of Asian Studies* Vol. 65 Issue4, 2006, p. 835.

37 Sŏng-mi Yi, *Searching for modernity: Western influence and true-view landscape in Korean painting of the late Chŏson period*, Seattle : University of Washington, 2015.

38 Joan Kee, "The measure of the World: Scene from a Journey to Kaesŏng," *Art History* Vol. 38 Issue 2, 2015.

39 Burglind Jungmann, *Pathways to Korean culture: paintings of the Joseon Dynasty, 1392-1910*, London, England: Reaktion Books, 2014, p. 144.

40 For example, see Jae Sook Kim, "Reading Traditional Korean Artistic Sensibilities through the Concept of Jin-gyeong," *Korea Journal* Vol. 42 No. 4, 2002; Hannah H. Kim, "Art beyond Morality and Metaphysics: Late Joseon Korean Aesthetics," *Journal of Aesthetics & Art Criticism* Vol. 77 Issue 4, 2019.

41 For example, Ahn Hwi-jun criticized the Chin'gyŏngshidae theory, arguing that the creation of a new Chin'gyŏng landscape painting style was not rooted in ideologies such as Chosŏn Neo-Confucianism or Chosŏn Zhonghua but was instead entirely the independent achievement of Chŏng Sŏn, and

therefore all credit should be attributed to him. See Ahn Hwi-jun, *op. cit.*, 2012, pp. 15-17.

42 Chang Chinsŏng, "Aejŏngŭi oryu: chŏngsŏne taehan p'yŏnggawa sŏsurŭi munje" (The fallacy of affection: Issues in the evaluation and narration of Chŏng Sŏn), *Misulsanondan* Vol. 33, 2011.

43 Ko Yŏnhŭi, "Kyŏmjae chŏngsŏn, kŭ myŏngsŏngŭi kŭn'gŏ kŏmt'o" (Kyŏmjae Chŏng sŏn: An examination of the basis for his renown), *Taedongmunhwayŏn'gu* Vol. 109, 2020.

44 Yi Gyeong-hwa, "Shingminji shigi chŏngsŏn hoehwaŭi tamnon hyŏngsŏnggwa sujip" (The formation of discourse and collection of Chŏng Sŏn's paintings during the Japanese colonial period), *Misulcharyo* Vol. 103, 2023.

45 See Cho Kyuhŭi, "Chosŏnshidaeŭi san'gŏdo" (Paintings of the 'dwelling in the mountains' of the Chosŏn dynasty), *Misulsahakyŏn'gu* Vol. 217·218, 1998; "Chosŏnshidae pyŏlsŏdo yŏn'gu" (Estate paintings of the Chosŏn dynasty), PhD diss., Seoul National University, 2006.

46 Cho Kyuhŭi, *Sansuhwaga mandŭn segye* (The world created by landscape paintings), Sŏhaemunjip, 2022.

47 Yi Seong-hyeon, *Noronŭi hwaga, kyŏmjae chŏngsŏn: tashi ilgŏnaenŭn kyŏmjaeŭi chin'gyŏngsansuhwa* (Kyŏmjae Chŏng Sŏn, the painter of the the Noron: rereading Chŏng Sŏn's Chin'gyŏng landscape paintings), Tŭllyŏk, 2020.

48 This argument seems to parallel with a trend of Chinese art history research in the West, as exemplified by James Cahill, who shifted away from idealized views of literati painting and instead emphasized the socioeconomic and historical significance of artworks. For example, see James Cahill, *The Painter's Practice: How Artists Lived and Worked in Traditional China,* Columbia University Press, 1994.

49 J. P. Park, *A new Middle Kingdom: painting and cultural politics in late Chosŏn Korea (1700-1850)*, University of Washington Press, 2018. For a recent academic critique to this study, see Kye Sŭngpŏm, "Ch'oegŭn chosŏnshidaesa yŏngŏgwŏn haksulsŏ hyŏnhwanggwa sŏnbyŏl pip'yŏng" (The current status and selective critique of English-language scholarly works on Chosŏn dynasty history), *Chosŏnshidaesahakpo* Vol. 108, 2024, pp. 92-95.

50 Hong Sŏnp'yo, "Kwangbong 40nyŏnŭi han'guk'oehwasa yŏn'gu" (Forty years of research on the history of Korean paintings since liberation) in

op. cit., 1999, p.105.

51 Ko Yŏnhŭi, *op. cit.*, 2020; Yi Gyeong-hwa, *op. cit.*, 2023.

52 Pak Kyeri, "Han'gungmisurŭi kŭndaejŏk chŏngch'esŏng suripkwa chŏnt'ongnon" (Establishing the modern identity of Korean art and the discourse on tradition), in *Tongasia misurŭi kŭndaewa kŭndaesŏng* (Modernity and modernism in East Asian art), ed. Hong Sŏnp'yo, Hakkojae, 2009, pp. 371-403.

53 Kim Kyŏngyŏn, "20segi huban tongyanghwaŭi hyŏndaesŏng mosaege taehayŏ: sansuhwaŭi chin'gyŏng kaenyŏmŭi pyŏnhwarŭl chungshimŭro" (Exploring the modernity of oriental paintings in the late twentieth century: focusing on the transformation of the Chin'gyŏng concept in landscape paintings), *Han'gukkŭnhyŏndaemisulsahak* Vol. 46, 2023, pp. 12–15.

54 For example, see 辻惟雄, 日本美術の見方, 東京: 岩波書店, 1992.

55 Chin-Sung Chang, "The Landscape before the Eyes: Mounts Geumgang, Fuji, and Huang," *Diamond Mountains: Travel and Nostalgia in Korea Art*, New York: Metropolitan Museum of Art, 2018, p. 100.

56 Hong Sŏnp'yo, *op. cit.*, 1999, pp. 300–301.

57 Cho Kyuhŭi, "Chŏngsŏnŭi kŭmgangsan kŭrimgwa kŭrim kat'ŭn shi-chin'gyŏngsansuhwa ŭimi chaego" (Chŏngsŏn's kŭmgangsan paintings and the picturesque poetry- reconsideration of the terminology, 'True-view Landscapes'), *Han'guk'anmunhakyŏn'gu* Vol. 66, 2017, pp. 214–217.

58 See Cho Kyuhŭi, *op. cit.*, 1998; 2006.

59 For example, see Jeong Dawoon, "17segi huban sŏinŭi hamgyŏngdo kyŏnghŏmgwa chŏngch'ihwaldong: kimsuhanggwa minjŏngjungŭl chungsimŭro" (The Sŏin's experiences in Hamgyŏng Province and political activities in late seventeenth century: focusing on Kim Su-hang and Min Jeong-jung), MA thesis, Sogang University, 2019.

60 See Burglind Jungmann, *Painters as envoys: Korean inspiration in eighteenth-century Japanese Nanga*, Princeton, N.J.:Princeton University Press, 2004.

61 Pak Ŭnsun, *op. cit.*, 2007, p.99.

62 Debates on Chosŏn Zhonghua ideology have been particularly active since the early 2010s. As representative monographs, for example, see Hŏ t'aeyong, *Chosŏnhugi chunghwaron'gwa yŏksainsik* (The Zhonghua ideology and historical consciousness of late Chosŏn), Ak'anenn, 2009; Kye Sŭngpŏm, *Chŏngjidoen sigan: chosŏnŭi taebodan'gwa kŭndaeŭi munt'ŏk*

(Time standing still: Chosŏn's Taebodan and the threshold of modernity), Sŏgangdaehakkyoch'ulp'anbu, 2011; U Gyŏngsŏp, *Chosŏnjunghwajuŭiŭi sŏngnipkwa tongasia* (The formation of Chosŏn Zhonghua ideology and East Asia), Yunisŭt'ori, 2013; Kim Yŏngsik, *Chunggukkwa chosŏn, kŭrigo chunghwa : chosŏn hugi chungguk insigŭi chŏn'gaewa chunghwa sasangŭi kuljŏl* (China, Chosŏn, and Zhonghua: The development of Chinese perception and the distortion of Zhonghua thought in Late Chosŏn), Ak'anenn, 2018.

63 Bae Usŏng, *Chosŏn'gwa chunghwa : chosŏni kkumkkugo sangsanghan segyewa munmyŏng* (Chosŏn and Zhonghua: The world and civilization dreamed and imagined by Chosŏn), Tolbegae, 2014.

64 For example, see Yŏksahak'oe ed., *Chŏngjowa 18segi* (King Chŏngjo and eighteenth century), P'urŭnyŏksa, 2013; No Taehwan et. al., *Chŏngjowa chŏngjo ihu: chŏngjo shidaewa 19segiŭi yŏnsokkwa tanjŏl* (King Chŏngjo and After: Continuity and discontinuity between the Chŏngjo era and the nineteenth Century), Yŏksabip'yŏngsa, 2017.

65 For another example, see Han Chŏnghŭi, Yi Juhyŏn, et al., *Kŭndaerŭl mannan tongasia hoehwa: tongasia hoehwa yŏn'gurŭl wihan saeroun mosaek* (East Asian painting encounters modernity: new approaches to East Asian painting research), Sahoep'yŏngnon, 2011; Pak Ŭnsun, Pak Haehun et al., *Chosŏnsidae hoehwaŭi kyoryuwa sot'ong : chosŏnsidae hoehwa yŏn'guŭi saeroun chŏpkŭn* (Exchange and communication in Chosŏn period painting: new approaches to Chosŏn art historical research), Sahoep'yŏngnon, 2014.

Korean Sources

An, Hwi–jun, *Han'guk'oehwasa* (History of Korean paintings), Ilchisa, 1980.

________, "Kyŏmjae Chŏngsŏn(1676~1759)kwa kŭŭi chin'gyŏngsansuhwa, ŏttŏk'e pol kŏshin'ga" (Kyŏmjae chŏngsŏn and his Chin'gyŏng landscape paintings: how should we view them?), *Yŏksahakpo* Vol. 214, 2012.

Bae, Usŏng, *Chosŏn'gwa chunghwa : chosŏni kkumkkugo sangsanghan segyewa munmyŏng* (Chosŏn and Zhonghua: The world and civilization dreamed and imagined by Chosŏn), Tolbegae, 2014.

Chang, Chinsŏng, "Aejŏngŭi oryu: chŏngsŏne taehan p'yŏnggawa sŏsurŭi munje" (The fallacy of affection: Issues in the evaluation and narration of Chŏng Sŏn), *Misulsanondan* Vol. 33, 2011.

Cho, Kyuhŭi, "Chosŏnshidaeŭi san'gŏdo" (Paintings of the 'dwelling in the mountains' of the Chosŏn dynasty), *Misulsahakyŏn'gu* Vol. 217·218, 1998.

________, "Chosŏnshidae pyŏlsŏdo yŏn'gu" (Estate paintings of the Chosŏn dynasty), PhD diss., Seoul National University, 2006.

________, "Chŏngsŏnŭi kŭmgangsan kŭrimgwa kŭrim kat'ŭn shi-chin'gyŏngsansuhwa ŭimi chaego" (Chŏngsŏn's kŭmgangsan paintings and the picturesque poetry- reconsideration of the terminology, 'True-view Landscapes'), *Han'guk'anmunhakyŏn'gu* Vol. 66, 2017.

________, *Sansuhwaga mandŭn segye* (The world created by landscape paintings), Sŏhaemunjip, 2022.

Ch'oe, Wansu, "Kyŏmjae chin'gyŏngsansuhwago" (A study on Chin'gyŏng landscape paintings by Kyŏmjae), *Kansongmunhwa* Vol. 21·29·35, 1981·1985·1988.

________, *Kyŏmjae chŏngsŏn chin'gyŏngsansuhwa* (Chin'gyŏng landscape paintings of Kyŏmjae Chŏng Sŏn), Beomwoosa, 1993.

________, *Kyŏmjae Chŏng Sŏn 1·2·3* (Kyŏmjae Chŏng Sŏn), Hyŏnamsa, 2009.

Ch'oe Wansu et al., *Urimunhwaŭi hwanggŭmgi, chin'gyŏngshidae* (The golden age of our culture: The Chin'gyŏng era) Vol 1·2, Tolbegae, 1998.

Ch'oe, Yŏngchin, "Uri munhwaŭi hwanggŭmgi chin'gyŏngshidae, kŭrigo kŭ ppurirosŏŭi chosŏnsŏngnihak: Ch'oe Wansu oe, *chin'gyŏngshidae*" (The golden age of our culture: The Chin'gyŏng era, and Chosŏn Neo-Confucianism as its roots: Ch'oe Wansu et al., chin'gyŏngshidae), *Tongashia munhwawa sasang* Vol. 1, 1998.

Chŏn, Hongsŏk, "Tongashia moderŭi chŏnhwan: chungsehwaron'gwa chin'gyŏngmunhwa-tongashia kukchegonggonggongsŏng mosaekŭl chungshimŭro" (Transition of the East Asian model: medieval theory and Chin'gyŏng culture-focusing on the search international publicness for East Asian), *Tongyangch'ŏrhakyŏn'gu* Vol. 76, 2013.

Chŏng, Okcha, *Chosŏnhugi chosŏnjunghwasasang yŏn'gu* (A study on Chosŏn zhonghua in Late Chosŏn period), Ilchisa, 1998.

Han, Chŏnghŭi, "Chosŏnhugi hoehwae mich'in chunggugŭi yŏnghyang" (Chinese influence on late Chosŏn paintings), *Misulsahakyŏn'gu* Vol. 206, 1995.

________, *Han'gukkwa chunggugŭi hoehwar: kwan'gyesŏnggwa pigyoron* (Korean and Chinese paintings: relationships and comparative theories), Hakkojae, 1999.

________, "17-18segi tongashiaesŏ shilgyŏngsansuhwaŭi sŏnghaenggwa kŭ ŭimi" (The rise of Silgyŏng landscapes in the seventeenth and eighteenth centuries in East Asia and its implications), *Misulsahakyŏn'gu* Vol. 237, 2003.

Han, Chŏnghŭi and Yi, Juhyŏn, et al., *Kŭndaerŭl mannan tongasia hoehwa: tongasia hoehwa yŏn'gurŭl wihan saeroun mosaek* (East Asian painting encounters modernity: new approaches to East Asian painting research), Sahoep'yŏngnon, 2011.

Han'gungminjongmisuryŏn'guso, *Chin'gyŏngmunhwa: Ch'allanhan uri munhwaŭi kkot* (Chin'gyŏng Culture: The gloriousness of our cultural heritage), Hyŏnamsa, 2014.

Hŏ, t'aeyong, *Chosŏnhugi chunghwaron'gwa yŏksainsik* (The Zhonghua ideology and historical consciousness of late Chosŏn), Ak'anenn, 2009.

Hong, Sŏnp'yo, "Chin'gyŏngsansuhwa yŏn'guŭi pip'anjŏng kŏmt'o" (A critical review of research on Chin'gyŏng landscape paintings), *Kanaart* July·August, 1994.

________, *Chosŏnshidaehoehwasaron* (Theories of Chosŏn painting history), Munye, 1999.

Jeong, Dawoon, "17segi huban sŏinŭi hamgyŏngdo kyŏnghŏmgwa chŏngch'i hwaldong: kimsuhanggwa minjŏngjungŭl chungsimŭro" (The Sŏin's experiences in Hamgyŏng Province and political activities in late seventeenth century: focusing on Kim Su-hang and Min Jeong-jung), MA thesis, Sogang University, 2019.

Kim, Chinkyŏng, "Kyŏmjae chin'gyŏngsansuhwae nat'anan nambukchong hwabŏbyunghabŭi tokch'angsŏng yŏn'gu" (A study on the originality of the fusion of Southern and Northern Schools' painting techniques in Kŏmjae's Chin'gyŏng landscapes), *Yangmyŏnghak* Vol. 34, 2013.

Kim, Chiyŏng, "18segi chin'gyŏngŭi yŏksajŏng ihae" (Historical understanding of Chin'gyŏng in the eighteenth century), *Han'guksasangsahak* Vol. 28, 2007.

Kim, Kyŏngyŏn, "20segi huban tongyanghwaŭi hyŏndaesŏng mosaege taehayŏ: sansuhwaŭi chin'gyŏng kaenyŏmŭi pyŏnhwarŭl chungshimŭro" (Exploring the modernity of oriental paintings in the late twentieth century: focusing on the transformation of the Chin'gyŏng concept in landscape paintings), *Han'gukkŭnhyŏndaemisulsahak* Vol. 46, 2023.

Kim Ulrim, O Tayŏn, Yi Jae-ho, *Chosŏnshidae shilgyŏngsansuhwa* (Silgyŏng landscape paintings of Chosŏn period), Kungnipchungangbangmulgwan, 2018.

Kim, Yŏngsik, *Chunggukkwa chosŏn, kŭrigo chunghwa : chosŏn hugi chungguk insigŭi chŏn'gaewa chunghwa sasangŭi kuljŏl* (China, Chosŏn, and Zhonghua: The development of Chinese perception and the distortion of Zhonghua thought in Late Chosŏn), Ak'anenn, 2018.

Ko, Yŏnhŭi, *Chosŏnhugi sansugihaengyesul yŏn'gu: chŏngsŏn'gwa nongyŏn'gŭrubŭl chungshimŭro* (Research on Travelogue and Real Scenery Painting of late Chosŏn centered on Chŏng Sŏn and Nongyŏn group), Ilchisa, 2001.

_______, "Kyŏmjae chŏngsŏn, kŭ myŏngsŏngŭi kŭn'gŏ kŏmt'o" (Kyŏmjae Chŏng sŏn: An examination of the basis for his renown), *Taedongmunhwayŏn'gu* Vol. 109, 2020.

Kwŏn, Kichun, "Chŏpch'okchidaerosŏ han'gung munhwajae kugoe chŏnshi: Han'gukkukpojŏn'(1957~1959) gwa han'gungmisul och'ŏnnyŏnjŏn(1979~1981)" (Overseas exhibitions of Korean cultural assets as a contact zone - The Korean National Treasures Exhibition

(1957-1959) and Five Thousand Years of Korean Art (1979-1981)), *Han'guk'akyŏn'gu* Vol. 72, 2024.

Kye, Sŭngpŏm, *Chŏngjidoen sigan: chosŏnŭi taebodan'gwa kŭndaeŭi munt'ŏk* (Time standing still: Chosŏn's Taebodan and the threshold of modernity), Sŏgangdaehakkyoch'ulp'anbu, 2011.

_______, "Ch'oegŭn chosŏnshidaesa yŏngŏgwŏn haksulsŏ hyŏnhwanggwa sŏnbyŏl pip'yŏng" (The current status and selective critique of English-language scholarly works on Chosŏn dynasty history), *Chosŏnshidaesahakpo* Vol. 108, 2024.

No Taehwan et. al., *Chŏngjowa chŏngjo ihu: chŏngjo shidaewa 19segiŭi yŏnsokkwa tanjŏl* (King Chŏngjo and After: Continuity and discontinuity between the Chŏngjo era and the nineteenth Century), Yŏksabip'yŏngsa, 2017.

Pak, Kyer, "Han'gungmisurŭi kŭndaejŏk chŏngch'esŏng suripkwa chŏnt'ongnon" (Establishing the modern identity of Korean art and the discourse on tradition), in *Tongasia misurŭi kŭndaewa kŭndaesŏng* (Modernity and modernism in East Asian art), ed. Hong Sŏnp'yo, Hakkojae, 2009.

Pak, Ŭnsun, "Chin'gyŏngsansuhwa yŏn'gue taehan pip'anjŏng kŏmt'o: Chin'gyŏngmunhwa, chin'gyŏngshidaeronŭl chungshimŭro" (A critical review of studies on Chin'gyŏng landscape paintings: focusing on Chin'gyŏng Culture and the Chin'gyŏng Era theory), *Han'guksasangsahak* Vol. 28, 2007.

_______, *Chosŏnhugi chin'gyŏngsansuhwa* (Chin'gyŏng landscape paintings of Late Chosŏn), Tolbegae, 2024.

Pak, Ŭnsun and Pak, Haehun et al., *Chosŏnsidae hoehwaŭi kyoryuwa sot'ong : chosŏnsidae hoehwa yŏn'guŭi saeroun chŏpkŭn* (Exchange and communication in Chosŏn period painting: new approaches to Chosŏn art historical research), Sahoep'yŏngnon, 2014.

U, Gyŏngsŏp, *Chosŏnjunghwajuŭiŭi sŏngnipkwa tongasia* (The formation of Chosŏn Zhonghua ideology and East Asia), Yunisŭt'ori, 2013.

Yi, Dong–ju, "Kyŏmjaeilp'aŭi chin'gyŏngsansu" (Chin'gyŏng landscape paintings by Kyŏmjae school) in *Urinaraŭi yetkŭrim* (Old paintings of our country), Pakyŏngsa, 1975.

_______, "Kyŏmjaeilp'aŭi chin'gyŏngsansu" (Chin'gyŏng landscape paintings by Kyŏmjae school) *Kyŏmjae Chŏng Sŏn* (Kyŏmjae Chŏng

Sŏn), Chungangilbo·tongyangbangsong, 1977.

Yi, Gyeong-hwa, "Shingminji shigi chŏngsŏn hoehwaŭi tamnon hyŏngsŏnggwa sujip" (The formation of discourse and collection of Chŏng Sŏn's paintings during the Japanese colonial period), *Misulcharyo* Vol. 103, 2023.

Yi, Seong-hyeon, *Noronŭi hwaga, kyŏmjae chŏngsŏn: tashi ilgŏnaenŭn kyŏmjaeŭi chin'gyŏngsansuhwa* (Kyŏmjae Chŏng Sŏn, the painter of the Noron: rereading Chŏng Sŏn's Chin'gyŏng landscape paintings), Tŭllyŏk, 2020.

Yi, Sŏng-Mi, "Uri munhwaŭi hwanggŭmgi chin'gyŏngshidae" (The golden age of our culture: The Chin'gyŏng era), *Misulsahakyŏn'gu* Vol. 227, 2000.

Yi, Tae-ho, "Chŏng Sŏn chin'gyŏngsansuhwap'ungŭi kyesŭnggwa pyŏnmo" (Succession and transformation of art styles of Chŏng Sŏn's Chin'gyŏng landscapes) in *Han'gungmisulsanonmunjip* (Journal of Korean Art History), Han'gukchŏngshinmunhwayŏn'guwŏn, 1984.

________, "18~19segi hoehwaŭi chosŏnp'ung, tokch'angsŏng, sashilchŏngshin" (Chosŏn style, originality, and realistic mindset in 18-19th century painting) *Yŏksabip'yŏng* Vol. 23, 1993.

________, *Chosŏnhugi hoehwaŭi sashilchŏngshin* (The realistic mindset in Late Chosŏn period painting), Hakkojae, 1996.

Yŏksahak'oe ed., *Chŏngjowa 18segi* (King Chŏngjo and eighteenth century), P'urŭnyŏksa, 2013.

Yu, Ponghak, *Shirhakkwa chin'gyŏngmunhwa* (Silhak and Chin'gyŏng culture), Shin'gumunhwasa, 2013.

Other Sources

Cahill, James, *The Painter's Practice: How Artists Lived and Worked in Traditional China,* Columbia University Press, 1994.

Chang, Chin-Sung, "The Landscape before the Eyes: Mounts Geumgang, Fuji, and Huang," *Diamond Mountains: Travel and Nostalgia in Korea Art*, New York: Metropolitan Museum of Art, 2018.

Choe, Wan-Su, edited translation by Pak Youngsook and Roderick Whitfield, *Korean true-view landscape: paintings by Chŏng Sŏn (1676-1759)*, London, England : Saffron, 2005.

Jungmann, Burglind, *Painters as envoys: Korean inspiration in eighteenth-century Japanese Nanga*, Princeton, N.J.:Princeton University Press, 2004.

Jungmann, Burglind, *Pathways to Korean culture: paintings of the Joseon Dynasty, 1392-1910*, London, England: Reaktion Books, 2014.

Kim, Hannah H., "Art beyond Morality and Metaphysics: Late Joseon Korean Aesthetics," *Journal of Aesthetics & Art Criticism* Vol. 77 Issue 4, 2019.

Kim, Jae Sook, "Reading Traditional Korean Artistic Sensibilities through the Concept of Jin-gyeong," *Korea Journal* Vol. 42 No. 4, 2002.

Kee, Joan, "The measure of the World: Scene from a Journey to Kaesŏng," *Art History* Vol. 38 Issue 2, 2015.

Park, J. P., *A new Middle Kingdom: painting and cultural politics in late Chosŏn Korea (1700-1850)*, University of Washington Press, 2018.

Park, J. P. , Jungmann, Burglind, Rhi, Juhyung, ed., *A companion to Korean art*, Hoboken: Wiley Blackwell, 2020.

Weidner, Marsha, "Korean Landscape Painting: Continuity and Innovation through thte Ages by Yi Song-mi," *The Journal of Asian Studies* Vol. 65 Issue4, 2006.

Yi, Sŏng-mi, *Korean landscape painting: Continuity and Innovation through the Ages,* Elizabeth: Hollym, 2006.

Yi, Sŏng-mi, *Searching for modernity: Western influence and true-view landscape in Korean painting of the late Chŏson period*, Seattle : University of Washington, 2015.

辻惟雄, 日本美術の見方, 東京: 岩波書店, 1992. *Encyclopedia of Korean Culture* (https://encykorea.aks.ac.kr/Article/E0054575).

Index

D

E

J

K

L

M

N

O

T

U

W

X

Y

Z

Contributors

Joon Hur is a lecturer at Underwood International College, Yonsei University. He has published a number of articles in Korean and English on the discourse of national identity in pre–modern Korea, Confucian culture and institutions, and political philosophy in the Chosŏn dynasty.

Seung B. Kye is a Professor in the Department of History at Sogang University in Seoul, Korea. His research centers on the political, intellectual, and socio-economic history of Chosŏn Korea, as well as Sino–Korean relations, all situated within the broader context of East Asia. He is particularly interested in how Confucian notions of Sinocentrism and their localized reinterpretations in Korea shaped the formation of the Chosŏn state, and how these historical legacies continue to influence contemporary Korean society.

Hyunchae Lim is a doctoral candidate in the Department of History at Sogang University. His dissertation examines the evolving perceptions of Japan among Korea's ruling elite across the period preceding, encompassing, and following the Imjin War—also known as the Hideyoshi Invasion of Korea.

Chaeyoung Choo received her Ph.D. in history from Sogang University, with a dissertation examining the politics and governance of King Yŏngjo during the mid-eighteenth century. Her research focuses on the political and cultural history of late Chosŏn Korea, with particular attention to historical narratives and their representations in visual media. She also works as a historical consultant for Korean period films and television dramas.

Karam Kim received her Ph.D. in history from Sogang University. Her dissertation explores the evolving conceptions of filial piety and unfilial conduct among Confucian elites in early Chosŏn Korea, focusing on their moral and legal applications to everyday life during the fifteenth and sixteenth centuries. Her broader research interests include the shifting interplay between male filial piety and female chastity, the Confucian social hierarchy grounded in the Three Bonds and Five Moral Relationships, and the changing identity and roles of women under Confucian rule.

Kunha Kim earned his Ph.D. in History from Sogang University, with a dissertation examining the transformation of military service institutions in the Chosŏn dynasty from a socio-economic perspective. He previously served as a research assistant professor at the Center for Digital Humanities and Social Sciences at KAIST, and is currently a research professor at Sogang University. His research integrates digital methodologies with Korean military and socio-economic history, contributing to the development of interdisciplinary approaches in historical scholarship.

Hohyun Nam is Associate Professor in the Department of History and Philosophy at the Republic of Korea Air Force Academy. His research explores the intersection of religion, politics, and law in late Chosŏn Korea, with a particular focus on the history of the Korean Catholic Church. He is especially interested in how Catholicism was received, regulated, and resisted within the Confucian sociopolitical order, and how these dynamics mirrored broader developments in Sino–Korean relations. His work also engages digital history, exploring how emerging methodologies can shed new light on patterns in Korean and East Asian religious history.

Dawoon Jeong is a doctoral candidate in the Department of History at Sogang University. Her dissertation explores the changing political situations reflected in paintings, situating them within the broader effort to reconstruct the political, cultural, and social dimensions of late Chosŏn Korea. She emphasizes the historical significance of visual materials alongside textual sources, with a particular interest in how visual culture contributes to our understanding of the period's political discourse.

Sogang Korean Studies 01